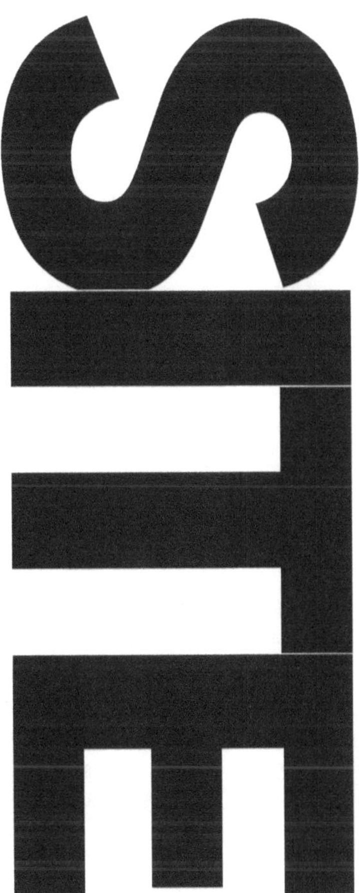

PUBLISHER & EDITOR:
Sven-Olov Wallenstein
EDITORIAL BOARD: Brian Manning
Delaney, Power Ekroth, Jeff Kinkle,
Trond Lundemo, Staffan Lundgren,
Karl Lydén, Helena Mattsson, Meike
Schalk, Susan Schuppli, Kim West
GRAPHIC DESIGN: Konst & Teknik +
Caroline Settergren

SITE
Box 19009
SE-104 32 Stockholm
Sweden

www.sitemagazine.net
info@sitemagazine.net

SUBMISSIONS: Text proposals to
be sent to info@sitemagazine.net

ISSN 1650–7894
ISBN 978-91-86883-20-1

Distributed by Axl Books

33.2013 Contents

Senses

Any definition of the aesthetic domain poses a challenge to thought: should aesthetics limit itself to the fine arts, and perhaps only to works that attain a particular and paradigmatic status, or should it aspire to formulate a general theory of what may count as an object of aesthetic appreciation, including everyday life and all aspects of our world that pertain to the senses? When the term *aesthetics* was coined in the first half of the eighteenth century, it was from the outset a multidimensional term, beset with tensions and conflicts — on the one hand a theory of the fine arts, which would coalesce into a "system" a few decades later; on the other hand, as was claimed by Baumgarten, who invented the term, an "art of thinking beautifully." Aesthetics was partly a theory of a new class of objects, but more generally also a profound upheaval of rationalist philosophy that took its cues from a re-evaluation of the sensible. From the moment of its emergence, aesthetics has oscillated between a subordinate position in the philosophical encyclopedia and a claim to explore the dimension of sense as such, beyond all particular disciplinary demarcations.

The first section explores this question in the past and present, beginning with an interview with Jacques Rancière, whose *Aisthesis: Scenes from the Aesthetic Regime of Art* constitutes one of the most significant attempts in recent times to chart the emergence of a new distribution of the sensible from the eighteenth century onward. Continuing with essays that address crucial moments in the first phases of aesthetics — Baumgarten, who is currently being re-read as providing a general theory of sensibility (Sven-Olov Wallenstein), Lessing, who gives aesthetic pleasure a particular twist by connecting it to a dimension of pain (Cecilia Sjöholm), and the later intertwining of aesthetics and fashion (Sara Danius)   the section proceeds to discussions of modern artistic forms: the role of law and guilt in Kafka (Howard Caygill), the question of filmic illusion (Gertrud

Koch), and the problem of whether art, and particularly the visual arts, can be understood at all on the basis of a generalized aesthetic (Morten Kyndrup). The status of a phenomenology of the sensible is at the center of the last three contributions, Pablo Bustinduy Amador's essay on painting, Marcia Sá Cavalcante Schuback's meditation on drawing, and finally Susan Kozel's interrogation of the challenge put to a phenomenology of dance by new types of somatic materialism.

Another dimension of the senses, the sensory and the sensible is the necessary intertwining with technologies of perception, storage, and transmission. 2011 was the centenary of the birth of Marshall McLuhan, whose writings were paramount in bringing the idea of "media" to the forefront of culture, and the second section explores the ramifications of this concept in contemporary media and communication studies and art criticism. Drawing on material presented at a symposium at Moderna Museet, this section contains contributions by Thierry de Duve, on Duchamp and the question of art in general; by Richard Cavell, on McLuhan's fundamental idea of remediation; by Wolfgang Ernst on the temporal structure of electronic media; by Staffan Ericson on the link between McLuhan and Walter Benjamin; and a review by Dan Karlholm of a recent book by Rosalind Krauss that develops her earlier analysis of the "post-medium condition" of the arts.

The third and final section contains a series of essays dealing with architecture and urbanism. Tim Anstey reviews a new book by Pier Vittorio Aureli on the possibility of an absolute architecture, Sten Gromark discusses Łukasz Stanek's recent work of Henri Lefebvre, Sarah Stanley probes the modernity of Japanese Metabolism, and Staffan Lundgren provides a critical take on the ideologies of parametric design. •

THE EDITORS

Aisthesis

Jacques Rancière
Sven-Olov
    Wallenstein
Kim West
Cecilia Sjöholm
Sara Danius
Howard Caygill
Gertrud Koch
Morten Kyndrup
Pablo Bustinduy
    Amador
Marcia Sá
    Cavalcante
    Schuback
Susan Kozel

Senses of the Sensible: Interview with Jacques Rancière

Sven-Olov Wallenstein and Kim West

SVEN-OLOV WALLENSTEIN: In your new book, *Aisthesis: Scenes from the Aesthetic Regime of Art*, you propose that the aesthetic regime is not a new concept of art, but a way of identifying objects. Could you explain this further? What does it mean to "identify objects"?

JACQUES RANCIÈRE: On a fundamental level, the book tries to identify what the word "art" signifies. So the problem is not to identify objects in general, but to identify the type of event, the type of interpretation of events, the type of relationship between form and signification that make it possible to understand objects, events or performances as belonging to a sphere of experience called "art". And I'm simply trying to say that what distinguishes the aesthetic regime from the representational regime is that, in the latter, there is a whole set of rules that define the conditions for including certain objects within an art form, an artistic genre, a hierarchy of artistic genres. At the same time, this way of defining objects as belonging to an art form is a way of defining a general structure of relationships between different forms of experience. The fine arts succeed the liberal arts, which are themselves opposed to the mechanical arts; the liberal arts and the mechanical arts were two completely distinct configurations of the realm of the sensible. The question is therefore which types of objects are understood as corresponding

to a certain practice, which is itself defined as corresponding to a certain type of human being, a certain type of experience.

What is important, then, is that in the representational regime certain objects, in the sense of forms, modes of expression or assemblages of words, forms and movements, can, on account of their properties, be identified as belonging to a specific artistic genre. In the aesthetic regime, this identification no longer works. Here, what is identified is a regime of sensible experience within which events that are called art take place, but paradoxically this is only possible on the condition that the criteria for identifying these events as a specific class of objects disappear. What is henceforth identified is therefore a mode of sensible experience that is at a distance from the general distribution of positions, where active subjects are distinguished from passive subjects, objects that belong to ordinary experience are distinguished from objects that belong to a form of art, and so on. That is how I understand identification, on the most general level. Either you identify objects directly, or you identify forms of experience.

sow: How should we understand your notion of the sensible? When you talk of this new distribution of the sensible, there is also a change in the very notion of sensibility, *Sinnlichkeit*, *sensibilitas*. Generally the sensible was thought of as something below the conceptual, the noetic, etc., but here we seem to be dealing with an expansion of the sensible: a sensible which is not placed below the conceptual, but which invades, encompasses the conceptual as well as the noetic.

jr: There are several aspects here. The sensible at the heart of the aesthetic regime of art is a sensible that, first of all, is opposed to two other regimes of the sensible, which we could call the "classical" ones. First, the sensible understood as opposed to the intelligible, as inferior in relation to the intelligible, and second, the sensible understood as an arrangement of sensible forms produced by an idea, produced by an intention. What is important with the definition of the new sensible, in Schiller for example, is the idea of a separation between three senses of the sensible: the sensible as an object of knowledge, the sensible as a realization of the will, and finally the sensible understood as something proper to the aesthetic judgment. I believe that this separation is central to Kant. Even though it is never pronounced, it contributes to what I find strange about the architecture of the first part of the *Critique of Judgment*, where there is on the one hand a definition of sensible experience which permits us to attribute and to form sensible judgments, and on the other hand a theory of the fine arts which is bizarrely attached to the analytic of the sublime, but where it is never clear how we went from the former to the latter. The heart of the matter is, I believe, that the sensible that is the object of the aesthetic regime of art is fundamentally divided between the forms through which sensible forms are considered or appreciated as beautiful, and the rules according to which the sensible forms are considered as products of art. In a sense my whole reflection has concerned the theme of the aesthetic idea in Kant, because this idea is the bridge, the connection between the experience of the beautiful and the rules of art. The aesthetic idea is the way in which the artist manages to produce a mode of sensible existence that is at the same time the opposite of the normal mode of sensible existence of an artwork, because an artwork is normally the form of sensible existence that results from the intentions of an author, whereas the aesthetic form must be judged independently of all concepts.

SOW: There is one essential reference here: Alexander Gottlieb Baumgarten, and the transformation of the notion of *aisthesis* that takes place in his work. He is not present in the book, but could you say something about him, and about the connection to the rationalist tradition that he represents? This is a big question, of course, but I believe that there is a reevaluation of Baumgarten today, both in Germany and in France, where the Kantian revolution is perceived as less radical than what is already present in Baumgarten, where we find precisely this expansion of the sensible, whereas in Kant there is a division between sensible and intelligible.

JR: For me, Kant is the point of departure, at least to the extent that philosophical and aesthetic origins can simply be assigned. But I do not relate him to Baumgarten, because Baumgarten remains attached to the Leibnizian notion of the sensible as confused intelligibility, which means that every reading of Baumgarten must take place within the framework of classical poetics, as concerns its objects as well as its modes of analysis. Kant never produces a single analysis of an artwork, because he is the one who actually names the sensible reality with which the aesthetic regime is concerned, which is a divided sensible reality. What is important in Kant is the division between the spheres of sensible experience. I understand that it makes sense to retroactively assign priority to Baumgarten, especially within a Deleuzian tradition that aims precisely to return to Leibniz, to return the opposition between the intelligible and the sensible to a matter of levels of clarity and obscurity, of distinction and indistinction, but for me the aesthetic regime is based on the Kantian division, which breaks with what remains traditional in Baumgarten.

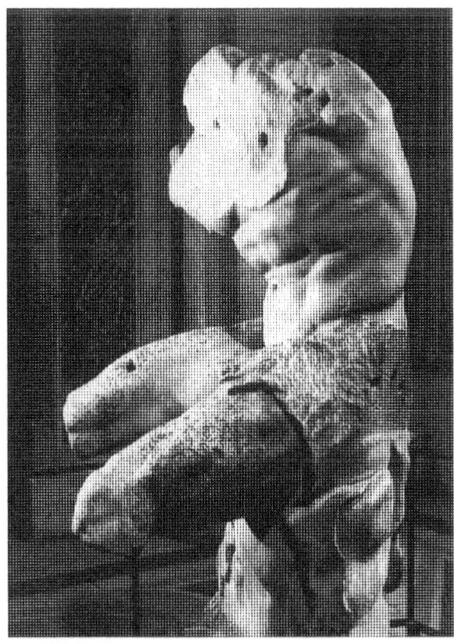

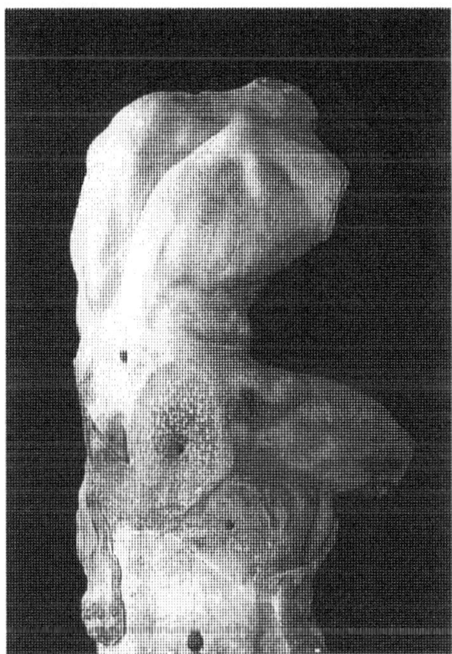

The Belvedere Torso, Museo Pio-Clementino, Vatican Museums, Rome.

SOW: In fact, you begin with Winckelmann before reaching Kant. Why?

JR: I couldn't say exactly why I begin with Winckelmann. I think I focused on him first of all because of the figure of the Belvedere Torso, and the question: how is it possible that a completely mutilated statue could be perceived not only as the highest achievement in art, but also as the highest expression of a people's liberty? What interests me is this double paradox where, first, the incomplete, the fragmented, the ruined becomes that which is perfect, and, second, the activity of a people becomes manifested in a mutilated body. So Winckelmann has been important for me for many reasons, but first of all because he points toward the ruin of a certain model of perfection. The classical model of perfection is the perfection of the human body with all of its parts, where the head rules, and so on. This is a model of perfection that has often been understood as properly modern — I am thinking of a whole analysis of modernity which sets the autonomous organism against the tradition of representation, the internal perfection of the work against the ideal of representation, an analysis that of course remains bound to the organic model. In some of my texts on literature I have attempted to challenge the Borgesian vision of the fiction as a closed totality where everything is interconnected, that presents itself as a perfectly organized body with all its parts. Winckelmann is essential in the same respect: he helps us conceive of modernity not under the sign of the self-sufficient work, but under the sign of the fragment that definitely remains a fragment. But he has also been important as a model of inactivity, in contrast to all conceptions of the politics of art as the passage from passivity to activity. Here, the torso is a counter-model, something

entirely inactive that is at the same time the expression of a
people's liberty. And then there is a third point, which is that
Winckelmann inaugurates art history as art history, that there is
a break here with the old ways of describing the life of painters
and artists or of studying art works as historical testimony. I
believe that it is important that the birth of art occurs through
the birth of art history: there is art because there is a history of
art, which undermines all attempts at opposing the pure autonomy of art to its historicity. It also seems important to me that
three terms here appear at the same time: art, history and
people. There is *art* when there is *history* of art, and there is art
when we can identify the history of art with the history of the
liberty of a *people* — which obviously places us at a complete
distance from all discourses about the autonomy of art, in their
various versions.

sow: In Winckelmann, this history is also a lost history. If we
think of the last lines of his *History of Ancient Art*, it is a history
that is lost. Greece is lost. If we would move a little bit further,
for example to German romanticism, this would be a question
of the history of the future, of the artwork of the future, but in
Winckelmann it is a lost art.

jr: Yes, but to say that Greece is a lost fatherland is also to say
that it is a fatherland that we could attempt to revive. What I
find important is the moment when we leave the classical relationship to antiquity, which used to state that we need to study
the ancient masterpieces according to the model of perfection,
as examples, but as examples which are nothing but examples.
Classically one studied the ancients in order to find models,
modes of expression that could suit for dramatic themes and
subjects, but at the same time there was a limit, where the
ancients remained the ancients. Let us think of the polemics
between the ancients and the moderns in late seventeenth
century France. Even for the champions of the ancients, it was
clear that there are the ancients and there are the moderns. The
ancients belonged to education, but at the same time there was
a rift between the productions of the ancients and those of the
moderns, and there was no possible contemporaneity. So what
does Winckelmann do? In the midst of the creation of a new
contemporaneity — and this is also connected to the archeologi-
cal excavations of the eighteenth century — we are no longer
dealing with the same Greece that used to be found in the manu-
als for the education of good taste, but with a country — and a
model of art — that is as real as an actually existing one. And this
is the condition for the desire, the utopia to resuscitate Greece as
a model for the relationship between a people and its art.

KIM WEST: Here we could perhaps approach the question of play, *Spiel*, which is evidently a central figure in the book. You find it already in Winckelmann, and then in Kant, Schiller, and so on. Perhaps we could say that what the book does is to trace the recurrences of this figure in what we normally call modern art, or with the appearance of the aesthetic regime of art. Would you say that this is a fair description?

JR: I wouldn't say that the project could be reduced to a history of the notion of play. At the same time this concept is of course capital, and it is essential that it was placed at the center of aesthetic perception, of the aesthetic perception of art, by Schiller, who took it from Kant, because this too means that there is art when there is a rupture of a certain distribution of the sensible, of the hierarchical system that placed activity on one side and passivity on the other, form on one side and matter on the other — a division which is also a division between different forms of existence and types of human beings. The notion of play is important because it breaks with all these hierarchical models, and because it presents this break, this third type of sensible experience, as the place of aesthetic experience, the place, in other words, where works may be appreciated as works of art, but where works of art may also function as models for a future community. This break is what is essential about the notion of play. This is not so present in the book, but it's there in the background, it's in the chapter on Winckelmann we just discussed, and it is the break with a whole vision of the opposition between different types of activity and inactivity. Play, as it is understood by Kant and Schiller, is opposed to the notion of play we find in Aristotle, who distinguishes between the leisure of free men and the rest of mechanical men. Play here belongs to the realm of free leisure which is opposed to the alternation of tension and relaxation pertaining to those who belong to the mechanical sphere. In Schiller, this whole complex of problems about tension and relaxation is completely transformed. Even though Schiller never refers to Aristotle in this regard, it is nevertheless important to rethink the relationship between tension and release, and all that this may imply as a redistribution of the relations between activity and passivity. What I see as essential to the aesthetic regime and to the political implications of the aesthetic regime is the appearance and the centrality of experiences of suspension of activity or of inactivity — which is what I argue in the chapter about Stendhal. I see it as very important that, at the very moment when the representational regime is criticized and begins to fall into ruin, an ethical counter-model appears, which is the model of the active spectator, the civic sentiment, etc. And at the same time there is the more or less contemporaneous counter-model of play, which is a way of escaping from the hierarchical realm itself, within which activity was opposed to passivity. I think that "play" is one of the possible names of this redistribution of relationships between the active and the passive which is at the heart of the aesthetic regime, but which can also be translated into philosophical terms as the redistribution of relationships between the conscious and the unconscious, for example.

SOW: If we connect this question about activity and passivity to the other question about Baumgarten and the reevaluation of the sensible, I remember a lecture you gave in Stockholm on Deleuze, where you said that aesthetics is not a part of philosophy in the same sense as logic, ethics, metaphysics, etc. Back then you didn't use the notion of the aesthetic regime, but you said that aesthetics is a new way of thinking, or in other words, that aesthetics is not a specific part of philosophy, not a subdiscipline within philosophy, but a transformation of the very notion of philosophy.

JR: I believe it is important not to think in terms of a division of the different parts of philosophy. I do not understand myself as a philosopher who would attempt to establish the correct relations between aesthetics and the other parts of philosophy. I believe that, at the time, I was mainly focused on the question of the relations between conscious thought and unconscious thought, and on the fact that, within the aesthetic idea, there is a dissolution of the foundations upon which the philosophical edifice as such is constructed. I looked at all the different formulations about the becoming-unconscious of the conscious, which we can find at the heart of the aesthetic thinking of Schelling and Schiller. I tried to follow this thread from romanticism up until Deleuze. In this book I am less interested in the properly philosophical intrigue about the relations between conscious and unconscious, and more in the archeology itself, in the construction of a sensible realm through which this disturbance is introduced into philosophy. What remains true is that the name of a discipline of thought is an idea of thought itself.

SOW: If we look at how this book is written we see that you omit the great names of philosophy: there is no chapter on Kant, no chapter on Nietzsche, etc. You begin with lesser known figures and then you work your way back to the philosophical issues. So the book is written in another way: it is not a history of philosophy, it is not a history of aesthetics, it is a way of rethinking aesthetics starting from certain events. Could you say something about the logic of the book's narrative?

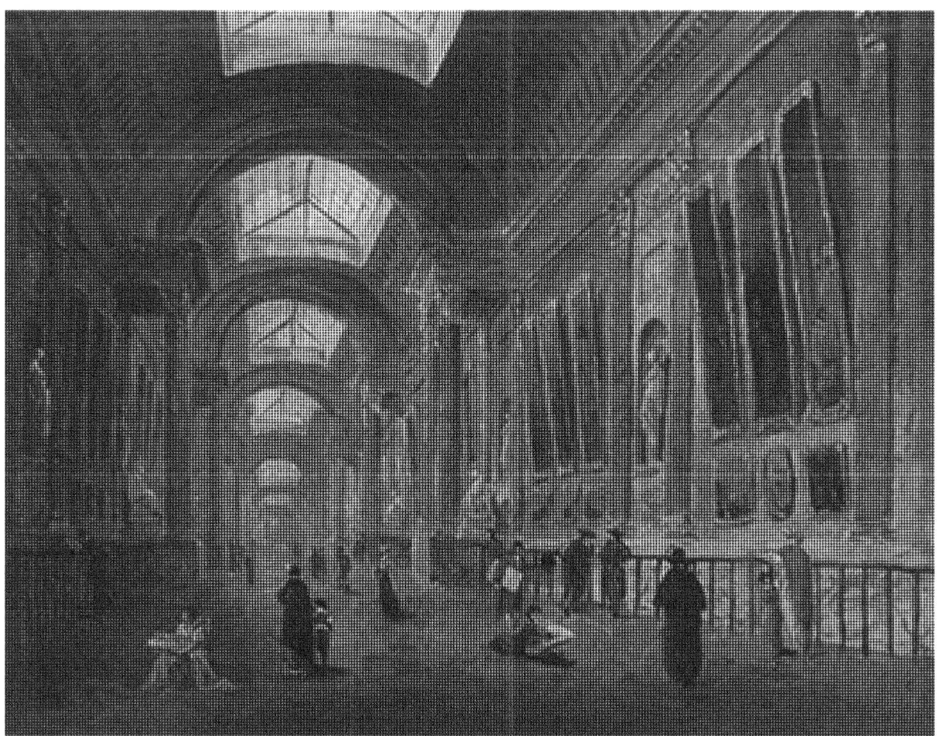

Hubert Robert, *Proposed Renovation of the Grande Galerie,* circa 1796–1798. Oil on canvas, Department of Paintings, Musée du Louvre, Paris (RF 2050).

JR: The logic of this book is essentially the same as the one I employed when I wrote about the life of the proletarians, that is: to rewrite social history not along the great themes of the development of class consciousness in relation to capitalism, but starting from the points of irruption around which individuals and groups restructure their sensible world. Here, in a sense, I operated in the same way. I have chosen a number of scenes where the fundamental question is: what do you do with a form, what do you do with a statue, with a painting, with a dance spectacle, with a photo exhibition; how are they seen, how could they be thought? It is for this reason that I approached Hegel not from the point of view of the development of his aesthetic theory, but from the point of view of what I find is an essential moment, the constitution of another image of modernity, more precisely the dissolution of the hierarchy of subject matter. Which means that we pose the question: what do you do with a canvas? In the last instance I've inscribed Hegel into the extension of the perfectly material experience of the directors of the Louvre welcoming the artworks stolen by the French armies during the revolutionary period, who saw those paintings as the achievement of free humanity, and who found themselves in front of Venuses, portraits of the king's mistresses, religious scenes, and so on, and were forced to ask themselves: what can we do to present all these paintings, with their stories of superstition and the turpitudes of the rich and noble, as manifestations of liberty? This is the same question as the one Hegel asks: he feels that there is something in these small genre paintings that can express liberty much stronger than how the great history paintings present their grand episodes, including the grand episodes from the history of liberty itself. Hegel is confronted with this new sensation, that freedom is there, the spirit is there, the spirit is not in the portraits of the philosophers, freedom is not in the representation of the freedom fighters, it is there, in these small genre scenes, and we must learn to think this presence. This is very important because it coincides with the moment I believe is fundamental for the possibility of rethinking painting, and therefore of making another painting, that is, the moment when the hierarchy of genres is overthrown, which will also mean that what the painting says is something else than what it tells, than the persons it represents. This is what I have tried to say several times, that abstract painting becomes possible from the moment when the process of abstracting the subjects of painting began.

SOW: The rereading of Hegel is astonishing, in the same sense as your rereading of Winckelmann. Hegel's lectures on aesthetics are of course in a sense the high point of the classic, with its hierarchy of the arts, its system of the arts in the development of the spirit, etc. In this sense, Hegel represents the closure of the classical system of art theory. You do not try to reconstruct this system, you do something else, an excavation: you find Hegel's experience in front of the genre painting. It's not the Hegelian system; it 's Hegel's experience.

JR: Yes, but that also means that it's the moment when the system breaks down, the moment when we are inside the classical theory of the fine arts and at the same time something else is expressed, which is not at all the type of sensibility and the modes of interpretation that used to belong to the classical theory of the fine arts. In other words, Hegel takes up the objects of the poetic arts or of the traditional discourses on painting, but not exclusively, because he also includes everything that appears with Winckelmann, everything that appears with this tradition of rereading the ancients. So when Hegel returns to Greek sculpture and to the development of painting from the renaissance until the Dutch golden age, he in a sense returns to objects that already exist, but his relationship to them is completely new — and this relationship is not only his, we also find it in a new sensitivity toward the works of these minor masters who painted genre scenes, a sensitivity which is no more the taste for the exotic that characterized the eighteenth-century aristocracy who bought those paintings. In a sense, there is a Hegelian logic inside Hegel's work itself, that is, the content explodes the form, there are new modes of sensibility regarding what takes place when one is in the presence of a statue or a painting. This is the reason the Hegelian closure is a closure that must be burst open: it is the very contradiction between the objects and the modes of interpretation of these objects. What interests me is therefore what passes through Hegel and points to accomplishments that Hegel may have thought or art forms that he could have known, such as photography.

sow: In your reading of Hegel you also make an essential connection: at the same time as Hegel presented his lectures on aesthetics in Berlin, Schinkel's Altes Museum was being built in front of the university. In other words, Hegel is the thinker of the museum. What he thinks in his aesthetics is the space of the museum.

jr: Yes, certainly. And the space of the museum is the space where works are, at one and the same time, entirely separated from their traditional function in the service of the church, the aristocracy, the monarchy, and arranged in such a manner that they must tell a story. I must say that I always find it striking that all the great museums have adopted this historical mode of presentation of their works. Which means that, in a fundamental sense, painting is the question of the life of the people. This is something extremely important: the museum is the space where works are separated from their destination, and they are presented to a spectator who does not know what they are about, what questions they pose, and what they talk about, and who will therefore resemble the spectator of the Louvre of the republic: he is forced to look at painting itself, because he can no longer know exactly what painting speaks of. But at the same time the presentation of the paintings tells a story, the story of the people.

kw: You started to discuss the narrative structure of your book. In this regard there is another essential name: Auerbach. *Aisthesis* is of course a reference to Auerbach's *Mimesis*, and in the preface to your book you refer explicitly to this work, which serves as a kind of model. At the same time there are obvious differences between the two projects, for example in your respective readings of Stendhal's *The Red and the Black*. In your reading, Julien Sorel becomes a figure who, in the end of the novel, experiences a certain pleasure in inactivity, in the way we just discussed. There is a direct connection to the notion of play. So, I'd like to begin with a general question: what is the relationship

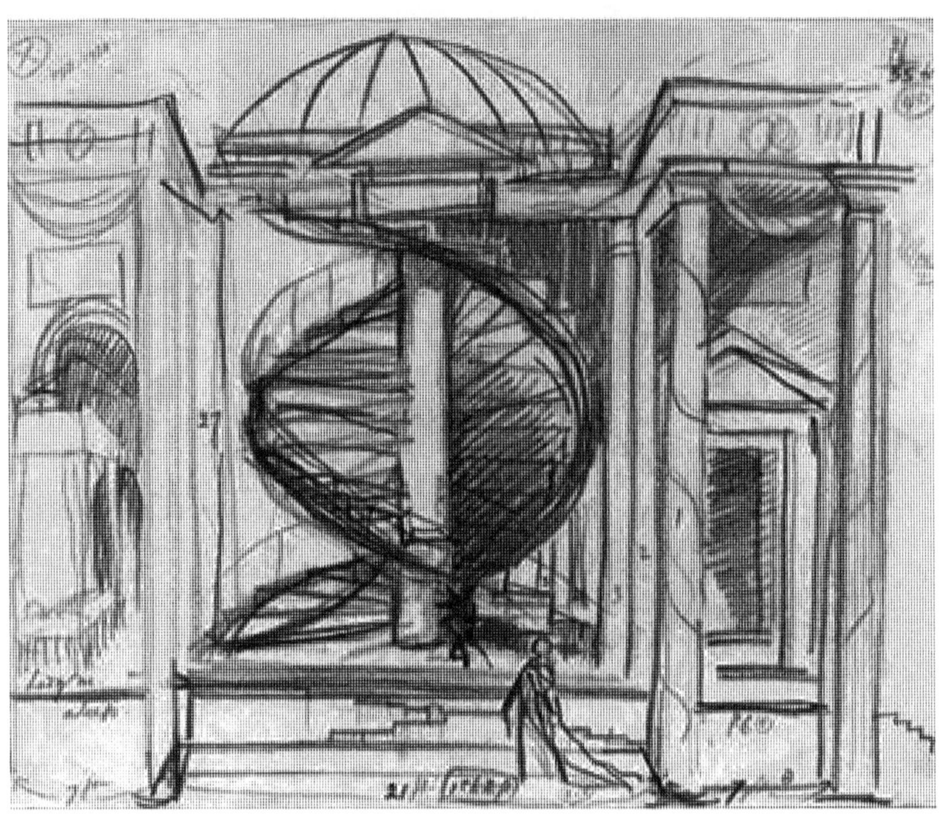

between *Mimesis* and *Aisthesis*, both the books and the concepts? Is *aisthesis* a more fundamental concept than *mimesis*? Should we understand the development of the new, aesthetic regime of art as the condition of possibility of literary realism, which is finally the subject of Auerbach's study?

JR: A vast question. Let's say that what I borrow from Auerbach are the modes of exposition, the small scenes where you concentrate upon a small text and attempt to develop all its implications. That said, my perspective is after all very different from that of Auerbach. The difference between our interpretations of Stendhal presupposes a more fundamental difference, because for Auerbach, *mimesis* is understood in the classical sense, as imitation. For him there is, at the heart of the notion of *mimesis*, a relationship to a referent called reality. And the progress of *mimesis* is a progress that concerns what type of reality we have access to. There is a historical teleology, which in a sense is parallel to others — I am thinking of Gombrich, for example — where literary writing becomes more and more apt to grasp a reality that on the one hand becomes more and more concrete, and on the other hand more and more detailed. For me, *mimesis* is not imitation.

Mimesis is a regime of identification of the arts, and what constitutes *mimesis* as an order is not a norm for the imitation of reality, but the fact that imitation or representation is included within a number of rules, within a whole division between what is artistic and what is not artistic, between the noble genres and the non-noble genres, etc. I understand *mimesis* as the classical order, a total order that subjects the representation of reality not only to a certain number of restrictive norms, but to a certain hierarchical model. So what I find important, and what separates me from Auerbach, is that the question of what is called "realism" is connected to the destruction of the fundamental model of Aristotle's poetics, where the work is defined first of all by its plot, and the plot is defined first of all as a chain of actions. What I tried to say in *The Politics of Literature* is that at the center of the model of *mimesis* there is the privilege of action, the idea of poetry as something that constructs an action or a chain of events, as opposed to history, which simply accounts for life and its developments. I believe that there is a fundamental opposition between action and life, which is an opposition between two types of humanity. As I see it, the birth of modern realism is not connected to how authors, as Auerbach states, began to take an interest in historical reality, in the relationship between the social classes at a certain point in history. It is connected to the destruction of the privilege of a certain model, the privilege of the model of action, of well-formed chains of action, over life in its proper developments. So what I see as central to Stendhal is not that he takes an interest in the specific tonalities of an aristocratic salon in the days preceding the revolution of 1830, but a basic contradiction according to which there are two ways of thinking the transformation of the sensible conditions of an individual who has a low position in the social hierarchy: either he climbs to the top of the hierarchy, or else he completely undoes the hierarchy as a whole. Stendhal's novel is structured around this fundamental opposition between two ways of conceiving of equality: as revenge against a certain condition, or as abolition of the opposition between different conditions in the sensible event or in the distribution of the sensible event. For me, this is the very heart of realism, which is why I find for example Barthes' analyses of the reality effect completely irrelevant. What is important about the realist novel in the nineteenth century is not, as he thinks, a sort of excessive manifestation of signs of bourgeois plenitude, but something completely different. If there are many things, if there are many descriptions, it is because the sensible moment becomes essential, which also means that the poetic model based on creating well-formed chains of actions is about to break down.

sow: Even if you prefer not to talk about the connection between aesthetics and politics, we must still pose the question. You've written a history of the worker's movement in the nineteenth century, which is also the history of a new experience of the sensible. So there is a politics of literature, and there is also, as you say in the book, a sort of lag or rupture between a model of activity and a model of passivity in the socialist movement. Could you articulate this connection?

jr: This is something extremely complex. If we talk about the point of departure, I believe that the moment when ideas of revolution or emancipation take center stage is the moment of a connection between an idea of an active transformation of society and an idea of a suspension, an interruption, where the main issue is to live in another realm of the sensible. What aesthetics does, and this is what we find in Schiller, is to propose another idea of the revolution: a revolution that does not want to kill the king and reform the laws, but to change the very forms of sensible life. And I think that this model is present not only as an opposition between the strategies of different political parties or movements, but inside of Marxism itself, for example it is clearly present in Marx's early texts where we find the romantic model of the human revolution as opposed to the political revolution, a revolution of the forms of sensible existence that goes beyond the scope of a political revolution. We can see how what is commonly called the economism of Marx is also a way of transforming this idea of the peaceful revolution of the forms of life. In Marxism there is always this tension between a peaceful revolution of the material forms of life, and the idea of an insurrection that must await the precise moment of the historical process. And we can see that the primacy of history in Marx is the primacy of the relationship between these two models. History is both the development of the material conditions of a new sensible world, and what must produce the moment in which we can act. I think that we see this fundamental tension when Marx finds himself in front of the German communists in Paris who want to live in a new sensible world. On the one hand, in the manuscripts of 1844, he insists on the fact that they gather together not only for the defense of their interests but as the achievement of a new sense of community. On the other hand, in their correspondence, Engels and Marx scoff at those idiots who ask whether they should not attach forks and knives together to really live as communists.

Of course he thinks that this is stupid, that what counts is to found a party that will create the possibility of communism in the future. But at the same time there is this tension in the heart of Marxism, and it remains central to a whole idea of the revolution, of social transformation. In short, there is a fundamental opposition between a vision based on the classical model of action, where events are interlinked in order to arrive at a result, and then a model based on the idea of a revolution of the sensible forms, which also means an abolition of the relationship between activity and passivity, a challenge of the model of action. And in the end this is where we still find ourselves, whatever opinion we may have regarding the movements that occupy the streets today.

SOW: One author who is situated at the extreme point of this development, this way of breaking the causal chain, the chain of actions, is of course Mallarmé. You have returned to Mallarmé several times, and you place him next to Emerson and Whitman, but you also in a certain way understand him as a consequence of Stendhal's revolution, of Julien Sorel's ultimate fate. Where should we locate Mallarmé in this history?

JR: My reading of Mallarmé has always been animated by a critique of the modernist conception of him as the poet of the impossible work, the poet for whom in the poem the language takes itself as its object, this doxa where Mallarmé figures next to Mondrian and Schönberg as the one who liberates art from the certitude of representation: Mallarmé, in short, as the model of the autonomy of art. What I've been trying to do since quite a while already — in fact, this is almost where I started — has been to return Mallarmé to his place as a spectator of small theater representations, as a spectator of Loie Fuller's dance, as a spectator of attractions and popular shows and fairs: a Mallarmé who, on the stage and in the spatial realm of the performance, searches for the elements that will help him rethink the spatiality of the written poem. This also means that I have tried to place Mallarmé closer to the republican context of the era, where the aim was not at all to withdraw into solitude and separation, but on the contrary to see how poetry, once it had lost its old glory, could be rethought and dignified as a mode of experience of the common world. In Mallarmé's reflections about the theater, the theater is the place where a common world is outlined, defined. And in his reflections on poetry, the forms of poetry can constitute the voice of a common world, without degenerating into Wagnerian nationalism. This is what I find essential in Mallarmé. It is not connected so much to the question of activity-inactivity, but to the question of the model of the work, of the relationship between art and non-art, the fact that art from this point on constitutes itself by a sort of reappropriation of everything that had normally been placed in the domain of non-art. And this is the reason that in this book I've placed Mallarmé in the same lineage as poets such as Gautier and Banville, who looked at tightrope walkers and musicals, who searched for the elements of a new form of theater that would break with the petrified and dying forms of the old.

sow: There is a presence of theater: Ibsen, Gordon Craig, Maeterlinck — the spatiality of theater plays a central role in the book.

jr: This is important because I also try to reestablish, in the reflection about what is called modernity, the essential role of the arts of theater, the arts of the spectacle, the performing arts: choreography, tightrope walking, pantomime, early cinema, etc. I think it is very important to admit that there is a whole idea of modernity that is based almost exclusively on painting and on the facile paradigm that painting can offer us. Everyone knows what an abstract painting is, but what is an immobile theater, what is an inactive theater? This, for me, is an essential scene, because it will reconfigure the very relationship between action and life. Theater is the place where the old model of theatrical action will be finally ruined. And the ruin of the old model of theatrical action can be thought antithetically, that is, in the form of the direct presence of bodies, a sort of direct action of the bodies on stage, as opposed to the interpretation of a dramatic text. This is something that I try to follow in the book: the ways that theater can transform itself. On the one hand, it can transform itself into a sort of cathedral of the future, a place for the gathering of a crowd, which poses another problem about the relationship between aesthetics and ethics. The other side to the same story is theater as something that, faced with the classical model of action, tries to conquer a certain immobility, a pictorial immobility in certain stage settings, or a sculptural immobility, which is what is happening in Gordon Craig's work, in a very fascinating way: the destruction of the model of the actor, because the actor is an impossible mediation between two arts, one which is that of the poem, and one which is the art of movement in space. Gordon Craig creates a theater where the scenes are without words and where the staircase is the principal actor, not the support for the action. This was something fundamental, and even though people like Craig were forgotten they gave to the standard conception of theater a new set of elements that , in a sense, were themselves completely oblivoius of their origins and their function. Today the staircase has become a sort of obligatory accessory for a whole series of theatrical scenes, without any trace of the dramatic and theoretic function it used to serve. For me many things happen in the domains that are left by the side, such as the theater stage or the crafts, where the scene is redistributed. If we limit ourselves to

the facile perspective of new painting and music, we forget
everything that permits us to see the transformation of the paradigms of action on the theater stage, or the transformation of
the paradigms of life in the arts and crafts, for example.

KW: In this discussion about what we call modernism, about a
certain formalist modernism, one critic has a strategic function
in your book, and that is of course Clement Greenberg, who in a
sense provides the history of your counter-history. What does
Greenberg represent in your book?

JR: Well, let's say that I have nothing particular against Greenberg. Earlier I have confronted modernism in its French
versions, both the vulgar ones, such as Jean Clair, and the sophisticated ones, such as Lyotard — or else by way of the question of
Adorno. Greenberg is in the book almost by accident, certainly
there is a model...

SOW: The book ends with Greenberg, after all.

JR: The book ends there, but it is a connection that I... I did not
at all have the intention of ending the book with Greenberg, in
the sense that I almost did not have any idea of the architecture
of the book, of where it would end. I could have continued, at
one point I had the idea of talking about the cinema of Godard

▼
**Frederick Glasier,
Portrait of Loie
Fuller, 1902.**

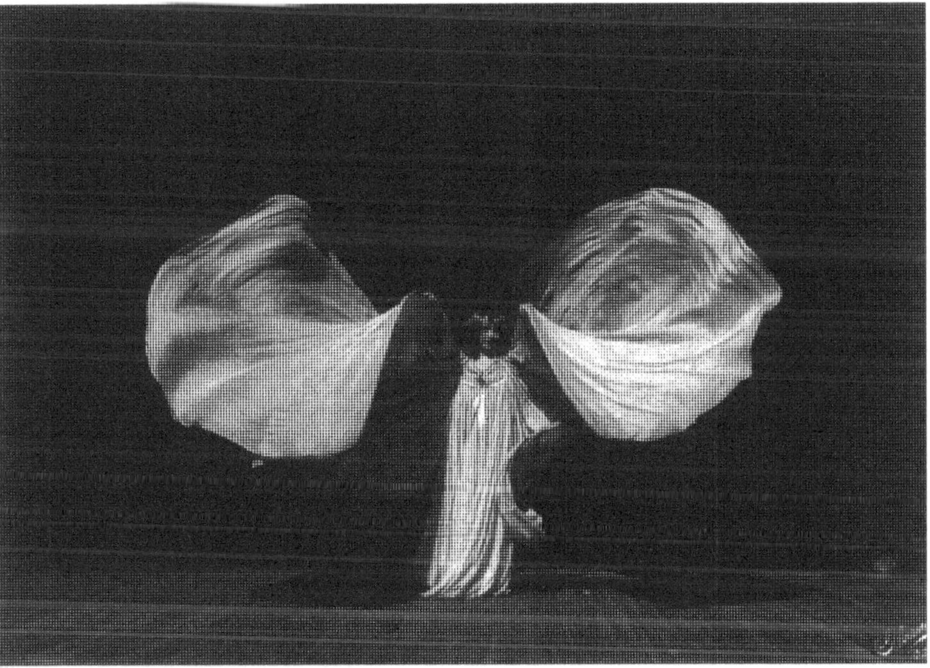

for example, but I had discussed it several times and I don't like to repeat myself. Anyway, at a certain moment, for reasons that had little to do with the structure of the book, I wanted to write something about James Agee's book, *Let Us Now Praise Famous Men*, with the idea that this could perhaps at some stage enter into my work. And then when I was working on Agee I came across an appendix where there is this controversy with the people behind the *Partisan Review*, who made a poll among their writers, and it was clear that the purpose of this poll was to announce that the model of the politics of literature can no longer be Whitman, can no longer be this democratic art, but must be Henry James and T.S. Eliot — and of course, Agee reacted strongly to this. Taking this into account, and thinking of the fact that Agee's book was started in 1936 and published in 1941, a lapse of time that also saw the publication of Greenberg's article, I constructed the final plot of the book, starting from the question: what happens in Agee's book? It is like the ultimate moment of a modernity that wanted precisely to renew art by including all the forms of experience that had been dismissed as trivial, as banal, as belonging outside of art. In a certain sense this is not only the story of Whitman — even though the story of Whitmanism in the US is very important, since it permits us to displace the emphasis from Mallarmé's European model — but it is also what is at play in Hegel in front of Murillo, in Théodore de Banville facing the acrobats, in Mallarmé in front of Loie Fuller, it is what is at play in Vertov, in Chaplin, in a whole idea of modernity as the abolition of the border between art and non-art — and we also find expressions to this effect in James Agee. And finally a moment arrives when people say, "OK, fine, we're tired of all that," and these people are of course Marxists, Trotskyists, who say that this is all Stalinism. I won't develop the Stalin-Trotsky aspect of this affair, but at one point I told myself that this was a possible ending, a provisional ending but a possible ending to the book: to show how the modernist ideology, such as it was thought by Greenberg, by Adorno, who played with it in a highly complex fashion, by Lyotard, who transformed it into a question of the rupture and the sublime, by people like Baudrillard, who transformed it into a paranoia regarding the great art conspiracy — to show, in other words, how this second modernity was constructed late, in opposition to the historical modernity, which wanted just the contrary: not at all to render art autonomous, but to make art a form of life, or to renew art by including everything, quotidian experience, newspapers, the accessories of life, everything.

SOW: In a certain way we could see this discussion in the *Partisan Review* as a sort of echo from or a parallel to the battle of expressionism in Europe in the '30s, with Lukács, Brecht and the others, a battle that is also in a sense the last movement of the period between the wars, and the end of the historical avant-garde, to use Peter Bürger's term. Could you connect these two, the Partisan Review with the *Expressionismusstreit* in Europe?

JR: As far as I've understood it, the question of realism in Europe, the way I perceive it through the Lukács-Brecht debate, concerns the way in which Lukács attempts to constitute a sort of progressive bourgeois tradition of realism in opposition to Brecht, who essentially — although it is of course more compli-cated — belongs to a dramatic tradition that tries to integrate the forms of the amusement park spectacles, to integrate the fragmentation of the plot, into the dramatic spectacle. After all what is important in Brecht is the way in which he takes up and reinterprets what had been at the center of interest of the aesthetes of the nineteenth century for popular theater, panto-mime, music-hall and so on: the fact that the "popular" perfor-mance, with its sequence of numbers is a break in relation to the classical representative logic and that it is the true form of "art for art's sake" since it "tells" nothing beyond the perfection of its own execution. Brecht takes up this re-evaluation and makes it a political project, when he conceives of epic theater as a suite of numbers. He inscribes himself into the tradition that has attempted to recuperate the popular spectacle as a spectacle without hidden significance, but he turns this "popular form" of "art for art's sake" into an instrument for denouncing a certain social system. On the opposite side, it seems to me that what Lukács tries to do is to mask the break with the model of action, which means that in a sense Brecht is the one who is sensible to this break, even though he tries to reestablish it by thinking that a sequence of numbers instead of a classical plot will be the reve-lation of a world that must be changed, which is after all an idea that, so to speak, was never verified historically. What is certain is that, when Lukács tries to build upon a model which is broken — and which happens to be the same model that Auerbach uses, the model of progressive history — what is at stake in the Euro-pean debate is ultimately the question: do we present the social-ist revolution as an extension of the progressive bourgeois model, with its supposed artistic forms, or do we play the game of rupture? Which is somewhat different from the way the debate is played out in the case of Greenberg, where you have T.S. Eliot and Hans Hofmann on one side and Whitman and the tradition of realist painters such as Thomas Hart Benton, Regi-nald Marsh and so on , the painters of American life, on the other.

SOW: What I wanted to say with this reference to .. expressionism, a battle that was constructed around an op̣p̣ tion between expressionism, which for Lukács included Joyce, Kafka, Woolf, in short modernism, and at the other end writers like Ernst Bloch and Brecht, who attempted to find a way to describe modernism as realism — what I wanted to say is that this debate, even though it may seem a bit bizarre and even though it disappeared very quickly because of WWII, had a very important effect in the sense that it established the program for a certain Marxist aesthetic discourse: we find it in Adorno in the 50s, in Fredric Jameson still today... So this debate was paradigmatic for a certain tradition where modernity and then postmodernity are thought on the basis of a theory of Marxism. And these old notions of realism and modernism still exist, even in Fredric Jameson. But your reading of realism is different: you break with this historicism.

JR: Certainly. What I try to say is precisely that realism is fragmentation. What Lukács does is to set realism, in the sense of the great narrative that unravels its meaning, against fragmentation, with the idea that fragmentation is expressionism, is bourgeois subjectivism, and in the extension of this we find Jameson. What is actually the heart of realism, among all the great realists, is the break with this model, and this is something that can be verified in everyone from Dostoyevsky and Tolstoy to Balzac, Flaubert and Stendhal.

SOW: You tell a certain kind of history... For example, if we wanted to compare your project with Peter Bürger's, for you the last part of the nineteenth century is very important: Symbolism, Mallarmé and so on. For Bürger this is the summit of aestheticism, the peak of the theory of art-for-art's-sake, perfected aestheticism: it is achieved autonomy. And then he describes the break that comes with the historical avant-garde, which wants to rejoin art and life. The history that you create is completely different.

JR: Yes, well, I don't know Peter Bürger very well and as you know I haven't taken a great interest in the problem of the avant-garde. Even though I attempt to establish connections to the notions of avant-garde and modernity, they are not my notions. On the contrary I have tried to show that this desire to rejoin art and life is something that runs through the whole of the nineteenth century, and that what is called art-for-art's-sake or autonomous art has always been a search for a certain type of inclusion of the new forms of life within the forms of art. Which is the reason that I have been especially interested in trying to challenge the perception of Mallarmé as the aestheticist poet who remains enclosed within his ivory tower, just as I have tried to change the perception of Flaubert as the novelist of the ivory tower: what is interesting is that the new form of the novel is only possible in correlation with the new forms of sensible experience, such as those we find in the scenes of Madame Bovary, with the women of the people who want to live a new life, to place art in their lives. And then, of course, Flaubert mocks this desire to aestheticize life. But his novel is not conceivable as an autonomous form, its syntax is only possible in correlation with the great social and cultural transformation as a result of which there is no longer a world of refined men and then a popular world below, but all of these forms of mediation, all of these forms of urban culture, all of these forms of culture propagated by newspapers and magazines, thanks to which a certain border can no longer be upheld. Let me remind you that this is all at the center of Greenberg's article: it is after all the culture of the poor that is responsible for the ruin of great art. What is important is that Flaubert makes great art with the culture of the poor: he denounces the culture of the poor and at the same time he proves the total solidarity between great art and the culture of the poor.

SOW: There are very few references to other thinkers in your book. There is Greenberg, but there is no Bürger, no Lukács, etc. Adorno appears once in a footnote. As *Aesthetic Theory* is lying there on the table, could you say something about Adorno? Your projects are very different but nevertheless there are certain parallels.

JR: It is very complicated, I am not sure that I have understood Adorno. There are authors that I haven't read so much, who do not interest me in a fundamental way, but Adorno is one of the authors that I have tried to come to terms with — not in the sense of taking position with or against him, but of attempting to understand what he said. Adorno is fascinating because on the one hand he incarnates a certain version of modernity, of the idea of the relationship between artistic modernity and political avant-garde, since modern art, autonomous art separates from the experience of aestheticized life, the experience of the culture industry; but there is also something that he lacks completely, with his rigid oppositions, which resemble those of Greenberg, between the real culture and the true art and then the aestheticized life, the culture industry, and so on. And at the same time he is someone who knows that, at the heart of modern and autonomous art there must be a fracture, in all the senses of the word, that is, an expression of pain and a persistence of childhood. So what I find interesting in Adorno, and what is

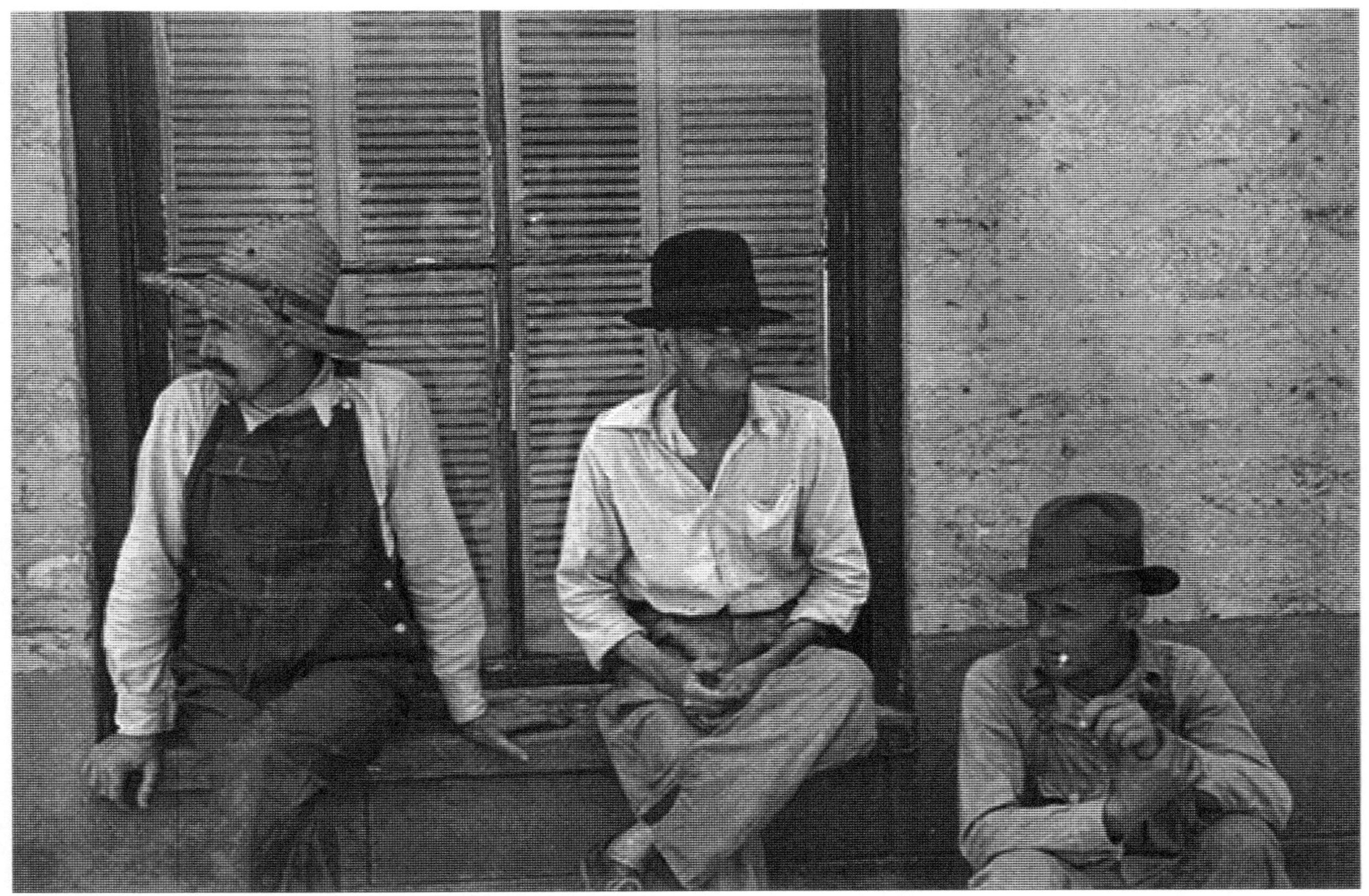

completely absent in Greenberg and has disappeared also in thinkers such as Lyotard, is this tension between a model that establishes an equivalence between autonomy, modernity and revolution, in so far as the word revolution still has a sense in the late Adorno, and a fractured model, and at the same time there is the fundamental idea that the distribution that makes art possible is connected to a social distribution which is in the last instance a separation between those who can listen to the song of the sirens and those who cannot. Which means that the autonomy of the work in Adorno must constantly be an autonomy that makes the fracture appear, the fact that behind it there is the pain of the division of labor, the pain of separation and social difference. And this is also at the same time the reappearance of the figure of childhood, the figure of the reconciled world, the world that thinks itself beyond all forms of social division. Think, for example, of Adorno's attitude to the figure of Chaplin, the double relationship that he could have to Chaplin: the positivity of the clown and at the same time the denunciation of *The Dictator* as a bad way of talking about Nazism. In a certain sense Adorno could just as well have understood *The Dictator* in the same way that he had understood the figure of Chaplin before, but at this historical moment he understands Chaplin as humanist denunciation. Fundamentally I think that there is an interesting tension in Adorno, but he also exhausts me a little.

sow: One thing that we do find in Adorno, and also in a different way in Heidegger, is the question of technology. For Adorno there is something in the modern artwork that is very important, its becoming-technical: serialism, etc. For him sensibility is something very suspect, because it implies a notion of immediacy, against which he sets the question of technical mediation. For you I would say that it is rather a question of a reevaluation of the sensible, whereas the question of technology remains in the background, it is not so important for you.

JR: Behind the whole question of the relationship between art and the transformations of technology or of technical mediation there is for me always the figure of the puppeteer, as in the Platonic myth. The puppeteer is the one who, since he creates popular culture, produces reality in a bad sense, the reality of the shadows, the sense of reality of the people who live in the cave. The puppeteer is the one who creates popular culture, and therefore he is bad, but at the same time he is bad as a technician, that is to say: the puppeteer is denounced on the one hand because he produces a vulgar sense of reality for the people, and on the other hand because he produces a false sense of reality which is finally nothing but manipulation. It is for this reason

there is this double discourse, which is very clear in the case of
Heidegger: the whole denunciation of media, of what media do,
of the new technologies, which are understood as producers of
images, but the image is here in fact two completely different
things: both the fate of people who are lost in the sensible, and
that which separates us from the true sensible, which is always
on the order of the immediate. I believe that this is what is
important: to think that behind the whole discourse on the role
of technology there is always this double game in relationship to
the very sense of technology, where technology is that which
produces both vulgar materiality and immateriality.

KW: The book ends with Agee, Greenberg, World War II, but if
you would have continued, where would you have gone? We
could think of any number of scenes where the play of activity
and inactivity returns. You mentioned Godard, but we could
also think of the Situationists, for example their notion of the
dérive, or of the rereading of the readymade among the New
Realists, and so on. Where would you have gone?

JR: The notion of play such as it was reappropriated by the New
Realists and the Situationists does not interest me a lot because
they take this notion too literally, too immediately. In other
words, what interests me with the notion of play is the notion of
a displacement of one form of sensible experience into another
form of sensible experience. On the other hand I of course see
that it is significant that this notion turns up in an iconoclastic
form among the New Realists and as a sort of anti-politics among
the Situationists. Let us say that play does not interest me as
much when it becomes identical with derision. There is a whole
way of thinking the politics of art according to the model of derision, where you question what is serious in art, and create different sorts of pastiche, an attitude that was important in defining
postmodernity, in Jameson for example. This does not interest
me. What would have interested me if I would have continued
would have been to work with events and forms of art that make
sensible forms pass over into other ones. And it is for this reason
that Godard's *Histoire(s) du cinéma* could have been interesting,
because they set everything into play: by the way in which
cinema is treated, where the images of cinema are connected to
news images, paintings, and so on; by the way in which the
movement of the film images is connected to the movement of
images in video art — all of this interests me. What I end in this
way is only this book: I have marked a phase, now I must go on.
And one can go on by turning back or by going further forward.
My problem is, in spite of all, that I am not so interested in all the
discourses that have become attached to the artistic events since

the '60s. I would say that with the network of discourses that has been created around Chaplin or around Loie Fuller I still have a certain liberty, but it seems to me that many of the artistic events since the '60s were events that in a sense were anticipated by their own discourses, which makes them less interesting. The discourses that accompany them render them this disservice. So the question would be if we could reestablish events from which some small scenes of discourse could be reinvented. What is interesting to me is to reconstruct a scene of discourse that has escaped. In late modernity, in the art from the '60s until today, there is such an almost obscene intrication of the discourses on art within the forms of art themselves, that for me as a researcher this art is not very interesting. It could place me in a position where I must judge between different interpretative systems, and not in the position of someone who could reestablish the discursive continent around an artistic event.

KW: In a sense this already answers my question, but I need to ask: "anti-Greenbergianism" already has a long tradition, how do you situate yourself within this tradition? From Rosalind Krauss to Thierry de Duve there is a great tradition of re-readings of Greenberg, which ask how Greenberg could miss the '60s, Minimalism, conceptual art, etc. What is your position in relation to these readings?

JR: I have read very little because it interests me very little. Again, I arrived at Greenberg not by way of Krauss or de Duve, but essentially — even though I had read texts by Greenberg before — by way of Agee, which is to say that I arrived at a Greenberg who marked the end of a certain American tradition, and not at someone by recourse to whom we could reevaluate the history of the art movements of the '60s. The art of the New Realists or conceptual art are not things that interest me as forms of art, and therefore they are not things that interest me as supports of discourses on art.

SOW: There is actually an astonishing proximity between what you say about Rodin, the surface of Rodin, the becoming-event of the surface in Rodin, and what Rosalind Krauss says in *Passages in Modern Sculpture*, where she reads Rodin's experiment in a way that is very close to yours.

JR: That is possible, but I haven't read this book by Rosalind Krauss. I am not a theorist of aesthetics, which means that there are things that I haven't read, and things that I have read very quickly, but I haven't at all tried to follow the development of aesthetic reflection as such. I arrived by transversal routes. •

Aisthesis

Baumgarten and the Invention of Aesthetics

Sven-Olov Wallenstein

1 • "Vom Begriff der philosophischen Ästhetik geht ein Ausdruck des Veralteten aus," *Ästhetische Theorie* (Frankfurt am Main: Suhrkamp, 1970), 491.

Reinventing the problem

"Aesthetics" and the "aesthetic" seem to have become concepts that in modern philosophy oscillate between a marginal and a central position — or perhaps even an exorbitant position. As *marginal*, aesthetics would be considered as only an addendum that does not address the central questions of ontology, epistemology, and ethics; as *essential*, there is something aesthetic at the heart of reason, to which works of art indeed point, although in a non-conceptual fashion that calls upon philosophy for clarification; and as *exorbitant*, finally, it occupies both positions at once, in a kind of antinomy, to be sure reminiscent of its Kantian ancestor, and yet impossible to solve with reference to a decidable philosophical architecture.

To cite one major example of this tension: Adorno, in the first draft for an introduction to his *Aesthetic Theory*, on the one hand notes that already the very word "philosophical aesthetics" gives the sense of something outmoded, and thus increasingly marginal.[1] And yet, we also know that aesthetics for him was a gateway to, if not simply identical to, a *prima philosophia* for modernity, in its capacity to suggest constellations of concepts and particulars that allow us to glimpse a certain truth otherwise inaccessible for philosophy as a mode of conceptual domination and subsumption. In this way it constitutes an indispensable part of negative dialectics, and not just one of several applications. And finally, in another passage he states the result of this logic, in a chiasma that decenters the circular relation, and can be taken as paradigmatic for a whole tradition of philosophy that extends far beyond Adorno's own work: "The true is unconcealed for discursive knowledge, but for this reason the latter does not possess it; the kind of knowledge that art is, has the true, but as something incommensurable to itself."[2]

But what is the origin of this strange quest, in which aesthetics overflows the bounds of a conceptual analysis and instead becomes a challenge to the very self-understanding of philosophy? Normally the inception of this tradition is situated in German idealism, in the debates that unfold from Kant to Hegel, where the Platonic conflict, the *diaphora* between art and poetry that already for Plato was something "immemorial," was opened again. Idealism in this sense made possible an "aestheticizing" of philosophy that became the main way in which Kant's strictures could be overcome. Subsequent to this we find Hegel's attempt to reinstate the rights of the concept, and to relocate art to the first movement of absolute spirit, but as such once more subordinated to philosophy, a move that is often seen as the first completion of a dialectical drama that would subsequently be rehearsed over and over again throughout modernity.

Here I would like to take a further step back to an even earlier historical period, where we find something like an "invention of the aesthetic". From Descartes to Baumgarten, who will be in focus here, there is a series of conceptual breakthroughs that precede and condition that later development leading up to Kant. For a long time Baumgarten was neglected, at least in the English-speaking world; recently, however, German and Italian scholarship has reintroduced him as a key figure.[3] In most textbooks he is credited with the invention of the very term "aesthetics" — the word appears in the penultimate paragraph in his 1735 thesis *Reflections on Poetry* — but then he is just as quickly dismissed as a belated echo of rationalism, and whose true insights would only become productive once they had been recast in a Kantian vocabulary. Here I will instead propose that a re-reading of Baumgarten may in fact provide us with a larger framework within which the subsequent development can be seen, and hopefully retrieve the idea of aesthetics as a *challenge*, as a *question* to thought, instead of just another academic discipline.

My proposal is thus not just to

2 • "Unverhüllt ist das Wahre der diskursiven Erkenntnis, aber dafür hat sie es nicht; die Erkenntnis, welche Kunst ist, hat es, aber als ein ihr Inkommensurables." Adorno, *Ästhetische Theorie*, 191.
3 • For a thorough survey of recent scholarship, see the translator's introduction in Baumgarten, *Ästhetik*, trans. Dagmar Mirbach (Hamburg: Felix Meiner, 2007). At present there is however to my knowledge no book-length monograph on his work in English.

unearth a piece of history, but to point to the origin of a certain articulation of concepts and sensibility that conditions the advent of idealism, and that has bearings on the present as well. In fact, what motivates the current interest in Baumgarten can be taken as our insecurity about the very meaning, status, and position of the aesthetic in the discourse of modern philosophy, and the question that I would like to resuscitate thus belongs to core of the definition of aesthetics today.

Drawing somewhat freely on the ideas of Jacques Rancière, I will propose that aesthetics should not be understood as a way to enclose the work of art, or the experience we have of it, in a particular sphere, as has been claimed by many 20th century thinkers, in the most far-reaching way probably by Heidegger, who inscribes it in mediation of Western metaphysics as a whole. But in spite of his attention to the historicity of thought, Heidegger's "destruction" of aesthetics remains strangely indifferent to the specific genealogy of the term itself, which he without further ado projects back into Greek philosophy.[4] Rather than as a late consequence of a set of initial, largely Platonic, metaphysical decisions — and thus as somehow predetermined by, or already contained in, the past — aesthetics is more productively seen as the irruption of an *expanded idea of thinking as such*, with implications that are metaphysical and epistemological as well as ethical and political. In this first phase of aesthetics, we find precise indications of what Rancière calls a new "distribution" or "sharing" of the sensible (*partage du sensible*),[5] i.e. on the one hand a reordering of the hierarchy between concept and intuition, understanding and sensibility, on the other hand an opening towards a dimension of intersubjective experience that allows for a togetherness in diversity.

But why speak of "invention"? Does this not somehow imply the

4 • As Christoph Menke argues, for Heidegger, modern aesthetics is based on the Cartesian subject and remains firmly entrenched in the ego cogito, which is a far too simple story; see Menke, *Kraft: Ein Grundbegriff ästhetischer Anthropologie* (Frankfurt am Main: Suhrkamp, 2008), 38ff. Symptomatically enough, in the inscription of aesthetics in the history of metaphysics that Heidegger proposes in the 1936 lectures on Nietzsche and the will to power as art, he proceeds directly from Descartes to Hegel, and ignores the whole eighteenth-century development, not only the specific formation of the term aesthetics, but curiously enough also Kant. I do not think that this simply invalidates Heidegger's reading, whose negative attitude, I think, is too influenced by what aesthetics *had become* during its development through nineteenth-century aestheticism and early twentieth-century formalism and neo-Kantianism. We should rather be aware of the possibility that what Heidegger calls the *destruction* of aesthetics — which, if we follow Heidegger's own lead, cannot be something negative, but just as the destruction of metaphysics delineated in *Being and Time* implies a setting free of hidden possibilities — is already part of the initial formation of the concept in relation to architecture of reason defined by a simplified rationalism. Rather than an extension and solidification of the metaphysics of subjectivity as inaugurated by Descartes, aesthetics initiates a "destructive" self-reflection of this very metaphysics, which thus already from the outset must be read according to its own stratification and inner insecurities.

5 • See for instance Rancière, *The Politics of Aesthetics*, trans. Gabriel Rockhill (London: Continuum, 2004).

artificial, vacuous, even "ideological" nature of the concept, as for instance Terry Eagleton claims?[6] After all, no one would speak of the "invention" of ethics or logic, even if they too indeed came into being as philosophical disciplines in particular contexts, and due to specific circumstances. As I hope to make clear, the word "invention" used in the title, should be understood neither as some creation *ex nihilo*, nor as the production of an ideological smoke screen, but rather in terms of what classical rhetoric called *inventio*. The idea of invention plays an important part in Renaissance theory, for instance in Alberti's use of *invenzione*, understood as the capacity of the painter to forge something new, an *istoria*, on the basis of a given material, while still retaining a certain recognizable quality that allows identities *and* displacements to be appreciated. In this sense the concept of aesthetics is an invention that draws on roots extending back to the inception of Greek philosophy, and reconfigures terms like *aisthesis*, *poiesis*, *techne*, and *phantasia* within the sphere of subjectivity, but also entails something new and unexpected that cannot be reduced to a set of sources and influences. It makes possible a new experience, both of works of art and of the thinking subject, and in this sense it belongs among the decisive "events" in philosophy. There is both continuity and discontinuity, and we should avoid both the theory of sharp epistemological breaks (nothing is the same after, say, Kant), and the continuity of origins (everything already lay dormant in Plato).

Aesthetics, as it emerges in the eighteenth century, is normally understood as a theoretical and philosophical description of a certain type of experience that we have in front of works of art, but also possibly including natural phenomena and utensils, if they are viewed from a certain perspective (the first systematic limitation of aesthetics to fine art and the exclusion of natural beauty occurs in Hegel's *Lectures on Aesthetics*). This description focuses on the subjective response of the viewer, which in turn impacts on the idea of creation that now begins to withdraw from the sphere of rules and instead comes to emphasize a particular type of indeterminacy. But, and this will be one of my proposals here, it also makes possible a different understanding of *thought itself*, not only of how it unfolds from intuitive manifolds, how it synthesizes and recognizes its objects, but also of how it *feels to think*, how thinking impacts, as well as draws on, a body no longer understood along the lines of a Cartesian *res extensa*, but as endowed with an irreducible life that overflows the bounds of intentional acting, and finally, it makes possible an understanding of subjectivity as resulting from a movement of repetition, contraction, and expansion whose synthesis is open-ended and belongs to time.

6 • See Eagleton, *The Ideology of the Aesthetic* (Oxford: Blackwell, 1990).

Within the rationalist tradition, this shift implies that knowing can no longer be understood as a deduction from evident axioms, or as an application of the model of a universal mathematics, the *mathesis* and/or *characteristica universalis* developed from Descartes to Leibniz, within which the particular and individual remains obscure, opaque, and devoid of rationality. But is also true that Baumgarten remains an heir to rationalism, and his suggestions must at first have seemed like marginal notes to the rationalist tradition. This is why Baumgarten's originality was disputed for a long time, and why for many historians, for instance Benedetto Croce and Réné Wellek, he is only nominally the inventor of aesthetics. Others acknowledge his originality, but instead claim that his discovery was such that it could only be integrated into the rationalist framework at the price of a contradiction and an inconsistency in his philosophy. Here I will argue against both of these reading. If many details in Baumgarten's work are heavily dependent on an unquestioned tradition, and some are admittedly obscure, this is because his work occupies a point of transition. This does however not prevent it from being both original and consistent, in fact, such a reading allows us to grasp it as a vantage point from which his rationalist predecessors as well as his Kantian successors appear a different light. In Baumgarten's breakthrough nothing was yet decided, which perhaps is what makes him relevant to our present uncertainties.

The evaluation of Baumgarten as unoriginal or inconsistent is in fact dependent on a stereotyped view of the rationalist theory of the continuity of nature, which was launched by Kant for largely polemical purposes. From Leibniz to Wolff, this theory is understood to have rejected sensible particulars as merely a diffuse mode of appearing of the intelligible, and to have reduced all knowledge to clear and distinct ideas — i.e., in principle, since such a reduction is not always possible for finite human beings, for instance in the case of contingent truths. To finite created minds a proposition like "Caesar crossed the Rubicon" seems contingent and random, whereas for God, the predicate "to cross the Rubicon" has always and necessarily been included in the substance bearing the signature "Caesar". For the field of experience later circumscribed as aesthetics, this would imply that "the pleasures of the senses are only intellectual pleasures perceived in a confused way," as Leibniz says at one point (*Principles of Nature and Grace*, § 17). For aesthetics to emerge, so the argument runs, this continuity would have to be abandoned in favor of the new opposition between the sensible and the intelligible, intuition and thought, which we find worked out in Kant.

But is this a sufficient view of rationalism? If this is *not* the case, then Baumgarten's rationalism need not introduce any inconsistency into his theory of aesthetics; in fact, it may be understood as prolonging and intensifying a tendency that we can unearth already in his predecessors. What we find upon closer inspection in the Cartesian turn to the "subject" will indeed make possible a whole set of other transformations that also include a new appreciation of art as referring to a particular mode of our sensibility, even though this is a quality that at first for Descartes disqualifies art and the sphere of imagination from being a topic for serious philosophical reflection, as he states in a famous letter to Mersenne. But in the next step, this rejection of the rational character of art — which also renders doubtful in advance the many affiliations that have been construed between Descartes and various forms of French Academic and classicist art theory — also paves the way for its *liberation* from the rules of poetics, which will make possible the emergence of a different understanding of rules, centered around the notion of subjectivity as a more fluid and open notion of experience that eventually comes to act as a kind of counterforce to the rule of Cartesian reason.

The next steps were taken by Leibniz, where we find not only a reworking of the Cartesian theory of ideas, which opens up the possibility of an analysis of clear and confused and yet not distinct ideas, the famous *je-ne-sais quoi* — which seems to imply an irreducible reference to a perceiving and embodied subject, whereas distinction refers to a disembodied conceptual knowledge — but also a new appreciation of that which eludes the active principle of consciousness ("small perceptions") and a way to unify consciousness through an inner and yet unknown principle. Aesthetics as a different way of understanding sensibility lies dormant here, folded into these minute perceptions: there is a principle at work in this seeming indeterminacy, although reason may not be sufficient to comprehend it, which perhaps also implies that reason itself must be thought differently, as necessarily related to a sensible multiplicity out of which it emerges, and that will always overflow it.

The turn towards the subject in Descartes is thus indeed a necessary, although not sufficient condition for the invention of aesthetics, as comes across in his unequivocal claim that the sensible and particular cannot be made into the object of science, whereas Leibniz in fact takes several decisive steps towards a new conception, which eventually would usher into the emergence of aesthetics as a new domain of philosophy. In this sense, the fact that Baumgarten continues a certain rationalist type of philosophy *and* opens up the territory of aesthetics need not involve him in any inconsistencies. What he invites us to do is to redefine the sensible in a way that will also affect the logical, which can be taken precisely as an invention that first

AESTHETICA

SCRIPSIT

ALEXAND. GOTTLIEB BAVMGARTEN

PROF. PHILOSOPHIAE.

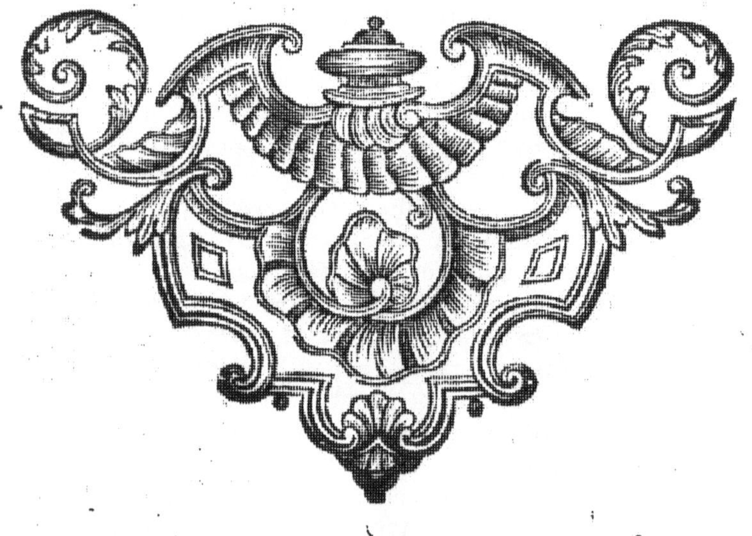

TRAIECTI CIS VIADRVM

IMPENS. IOANNIS CHRISTIANI KLEYB

CIↃCIↃCCL.

◄

**Frontispiece
from *Aesthetica*,
Alexander
Gottlieb
Baumgarten,
printed by Ioannis
Christiani Kleub,
1750.**

seems to introduce a certain disorder among the faculties, but also, in a more positive vein, can be taken as a "redistribution" of the sensible, both a *division* and a *sharing*. This does not mean that a new object emerges that had been simply lying there, dormant throughout history, but signals a transformation of the idea of a hierarchy of the faculties as such.

The project of a new science

Baumgarten's *Reflections on Poetry* is a dissertation, presented by the 21-year-old student at the philosophical faculty at the University of Halle in 1735, and at first it went almost unnoticed. In these dense 117 paragraphs, posterity has however been able to detect a decisive shift, where the arts (in the thesis the analysis is restricted to poetry, which will remain Baumgarten's main source) for the first time became the object of a particular philosophical discipline, and a new determination of sensibility emerges. In this the field of aesthetics not only appears as a hitherto dormant possibility of inquiry, but also as something that has repercussions on the structure of philosophy itself. Even though this was at first largely implicit, the logic of the sensible that Baumgarten projects has one side turned towards the arts and their particular qualities, another side towards the relation between the sensible and intelligible in general, and it is in this sense that we may understand it as a redistribution and a sharing that not only identifies a new type of objects, but also reconfigures the links between the faculties of the mind. The project of a new science in this sense also implies the larger project of a new determination of science as such, a rethinking of philosophy's own self-understanding.

The theses on poetry in the first treatise from 1735 would soon be explored in a series of writings, where aesthetics was to be expanded to include all of the arts (even though this was never worked out but remained a promise), and is connected to the problems of metaphysics, logic, and ethics. This movement culminates in the monumental although unfinished *Aesthetica* (two volumes were published in 1750 and 1758), where the term "aesthetics," in the first treatise only introduced as if *en passant* in the next-to-last paragraph, now becomes the main title. This later work however for a long time remained less known, partly because of its obscure Latin style, judged by Baumgarten's contemporary, the philologist Johann Matthias Gessner, to be "horrible beyond comparison,"[7] but also, and perhaps more importantly, because of the constant references to classical poetics and poetry that tended to obscure its originality. Thus, for a long time the more succinct and accessible text from 1735 was the main reference, and it is also, significantly enough, still the only of his works to have been translated into English.[8]

Between the *Reflections* and the *Aesthetica* there also lies a series of works, above all the *Philosophische Brieffe von Aletheophilus* (a philosophical weekly published by Baumgarten in 1741, discontinued after the first year) and the *Metaphysica* (1738), where we find the intermediary steps that would lead to the final conception. Baumgarten also published many other works, comprising treatises on moral philosophy and logic, which, however, lie outside of my focus here, and I will limit myself to delineating the main steps in the particular trajectory that takes him from the first treatise on poetry to the attempt to create a systematic aesthetics in the last years.

In the brief autobiographical sketch that opens the *Reflections*, Baumgarten provides some clues to the context of his dissertation, above all his early interest in poetry and humanist scholarship, and his unshakable faith that they provide both pleasure and instruction, according to the venerate Horatian formula, *delectare et prodesse*. He also points to the preparatory classes he had been teaching the future students at the university, where his guiding question took form: can poetry be given a proper philosophical foundation, and furthermore, is this because there exists an even more profound unity of philosophy and poetics? The first proposal extends the program of Wolffian philosophy, although remaining within its orbit: to provide an a priori foundation for those sciences that rely on empirical and historical evidence (or practice and imitation, in the case of poetry). The second, announced in the clam that philosophy and the science of the making of poetry are not "entirely antithetical" (*dissitissimis*), but in fact "linked together in the most amiable union" (*amicissimo iunctas*), is a more daring step, and as we will see, it also entails a rethinking of the relation between concepts and sensibility, which will be the task of aesthetics.

Such a theory, a combination of Wolffian rationalism and a poetry influenced by Baumgarten's teacher Martin

Aisthesis

---

7 • Cited in Pietro Pimpinella's preface to the Italian translation of the *Reflections, Riflessioni sulla Poesia* (Palermo: Aesthetica, 1999), 7. The lectures held by Baumgarten, where he commented the text of the *Aesthetica* paragraph by paragraph, are much more clear and accessible, although they for a long time remained unpublished. A manuscript, probably dating from 1750–51, was published in 1907, as *Kollegium über Ästhetik*, appendix in Bernhard Poppe's thesis *Alexander Gottlieb Baumgarten: Seine Bedetung und Stellung in der Leibniz-Wolffischen Philosophie und seine Beziehung auf Kant*. These lecture notes have also been translated and edited in Italian by Salvatore Tedesco, as *Lezione di Estetica* (Palermo: Aesthetica, 1998).

8 • *Alexander Gottlieb Baumgarten's Meditationes philosophicae de nonnullis ad poema pertinentibus: Reflections on Poetry*. Translation, introduction, and notes by William B. Holther and Karl Aschenbrenner (Berkeley: University of California Press, 1954). All references to the *Reflections* are with paragraph number. I have also benefited greatly from three other translations: by Heinz Paetzold, *Philosophische Betrachtungen über einige Bedingungen des Gedichts* (Hamburg: Meiner, 1992), by Pietro Pimpinella, *Riflessioni sulla poesia*, and by Jean-Yves Pranchère, *Méditations philosophiques sur quelque sujets se rapportant à l'essence du poème*, included in Baumgarten, *Esthétique* (Paris: L'Herne, 1988).

Christgau, must at the time have seemed like an impossible idea, as Herder would later note.[9] And yet this is precisely what Baumgarten projects, even though the ramifications of this idea were probably not evident to him at first: not only to rationalize Horace's *Ars poetica* and provide it with a deductive form, but also to attain the moment when poetry, or a certain experience of language and concepts that poetry conveys, becomes essential for logic itself, since it must be able to incorporate a relation to sensible particulars. Extending some of Baumgarten's claims, we might say that there is finally nothing purely logical, no pure conceptual relations that would be independent of the medium or sensible element in which they are immersed.

By giving his dissertation the title "meditations" (which is lost in the English translation "Reflections": the Latin title, *Meditationes philosophicae de nonnullis ad poema pertinentibus*, might be rendered more literally as "Meditations on some things pertinent to the poem"), Baumgarten inserts his treatise in the tradition from Descartes's *Meditations on First Philosophy*, with the intent to probe deeper and deeper layers in search of a foundation upon which we may ground and rebuild what we in our everyday understanding assume in a non-reflected way. As we will see, here too the problem will be how to relate the two moments in the Cartesian definition of truth: the clear and the distinct. For Baumgarten, there will appear a limit to the Cartesian project, or more precisely, the possibility of investigating a space left blank by Descartes, in a way that neither simply opposes nor subscribes to the predecessor's claims, and this will be the space of the "aesthetic". Rather than taking us down to a *fundamentum inconcussum*, these meditations will lead us into a space of exchange between the sensible and the intelligible, where their respective determinations as "higher" and "lower" largely remain nominally intact, to be sure, although a different kind of articulation is at work below the inherited vocabulary.

Baumgarten provides us with a plan for what is to come, a deductive structure in the Wolffian tradition, but one which also revives a rhetorical tradition.[10] These five main sections, which do not correspond to any graphic markers in the text, are as follows: A (§ 1–11), definition of the poetic idea, and its relation to other ideas; B (§ 12 64), development of the poetic thought (*cogitatio poetica*) and its constituent parts; C (§ 65–76), description of the poetical method; D (§ 77–107), analysis of the poetic mode of expression

9 • "Ein *Wolfischer* Philosoph und ein *Christgauischer* Poet in Einer Person," Herder writes. See "Vom Baumgartens Denkart in seinen Schriften" (1767), in *Werke* (Munich: Hanser, 1987), vol. 2, 20. Martin Christgau (1698–1776) was from 1727 the headmaster at the gymnasium in Berlin, and Baumgarten's father had early on entrusted Christgau with the intellectual upbringing of the young Alexander.

10 • Baumgarten's division of the text can be taken as corresponding to the rhetorical three-part structure *inventio, dispositio,* and *elucutio,* and a similar plan also organizes the *Aesthetica.* See Paetzold's introduction to the German translation, XLIII.

in relation to other types; and E (§ 108–117), concluding remarks, first on the role of mimesis, and then on the necessity of a new discipline named aesthetics.

A) The idea of the poem. Baumgarten begins by defining one of his key terms, *discourse (oratio)* as a series of words that designate connected representations. Here he moves on well-established rationalist ground: representation is the most general term for the contents of the mind,[11] and inversely, such connected representations may be discerned through an analysis of discourse. Discourse and representation in this sense mirror each other, they are mutually implicative, and we can follow this analysis from the singular representation and its connections down to the minute details, words or articulate sounds, represented by letters that form the signs for the representation in question.

The kind of representations that we are dealing with in the case of poetry are however "sensible" (*sensitivae*),[12] which, unlike in the case of Wolff, does not mean that they are specifically related to the faculty of desire, instead they are just as much connected to knowledge. This implies a restructuring of the hierarchy, within which we see the sensible acquire a new type of perfection, expressed in a reordering of the clear and the obscure, the confused and the distinct. Such a sensible moment, Baumgarten adds, exists in all forms of discourse, even the most abstract and intellectual ones like philosophy, and it can never be entirely reduced. In a *perfect* sensible discourse, however, the constituent parts are uniquely directed towards sensible representations and the awakening of such representations, and this type of discourse is the *poem*.

The idea of perfection here plays a crucial role, and it will be one of the motives behind Kant's criticism in his *Critique of Judgment*, since it appears to link aesthetic experience too closely to a cognitive claim and reduce its specificity. In later writings too, both in the *Metaphysica* (§ 662) and the *Aesthetica* (§ 14), perfection will be taken as synonymous with beauty, and Baumgarten seems to adhere to a traditional ontological idea of beauty as unity in variety, which we can find eloquently developed in Leibniz' various claims about harmony, but can also be traced back through medieval philosophy to Plato. The role of the argument in this context seems, however, to be to specify the particular nature of the poem with respect to discourse in general: the more

11 • Even in Kant, everything from concepts of the understanding to space and time as intuitions, are subsumed under the general concept of "Vorstellung": see *Critique of Pure Reason*, A 320/B 376f.
12 • Aschenbrenner and Hold' translation *sensate* seems uncalled for, just as Paetzold's "sensitiv." Dagmar Mirbach, in her recent translation of the *Aesthetica*, opts for "sinnlich," and in the following I will use "sensible" in English. "Sinnlich" is also how Baumgarten renders the term in German in the *Kollegium* text.

the parts of a poem awaken sensible knowledge of particulars, the more it is perfect, whereas other forms of discourse — for instance rhetoric, as we will see towards the end of the dissertation — always subordinate this sensible perfection to some other aim, for instance transmission of conceptual knowledge or persuasion. The "poetic," Baumgarten continues, can be determined as that which contributes to the perfection of the poem, and the poem itself can be understood as a perfect sensible discourse.

B) Poetic thought. The second part then proceeds to develop the idea of a poetic thought, in two steps: first by discussing the concept of extensive clarity, where we find the essentials of Baumgarten's reception and reformulation of the debate on the status of the idea from Descartes through Leibniz to Wolff, and then by applying these general concepts to the structure of the poem.

The Cartesian definition of truth, based in the dual criterion of clarity and distinction, had already been pried apart by Leibniz, who introduced a whole set of degrees and dynamisms in the monad, a work that was continued in Wolff, who proposed even further distinctions. For Baumgarten, an obscure cognition (*cognitio obscura*) implies that we cannot recall a particular impression and separate it from others, since we do not possess a sufficient amount of characteristic marks (*notae*). In clear cognition (*cognitio clara*), however, we possess such marks, and we are able to hold on to them. These clear ideas contribute more to the richness of the representations to be communicated, Baumgarten adds, and they are in this sense more poetic than obscure ones. Obscurity as such, he repeatedly claims, cannot be a criterion of poetic value, which on the one hand obviously testifies to his adherence to a classicizing tradition (in this respect, Baumgarten is not a proto-Romantic, but firmly entrenched within the Horatian camp), but on the other hand constitutes a necessary move for the formulation of the aesthetic concept of clarity.

Unlike clear cognition, distinct cognition (*cognitio distincta*) means that we are able to analyze the marks contained within representation into their constituent parts, and it can be augmented to the level of adequate, symbolic, and intuitive knowledge (with terms that all derive from Leibniz). If we are able to distinguish the conditions of the terms used, cognition will be adequate; if these conditions contain a priori concepts, it is either symbolic or intuitive, where symbolic means that we operate with complex concepts that we cannot see through (operations carried out by a "blind cogitation," *cogitatione caeca*, as Leibniz says,[13] which is most often the case in mathematics and geometry), whereas intuitive cognition would be that rare case when we are able to have a direct access to the ultimate foundations, which are normally unavailable except to divine thought.

From this Baumgarten draws two conclusions. The first is that poetic representations cannot be those that are distinct, complete, adequate, and profound at all levels, since they belong to the order of conceptual knowledge, instead poetic representations must be confused. These can in turn be obscure or clear, and the latter are the ones that contribute to the perfection of the poem in making the poetic image more comprehensible, whereas obscure ideas only provide a kind of underlying resonance and ulterior associative ramifications.[14] The second consequence is that a further specification of the concept of clarity is possible: by a further analysis of the marks contained within clear representations, they can either be augmented so as to reach a state of distinction, or they can remain in a state of confusion.[15] But even in this state of confusion they allow for a recognition of objects, although not through concepts, and typical cases of this would be smells, sounds, colors, and faces, as Leibniz had already suggested. To this Baumgarten now adds a further distinction, which allows him to delineate the space of the poem more precisely than his predecessors, and may be taken as one of his essential inventions: clarity can be increased by the addition of new marks without these latter being further analyzed, which results in *extensive clarity*, whereas a clarity increased through an analysis of the various parts would be *intensive*. The former is the properly *poetic* domain: an extensive clarity that increases the amount of marks while still being able to retain the individuality of the representation, which is the true sense of perfection as unity in variety. Intensive clarity, on the other hand, approaches distinction and concepts, and belongs to cognition in the theoretical sense.

But how is this to be applied to the poem? Baumgarten develops this in three steps, first through what we could call a *logic of individuality*, and then through an account of the role of *affects* and *fictions*. The first step has to do with the fact that poetic thought first and foremost refers to something individual.[16] Individuals, he writes, are determined in all respects, and singular representations

13 • See for instance "Meditationes de Cognitione, Veritate et Ideis," in *Die Philosophischen Schriften*, ed. Gerhardt, IV, 424. On the nature of this blindness, which opposes the formalism of Leibniz to what we could call the "intuitionism" in Descartes, and in this way introduces a much more complex classification of mental acts, see Michel Serres, *Hermes I: La commiunication* (Paris: Minuit, 1968), 127–53, and Yvon Belaval, *Leibniz: Initiation à sa philosophie* (Paris; Vrin, 1969), where the theme is traced all the way back to the early text *De Arte Combinatoria*.

14 • On the shifting role of the obscure, which seems to be more important as Baumgarten's work progresses, see Ursula Franke, *Kunst als Erkenntnis: Die Rolle der Sinnlichkeit in der Ästhetik des Alexander Gottlieb Baumgartens* (Wiesbaden: Studia Leibnitiana, supplement IX, 1972), 46f.

15 • Here we must avoid to see this confusion simply as a lack of distinction, although Baumgarten's own translation in the *Kollegnachschrift* of the term as *verworren* might seem to indicate this. The emphasis must rather lie on the dimension of fusing, blending, and merging, and not on any simple disorder.

can thus be taken as poetic in the highest degree. Representations at a lower level of abstraction are always more poetic than those on a higher level, and abstractions must be endowed with individual traits and be personified in order to appear vivid. There is also a rhetorical background to this argument, in the idea of the *exemplum*, i.e. a representation of something more determinate that is added to enhance clarity.

The second aspect relates to *affects* or "sense impressions" (*sensualibus ideis*),[17] which also contribute to extensive clarity by producing changes relating to the sphere of practice and desire in the representing subject. Setting affects in motion, Baumgarten concludes in this second and brief point, is highly poetic.[18]

The third application has to do with *fictions* and the use of fantasy. Imaginations (*phantasmata*) too belong to the sensible representations, and they contribute to extensive clarity in several ways: by substituting part for whole, by an expanding movement in space and time, by shifting the relation between genus and species, and by introducing similes. They also have the capacity to produce wonder by the introduction of foreign elements, although these have to be tempered by familiar ones.

This restrictive and classicizing tendency permeates Baumgarten's writings, and it can be taken to show that his taste, notwithstanding the radicalism of his invention of aesthetics, undoubtedly remains firmly entrenched in the tradition. Even though he acknowledges the usefulness of elements that are altogether fantasized, *figmenta*, themselves composed by imaginations, this is always within the framework of a discussion of the bounds of the poet's imagination. He understands these bounds on the basis of his metaphysics, which draws on Leibniz' theory of possible worlds, where the best of all possible is selected on the basis of the principle of maximum compossibility (the being possible *together*, *com*-possible) of variations within one and the same world.[19] It is through this metaphysical argument, rather than through a claim to uphold a particular

16 • Here too we might discern yet another motif from Leibniz, where individual and concept enter into a new constellation, so that the fully determined and specified concept itself is an individual (Caesar who contains all his predicates: to cross the Rubicon in 49 BC, to be stabbed to death by Brutus...), and the individual is that which envelops all of its past, present, and future predicates. The power that unfolds through and as the individual is a striving to attain as high a level of determination as possible, the "living force" that drives the monad from one perception to another, and to unfold and explicate that which is enfolded and implicated in its dark backdrop, the *fuscum subnigrum*.

17 • By *sensualibus* Baumgarten here and in the following seems to refer to "ideas" particularly related to direct sense perceptions instead of imagined ones, although his use of this adjective is far from consistent, and sometimes creates a confusion with "sensitivus."

18 • We should note that the theory of affects too is part of the rhetorical tradition, and that it had been systematized in the seventeenth century, especially in the theory of music. Important contributions were made by for instance Descartes' interlocutor Mersenne, in his *Harmonie universelle* (1636).

decorum, that he first distinguishes between true figments (*figmenta vera*, § 51) which are possible within this world, and "heterocosmic" ones (*figmenta heterocosmica*, § 52), only possible in other worlds, and proposes that these two, each in their respective way, contribute to the poetic, whereas the third type, utopian figments (*figmenta utopica*), violate the possibility of the world as such. In this way the poet cannot be said to be a creator of a world to the fullest extent, since his task is to reveal the order of this world, and the beauty and pleasure of the poem will always have to do with the beauty and pleasure we take in the world.

C) The order of the poem. After having uncovered the idea of the poem as distinguished from other ideas (or forms of discourse), and having determined the structure of the *cogitatio poetica*, Baumgarten proceeds to discuss the internal order of the poem. This task also has two aspects: the analysis of the *theme*, i.e. the basis for the unity of the poem, and a presentation of the *method* of poetry. The theme is that which contains the sufficient reason for the other representations in the series that makes up a poem. As such it is not a representation among others (it need not be explicitly stated in the poem), but what provides the sequence of representations with their unity, and this is why it is better, Baumgarten suggests, to have one and not several themes. Order (*ordo*, § 69), i.e. the way in which the various parts are determined through the theme, is thus to be understood as a fundamental aesthetic category. This may on the one hand be read as if the poet would create his theme, and in this sense be the sole legislator over the world that he has engendered; on the other hand, and in line with the Leibnizian restriction on fantasy that concluded the previous section, for Baumgarten it is the unity of the world that is reflected in the theme, which once more limits the idea of a radical and unfettered worldmaking.

What, then, is the method of poetry — the "lucid method" (*methodus lucidas*) that Baumgarten no doubt picks up from Horace's *lucidos ordo*,[20] and which seems to relate him so closely to the tradition of ancient poetics that some in these *Reflections* have seen simply an attempt to rewrite the *Ars poetica* in the language of Wolffian rationalism? Later, in the *Aesthetica*,

19 • The notion of compossibility in Leibniz should be distinguished from that of logical contradiction, in that not all logically possible states are compossible within the same world. Deleuze suggest the term "vicediction" instead of "contradiction" to describe this; see Deleuze, *Le Pli: Leibniz et le baroque* (Paris: Minuit, 1988), 79. As Deleuze notes, Leibniz himself ultimately presents the idea as a mystery, hidden deep inside the mind of God.

20 • "Cui lecta potenter eris res, nec facundia deseret hunc nec lucidus ordo" ("A man who chooses a subject within his powers will never be at loss for words, and his thoughts will be clear and orderly"). Horace, *The Art of Poetry*, 40–41. trans. T. S. Dorsch, in *Classical Literary Criticism* (London: Penguin,

Baumgarten would speak of an "aesthetic light" (*lux aesthetica*) that makes the work accessible and comprehensible to the senses, and derives from the interplay of extensive clarity and unity. In the *Reflections*, he says that the rule of the lucid method is that poetic representations should follow upon each other in such a way that *the theme gradually becomes more extensively clear* (§ 71). It is only in the light of this emergent unity that the theme can transpire in all of its clarity, and each part must contribute to this goal.

The more precise analysis of this method is only sketched out, and Baumgarten does not seem to have given much thought to the interrelations between its different aspects: it can consist of a relation between premise and conclusion, i.e., a strictly rational method and a logical instead of sensible connection (which contradicts the initial determinations in the first part of the text, although Baumgarten seems not to notice it); it can be a "historical" method that creates connections according to the laws of fantasy and perception, in their turn grounded in memory; and finally, it can be a method of "wit" (*ingenium*), which lets like follow upon like. To these rather loose descriptions Baumgarten adds a demand for brevity: the poet must avoid digressions that lack connection to the overall theme.

D) Poetic expressions. In the fourth part, Baumgarten descends further down into the structure of the poem, and investigates the nature of poetic expressions, as well as our response to them. Here he discusses four particular aspects: the relation between language and poetry in general, poetic tropes or figures, the capacity for sensible judgment or taste, and finally poetic meter.

The poem, Baumgarten underlines, does not only consist of a poetic thought and connections between representations, but also of *words*, which in turn have both a semantic and an acoustic dimension. To be poetic means to pay heed to both of these aspects; the first, semantic quality, points to the theory of tropes, whereas the second, the acoustic quality, to an analysis of sound, and also to *taste* as the capacity of sensible judging, within which he also locates meter.

The poetic figures give us a semantic complexity in drawing on an "improper signification" (*significatus improprius*, § 79), and in this their multidimensionality brings us close to the senses, although here too Baumgarten once more stresses that obscurity must not be an end in itself, but always be subordinated to the demand for clarity. He provides us with a rather conventional account of the tropes, drawing on Aristotle, Quintilian, Cicero, and their Renaissance commentators, and discusses epithets and allegories. An original stroke is however added in § 89, when he notes that proper names in themselves can be poetic, since they denote an individual, which, as we have seen, for Baumgarten is not simply the bearer of properties, but following Leibniz is understood as containing a particular perspective on the world that can be unfolded.

The discussion of taste provides a more original account, although Baumgarten here too draws on discussions whose roots lead as far back as the Renaissance, if not further. Taste, he suggests, is a sensible capacity for judging, and it judges the sensible as such, the sensual ideas (*ideas sensuales*, § 91) produced by words in our mind. The "judgment of sense" (*iudicium sensuum*)[21] is a confused judgment, relating to the perfection of the senses, which means that the capacity for judging does not belong exclusively to the understanding (as was the case in Descartes and is still upheld by Kant). This judgment of the ear can produce pleasure (*voluptas*) or displeasure (*taedium*), and to produce such sentiments is the task of poetry. The more we experience a harmony, the more pleasure we get, which also heightens our attention.

If a poem produces a pleasure of the ear through a series of articulated sounds, this is because it also possesses a unity on a pre-semantic level, beneath the layer of explicit signification. In order to possess such a unity, a poetically worked-through linguistic structure needs purity (*puritas*), a harmony of parts (*concinnitas*), an ornamentation of the figures (*ornatus figurarum*), all of which comes together in a euphony or a "sonority" (*sonoritas*). These aspects exist in all uses of language, although poetry is the only one to focus on them in such a way that the communication of a particular content may be relegated to a secondary status. To this Baumgarten adds a discussion of poetic meter, whose use of syllable length and syllable quality generates a similar euphony and unity beneath the level of signification, by making the series of sensual ideas accessible in a temporal order.

E) The principles of poetry: mimesis and aesthetics. After having traversed these steps, which proceed in a descending order from the specific idea of poetry as a part of discourse in general, to poetic thought as based in extensive clarity, and its application to the poem, then to the internal order of the poem, based in the theme and the lucid order, then to poetic expressions and their use of words, both as semantic and acoustic phenomena, we finally arrive at the conclusions, which deal first with the idea of mimesis, and then with the consequences for philosophy in general.

Aisthesis

21 • The idea of a judgment of sense has a long history before Baumgarten, as is demonstrated in great detail in David Summers, *The Judgment of Sense: Renaissance, Naturalism and the Rise of Aesthetics* (Cambridge: Cambridge University Press, 1987).

Imitation, Baumgarten proposes, occurs when something produces a similar effect, which in the case of poetry means that its imitation of nature must produce an effect that is similar to nature. In order to grasp this we must once more note the proximity of Baumgarten's concept of nature to that of Leibniz: nature is not an external object in space and time to be depicted or copied, rather it is the internal principle of change in the universe, reflected in each monad, extending from the most obscure and confused level of sensibility to the highest clarity and distinction. This is why Baumgarten can determine the logic of mimesis as a double process, where nature and art mirror each other, since they produce similar representations. If poetry is an analogy to nature, as he had claimed earlier (§ 68), then we can also say that art imitates because nature is itself a process of production of sensible representations.

Aesthetics, finally, will demand a transformation of the idea of philosophy, since the latter cannot simply incorporate it as one more object of study to be ranged among the others, although this is not developed until the later writings. The case of poetry shows that there is a specific domain of sensible cognition that must be investigated in a different fashion than is done by traditional logic, i.e. a logic of sensibility that must incorporate the findings of "psychology" (which, as we will see, for Baumgarten is the discipline that investigates the depths of the soul as that out which representations emerge). This will not just entail a new appreciation of language, as in the humanist reevaluation of rhetoric, but the founding of an entirely new discipline.

Already the ancient philosophers and the Patristic thinkers made a distinction between that which belongs to *aisthesis* and *noesis*, Baumgarten notes, where the former was the object of logic. A study of *ta aistheta*, those things that belong to sensibility, must however not limit itself to an analysis of perceptual structures, but also include fantasy and fiction, i.e. the whole domain of art.

In a certain way philosophy, poetry, and rhetoric share a common ground, although this does not mean that they merge into some indistinct unity. Philosophy, Baumgarten suggests, does not direct its attention to the expressions as *aistheta*, whereas rhetoric and poetics, as parts of aesthetics, focus precisely on this aspect. Rhetoric, he concludes, is the science of how to present sensible representations in an imperfect way, whereas poetics investigates them with respect to perfection, since the former uses these representations in order to convince the listener of a content that can be defined outside of them, while poetry intends to develop our capacity for sensible representations as such.

Metaphysica and the Letter from Aletheophilus

In the wake of the *Reflections*, Baumgarten would constantly return to the questions that his youthful dissertation had opened up, develop them in new systematic contexts and attempt to provide the metaphysical framework that remained implicit in the first text. This first takes place in the *Metaphysica* (1739),[22] where he, in a section called "empirical psychology," presents a more detailed analysis of the lower cognitive faculty, which he now determines as the seat of sensible representations.

Baumgarten's *Metaphysica* had a huge impact: seven editions were published between 1739 and 1779, after Baumgarten's death it was translated in 1776 in an abridged form by his pupil Meyer, which meant that it also gained a wide popular readership. Kant would later use this text as the point of departure for his lectures on logic and metaphysics, even though he in the *Critique of Pure Reason* rejects Baumgarten's use of the term aesthetics to discuss taste,[23] and wants to reserve this term for a treatment of space and time as the sensible conditions of experience. After Kant the work has however sunk into oblivion, and was for a long time rarely cited, and it has still not been translated in its entirety into any modern language.

In the *Metaphysica* Baumgarten presents the basic outlines of his system, once more drawing on Wolff and Leibniz, and for our present intent, it is crucial how he develops and generalizes his aesthetic theory by providing it with a conceptual underpinning. The relevant part is the section on "empirical psychology," where he provides us with a detailed account of the lower cognitive faculty. Following the model established in the Wolffian school, the book as a whole is divided into cosmology, psychology, and theology (which corresponds to the old division between *metaphysica generalis*, dealing with the general features of being as such, *ens commune*, and *metaphysica specialis*, dealing with the three "special" and eminent domains, the world, the soul, and God), and psychology is in turn divided into a rational

Aisthesis

22 • The text is cited from the Latin-German edition in Baumgarten, *Texte zur Grundlegung der Ästhetik*, ed. and trans. Hans Rudolf Schweizer (Hamburg: Felix Meiner, 1983). For discussions of the *Metaphysica* in relation to the earlier thesis, se Ursula Franke, *Kunst als Erkenntnis*, 37f, and Hans Rudolf Schweizer, "Einführung," in Baumgarten, *Texte zur Grundlegung der Ästhetik*, X-XV. For Baumgarten's conception of metaphysics, see Baumgarten, *Die Vorreden zur Metaphysik* (Frankfurt am Main: Klostermann, 1998), ed. and trans. Ursula Niggli.

23 • "The Germans are the only people who currently make use of the word 'aesthetic' in order to signify what others call the critique of taste. This usage originated in the abortive attempt made by Baumgarten, that admirable analytical thinker, to bring the critical treatment of the beautiful under rational principles, and so raise its rules to the rank of a science. But such endeavors are fruitless." (A 21/B 35f, trans. Norman Kemp Smith) These statements remain the same in 1781 and in 1787; as is well known, three years later Kant will have changed his mind about the term "aesthetics," although not about Baumgarten's contribution.

and empirical part. Rather than indicating the marginality of
aesthetics, the architecture of the *Metaphysica* in fact testifies to
the gravitational pull of this new entity: the empirical part of
psychology comprises 235 paragraphs, the rational part only 59,
and in the former, the lower faculty of knowledge receives a
much more substantial treatment (104 paragraphs) than the
higher (29 paragraphs).

These merely quantitative remarks are obviously as
such superficial, but when compared to a work like Wolff's
Psychologia empirica, published only seven years earlier, they still
indicate an important shift in emphasis, which also comes across
in the new, diversified terminology in Baumgarten. In the 1735
thesis on poetry he still spoke of the "lower part of the cognitive
faculty" (§ 3), whereas this now has become an autonomous part
referred to as the "lower cognitive faculty" (*facultas cognoscitiva
inferior*, § 520), and the object of a "lower doctrine of knowledge"
(*gnoseologia inferior*, § 533). This faculty — to be sure still inscribed
in the high-low dichotomy, but nevertheless now a faculty of its
own — acquires several new features, for instance "perspicacity"
(*perspicacia*), "foresight" (*praevisio*), "judgment" (*iudicium*, which
was related to the concept of taste in the treatise on poetry), the
capacity for "expectation" (*praesagitio*), and "the faculty of desig-
nating" (*facultas characteristica*). As Hans Rudolf Schweizer points
out, these capacities have both a temporal dimension in being
directed to the future, and a focus on expression and evaluation,
which emphasizes their active aspect.[24]

While branching out in many directions and indicating our multifaceted take on the work, they all derive from the
soul as the power of representation (*vis reprasentativa*, § 505),
with a term that comes straight from Leibniz, and points to an
underlying structure that was only hinted at in the 1735 thesis.
Just as the monad has an obscure ground from which perceptions emerge gradually, develop, and are integrated into larger
unities, Baumgarten's soul plunges into a dark ground or foundation, a *fundus animae* with its *perceptiones obscurae* (§ 511), which
is a rich reservoir that holds both past and future experiences,
creating a dynamism that is both temporal and related to grada-
tions of presence. Later, in the *Aesthetica*, Baumgarten would
speak of this dynamic as an "aesthetic impetus" that provides
depth and a temporal movement to the soul: "Psychologists
know that the soul under such an impetus intensifies all its
faculties, above all the lower one, so that almost the entire
ground of the soul is raised up a bit higher and is filled with a
deeper breath, and therefore willingly offers us all that we have
forgotten or not yet experienced, and that
we, and even more so others, never seem
to have been able to predict" (*Aesthetica* §

80).[25] Just as in Leibniz, for Baumgarten this ground is in a *positive* way related to the position of the body (§ 512), which opposes both of them to Descartes, for whom the body is a negative limit that only obscures the soul's clear and distinct perceptions of the world, whereas it here constitutes a condition for the exploration of the world, so that it can be as rich and varied as possible while still respecting the demand for unity.[26]

Aisthesis

In the general model for the dynamics of the soul presented in the *Metaphysica*, there is an explicit upgrading of the role of "obscure" representations, whereas they, as we noted earlier, in the 1735 thesis, with its normative perspective on poetry, play a subordinate role in relation to extensive clarity. With terms borrowed from Wolff, Baumgarten now opposes a "kingdom of light" (*regnum lucis*, § 518) to a "kingdom of darkness" (*regnum tenebrarum*), although not in the sense of a dualism or of a gradual fading away of light as it descends into matter, where the latter at the limit would be only the negation or absence of the luminous principle, as in Neoplatonism. Darkness is rather the source or obscure ground from which light emerges in a continual movement of intensification. This corresponds to the Leibnizian idea that nature "makes no leaps," which, as we noted earlier, is often cited as one of the main reasons for the absence of a coherent aesthetic theory in rationalism, since it would require a strict division — often understood along Kantian lines — between concepts and intuition, reason and sensibility. But in fact, it is precisely within such a hypothesis of ontological continuity that aesthetics emerges in Baumgarten, and not only as a mere extension of conceptual analysis as it had been practiced, but as the very *element* of the concept, that out of which it draws its power, yet without being able to exhaust it. This is why aesthetics — not primarily as a theory of the fine arts but rather as a reevaluation of the sensible in the widest sense, as the domain of *sense* — plays such a surprising role in a work that claims to survey metaphysics as a whole, and from the second edition 1742 onward it is applied to a whole set of topics that lie outside poetry and the fine arts.

In § 533 we find the definition of the term that picks up the thread from the treatise on poetry: "The science of this sensible knowledge and speaking is AESTHETICS (the logic of the lower cognitive faculty, the Philosophy of the graces and the muses, a lower doctrine of knowledge, the art of thinking beautifully, the art of analogy to reason)."[27] These

25 • "Psychologia patet in tali impetu totam quidem animam vires suas intendere, maxime tamen facultas inferiores, ita, ut omnis quasi fundus animae surgat nonnihil alius, et maius aliquid spiret, pronusque suppeditet, quorum obliti, quae non experti, quae praevidere non posse nobis ipsis, multo magis aliis, videbamur."
26 • There is in Leibniz a complex "demand" for a body, Deleuze suggests, because the soul has both dark zones and clear ones, which together make up body's as a relation to the world; se Deleuze, *Le Pli*, chap. 7.

formulas have however passed through several revisions, where we can see how Baumgarten struggles with the question of the extension that is to be given to the new science. In the first edition from 1739, rhetoric and poetics were placed on the same level as aesthetics, in the second edition from 1742 they have been replaced by the first part of the phrase in the parenthesis, "the logic of the lower cognitive faculty," and from the fourth edition 1757 onwards the remaining parts of the parenthesis were added, so that the definition in principle coincides with the one proposed in *Aesthetica* § 1.

Particular attention must here be given to the term *analogy*.[28] The claim that aesthetics is "the art of analogy to reason" (*ars analogi rationis*) may give rise to the impression that aesthetics is still understood *only* as a modification of the understanding, as a likeness or resemblance that remains regulated by and subordinate to its model. But this relation is not just one of submission: aesthetics forms a parallel structure with its own features, particularly those pertaining to sense, fantasy, and the faculty of fictions, whereas all the other subsections have the correspondence in the higher part, where they are qualified by the attribute "intellectualis". There is more in the lower part than in the higher, and the analogy invites a double reading, which does not remove the hierarchy, whose insistence comes across in the constant use of terms like high and low, but allows for a circulation of terms that on many points renders the high-low vocabulary fluid and uncertain, so that the higher might be understood as arising from, founded on, or even as immersed in, the lower.

In 1741, Baumgarten, under the pseudonym "Aletheiophilus" ("The friend of truth"), engaged in the publication of a weekly journal entitled *Philosophische Brieffe von Aletheiophilus*. It was modeled on other more widespread publications like the English *Spectator* and the German *Discourse der Mahlern* och *Critische Beyträge*, and with them it shared the project to spread philosophical and academic debates to a wider audience (it is one of Baumgarten's few substantial publications in German).

---

27 • "Scientia sensitive cognoscendi et proponendi est AESTHTETICA (logica facultatis cognoscitivae inferioris, Philosophia gratiarum et musarum, gnoseologia inferior, ars pulchre cogitandi, ars analogi rationis)."

28 • This analogy has a long history, even though the immediate context is the development from Leibniz to Wolff, and the debate whether animals could be endowed with an activity "resembling reason," which Descartes had famously denied. For Leibniz, everything that exists, and not only living beings, is understood as a representing and perceiving activity, and there is a gradual transition from the almost wholly obscure perceptions of matter and the barest forms of life without consciousness to the "apperceptive" consciousness of man, who is conscious both of himself and higher truths of reason. See for instance Leibniz, *The Monadology* § 26 (the dog remembers the pain inflicted on it by the stick, and runs away upon seeing it again), an example taken up again by Wolff, *Psychologia rationalis* § 765 (the dog has a way of thinking that is "analogous to reason," "canis analogum rationis habet").

Largely devoted to the quarrels around Wolffianism, the relation between ancients and moderns, and moral philosophy, these *Letters* also touched upon specific problems in art, such as the role of rhyme in poetry. The journal was however unsuccessful, and was discontinued during its first year, after 26 issues. For our present topic the second letter is of great interest, and here we find Baumgarten delineating a plan for a philosophical encyclopedia that he feigns to have received from an anonymous friend,[29] and in which the place of aesthetics in relation to the other parts of the system is specified.

The letter describes how "organic philosophy" — i.e. philosophy considered as tool in the Aristotelian sense, *organon*, or "instrumental philosophy" — may serve to improve human knowledge. In order to do this, it must go beyond the kind of logic that is only based on understanding, *Verstand*, in the narrow sense, and incorporate aesthetics as a program for an expanded logic, corresponding to the "logic in a more general sense" that had been proposed in the treatise on poetry (§ 115), just before the first mentioning of the term "aesthetics". This question of the relation between aesthetics and logic traverses all of Baumgarten's writings, and we could find equal support for a division between aesthetics and logic "in the narrower sense" as for the necessity of including both in a logic "in a wider sense" — both of which in the end may be compatible, and yet seem to place the emphasis differently. Here one must also bear in mind that "logic" in the tradition to which Baumgarten belongs, and that still remains present in Kant, does not refer to a purely formal discipline, but to rules for how a given faculty is to be exercised in the most efficient way. What Baumgarten seems to be looking for could perhaps be called a logic of the sensible, even though this expression does not appear as such in his writings.

This new aesthetic science, which, he says, has already appeared "in a few printed academic works" (i.e. Baumgarten's own previous publications), is here presented mainly as an aid to already formed knowledge, particularly to its transmission. Baumgarten emphasizes rhetorical and pedagogical aspects,[30]

Aisthesis

29 • This sketch for an encyclopedia was written by Baumgarten, but was published only after his death by his friend Johannes Christian Förster in 1769, under the title *Sciagraphia encyclopaediae philosophicae*. See also the sketch for a *Philosophia generalis*, § 147 (1742; partial German trans. in Baumgarten, *Texte zur Grundlegung der Ästhetik*, partial French trans. in Baumgarten, *Esthétique*).

30 • This pedagogical aspect also appears in his installation lecture at the Viadriana university in Frankfurt and der Oder in 1740, *Gedancken vom vernünfftigen Beyfall auf Academien*. Here Baumgarten presents the program of aesthetics in its twofold dimension, sensible knowledge and sensible presentation, by in turn analyzing thoughts, their connection, expression, speech, the voice, and finally the position of the body. See Salvatore Tedesco, "Sistematica e didattica dell'estetica," appendix in Baumgarten, *Riflessioni sulla poesia*.

and takes his point of departure in the concept of "attention," whose general structures had already been explicated at length in the *Metaphysica*, but is here also dealt with as a concrete everyday phenomenon: how should a teacher do in order to get the attention of his students? Does it suffice to demand that they open their ears and eyes? In order to correctly use the "weapons of the senses," Baumgarten continues, we need to immerse ourselves in "aesthetic empirics" (*ästhetische Empirik*), which involves all aspects of the situation, from the purely physiological responses of the body to technical instruments like microscopes and telescopes, barometers and thermometers, which all have in common that they prolong and expand our senses. In this way, aesthetic empirics trains our perception and heightens our senses, just as Baumgarten later in the *Aesthetica* will underline that "exercise" (*exercitatio*, § 47) is an essential moment in aesthetics, and that it is less an already a priori given faculty than an inherent capacity to transform the subject.

Aesthetics, the form of thought, and the subject

In the large and unfinished *Aesthetica* the preceding formulas are drawn together in the introductory definition: "Aesthetics (the theory of the fine arts, the lower doctrine of knowledge, the art of thinking beautifully, the art of the analogy of reason) is the science of sensible knowledge" (§ 1).[31] While this complex definition may seem to simply juxtapose all the aspects whose inner relations ought to be determined, we should note that it emphatically comprises both a theory of the sensible dimension of thought, as well as the art of making sensible presentations, receptivity as well as productivity. Further on, § 553 will state this even more clearly: "Aesthetics is the science of sensible knowledge as well as of sensible presentations" ("Scientia sensitive cognoscendi *et proponendi* est aesthetica"), which indicates the wide scope of his theory, which goes far beyond the fine arts, even though these applications were not addressed in the volumes that were completed by the time of Baumgarten's death in 1758.

Ever since Kant's rather unappreciative remarks on Baumgarten's theory in the *Critique of Judgment* (he is never mentioned by name) it has often been assumed that beauty in Baumgarten is only the representation of objective perfection, and that his conception cannot resist subsuming it under concepts, to which Kant responds with his theory of an indeterminate harmony between the faculties as the true locus of beauty. It is

31 • "Aesthetica (theoria liberalium artium, gnoseologia inferior, ars pulchre cogitandi, ars analogi rationis) est scientia cognitionis sensitivae." I use the text established by Mirbach, as in note 3. There is also an integral translation into Italian by Francesco Caparrotta, Anna Li Vigni, and Salvatore Tedesco, with additional revisions by Elisa Romano, L'Estetica (Palermo: Aesthetica, 2000), as well as a partial French translation in Baumgarten, Esthétique.

true that Baumgarten lays claim to perfection, but it is a perfection that branches out in many directions, that resists closure, and evokes a kind of density in our experience that is not the same as conceptual knowledge. Beauty belongs to sensible representation as such, which he determines through a whole network of concepts such as "richness," "magnitude," "truth," "clarity," "certitude," "liveliness in knowledge" (*ubertas, magniudo, veritas, claritas, certitudo, vita cognitionis*) (see §§ 22–25). Just as was hinted at in the 1735 treatise, philosophy and poetry must be understood as choosing different paths on the basis of the same representation: philosophical analysis leads us towards precise distinctions, a distinct knowledge based on definitions, whereas poetry unfolds as a field of associations that is nevertheless clear and unified, although in a different way. Philosophy opts for distinction, poetry for clarity, and the series of concepts that Baumgarten mobilizes in order to account for the latter indicates that he did not see it as less "reasonable," although just as little as reducible to a narrow definition of reason. The liveliness claimed in the above series of terms also point to the inclusion of our bodily existence, our whole being, in aesthetic experience.

The underlying question that we have followed, how the position of the aesthetic is to be understood — subordination, juxtaposition, analogy etc. — here becomes even more pressing, and in some formulations Baumgarten may be taken to imply that it in fact holds a certain priority over logic and conceptual knowledge. Subordination and juxtaposition are still options that exert a considerable attraction in many passages, but sometimes a different perspective opens up (even though it is just as quickly closed by what follows, and in this respect Baumgarten's text seems to hesitate, or at least not to be entirely sure about what its arguments imply), and there emerges the possibility of an aesthetic domain that would not just be subordinated or juxtaposed to logic and concepts, or precede them in a *merely* empirical sense. When we represent objects in aesthetic clarity, Baumgarten suggests, they acquire a density and depth of their own, a "beautiful plenitude" (*venusta plenitudo*, § 558) that forever will remain out of reach for logical concepts. This argument eventually leads Baumgarten to venture the question that would echo in German romanticism, and subsequently in a whole tradition of modern aesthetic theory: "What is abstraction, if not a loss?" (*quid enim est abstractio, si iactura non est?*) (§ 560) Logical analysis loses something, it tears asunder a primordial interweaving in language, where the respective paths of philosophy and poetry as determined disciplines have not yet diverged. The question then becomes what type of language may be capable of doing justice to this density; for Baumgarten, at least as far as we can read in the *Aesthetica*, it is no doubt the language of poetry; the other arts remain in the shadow in the parts of the book that were finished, although the work was planned to include the other arts as well, which no doubt would have further complicated the structure, and even questioned the general value of a term like "abstraction," which still relies on the relation between a first linguistic density that it is then reduced, rather than on domains that as such are extra-linguistic. For us, however, the question not only relates to the diversity and difference of the modern arts, but must also bear on the language of philosophical discourse as such, a problem that would become explosive after Kant, both as a continuation of themes opened up in the third *Critique*, and as an attack on Kant's founding ideas.

When Baumgarten says that aesthetics, among other things, is "about the art of thinking beautifully" (*de arte pulchre cogitandi*), we must thus hear something more than the introduction of a new object or field — it is a transformation of the idea of thought, whose consequences extend beyond those objects that at roughly the same time were being assembled under the generic name "the fine arts," "les beaux-arts," or "die schönen Künste". Aesthetics does not enter as yet another book to be classified in the library of pure reason, or as a new "regional ontology," to use the language of early twentieth-century phenomenology, but as a subversion of the hierarchies of thinking, a possible deregulation of its faculties, powers, and capacities. Kant would later attempt to restore order, first of all by distinguishing between the ruling faculty, *Vermögen*, and a subordinate power, *Kraft*, although here too the power of aesthetic judgment, *die ästhetische Urteilskraft*, would prove unruly once again, making possible both Romanticism as well as Rimbaud's prophetic "deregulation of all the senses," as Deleuze notes.[32]

Furthermore, this new idea of thought also implies a new relation to the self as something that must be made through sensible practices, a kind of aesthetic self-fashioning or subjectification, as when Baumgarten reflects on the "character of the happy aesthetician" (*felix aestheticus*) (*Aesthetica*, § 27). This happiness, he proposes, does not only require a natural disposition (innate ideas), but practice and training (*exercitatio*, § 47), otherwise it inevitably dwindles. It cannot be learnt once and for all, like the application of abstract concepts or a rule for the direction of the mind that can be defined as distinct from the subject matter, as proposed by Descartes; it is "mastery" (*imperium*), not a "tyranny" (§ 12).

It has even been claimed that Baumgarten in this context introduces the idea of the "subjective" into the

32 • See Deleuze, "Sur quatre formules poétiques qui pourrait résumer la philosphie kantienne," in *Critique et clinique* (Paris: Minuit, 1993).

philosophical vocabulary, a term which later becomes a key concept in Kant, Hegel, and a whole subsequent tradition to such an extent that it appears to have always existed.[33] The subject is a force, capacity, and aptitude (*vis, facultas, habitus*) that must be cultivated, and no longer just the underlying bearer of properties and predicates, as is the case of the Aristotelian *hypokeimenon*, translated into Latin by Boethius as *subiectum*, and then reformulated by Descartes as a "thing that thinks," a *res cogitans* that has *thoughts* as its predicates. If Descartes rejects that "man" could be an answer to *what* or *who* this thing is that thinks, then Baumgarten's inclusion, at the beginning of *Aesthetica*, of sensible knowledge shifts the terms of both question and answer: "A philosopher is a man among men, and he would be mistaken if he thought that such a huge part of human knowledge would be inappropriate for him." (§ 6)

Rather than a given ground or underlying X that remain identical, as the condition for the unfolding of differences, the subject is practical, it is there because it is able to do and perform: my soul is force (*vis*), or a power to *do* something (*Metaphysica*, § 505), only then is it also capable of knowing and entertaining an epistemic relation to itself, and also to understand itself as free. Freedom is the actualization of a power, and conscious decisions only integrate processes already underway in a final approval (here too Leibniz is a precursor: small perceptions gradually coalesce into a conscious act that as it were seals the nascent unity of the will). These capacities are, however, not something internal in relation to an outward actualization, but exist as being exercised, in actualizing themselves (just as the capacity to play violin does not preexist the process of training and formation, but comes into existence in being practiced), and in actualizing themselves in a shared sphere of social action, where the subject's capacities always exist in relation to those of other subjects.

If we read the passage from Leibniz to Baumgarten in this way, as an opening up of the subject towards practices of self-fashioning and the cultivation of powers and capacities, then we can see that the invention of aesthetics is the invention of a different concept of experience, which not only makes possible a new relation to artworks, but also implies a transformed idea of thinking and subjectivity as such. As I proposed initially, this can be understood as sharing or distribution of the sensible, a capacitating of subjects in their constitutive difference and plurality. ●

33 • See *Metaphysica* § 527, and the note by Hans Rudolf Schwezier, in Baumgarten, *Texte zur Grundlegung der Ästhetik*, 89.

Revisiting Laocoon; Site-Specific Imitation

Cecilia Sjöholm

In Laocoon (1766), Gotthold Ephraim Lessing offers a study of a Roman sculpture depicting the Trojan priest Laocoon as he and his sons are strangled to death by an enormous snake. Lessing grapples with the question of how an expression irreducible to linguistic meaning may still achieve signification; we experience the scream coming out of the hollow mouth of Laocoon with extraordinary nuance, even though it is not described to us. Among the sources of Lessing's text we find works on psychology, such as his own translation of the renaissance Spanish psychologist Huarte. We find the tradition of *ut pictura poeisis*, transposing works of art into language. We find the theory of affects forwarded by Spinoza, the Roman tradition of rhetoric, etc. We find the practice of imitation that took place at the Belvedere Court in the Vatican, training artists in drawing the body of Laocoon during the time of Michelangelo. And we find the emergence of the public sphere, debates in various journals. These are only a few of the sources to what will become what one might call the aesthetics of Lessing.

With the apparition of Winckelmann's work, Kant's *Critique of Judgment*, Hegel's philosophy of art and the critical tradition pursuing the work of Diderot, much of the tradition of aesthetics has been focused on judgment as a central cultural concern. How do we value art? How do we relate what is beautiful to cultural presuppositions? How is judgment formed, and how de we form a *sensus communis*? Lessing's work on Laocoon has also been inserted in this discussion, not least through the resurrection of his name in the modernist debate through Eisenstein, Greenberg, Fried, etc.[1]

But to Lessing there is no work of art "an sich". The discipline of *Ästhetik* is the study of sense perception, tied in with psychology. The work of art is characterized in an indirect manner, through the effects it has on the reader or the viewer. The perspective on Lessing, therefore, can be shifted from discussing how he perceives the work of art, and the semiotic issues attached to it, to how he perceives the viewer. Here, the question of embodiment is crucial. How does the embodied mind respond to the image of a human body? To the tradition of imitation of the renaissance, this was a focal point. What I will do now is to look at Lessing's relation to that tradition and suggest ways in which we might consider the aesthetic subject to be constructed out of it.

Lessing is not so much concerned with judgment or theories of beauty. He takes for granted that beauty is the essence of art, but talks a lot more about ugliness, disgust, and the horrible. His study opens the gates to a pre-Kantian universe where embodiment and visual stimuli are studied through the grid of affects. The corporeality of the figure of Laocoon is always in focus; less with regard to judgment and more with regard to the observation of affects. If Kant's aesthetic turn was included in a quest for a critique of the limits of metaphysics, and the limits of human reason, Lessing rather was interested in the way in which aesthetic expression promotes the emotional and intellectual education of its audience. This is also why the stakes were so high in his diligent debate with Winckelmann.

The history of the group

As Lessing says himself, the experience of a work of art presumes a distinct knowledge of the world of myths and tales that is present in the work, but not always fully exposed. This is certainly true for Laocoon. Laocoon was a Trojan priest, of Neptune or Poseidon. He warned the Trojans that the Greeks would be hiding in the wooden horse. For this, Athena sent two great snakes that killed him and his sons. The scene of this killing is gruesome, and it has been interpreted in wall paintings in Pompeii, in Virgil, in ancient poems, in a lost tragedy by Sophocles, in Hellenistic art, in Renaissance art, and so on.

There are different versions of the story, and literature and art vary in

1 • Babbitt suggests that the most important aspect of *Laocoon* is when Lessing asserts the value of criticism, speaking against those who say it kills genius. See Irving Babbitt, *The New Laokoon: An Essay on the Confusion of the Arts* (Cambridge: The Riverside Press, 1910), 35.

Aisthesis

their account. In some, the sons are dying before the father, in others, at the same time. Not only is he not heard, in some versions he is also killed. And in some versions Athena sends two snakes to kill not only him, but also his two sons. There are also different versions cast of how Laocoon's body is depicted: naked or with clothing, and different versions of how he holds his arms. One may surmise, however, a common theme. In all versions, he represents the unbearable injustice that comes with his fate: attempting to warn his own people, the Trojans, for the death that awaits them in the Trojan horse. What is tolerable and what crosses the barrier into the intolerable? The various depictions of Laocoon, whatever media may be used, tend to give his pain a central role. The figure of Laocoon represents, above all, multiple ways of depicting and enduring pain. First, it is about corporeal pain, the pain that tortures the muscles, and makes the body twinge. The bite of the poisonous snake is tortuous. Secondly, it is about the pain of being quieted despite all the knowledge one has of events, and knowing that one's people are about to die. Thirdly, it is about knowing that one's children are also dying.

The episode with the sons dying as well as the priest has to do with divine fury and punishment. In older versions of the myth, Laocoon is sleeping with his wife Antope in front of the image of Apollo. Apollo sends snakes to take away the fruit of that union. One of the sons, however, escapes. In this version of the story, we find an allegory of the escape of Aeneas. There is also a tragic version to be found in a fragment by Sophocles, who lets both the sons die and Laocoon live. In the *Fall of Troy*, or the so-called Posthomerica from the 4th century by Quintus Smyrnaeus, Laocoon is first warned by Athena:

> Straight terror fell on him, and trembling bowed the knees of the presumptuous: round his head horror of darkness poured; a sharp pang thrilled his eyelids; swam his eyes beneath his brows; his eyeballs, stabbed with bitter anguish, throbbed even from the roots, and rolled in frenzy of pain. Clear through his brain the bitter torment pierced even to the filmy inner veil thereof; now bloodshot were his eyes, now ghastly green; anon with rheum they ran, as pours a stream down from a rugged crag, with thawing snow made turbid. As a man distraught he seemed: all things he saw showed double, and he groaned fearfully; yet he ceased not to exhort the men of Troy, and wrecked not of his pain. Then did the Goddess strike him utterly blind.[2]

2 • Quintus Smyrnaeus, *The Fall of Troy*, trans. Arthur Sanders Way (London: William Heinemann / Loeb Classical Library, 1913), vol. 19, book 12

Here, Laocoon becomes a figure like Cassandra. When he still insists on warning the people against the deceit of the Greeks, Athena sends two snakes from the sea, killing his sons. Laocoon himself survives, blinded, like the seer in tragedy. The fate of Laocoon then can be interpreted according to various notions that one has of pain. In Sophocles's version, the biggest pain is the killing of one's offspring, but not necessarily the torturing pain of the body itself.

We find a famous place in Virgil, depicting the killing of the Trojan priest. In Virgil, the scene is gruesome. The two snakes breach the waters approaching the priest and his sons in fire: "Their bosoms rise amid the surge, and their crests, bloodred, overtop the waves; the rest of them skims the main behind [...] with blazing eyes suffused with blood and fire, were licking with quivering tongues their hissing mouths." Here we must note two details. First, the snake kills the two sons. When the father is attempting to save them, they kill him. Virgil is also very graphic: the snakes tower over him, he says. They are large and terrifying, and they always do things doubly, strangle two boys; they roll around the waist and around the throat. The father gasps, Virgil says. Then he roars. This is both horrifying and enigmatic: how can he roar after gasping? Who roars? And why does he roar, from pain, over his sons, over his failure? Again there is clearly a moral aspect to the killing and to the pain endured — the pain cannot be conceived as only physical.

We have the first mention of the sculpture group of Laocoon in Pliny's *Natural History*, XXXVI 37: "Out of one block of stone the consummate artists, Hagesandros, Polydoros, and Athenodors of Rhodes made, after careful planning, Laocoon, his sons, and the snakes marvellously entwined about them."[3] The group remained a myth for centuries, undiscovered. Then in 1506 it was found under the palace of Titan. Michelangelo was involved in the discovery. It was placed in the Belvedere Court in what is now the Museum of the Vatican in the 16th century. The statue immediately caught the attention of the artists and writers of the day and was revered above all for the way in which it expressed the emotion and the pain of the figures it represented. The garden of sculptures at the Belvedere Court was consciously displayed architecturally, created not just for art. The garden was also an academic arena, gathering musicians, poets and artists alike, poetry was declared and music composed and the works themselves made the object of imitation. Poetry was composed to the sculptures, and they were imitated by

3 • Cited in Margarete Bieber, *Laocoon: The Influence of the Group Since its Rediscovery* (Detroit: Wayne State University Press, 1969), 12. In 1967, Margarethe Bieber published a short comparative study in which she shows that there is both a literary and a pictorial tradition of *Laokoon*, and she also shows how they differ.

training artists.[4] As art historian Peter Gillgren has put it, the sculptures became performative forces that produced a cooperation between the arts in different medias such as drawings, paintings, poetry, and music.[5] The first-known poem dedicated to the group was written by Sadoleto, whose empathy cannot be mistaken as he interprets the whole scene as a father's shriek to his sons, after he has been attacked himself:

> His sons no less the same wild strength attacks,
> And strangles them with swift embrace and tears
> Their little limbs: even now the gory breast
> Of one whose dying voice his father calls
> Has been its pasture, round him wrap its coils
> And crush him in the mighty winding folds.
> The other boy, unhurt, unbitten yet,
> Uplifts his foot to unloose the serpent's tail;
> His father's anguish seen as he stands aghast,
> Transfixed with horror — his loud wailings stay,
> His falling teardrops stay — in double dread.[6]

In this image, like in Sophocles, it is not the father, but the sons that die. Laocoons' tears are over them, and not so much over himself, or over his pain. In painting, the pain of Laocoon was depicted in a more graphic and less mythic ways, by El Greco for instance. In drawings by Rubens one can see the same phenomenon. In the period of the baroque, what was most interesting was the way in which the muscles of the group were depicting a tormented soul. Here, Laocoon's pain is not the suffering of a bereaved father, but a very real, inflicting pain, which has to do with the attacks of the snake.

When Lessing writes his *Laocoon*, then, the figure is already involved in a debate over expression, affect, and morality. The sculpture group is already a contested object of imitation, not just by other sculptures, but in various media. *Laocoon* has already, over centuries, come to raise the question of how various media approach the same object. Even if Lessing's insights are new, they have been prepared for during many years of intertwined and conflicting artistic practices at the Belvedere Court.

The debate between Winckelmann and Lessing

In the 18th century, part of the critical debate includes the question of what was first created: Virgil's epic or the statue. This is a question Lessing engages, but it

4 • See Sylvie Deswarte Rosa, "Francisco de Holanda et le Cortile di Belvedere," in Matthias Winner, Bernard Andreae, and Carlo Pietrangeli (eds.), *Il Cortile delle statue. Der Statuenhof des Belvedere im Vatikan* (Mainz am Rhein: P. von Zabern, 1998), 390–410.
5 • Peter Gillgren, from a work on Michelangelo under publication.
6 • Cited in Bieber, *Laocoon*, 14; the poem of Jacobus Sadoletus cited in the trans. by H S Wilkinson.

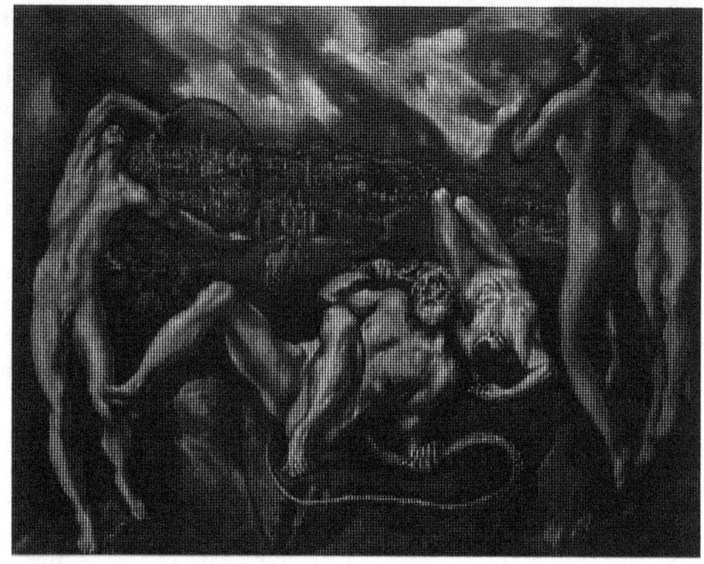

then deflates as he is showing that the one cannot be said to properly be an imitation of the other, since they are created in completely different media. It is interesting to consider what version they saw. When they found the statue in 1506, the arms of the Laocoon and the younger son were missing. The arms were replaced, but in a different version than in the original. In the 18th century, all the viewers that saw the sculpture saw Laocoon with his hand held high. Winckelmann saw the statue in poor light, since it was not fully exposed; it was kept in a box and could only be seen with a candle. Goethe, in turn, saw the statue in 1786 when it was in daylight. He deplored it greatly since he thought it would have been much more beautiful if he had seen it only in candlelight. The statue was brought to Paris by Napoleon, and returned to Rome in 1815.[7]

There is no evidence that Lessing ever saw the sculpture himself. It is interesting to compare his description of the group with that of art historian Jonathan Richardson, whose book on Roman art was widely read. The book is describing the statues in Rome in detail, but without any pictures. Richardson describes how an arm has been lost, and how therefore one of terracotta has been substituted in its place. He describes also how Michelangelo has started on another arm and how that arm lies in front of the piece, without having been placed on it.[8] There is no mention of this in Lessing. If he did not see it, or at least a copy of it, why would it be described with arms in the air? Why

7 • Simon Richter, *Laocoon's Body and the Aesthetics of Pain* (Detroit: Wayne State University Press, 1992), 23–25.
8 • Jonathan Richardson, *An account of some of the statues, bas-reliefs, drawings and pictures in Italy* (London, 1728).

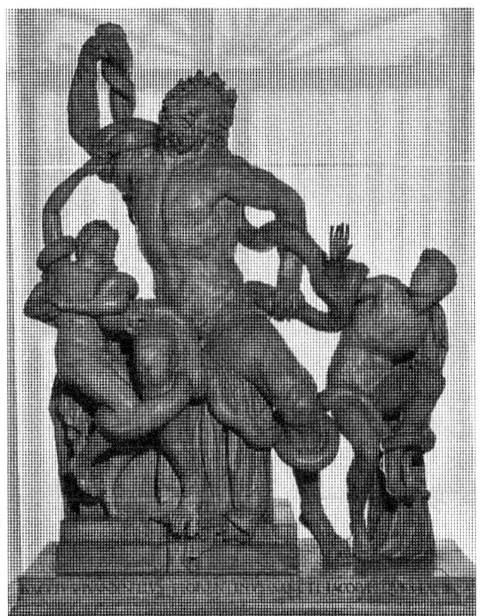

▲

**Baccio Bandinelli,
Laocoon, 1520–
1525, White
Marble, Uffizi,
Florence.**

did he not follow Richardson's description of a broken figure? He certainly knew the famous engravings of Montfaucon, for instance.[9] These are not faithful to the original. The arm should not have been held up but bent, which is also how Michelangelo wanted it.

Winckelmann and Lessing

How the statue is to be perceived has been subject to disputes, not least between Winckelmann and Lessing in the 1750s and 1760s. To Winckelmann, the group of Laocoon is an example of the difference in quality between the Greek and Roman soul. The sculpture does not depict a scream, Winckelmann argues, which is how it is depicted in Virgil. Laocoon suffers rather like Sophocles' Philoctetes says Winckelmann, with a restrained pain that is dignified. *Thoughts on the Imitation of Greek Works in Painting and Sculpture* (1755), introduced his famous motto of "noble simplicity and quiet grandeur." He sees no cry, but a sigh that is stifled.[10]

To Winckelmann, then, what was important was not the way in which the cause of pain was depicted, but rather the way in which we experience the figure of Laokoon as dignified. In this he draws not so much on the myth of Laocoon, as on the text of *Philoctetes*.[11] What we have here is an image of unbearable, unjust suffering, like that of Ixion attached to the wheel. To Lessing, however, Winckelmann makes the suffering *too* dignified: it is quite clear that Philoctetes screams and whines loudly on the island. His fellow soldiers cannot stand his heavy groans and complaints, and they cannot stand his odours either. Where is the dignity?

The reason for not depicting the scream of Laocoon is not a moral one; it is aesthetic: "Try to open the moth of

9 • Bernard de Montfaucon, *L'Antiquite expliquée et representée en figures* (Paris: De Laulne, 1719–24).
10 • Lessing resumes and criticizes Winckelmann in the third chapter of *Laocoon*.
11 • By Sophocles, in which the question of suffering and pain bears upon the question of dignity. Such as it is expressed by the chorus in *Philoctetes*:

> Since proud Ixion, doomed to feel
> The tortures of th' eternal wheel,
> Bound by the hand of angry Jove,
> Received the due rewards of impious love;
> Ne'er was distress so deep or woe so great
> As on the wretched Philoctetes wait,
> Who ever with the just and good,
> Guiltless of fraud and rapine, stood,
> And the fair paths of virtue still pursued;
> Alone on this inhospitable shore,
> Where waves for ever beat and tempests roar,
> How could he e'er or hope or comfort know,
> Or painful life support beneath such weight of woe?

Laocoon in imagination, and judge for yourself! In sculpture a mere widening of the mouth is a hollow that produces the most repulsive effect in the world."[12] What we see is movement, and the presupposition of a scream, the moments of anticipation before it will actually occur, thus the sequence taking place in which the scream can be anticipated but not quite disclosed.

Imitation and mimesis

Laocoon is perceived through the strong emotions it arouses through the opening of the mouth, the pain, and the scream that is never heard. The methodical coherence with which Lessing performs this task is remarkable. Although he himself is quite aware of relating to a newly formed discourse, that of aesthetics, we can also look at the way in which it ties in with that of psychology and physiology.

Lessing was the translator of *Examen de ingenios para les ciencias* (1575) by Juan Huarte. In this work, which was widely spread throughout Europe until around 1800, Huarte connects psychology and physiology, arguing that the mind creates its own conceptions using the resources of space and time, as well as concepts of causality and figurability. This gives us internal conceptions of phenomena that are not simply reflections of the outer world.[13] Huarte then shows that there are different dispositions or different "geniuses" in human beings, and points to a creative aspect in humans that cannot be assessed in a schematic way. In looking closer at the way in which Lessing approaches Huarte's book, it appears to belong to the genealogical roots of Lessing's text. We can reconsider it in relation to the tradition of the imitation of the *Laocoon* at the Belvedere Court, as performed by painters.

The aesthetic ideal of the Renaissance, as we know, is imitation. Lessing inserts himself into the tradition of *imitation* and *aemulatio*, attempting to triumph over his predecessor

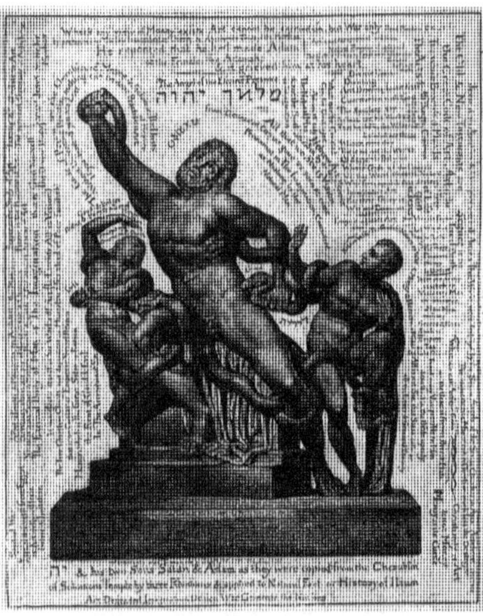

▲

William Blake, *Laocoon*, 1826–1827, Annotated Print.

12 • *Laocoon*, chapter II.
13 • Herder discusses Huarte in *Vom Erkennen und Empfinden der menschlichen Seele: Bemerkungen und Träume* (1778). He is mostly interested in the irrationality of nature, and the fact that human nature or character cannot be fully assessed on a schematic or scientific ground. See Martin Franzbach, "Lessings Huarte-Übersetzung (1752): Die Rezeption und Wirkungsgeschichte des "Examen de ingenious para les ciencis" (1575) in Deutschland," *Hamburger Romanistische Studien* No. 29 (1965): 134.
14 • Irving Babbitt, *The New Laokoon*, 44.

Winckelmann in his understanding of an aesthetic response to the Laocoon group. But what is being imitated here? It may well be that Lessing appears as a Renaissance Aristotelian in that he discusses art as imitation of action.[14] But what is being imitated is, like in drawing, the body. Painting uses figures and colours in space, whereas poetry articulates tones in time. Bodies, this time regarded both as human bodies and objects, exist next to each other. But bodies exist also in time and can imitate actions. Poetry imitates sensible aspects of bodies too, in a sustained figure of imitation. This is described, for instance, through the scene in which Agamemnon is dressed in the *Iliad*, how his body is made tangible through the layers of cloth put on it. Action becomes body, and poetry becomes painting.[15] The beauty of Helen of Troy is also an imitation of a body: "The poet said all his art could say to make beauty palpable to us, in order that, in imitation of him, the painter also should aim at the highest expression of it in his."[16] Beauty becomes sensuous and corporeal through the way in which the body is made palpable in the poem, as sensuous in literature as in painting.

Imitation, to Lessing, is far from copying, but it is not Aristotelian mimesis either. It is not a relation to an action, or what we might call the real. It is a relation to something that is already a representation. The object of imitation is not only a thing, but an affect, a myth. The relation becomes arbitrary, enacting the kind of displacement and condensation that psychoanalysis has shown to be ingrained in all creation of meaning. As the object is created, although it may be a product of imitation, the way it structures the sensible will always be a displacement in relation to what it imitates. It will be inscribed in a chain of imitations, in a chain of displacements and condensations.

Imitation is a re-presentation of a representation, seeing something that is already seen, and making it appear as corporeal and palpable and tangible. As all the versions of the story of Laocoon show, there is no original present. This does not mean that what is produced is emerging from nowhere. It means that it is a re-production of what has already been produced, a repetition of what has already emerged, although in a new way.[17]

In Lessing, imitation becomes a response to the sensible aspect of being. The figure of Laocoon figures the greatest pain, an affect that appears to be the very object of imitation in all the versions of Laocoon that we have at hand. At the same time, the movement of the figure displaces the affects of pain to the

15 • Lessing, *Laocoon*, chap XVI.
16 • Ibid, chap XXI.
17 • Samuel Ijsseling has argued for an ontological understanding of *mimesis* which makes it a pre-supposition of difference rather than a rendering of a difference; *mimesis* as the displacement of representation with regard to ontological difference. See Ijsseling, *Mimesis: On Appearing and Being* (Brussels: Peeters, 1997), 20–21.

sensibility of the imitation. Imitation structures the sensible while working with or against the aspect of figurability. As a product of imitation, the body of Laocoon crosses the limits between figure and movement. The way in which the head is tilted, the mouth half-open, the arms held high, the body twitching; all of these details imbue the body with a pain that we cannot fully fathom. The arms, Lessing writes, are the most active where the pain is the hardest to bear. Had the arms not been moving we would not have experienced pain. The figure would have lacked movement and appeared uninteresting if Laocoon had appeared with his arms straight down tied to his body, as if he was already dead. Lessing demonstrates its movement and indicates the horrible aspect of the immobility of the statue at the same time — there is something inhuman and monstrous over the way it appears fixed, and yet at the same time attempting to escape, situated in a moment of time, and a state of affect from which it will never be released. In responding to this aspect of imitation, the sensational aspect of movement and affect, the aesthetic subject is born. It is a subject that is less talked about in terms of taste, or pleasure, and more in terms of affectivity and sensibility. In discussing aesthetic judgment, Kant has described the pleasure that arises in a judgment of taste, where the thought touches itself, so to speak, detached from an object that may be the source of a reflective judgment but not a direct cause; objects do not in themselves cause pain or satisfaction. This means, to Kant, that the most dignified expression of art is that of the sketch, in contrast to the *Reize* or vivid stimuli of explosions of color or movement. Pure judgments of taste can be posited with regards to the composition before the music, the lines before the painting; positing a pure state of beauty that may never be at hand.

Is it then possible to posit a reflection beyond the *Reize*, if we are to consider the aesthetic response of the embodied being? Can we as embodied subjects conceive of aesthetic reflection beyond the relation we have to our own bodies as judging and reflecting subjects? The discussion of Laocoon is just as much a discussion about the reflective capacities of the embodied being, as it is a question of imitation.

In his famous essay "The Philosopher and his Shadow" (1959), Merleau-Ponty has described how in every philosopher there appears to be something unthought. To think is not to command an object, but rather to "encircle an area that we are not yet thinking."[18] The shadow of the philosopher is constituted by the history of philosophy itself, creating the objects of thought that can never become fully transparent. In Husserl, to whom Merleau-Ponty's essay is dedicated, the

18 • Maurice Merleau-Ponty, *Signs*, trans. Aphonso Lingis (Evanston: Northwestern University Press, 1964), 160.

unthought is unravelled on the way towards the phenomenological reduction where it is displaced by meaning. Here we see a
double movement: in leaving oneself one returns to oneself in a
reflexive moment. Here we also see a conflict: in the moment of
reflection, through which meaning is created, the aspect of
embodiment is left out. It reappears, however. The question of
how embodiment conditions meaning becomes the big question
in Husserl, and the question of one's own body in particular.
The unthought in Husserl, Merleau-Ponty says, constitutes itself
in the gap between the body of oneself and the body of the
other; the other body of perception, through which things
appear meaningful but which in itself will be imbued with an
aspect of foreignness and muteness.[19] The shadow of the
unthought is the body of the other that cannot be thought
through the means of phenomenological reduction.

Aisthesis
We might here consider the difference that Lessing
shows in the gap between the movement and the figure of
Laocoon. Winckelmann saw a figure. Lessing, on the other hand,
sees a movement that drags us out of the figure and beyond the
schema of the body, through which we could relate to a moment
of aesthetic pleasure. Pain is experienced and yet fleeing our
grasp.

The body in pain is the fleeing object of *imitatio*. Much
is made of Laocoon's nudity. The torn body is more interesting
without clothes. Just like Michelangelo made his pupils put
great emphasis in depicting the twitching of the muscles, so
Lessing puts great emphasis in finding the right expression to
explain the experience of the body through the eyes of the
viewer. He performs a kind of *aemulatio* that was also part of the
training of the artists, adding to, triumphing with his description, showcasing the sensation not only of the beauty of the
work of art but of the nude body as such. His observations do
not perform an imitation in the passive sense of the word, but
bring forth a human body, less in the way it may be seen as beautiful at an imaginary level and more in the way it may be
touched and felt.

This is also the reason why in Lessing we do not find
ourselves studying a work of art. What we reflect on is ourselves.
What we see in the body of Laocoon is not a work of art. What
we see is ourselves. We do not find ourselves imitating nature, as
the older doctrine of imitation would have it. We find ourselves
studying the imitation of a human body. The imitated body,
then, is not so much a product of art, as it is a bundle of affects
produced through the eyes and the sensibility of the spectator.
What we are witnessing here, through the imitation of the body
of Laocoon, is the birth of the aesthetic subject. It is not so much
produced through the work of art, as it produced through the

19 • Ibid, 73.

process of imitation. It is a subject through which the observations of the human body are tied up with emotions and affects, sensing the other body through the kinaesthetic effect it has on one's own.

In many ways, Lessing does the same thing as the art historian Richardson: describing an object that is not there. But Lessing, through his insights into the true nature, offers us something that is much more than a description, which has to do with the fact that the objects are not easily available. Lessing's text gives us an acute sense of bereavement: the magnificent shape and body of the statue is forever absent, but the experience remains through the process of imitation. The experience that comes to the fore is not the beauty, but the physical presence of the work, arising before one's eyes. The best way to make a work appear is through the aesthetic experience of an onlooker. What we see produced in Lessing's text, then, is a subject who reflects on himself through the passions figured in another body. It is a subject that is expecting the sensation being explored through the impressive figure of works of art, whether one sees them or not. And it is, above all, a subject through which works of art can teach us something about the way in which a human body experiences pain, grief, joy, tenderness and other affects. ●

Cecilia Sjöholm is Professor of Aesthetics at Södertörn University. Recent books include *Aisthesis: Estetikens historia del 1* (ed. with Sara Danius and Sven-Olov Wallenstein, 2012) and *Kristeva and the Political* (2005).

A Button is Never Just a Button: Realism, Fashion, and the Discovery of Society

Sara Danius

In this essay, I'd like to make five propositions. First proposition: the political is immanent in the aesthetic. Second: the novels of the founders of nineteenth-century realism, Stendhal and Balzac, are a case in point. Third: the more ephemeral the realist novel is, the more political it is. Fourth: to appreciate the political dimension of the realist novel, one should take a closer look at an unlikely theme — fashion. Fifth: to explore fashion in the realist novel is to explore how the novel makes the world visible and, even more important, legible.

I

Novels are like department stores. If you look long enough, you'll find everything. You'll find elevators (Proust). Slippers (Flaubert). Yellow soap (Joyce). Brown yarn (Woolf). Bugs (Kafka). And of course you'll find fashion. Every department store worthy of the name features an impressive clothing section. That is to say: all great modern novelists are generous with wardrobe details. It all begins with Stendhal's *The Red and the Black* (1830).[1]

But why should we bother about fashion? Scholars have also not bothered very much.[2] Literature and the arts are supposed to aim at the general, not at the particular. Exit lace, silk parasols, muslin skirts, long stockings. We don't want to get pulled down into the swamp of particularity. The idea is easy to understand, yet it

1 • Stendhal, *The Red and the Black,* trans. Roger Gard (London: Penguin, 2002). Page references are given parenthetically in the main text.
2 • But see, for example, Mark Anderson, Kafka's *Clothes: Ornament and Aestheticism in the Habsburg Fin de Siècle* (Oxford: Clarendon Press, 1992).

is a strange one. What's more, it's contested by the modern novel itself. It's enough to look at two monuments in the history of the modern European novel, and you quickly realize that you'd be guilty of intellectual sloppiness if you were to claim that clothes are mere props. In the modern novel, clothes are of crucial importance. They are as vital as identification documents at a frontier.

Consider *The Red and The Black* by Stendhal. In the beginning was a jacket. Then there was a short period spent in a black suit. After which followed a short intermezzo spent in a black frock, as worn by priests and priest wannabes, then a blue frock — and death. Intermittent day dreams revolving around red, Napoleon red. In describing the textile transformations of the protagonist, I have summarized an essential part of the plot. This fact alone testifies to the importance of dress in Stendhal's novel.

Anyone who's read *The Red and the Black* will remember that it is a *Bildungsroman* telling the story of a handsome young man of low station exploring the ways of the world. Julien Sorel, as he is called, is a richly talented individual. Among his gifts is his aggressive envy. He reveals himself to be quite adept at climbing the social ladder, eventually reaching the top: the aristocracy in Paris. The end result is a panorama of French society circa 1830. Stendhal takes us through three basic social contexts or, if you wish, estates or, indeed, classes: the bourgeoisie, the church, and the aristocracy. In this world, at least as described by Stendhal, the password is dress. Julien's journey through society presupposes an impressive number of changes of dress. After all, what is clothing other than a visually based class code? And what is Stendhal's novel other than a study in the formation of social identity? It's interesting to note that every time new clothes are introduced, they are represented as enigmatic objects. They may well be visible, but their meaning is far from legible.

Julien has emancipated himself from his class origins and begun to circulate in social contexts where he doesn't belong: the provincial bourgeoisie, the catholic seminary, the aristocracy in Paris. Naturally, dress turns into a problem. But dress is also an opportunity. No one moves with such intelligence through the social spheres as does Julien. No one handles textile transformations so well. No one is as dexterous when it comes to manipulating social codes.

Yet it must be remembered that Julien's success as transgressor presupposes a society that, sociologically speaking, is strictly stratified. Dress must carry social meaning. Dress must communicate social station, and it must do so in a relatively unambiguous way. Or else Julien's masquerade would be without social consequences. It's quite another thing that he's incapable of feeling at home anywhere in the world. Hence the tragic undercurrent in the novel. But the irony goes deeper. There's no difference in kind between Julien and the rest of the world, only a difference in degree. Julien's years of *Bildung* — formation — revolve around his ability to fill social functions. He successfully inserts himself into the most unlikely contexts by way of imitation. The novel describes an astonishing propagation of identities, with Julien in the test tube and his intrepid social ambitions as nutrient fluid.

Is such a world a desirable one? The narrator refrains from making moral judgments. All we have is the narrator's irony, a crushing yet redeeming irony. But what is even more remarkable is that the pattern laid bare by Stendhal makes itself felt just about everywhere. Bishops, priests, mayors, principals, politicians, Julien himself, even young aristocratic women: all fill functions, all copy and imitate in one way or another. Does this mean that the world is a theater? That social life is devoid of substance, authenticity, truth? That all is pretense? Such a conclusion would be rather banal. Besides, it's not true. Stendhal wouldn't be Stendhal unless the truth was a complex affair. There are identities, and there are plenty of them. But the notion of a true identity doesn't appeal to the author of *The Red and the Black*. The world is no peach. The world is an onion.

Social distinction is expressed by way of dress, Stendhal intimates. If you want to control the way in which people read social status, then you should manipulate your attire in particular. Stendhal's novel is a monument to this insight. That's the kind of world Stendhal seeks to make visible. What does this mean, exactly? To be sure, the world represented by the novel is made visible, that is, it appeals to the sense of sight, and Stendhal puts a great deal of emphasis on visibility. He wants precision, sensuous precision. But the world he depicts is anything but transparent. It's opaque. And now we're approaching the heart of the novel. Stendhal himself called it a novel about the civilization of the 19th century: postrevolutionary society, in other words.

What is it that Stendhal seeks to do? It may seem obvious. The world is to be made accessible to the senses. To this end, Stendhal selects a number of particulars. But if you look a little closer, you'll discover yet another level. Because at the very moment Stendhal makes the world visible, he also makes visible the discrepancy between sign and meaning, between individual and social status. That difference is constitutive of the social world described by Stendhal, that is, precisely, postrevolutionary society.

Few nineteenth-century writers, at least in France, are as interested in describing clothing as Stendhal. The only other writer I can think of is Balzac. Yet it can't be said that clothing is a crucial issue in Balzac. Or to be more precise: he explores fashion, not clothing. The new is everything. If Balzac is obsessed with the appearance of his characters — and obsessed he is — then he approaches their clothes as more or less successful expressions of the new. The shape of a collar may well define the destiny of a given character. Modern? Obsolete? The difference is subtle yet fateful. It may happen from one day to the next and determine how an individual fares in society. That's the kind of distinction that interests Balzac.

In Stendhal, you dress in order to pass and to belong to a particular class or social community, no matter how temporary this may be. In Balzac, individuals dress in order to compete with others and to differentiate themselves. If there's a primal scene in Balzac, it's the opera.

All of this can be put a little differently. In Stendhal, dress is about social distinction — with personal consequences. In Balzac, dress is about personal distinction — with social consequences.

II

To understand fashion — its nature, its logic, its historical emergence — one would do well to read writers and thinkers such as Baudelaire, Mallarmé, Veblen, Simmel, Benjamin, Elias, and others.[3] Yet one would do equally well to begin with Balzac. Not the novelist, but rather the theorist.[4] I am thinking, in particular, of *Treatise on Elegant Living,* a little known text that reveals Balzac as the insatiable and sharp observer of collective human behavior that he always was.[5] Written a few months after the July Revolution, *Treatise on Elegant Living* was published in installments in the review *La Mode* in October-November 1830.[6] As a treatise, Balzac's essay comes with all the ambitions traditionally associated with philosophical inquiry, complete with prolegomena, doctrines, and axioms. As a textual construction, it is wonderfully improbable. Written in a rigorously breezy style, it indulges in aphoristic wisdom ("Negligence of clothing

---

3 • The classic statements by Baudelaire, Simmel, Elias, and others have been collected in The Rise of Fashion, ed. Daniel Leonhard Purdy (Minneapolis: The University of Minnesota Press, 2004).
4 • For a handy summary of how Balzac approached dress in his novels, see the excerpts collected in Le vêtement chez Balzac, ed. François Boucher (Paris: Editions de l'institut français de la mode, 2001).
5 • Balzac, Traité de la vie élégante (Paris: CRLMC, 2000); translated by Napoleon Jeffries under the title Treatise on Elegant Living (Cambridge, Mass.: Wakefield, 2010). Page references are given parenthetically in the main text. In addition to the treatise, Balzac published Physiologie de la toilette and several other texts on appearance.
6 • For an excellent discussion, including contextualizing perspectives, see Rose Fortassier, "Balzac, pape de la modiphilie," in Les écrivains français et la mode. De Balzac à nos jours (Paris: Presses Universitaires de France, 1988), 43–62.

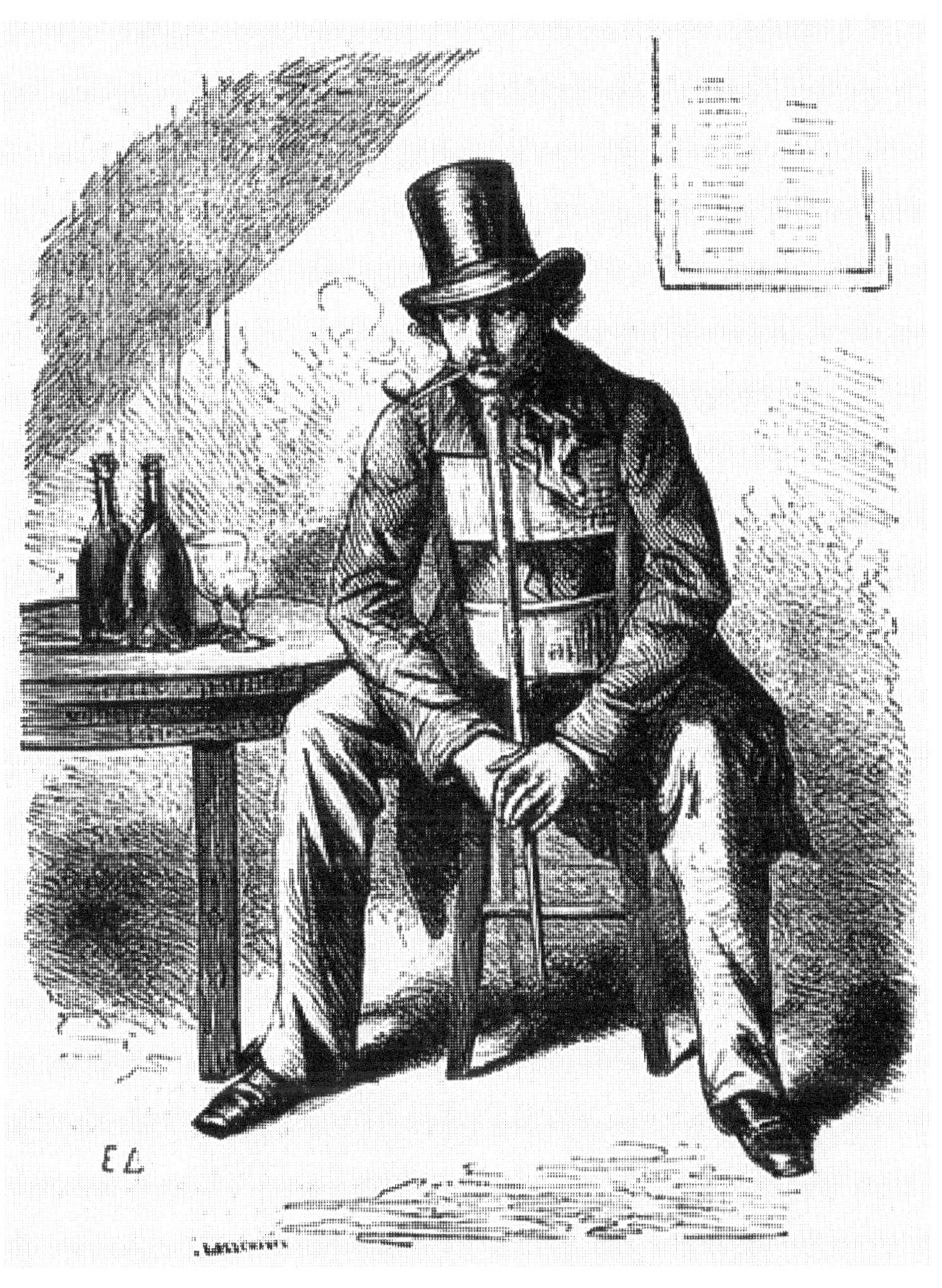

"He was a tavern dandy, one
of those tricksters who are the
despair of policemen." Eugène
Lampsonius (Eustache Lorsay),
from *Œuvres illustrées de
Balzac,* vol. 3–4,
Paris, 1857.

is moral suicide"), idiosyncratic reasoning, bizarre notions ("If privilege exists, it stems from moral superiority"). Yet it aspires to having established — scientifically — the laws governing *la vie élégante*. To be sure, Balzac may not live up to his scientific pretensions, but he manages to review virtually all the issues inherent in what is now known as fashion studies. Even more striking, Balzac's text is an unabashed celebration of the phenomenon he has turned into an object of inquiry.

    Treatise on Elegant Living has been handed down as a pioneering reflection on dandyism; it is well known that it exercised a considerable influence on Barbey d'Aurevilly, Baudelaire, and other writers concerned with that new sociological figure, the dandy.[7] After all, the centerpiece of Balzac's book is a portrait of Beau Brummell (1778–1840), the British dandy who turned into a celebrity in the 1820s. Balzac even goes so far as to include a fictitious conversation with Brummell, a conversation in which the latter gets to elaborate, at some length, his approach to attire, comportment, and manners — in short, his philosophy of elegant living. At the center of this philosophy is dress. "Clothes," Brummell maintains accordingly, "are the most tremendous modification social man has experienced: they influence all of existence." (38–39) Why? "There is one fact that towers over all the others," Brummell explains. "Man dresses himself before acting, before speaking, before walking, and before eating: the actions belonging to fashion, deportment, conversation, etc., are always just the consequences of our clothes." (38) Such a notion — that clothes influence all of existence — may appear as a splendid example of dandyesque philosophy, and if Balzac approves of Brummell's observation, which he certainly does, it is not so much because he subscribes to dandyism and elegant living, which he certainly also does, but rather because his point of departure is a genuinely sociological one — *avant la lettre*. Indeed, for Balzac fashion is a newly discovered yet perfectly natural object of social reflection. By the end of the book, garments, accessories, and gait all appear as a legitimate objects of systematic social inquiry, in particular if you are interested in the expansion of bourgeois culture in the decades following the revolution and its aftermath.

    For this and other reasons, to designate Balzac's treatise as an essay on dandyism seems a limiting description.[8] As the title of the book suggests, the enterprise Balzac felt impelled to

7 • As Rose Fortassier emphasizes, Balzac's treatise inspired a whole series of texts on elegance, for example, Eugène Chapuis, La théorie de l'élégance (1844), Mortemart-Boisse, La vie élégante (1844), and Eugène Marsan, Savoir vivre en France et savoir s'habiller. Incidentally, Barbey d'Aurevilly, in an article published in 1853, celebrates Balzac for having inaugurated a wholly new genre in writing the Traité: "personne avant lui n'avait eu l'idée d'un Esprit des lois de la vie élégante". See Fortassier, Les écrivains français, 57, 58.
8 • See the otherwise excellent introduction by Napoleon Jeffries. Besides, Balzac himself asserted that dandyism is "a heresy of elegant life" as well as "an affectation of fashion" (58).

undertake was a far more ambitious one. Originally intended as a theoretical cornerstone of *La comédie humaine*, *Treatise on Elegant Living* was part of a section titled *Pathologie de la vie sociale*.[9] And anyone with even a superficial knowledge of Balzac's plans for *La comédie humaine* will recognize that *Treatise* is marked by the urgent Balzacian impulse towards discovering the scientific laws governing human life in general and nineteenth-century French society in particular. But Balzac is inhabited by numerous theoretical creatures. He also emerges as a fashion theorist. The theory may not be a full-fledged one, to be sure, and the text itself never became more than a torso, but Balzac offers a theory of fashion no less. What makes his approach particularly interesting, even original, is that he operates with the assumption that fashion cannot be dissociated from society. This may sound obvious enough, especially today, but seen from the point of view of theories of modernity, Balzac's approach is a pioneering one.

Balzac is not saying that clothing is a distinctive characteristic of contemporary society. His argument is more radical than that. Clothing, he states, is "how society expresses itself" (65).[10] As it happens, Balzac himself thought that the science of fashion was the most far-reaching of all sciences. Why? Because fashion is that "which occupies every moment of our life, which governs every act of our waking hours and the instruments of our sleep" (40). Not only did he set out to offer such a science; Balzac also wanted to accomplish its universality. What he had in mind was an *elegantology*; a theory of elegant living, as he called it; at the same time, he wanted to provide something like a *clothingonomy*, much in the spirit of physiognomy, the art of deriving social character from appearance. At the time, physiognomies were vastly popular, and as numerous scholars have pointed out, the need typically arises in the wake of social changes. In Balzac's case such change has a name: the 1789 revolution.

When Balzac conceived his treatise, forty years had passed since that historical event. It may seem like a long time. Yet the text is everywhere animated by a sense of urgency, as though the changes ushered in by the revolution were still making themselves felt.[11] This much is in any case true: in Balzac's historical scenario, fashion is a key phenomenon. For he is not out to describe some timeless law governing the

9 • Begun in 1833 and published in 1839, "Pathologie de la vie sociale" consists of three essays: "Traité de la vie élégante," "Théorie de la démarche," and "Traité des excitants modernes." See Balzac, La comédie humaine. 23, Etudes analytiques... (Paris: Garnier, 2009), 00–00.
10 • Balzac refers to a certain M. Auger, who uttered these words. Balzac continues: "This maxim sums up all our doctrines and virtually contains them to such a degree that anything more that can be said is just a further development of this learned aphorism" (65).
11 • The July revolution, incidentally, has left few traces in the treatise.

workings of fashion; he sees things very differently. Fashion, for him, is a radically new occurrence. Driven by innovation and change, it presupposes a post-feudal society, including newly emergent forms of social mobility. Fashion is even a vehicle of such mobility. More than anything else, *Treatise on Elegant Living* is a protracted meditation on fashion as a distinctive feature of modern society. Balzac's theory of fashion, in effect, is at the same time a theory of modernity, although that is a word he never uses.

If, before the revolution, the social body was made up of the three estates, the postrevolutionary age calls for new typologies. Here's Balzac's contribution to the art of making the world legible. Society, he says, is now made up of "the man who works, the man who thinks, the man who does nothing" (3). This social taxonomy then yields another: "the busy life, the artist's life, the elegant life." In the end, Balzac concludes, the world can be divided into two populations: leisured people and working people, or, alternatively, the rich and the poor. Clearly, if we're looking for analytical subtlety, Balzac may not be our man, but if we're looking for the big picture, he definitely is.

If fashion, historically speaking, is a recent phenomenon, then to inquire into its history is to discover the sociology of modern selfhood. Indeed, Balzac intimates that elegant living is an essentially postrevolutionary phenomenon. This would have been unthinkable before 1789. (17) The emergence of *la vie élégante* presupposes a society in which feudal distinctions, along with those clothing ordinances that determined what each estate could wear, have long given way to a radically new order: one in which the individual is at the center. If, for hundreds of years, fashions had been set by the court, trends could now be set by individuals of no particular significance in terms of class and wealth. Or as they say: individuals of no consequence. The dandy is a case in point. Put simply, fashion has become a matter of personal expression, that is, style. As a means of distinction, it is no longer associated with social rank, estate, or class, at least not primarily. Money certainly helps, but as Balzac states, "fashion is no longer determined by a person's wealth" (26).

Fashion, indeed, is a key feature of modernity. This is the idea emerging between the lines. From Baudelaire' *Painting of Modern Life* onwards, this idea has been explored by a growing number of writers and thinkers such as Mallarmé, Simmel, and Benjamin. Yet Balzac's contribution to this tradition of inquiry has gone largely unnoticed, in cultural studies in general and fashion studies in particular. In the final analysis, the point is not just that Balzac helped pioneer a historicizing perspective in which modernity is everywhere

11 • The July revolution, incidentally, has left few traces in the treatise.

implied. There is more to Balzac's approach: what sets his analysis apart from that of writers such as Baudelaire, Mallarmé, Simmel, and Benjamin, is that he operates on the assumption that the rise of fashion cannot be dissociated from recent social history; in short, he insists on the question of class. Alluding time and again to a historical narrative in which the 1789 revolution plays a fundamental role, *Treatise on Elegant Living* is a pioneering attempt at understanding the rise of fashion in socio-historical terms. To put things a little differently: not only does Balzac take material culture seriously, treating fashion as a proper object of scientific inquiry; the perspective that he applies in order to explain the emergence of fashion is essentially a historical-materialist one. After all, he places questions of class in the foreground. Yet it would be unwise to expect a critical perspective on class relations. Balzac provides nothing of the sort. If anything, the treatise is an unashamed affirmation of the topic under discussion, elegant living or, if you wish, fashion as a means for individual members of the leisured classes to distinguish themselves. Balzac offers little in the way of progressive politics. This doesn't make his attempt at understanding fashion any less interesting.

Balzac's subject matter, strictly speaking, is not fashion, nor clothes, but rather what he calls *la vie élégante*, a certain way of living. What does he take that enigmatic expression to mean? It includes dress, accessories, taste, deportment, attitude, manners; in short, *appearance*, in the widest sense of that word. The closest equivalent would perhaps be *style*, a word even more difficult to define. Yet it takes us to the core of the treatise. Balzac never says as much, but in approaching fashion as a distinctive feature of postrevolutionary society, he traces a transition that serves as an illuminating parallel to an equally momentous one — in the sphere of literary language. As numerous literary scholars have suggested, Balzac's period witnesses the emergence of the modern notion of *style,* a process whose first stirrings can be observed during the second half of the eighteenth century. In short, style is substituted for rhetoric. Style now begins to be understood in the singular. Style is no longer thought of as a set of discursive registers available to the writer, but rather as something that is irreducibly individual. Style is the writer's personal signature, his or her unique fingerprints. In this process, incidentally, Flaubert is a key figure, and novels like *Madame Bovary* and *L'éducation sentimentale* mark the full-blown emergence of style. We might say, then, that just as in the sphere of literary language style is substituted for rhetoric, so in the sphere of clothing fashion is substituted for dress.[12]

12 • See Danius, *The Prose of the World* (Uppsala: Acta Universitatis Upsaliensis, 2006), 33–34.

III

Balzac's novel *Lost Illusions* (1837–1843), perhaps his greatest
work of narrative fiction, tells the story of a handsome young
man, Lucien de Rubempré.[13] Lucien is the son of a pharmacist
and a native of a small provincial town. He makes that classic
nineteenth-century journey from the provinces to the metropolis. His ambition is as classic: he wants to make a name for
himself. As soon as he has arrived in Paris, he acquaints himself
with the city by visiting public urban spaces such as streets,
squares, and parks, places to see and be seen. He makes sure to
wear his very best clothes. These cost his family back in
Angoulême a minor fortune.

Yet it takes only a few moments for him to realize that
people perceive him as a silly provincial. Nothing has been said,
yet he comes to understand what his exterior signifies in the
eyes of others. The insight is chilling. Without quite knowing it,
he's made the gaze of the other into his own. Paris has made him
see, and he doesn't like what he sees.

> Lucien spent two hours of torment in the Tuileries: he
> angrily took stock of his own appearance and
> condemned it. In the first place, not one of these
> elegant young men was wearing a cut-away coat: if he
> saw one at all it was worn by some disreputable old
> man, or some poor down-at-heel, or a *rentier* from the
> Marais quartier, or a commissionaire. Having realized
> the difference between morning and evening wear,
> this highly sensitive and keen-sighted poet recognized
> the ugliness of his own apparel, which was fit only for
> the rag-bag, the out-of-date cut of his coat, its dubious
> blue, its outrageously ungainly collar and its tails
> nearly meeting in front through too long usage; the
> buttons were rusty and there were tell-tale white lines
> along the creases. Also his waistcoat was too short and
> so grotesquely provincial in style that he hastily
> buttoned up his coat in order to hide it. Lastly, only
> common people were wearing nankeen trousers. Fash-
> ionable people were wearing attractively patterned or
> immaculately white material! Moreover everyone wore
> gaitered trousers; the bottoms of his fell in ugly crin-
> kles on the heels of his boots. He wore a
> white cravat with embroidered ends [...].
> Only grave personages, a few aged finan-
> ciers and austere public officials wore
> white cravats; worse still, the unhappy
> native of Angoulême saw a grocer's
> errand-boy with a basket on his head

13 • Balzac, *Lost Illusions*, trans. Herbert J.
Hunt (London: Penguin, 1971). Page references are given parenthetically in the main
text.

passing along the other side of the railings on the
pavement of the rue de Rivoli, and he was wearing a
cravat with its two ends embroidered by some adoring
shop-girl. For Lucien this was like a blow in the chest
[...]. (164–5)

This passage is a mere fragment of the episode that renders how
Lucien comes to see himself with the eyes of others. Yet the
comedy of these pages should be clear, and the formidable skill
with which Balzac's narrator approaches the descriptive task he
has set himself. For what Balzac achieves here is something
remarkable. The passage appears at first glance to offer an elaborate characterization of Lucien's appearance and little more. But
Balzac in effect accomplishes two things at once. The scene also
manages to expose — to make visible — the very parameters
that govern the fashion system in relation to which Lucien's
exterior takes on meaning.

And it does so in brutal detail. A button is never just a
button. It quickly dawns on Lucien that he is the unwitting
carrier of so many signs that have already assigned him a place
within a visually determined signifying system, that is, a herme-
neutics of class. And when Lucien discovers what kind of place
he occupies within this very signifying system, the gap between
his self-image and what he represents in the eyes of others
begins to yawn terrifyingly.

"I look just like an apothecary's son, a mere shop-assis-
tant!" he told himself, as he watched the passers-by,
graceful, smart, elegant young men of the Faubourg
Saint-Germain: all of them having a certain *cachet*, all
alike in their trimness of line, their dignity of bearing
and their self-confident air; yet all different thanks to
the setting each had chosen in order to show himself
to advantage. The best points in all of them were
brought out by a kind of *mise en scène* at which the
young men of Paris are as skilful as the women. (165)

It is as though Lucien, in casting a critical eye on his own appearance, has stepped out of himself. He has been pulled into a
strange dialectic: he is both the subject of perception and its
object. Lucien, after all, is indeed the son of a pharmacist, but
what he now discovers — what Paris makes him see — is that he
is a *mere* apothecary's son. As he looks at the others, he also looks
at himself — and then turns into an other in his own eyes.

Balzac here performs an exercise in comparative criticism. What is more, he crafts a passage that, in its accumulation
of tell-tale detail, recreates on the stylistic level the very

distinction about which it speaks. A whole series of particulars, all pregnant with unexpected social significance, parade before our eyes: the look of a button, the shape of a collar, the texture of a cravat, the cut of a waistcoat, the length of a trouser pant. In fact, *Lost Illusions* is more than just a novel; it's also a fashion guide, complete with listings of what's in — and out. That is to say, Balzac makes the fashion system legible, including the social context in which that system is operative.

For Lucien there is a simple lesson to be drawn. On learning how he appears in the eyes of others, Lucien is filled with desire for revenge. He decides to refashion himself. After a series of overly ambitious changes of dress, along with so many public humiliations, Lucien is ready for his Parisian career. He's filled with rage. It is powerful enough to carry him through six hundred pages. The result is *Lost Illusions*.
What Balzac does here is craft an archetypal tale of how a provincial arrives in the metropolis, discovering a social force field that is as vast and complex as it is opaque. And this discovery necessarily subjects the protagonist's previous experiences, convictions, and beliefs to painful relativization. Such relativization is another word for "lost illusions," and this, of course, is what *Lost Illusions* is all about. From now on, life will be a sequence of battles, and Balzac's handsome hero rises to the challenge.

This is a paradigmatic story, one that both Stendhal and Balzac rehearse, each in his own way. At the heart of the story is language, codes of behavior — and clothing. Indeed, in both writers dress is an integral part of the narrative fabric. In fact, it cuts to the thematic core: the discrepancy between visibility and legibility. What are the protagonists of Stendhal and Balzac other than narrative pretexts for exploring postrevolutionary society? Both writers represent this society as a world in which things may well be visible, sometimes excessively so, but not necessarily legible.

Yet there is a feature that sets Balzac's version of the story apart from that of Stendhal: the essentially modern way in which the former approaches the question of dress. Balzac is concerned with clothing as a means of expressing one's individuality; Stendhal is not. This is not to say that Balzac is the more interesting writer; far from it. My point is a simple one: the difference between Balzac and Stendhal usefully directs our attention to a slow but momentous change in the social history of clothes, a change that makes itself felt in this historical period: the rise of fashion.

IV
"Politics in a literary work is like a gun shot in the middle of a concert," Stendhal writes in *The Red and the Black*. This sounds

like an apology for the notion that art belongs in a realm above and beyond the political. Yet few nineteenth-century writers have done as much as Stendhal to push the novel towards the center of society. He was one of the first intellectuals to connect the question of style with the question of politics, as Yves Ansel has shown. But Stendhal's achievement is even greater: his work testifies to the discovery of society as such, postrevolutionary society. The same is true of Balzac. Accelerated social mobility is in the process of changing the face of the nation, including those very systems of signification that help make individuals, social groups, and actions legible.

The world that emerges in Stendhal and Balzac is no doubt visible. But it is not transparent. Society is a cipher, a rich cipher. It falls on the writer to make it legible. It is no coincidence that Stendhal is so busy with dress, disguises, and masks, just as it is no coincidence that Balzac places the semiotics of fashion right at the center of the social career of his protagonist, forcing him to learn how to navigate a world in which dress is a primary vehicle of individual distinction. What we're catching a glimpse of here, what is emerging on the literary horizon, is something like a sociology, well before the word exists. And it is in this newly discovered vacuum, long before sociology, ethnology, and psychology have even been thought of as possible modes of academic inquiry, that the early nineteenth-century realist novel makes sure to carve out a space, a radically new space, one in which the political is immanent in the aesthetic. •

Sara Danius is Professor of Aesthetics at Södertorn University. Recent books include *Den blå tvålen. Romanen och konsten att göra saker och ting synliga* (2013) and *Aisthesis: Estetikens historia del 1* (ed. with Cecilia Sjöholm and Sven-Olov Wallenstein, 2012).

Aisthesis

Accident and Absolute Guilt: Kafka's Jurisprudence

Howard Caygill

1 • To be found in *Franz Kafka Amtliche Schriften* ed. Klaus Hermsdorf (Berlin: Akademie Verlag, 1984) 134–141 or in the more recent *Kritische Ausgabe* edition edited by Klaus Hermsdorf and Benno Wagner (Frankfurt Am Main: Fischer, 2004). Hermsdorf's introductory essay to the earlier edition "Arbeit und Amt als Erfahrung und Gestaltung" remains one of the most insightful understandings of the relationship between Kafka's official and fictional authorships. A selection of these writings has recently been translated as *Franz Kafka: The Office Writings*, eds. Stanley Corngold, Jack Greenberg and Benno Wagner (New Haven: Princeton University Press, 2009).

Capitalism is probably the first instance of a cult that creates guilt (Schuld), not atonement. In this respect, this religious system is caught up in the headlong rush of a larger movement. A vast sense of guilt that is unable to find relief seizes on the cult, not in order to atone for this guilt but to make it universal, to hammer it into the conscious mind, so as once and for all to include God in the system of guilt and thereby awaken in him an interest in the process of atonement.

Walter Benjamin,
Capitalism as Religion

The relationship between Kafka's day-job as an expert in industrial accident insurance and his nocturnal fictional writing has been noted by critics but its implications remain to a surprising extent unexplored. The short story *In the Penal Colony* written during the autumn of 1914 is unsurpassed for its technical description of an industrial accident: the botched auto-execution of the presiding "Officer." The description of this death at work uncannily recalls the illustrations of industrial injury in Kafka's 1909 report on *Regulations for Accident Prevention with Wood-Planing Machines*.[1] Further descriptions of hazardous work environments can be found throughout Kafka's writings, most prominently in his abandoned first novel *The Lost One (America)*, notable also for its intimation of a society dominated by the motor car (Kafka was a pioneer in the emerging field of car insurance).[2] However, beyond the transfer of descriptive material from the official to the fictional authorship it is also possible to see the latter as fictional explorations of a new notion of *Schuld* (guilt/liability) emerging with industrial modernity and central to the development of the institutions of accident insurance.

At one point during the conversation between the Officer and the Researcher that makes up the first part of *In the Penal Colony*, the Officer — last remaining disciple of the late commandant and legislator of the Colony — describes the jurisprudence that informs his judicial decision to condemn the soldier awaiting execution. It comprises a principle and a procedure seemingly alien to the history of Western law: "The principle according to which I decide is: guilt (*Schuld*) is always without doubt. Other courts may not follow this principle, for they have many heads and have higher courts above them. This is not the case here, or it wasn't at least with the previous commandant."[3] The latest, "enlightened" commandant is turning away from this principle and deliberately neglecting the old law and its procedures. After lamenting this neglect, the Officer turns to a long and loving description of the *Apparat* or machine of execution that inscribes on the body of its victim the name of the crime of which he is deemed guilty. The moment of death coincides with the victim's ecstatic recognition of their guilt, or rather the crime of which they are guilty. The principles of this jurisprudence are clearly outlined in the fiction: guilt is always without doubt, a single judge "decides" each case according to this principle, and the victim is not only denied a hearing but is even ignorant of the crime of which they are accused, ignorant, that is, until the last ecstatic moment of the trial/punishment. Trial and execution are folded into each other, the judicial decision consisting not in the ascertainment of guilt, but in the choice of who is to be guilty.

Kafka wrote *In the Penal Colony* at the same time as *The Trial,* abandoning the latter on January 20, 1915. The parallels and contrasts between the two fictions are striking, with the Officer seeming to refer to the Court of *The Trial* with its esoteric hierarchy of instances when he refers to the "other courts" with "many heads" who obey a different jurisprudential principle due to the absence of unitary decision. The guilt of Josef K., the victim of the *Gericht/Apparat* of *The Trial,* seems always in doubt, and his journey through the machinery of law concludes with an execution in which he is not, as in the penal colony, enlightened as to his crime before a rapt public but experiences confusion and sense of a shame that will

2 • See Kafka *Amtliche Schriften*, 124–132.
3 • Kafka, *Die Erzählungen* (Frankfurt am Main: Fischer, 2007), 171.

survive him. Yet there is a strong sense in both stories that the incidence of absolute guilt is accidental, it happens to individuals like the insubordinate soldier and Josef K. not for any reason beyond their being subject to accusation, and the accusation can fall upon anyone.

In *Capitalism as Religion* Benjamin notes the "demonic ambiguity" of the word *Schuld,* an expression he also uses in the "Critique of Violence": "consider the demonic ambiguity of this word." Some of this ambiguity is evident in the equivocal possibilities available for translating *Schuld* as guilt, or debt, obligation, blame and even sin. As a word that intrinsically exploits its ambiguous location in economic, moral or religious contexts, *Schuld* is a concept central to Benjamin's radicalisation of Weber's protestant ethic thesis in the fragment *Capitalism as Religion* and later in the notion of "Fetish Commodity" in the *Arcades Project*. Benjamin's proposal that capitalism creates *Schuld* can be understood at once in terms of its creating debt, liability, ethical wrong, responsibility and religious guilt. Weber of course focused on the role of religious guilt in the formation of the "calling" (*Beruf*) that he sees at the origins of capitalism. Benjamin's condemnation of capitalism for its *Schuld* involves at once economic debt, moral responsibility for exploitation and religious guilt; however his emphasis on the ambiguity of the term also allows us to situate Kafka's notion of absolute guilt more precisely. The "larger movement" of capitalism that creates *Schuld* may also be understood in terms of the development of an economic and technical system that creates accidents, with victims who in terms of intention are innocent but once being called or arrested enter a context of absolute liability.

The term *accident* (*Unfall*) shares with *Schuld* the property of extreme ambiguity. Etymologically emerging from Latin "to fall," it describes an event without cause, one which can generate liability or guilt, something that occurs by chance, something fateful and yet nevertheless — and this is its philosophical sense — a somehow inessential attribute. In all senses, an accident befalls its victim and is neither intended nor forms part of their essence, but once having taken place becomes necessary and fateful. In Kafka's fragment from early 1917, *The Hunter Gracchus,* the dead but undeparted hunter literally suffered an accident, a fatal fall while hunting in the Black Forest. Arriving in a small lakeside port centuries later, Gracchus relates to the mayor who was expecting him: "Many years ago, it must be very many years ago, I fell off a cliff in the Black Forest, that's in Germany, as I chased a chamois. I've been dead since."[4] The hunter Gracchus relates how after his fall he travelled the countries of the world in a barge stranded between life and death. Gracchus is tormented by trying to justify the necessity of his accident — was he guilty as a hunter and was the accident thus punishment? He tells the mayor "I was a hunter, is that some kind of guilt (*Schuld*)." The mayor (not incidentally called Salvatore — saviour) replies that he is not required to judge Gracchus — "I am not called to decide that" — but confides that to him it seems as if there is no *Schuld.* He then immediately retracts this opinion, specifying that while Gracchus himself bears no personal *Schuld* for his accident, someone must nevertheless be *schuldig*, it could not just have been an accident: "'But who then does bear the guilt?' 'The boatman' said the hunter." Yet it is the very pursuit of the fateful yet erroneous question of who is guilty that holds Gracchus suspended between life and death: what prevents his dying is the pursuit of a meaning to his accident, the compulsion to situate it in a context of guilt involving intent and responsibility. His situation is parallel to that of Josef. K in *The Trial.* For Gracchus, someone must be responsible for his accident, he himself or perhaps the boatman; it cannot just have been a meaningless accident. Josef K. too is convinced of his innocence and pursues it to the end, his very conviction of being innocent trapping him inextricably in a nexus of guilt and innocence from which the only exit is death.

Kafka's work in industrial insurance brought him into daily, professional contact with accidents, issues of liability and accident statistics. His collections and series of accident statistics in various branches of industry show awareness that accidents occur in a population with a predictable regularity. Their predictability holds, however, for the population and not for the individuals who make up a population. His insurance work and his fictions take place in the biopolitical zone between the population and the individual. The industrial system generates a statistically regular number of accidents, but the issue of individual liability for these accidents was by no means clear. Much of Kafka's professional work involved the management of such liability. In the course of his career he devoted his attention increasingly to accident prevention, in order to reduce the incidence of accidents, but was continually forced to return to the problem of the *Schuld* for such events. Many of his earlier official writings represent industrial insurance and the work of his employer — The Workers Accident Insurance Institute — as mediating not only between the interests of the workers and the employers — balancing liability — but also between employers. Part of Kafka's work was to grade companies according to their statistical rates of industrial accidents and to determine their financial contribution to the common pool accordingly. Issues of intention and negligence were not central to the work of the Institute whose primary role was to distribute the *Schuld* of the accident rates among all the parties. Indeed, the pursuit of individual guilt or liability would obstruct the work of the Institute and blur its focus on managing a statistical population of accidents rather than the intent or negligence of individual perpetrators and victims.

Kafka thus worked with a systemic understanding of *Schuld* as a statistically predictable and definable property of a system or *Apparat,* in his case branches of industrial production and transport. In a sense his insurance work was parallel in its method and guiding intuitions to the sociology of Durkheim. In *Suicide* the sociologist's attention is fixed upon differential statistical rates of suicides and not the individual intent or decision to take one's own life. Durkheim would even speak of "suicidal waves" sweeping European societies with almost predictable regularity and carrying away vulnerable individuals. The prognosis of the sociologist, however, can only extend to the inevitability of a determinable suicide rate, it cannot specify or predict who the individuals will be who will make up that population. Similarly, it is rare in Kafka's official writings for the incidence of statistical rates on individual fates to be given much consideration, even though he spent much of his professional life in discussion with individual employers and victims of industrial accidents. A notable exception, and perhaps not to be included as part of his official writings, is a newspaper articles on psychiatrically damaged soldiers of 1917, where Kafka's recommendations for rehabilitation show a full and sensitive appreciation of the individual consequences of what appear as statistical casualty rates.

It is in his fiction that Kafka explores with exemplary rigour the question of the incidence of statistical regularities on individual lives. His fiction is nothing less than a catalogue of accidents that befall their protagonists: the hunter Gracchus falls from a cliff, the ape Rotpeter is captured by the entertainment industry in *A Report to an Academy*, the anti-hero Karl Rossman undergoes an escalating series of accidental misfortunes in *The Lost One (America)*, a salesman wakes up to find himself metamorphosed into an insect and the land-surveyor K. finds himself summoned to the Castle through an administrative error that no-one remembers and for which no one wants to admit responsibility (*Schuld*). These accidents befall an individual, selecting him or her without reason but according to a necessity subsequently described by statistical regularities. There is a necessity to the chance accident, but one which should not be sought in the intent or negligence of that individual — they are the victims, or the chosen ones, of a systemic propensity to generate accidents. What is important in the individual fates that Kafka imaginatively explores in the fictional complement to his insurance work are the consequences that follow for them from their

accidents. Many of Kafka's characters are blocked by an inappropriate interpretation of *Schuld* seeking behind their accidents a
malign intent or careless act of negligence and not understanding the random necessity that has called them to embody a
systemic property. The hunter Gracchus is condemned to
wander the earth between life and death not because of some
guilt that provoked the accident that happened to him, but
precisely because of his insistent search for a meaning to the
event in terms of guilt. His very syntax points to an
inability to distinguish between what is essential
and what accidental — he fell in the Black Forest,
adding unnecessarily the information "which is in
Germany," an accidental detail which shows he has
not grasped the essentials of his case.

It is in the fiction of the autumn of 1914
— *In the Penal Colony* and *The Trial* and *Before the
Law* — that we can appreciate the full implications
of Kafka's jurisprudence of *Schuld*. In the case of the
former, which is also in many respects a fable of
messianic misrecognition, the *Apparat* as combined
court and machinery of execution demands as a
reason for its existence a determined number of
victims. As the Officer explains, the *Apparat* is a
disciplinary technology, it selects victims according
to a timetable, and the very fact of selection
confirms the *Schuld* of the victim. The "doggishly submissive"
condemned man, who throughout the Officer's explanation of
the *Apparat* to the Researcher (*Forschungsreiser*) behaves like a dog
and whose job was to guard his own superiors' door like a dog,
is to be executed for insubordination. However, he has been
chosen not because of his offence, but because the *Apparat*
required a victim for the purpose of demonstrating its working
to the Researcher. He is spared by an industrial accident from
the fate of dying from the inscription upon his body of the
phrase "Honour thy superiors." It is crucial to the disciplinary
workings of the *Apparat* that its victims could be anybody —
in the penal colony all are guilty but not all are tried — and that
it be witnessed by the erstwhile crowds of the penal island
community and now by the Researcher.

The horrific death of the Officer who substitutes
himself for the insubordinate soldier underlines that the *Apparat*
is a system that randomly selects its individual victims; they
cannot *choose* to become accidents. This is the error of the officer
who attempts to have himself executed, in an act of misplaced
fidelity that fundamentally betrays the jurisprudence of the
Apparat. The Officer attempts to introduce a logic of sacrifice
into the workings of the *Apparat* which it refuses by provoking

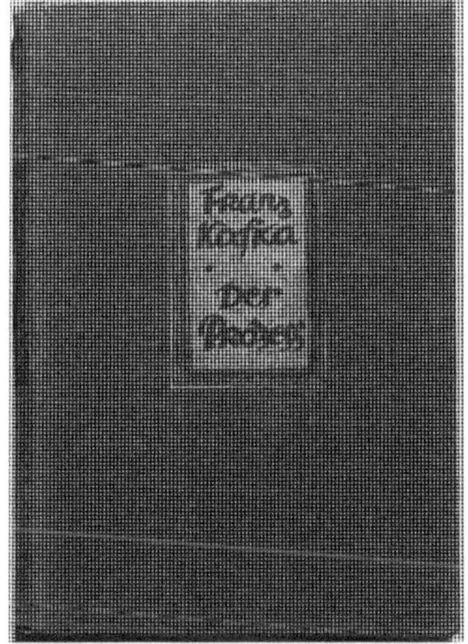

▲

**Franz Kafka, *Der
Prozess*, 1925, First
Edition.**

an even more spectacular accident that destroys both it and the Officer. Upon realising that the enlightened researcher is appalled by *Apparat* the Officer accepts this as condemnation and programmes the machine to execute him, under the eyes of the researcher (who now assumes the role of enlightened judge, hearing first the case for the *Apparat* and then condemning it) programming the inscription "Be just." The Officer imagines himself and his *Apparat* condemned as unjust, and tries to vindicate the *Apparat* by sacrificing himself — he intends to be executed by the *Apparat*, confirming at once his individual guilt but also the essential justice of the system. The result is mutual destruction: "The harrow did not write, it just stabbed, and the bed did not turn the body but lifted it shaking into the needles. The Researcher wanted to intervene, possibly bring the whole thing to a standstill, that was surely no torture as sought by the Officer, but just direct murder."[5] Programmed to perform a sacrifice rather than a random execution the machine destroyed itself and took the Officer with it.

The inappropriate attempt by the Officer to justify the *Apparat* by sacrificing himself to it as a guilty individual rather than as an accidental victim of its systemic guilt in this case destroyed the *Apparat*. This unexpected outcome is provoked by the complicating messianic confusions surrounding the Old Commandant and the Researcher. The latter is misrecognised by the Officer and by other secret followers of the Old Commandant as a Messianic figure who is thought to bring atonement to the guilt producing *Apparat*.[6] The Officer's self-immolation according to what he considered to be the sentence of the Messiah/Researcher was intended to redeem the justice of the machine, with the officer taking literally on his own back the systemic guilt of the *Apparat*. The mutual destruction of Officer and Apparat was possible due to the presence of the Researcher or accidental messiah who, however mistakenly, is considered to bear the promise of a new law. In the face of the Researcher's growing realisation of this misrecognition on the part of the islanders the story ends with him desperately fleeing the island. In the summer of 1917 Kafka returned to the ending, putting into question the Researcher's escape with sketches of alternative endings which represent traumatic, dreamlike returns to the scene of execution and failures to leave even the scene of the *Apparat*.

The Trial does not possess the messianic complications of *In the Penal Colony* and the complex stratifications of the court survive their victim Josef K. Yet the principle of systemic guilt attached to the *Apparat* also holds for the *Gericht*. The court generates *Schuld*, falling upon its victims apparently

Aisthesis

5 • Ibid, 195.
6 • See my "Kafka's Exit: Exile, Exodus and Messianism," in Peter de Bolla and Stefan H. Uhlig (eds.), *Aesthetics and the Work of Art: Adorno, Kafka, Richter* (Basingstoke: Palgrave Macmillan, 2008).

without reason; they are accident victims, a quota of individuals who are brought before the law. This is apparent already in the opening lines of the novel, according to which "someone must have slandered Josef K. for without having done anything bad he found himself arrested one morning."[7] Thereafter, instead of realising that the arrest was an accident with little to do with issues of guilt or innocence, Josef K. pursues a quest to establish his innocence. He was of course never guilty in sense of doing anything wrong or pursuing a criminal intent, and it is his persistence in pursuing a legal logic of guilt and innocence in the face of repeated advice to pursue diverse strategies, whether deference or procrastination, in order to divert the machine from executing its sentence, that will lead to his downfall. Josef K inappropriately sought atonement for a guilt which was not his but that of the court. The strategy of seeking meaning for the accident of his fall that left the hunter Gracchus suspended between life and death led Josef K. to an execution like a dog (akin to the doglike soldier condemned in *In The Penal Colony*) and a "shame would survive him" or in other words, one that, like the hunter, would live on.

Josef K. had received a clear and final warning against accepting individual responsibility for systemic guilt in the parable and commentary *Before the Law*. Many of the commentaries upon this parable, including the versions of Derrida's intense "Devant la loi" and "Prejuges devant la loi" miss this aspect of the parable by remaining fixated upon the problem of entry to the law. They share this with the "man from the country" who passes his life before the gate of the law trying to find a way to gain entrance and even Josef K. who could not walk away. For the point of the parable is less the entry to the law than an exit from the country. The gateway to the law is an obstacle to this escape, a distraction from the task of evading the incidence of the law. The Researcher of *In the Penal Colony* flees the proximity of the *Apparat* and the insidious way in which it was drawing him into its logic; the man from the country, however, is blocked by his fascination for the law. As he loses his sight and approaches death, he learns the door was just for him, and by waiting upon it he has fulfilled its sentence and become a victim of the law.

The parable appears three times in Kafka's *oeuvre*: towards the end of *The Trial*, as a free-standing parable, and among the stories of escape and fascination that made up the 1917 collection *A Country Doctor*. In *The Trial* it is related to Josef K. by a clergyman in the Cathedral, and is given an exegesis that serves also as a warning. Josef K. is effectively told not to wait for the law, but to flee its logic according to which guilt,

7 • Kafka, *Der Prozess*, ed. Malcolm Pasley (Frankfurt am Main: Fischer, 2008), 9.

however deferred, is inevitable. As Josef K. leaves the now dark Cathedral, hardly able to see, like the man from the country at the end of his wait before the law, he is left with a sense that there is something he has not understood, that the clergyman wants something from him. The clergyman explains that he belongs to the court and the asks "why would I want something from you. The court wants nothing from you. It takes you when you come and releases you when you go."[8] The point, however, is to go — for Josef K. to turn his back on the law and its nexus of guilt and innocence and resume his interrupted life. The intensification of *Schuld* mentioned by Benjamin in *Capitalism as Religion* introduces it into all areas of life — it consumes not only the life of the "man from the country" but even the death of the hunter Gracchus and Josef K. It does not, in Kafka, "awaken God's interest in salvation" — Benjamin's last chance — since God is nowhere implicated in *Schuld*.

Much of Kafka's professional life in industrial insurance was spent untangling the legal complications that arose following industrial accidents. As a systemic property of industrial modernity the incidence of industrial accidents were, as the clergyman of *The Trial* would put it, necessary. Their effects and the suffering they caused were complicated and exacerbated by attempts to accommodate them according to a legal structure founded on the ascertainment of subjective guilt, innocence and liability. Kafka's growing professional interest in accident prevention in the lumber industries and in quarries marks an attempt to reduce the incidence of accidents by reducing systemic propensity to *Schuld* or risk. Avoiding the recourse to law by means of reducing the risk of accidents or when they inevitably occurred by managing their consequences in terms of absolute *Schuld* or liability at least reduced the "demonic ambiguity" of *Schuld* and allowed life for its victims to go on free from the debilitating pursuit of individual guilt or innocence within a guilty system. •

Howard Caygill is Professor of Philosophy in the Centre for Research in Modern European Philosophy, Kingston University. His most recent book is *On Resistance: A Philosophy of Defiance* (2012).

8 • Ibid, 235.

Must We Believe What We See? On the Filmic Aesthetics of Illusion

Gertrud Koch

With reference to film perception and its theory, the question in this essay's title is less trivial than it may sound. It is my thesis that the perception of film is a complex interaction of believing and seeing, the normative context of which is discursive and determined performatively on the inside. The first aspect of "must" arises from the concreteness of the filmic image and lies with the communicative level in the sense that we cannot see nothing, but always have to see something. The second aspect of "must" has a normative quality: We do not have to believe in what we think we see, in front of a picture we can believe that we recognize a unicorn within it without believing in unicorns, consequently, we are making a statement with reference to what we see. The third aspect of "must," which lies beyond the normative "ought to," refers to a law of nature dimension of objective, perceptive-physiological illusion, for example, we have to see motion on the screen, even if we believe that a film consists of stills which contain mere stages of a movement, but not motion itself.

I would prefer "believing" understood as a pragmatic act here. In a situation which cannot be resolved by reverting to the knowledge of something, but nevertheless compels an action which refers to something, believing gains relevance as a form of "as if" knowledge — the situation of someone who has to decide which way to take at a crossroads can serve as an example here — even if he knows that he doesn't know, he has to believe that the chosen way is the right one, otherwise he would have chosen the other. Within the context of the aesthetic creation of illusion, this can be understood as a variation of the "as if" character: I know that I am acting to a fiction, and yet I believe so strongly in the viewed in the act of perception that it seizes me. Believing refers to the absoluteness of a world that only emerges vividly in the illudation of its viewer but forces me to recognize it in so far as I would disturb my own illudation in rejecting it. Inasmuch phenomena of appearance cannot claim knowledge, they challenge belief. Filmic illusion does not force a (mis)judgement of the empirical world on me in the act of believing in what becomes manifest within it, but it establishes a ratio in which I have to act with regard to the object as it appears, i.e. towards the way of its manifestation. Illusion as a whole is neither pre-reflexive, nor does it demand non-knowledge to be able to deceive. All aesthetic illusion wants is to be believed in its manifestation.

Three aspects of must-believe interact in film perception. In my opinion, this is as constitutive for a theoretical aesthetics of film as it is for the differing aesthetic methods of film and its poetics. The respective rules of this interaction enable the recognition of something within the viewed, the belief in it as a fiction and the acceptance of its possibility in the illusion of the perception of motion. Different film theories and aesthetics are constituted through this. I subsequently would like to discuss some of the consequences arising from the questions asked in the beginning, this with reference to the illusionary effect of film, which is undergoing various discussions.

With reference to film theoretical paradigms, the following typology can be opened up:

A) Cognitive, analytic film theory partly argues within the referential frame of cognitive psychology and its constructions of knowledge, but partly also within the referential frame of a carefully graded phenomenological realism of analytic philosophy. For either option, illusion is not an applicable concept. In his chapter on the "Myth of Illusion" Gregory Currie has put forth several of these arguments, with the assistance of which the phenomenon of the creation of illusion can be approached — and, as he thinks, left behind.[1] The first differentiation he makes is between "cognitive" and "perceptive" illusion. The most unambiguous case for a perceptive illusion are all phenomena which are called "objective illusion" in cognitive psychology — delusions of perception that we are subject to even if we are convinced to succumb to a delusion. This kind of perception proves cognitively

1 • Gregory Currie, *Image and Mind: Film, Philosophy and Cognitive Science* (Cambridge: Cambridge University Press, 1995).

impermeable. Currie uses the so-called Müller-Leyer illusion as an example. Two lines of the same length with arrowheads on their end: The arrowheads of one line are directed outwards, the ones of the other line inwards. Even if we know this scheme and are convinced that the lines are of the same length on the cognitive level, we are seeing lines of clearly different length. Another well-known example is the figure of gestalt switch. One figure contains two figures, of which we only see one at a time. We can never see both figures simultaneously, but only successively, even though we know that we are dealing with a gestalt switch. According to Currie, these cognitively impermeable illusions are of no interest to a cognitively tenable film theory, although they can occur in film as well. For we see motion because there is actually motion on the screen — that of the light rays moving across the screen and making objects appear on different parts of the screen. We experience this motion as real, in so far no creation of illusion takes place in perceiving the moving images of film. Not only do we not have to believe that there are indeed trains driving across the theatre because we can see a train drive across the screen. We are not even seeing an illusion of a movement on screen, but a real movement — thus, we can neither speak of an epistemic crisis nor of the belief in illusion as a manifestation.

B) Psychoanalytic film theory explores the ratio of sensory perception and intentionality as one of concealment and revelation, denial and imaginarization which become intertwined on different levels of consciousness. This process of processing sets a dynamics in motion in which compulsion and projection, derealization and recognition of error, wishful thinking and thought experiment, the principle of reality and interaction interlock.

In projection we see what we think we have to see, in denial we do not believe what we had to see, etc. The prototypical case in Freud's assumption of the visibility of the difference between the sexes is the male child who cannot believe what it sees and who imagines what it believed it had to see elsewhere in something else. What we see becomes our thought; we tell and explain to each other what we believed to have seen. Knowledge and prejudice are thus adjacent. Hypnosis, hallucination, dream and illusion are as much *states* of consciousness as they are part of the system of consciousness with its different layers and levels.

C) Phenomenological film theory reverts to perception's close connection with the body, thus asking the phenomenological questions on another level than that of semiotization. Material foundations are taken into account here as much as questions of relating to the world. Roughly summarized, the proposal is that illusion be comprehended not as a referential, epistemic problem, but as an aisthetic phenomenon of perception in itself.

D) Finally, The Nietzschean aesthetics of appearances circumscribes the connection between illusionization and reference to reality as complementary and demands an own status of recognition for aesthetic experience. For film aesthetics, Hinrich Fink-Eitel succinctly argues in a short essay:

> Another interpreter of dreams, Friedrich Nietzsche, invented the deity of film, Apoll. His realm, the "beautiful appearance of dream worlds," is the origin of all art. The first meaning of the term appearance, the basic category of classical aesthetics, is "to shine". Apoll is the one who shines, the God of light and thus of the art of light, of film. This gleam is beautiful, it renders splendor and shimmering colours to the world. Second, appearance means a fiction or an illusion. Non-reality, non-being. Thus, the term refers to what is not at the same time: to reality and to the being.[2]

Within an aesthetics of appearance, we do not have to believe that what we see is actually real, but we ought to believe in what we see, the reflexive refraction of reality within the illusionary image. The illusionary image is a reflexive image.

Different ways of creating illusion
With regard to film, the category of "objective illusion" is frequently applied with reference to the perception of motion. I would like to take this into account here first, because I assume that films differ from other images especially due to the fact that we see them as images of movement (e.g. tracking shots, walks etc.), which are also put into motion themselves (e.g. through the projector with a speed of 24 frames per second or already in the process of recording them with a camera) — which emerge especially through the movement of the camera during the process of shooting them.

The crucial point at which the term of illusion as opposed to fiction is brought up for film aesthetics is the point at which the stills, put into motion in projection, allow us to see motion. From the point of view of perceptive psychology, this is what is called an "objective illusion". An optical delusion which becomes apparent independently from the will of its observer, the function of which consists the prerequisite *that* we see the individual

2 • Hinrich Fink-Eitel, "Lust und Weisheit des Scheines: Die Alptraumwelt Alfred Hitchcocks," *Deutsche Zeitschrift für Philosophie* 43 (1995): 546

frames as a continuous movement. A realistic argument aims at the question of reproducing real motion. Accordingly, everything is half as exciting: We see phase-images of a real movement, which has taken place for real in front of a camera within the profilmic continuum. Within filmic projection, we supplement these phase images through the technical as well as through the perceptive-physiological apparatus, thus eventually completing them into a continuous, uninterrupted motion again. This assertion is based on the assumption that film does not create an illusion of motion, but rather reproduces real motion. Consequently, we may well believe in what we see. Where we see motion, there were movements, the succession of which our perceptive apparatus can synthesize from the individual phase-images. Instead of speaking of a delusion or an illusion, we rather ought to speak of the ability and the performative competence of the perceptive apparatus to create a complete image of motion from incomplete information. This position is occasionally characterized as the argument of transparency: Behind the images, we see something pre-filmic, a world which was in motion in front of the camera at the exact time when the images were shot. This thesis has it that film is as indexical as photography. It can be supplemented with yet another realistic argument which denies the illusionary aspect of the filmic vision of motion, insofar as the vision of motion is a general property and that it's not only in film that it is not based on a continuous perception of motion: The vision of motion depends on eye movements, but even if the blink of the eyelid rhythmically interrupts the transfer of sensory data, we do not see motion, but create it in the first place as a cognitive synthesis. It is the old philosophic problem that motion can only be comprehended functionally within the continuum of space and time that re-emerges here. I would like to point out here that in Xenon's "standing arrow" paradox or the one of Achilles the latter will never manage to overtake a turtle because the initial distance between the both of them cannot be suspended as long as space is comprehended as a constant and thus an indefinitely divisible quantity: So the spatial distance will become ever shorter, but it will always persist. Thus, also the arrow has to stand still in the airspace if we comprehend its movement as a flight through an indefinitely divisible, spatial distance. This paradox can be narrated for film as well if the phase images are accepted to lie at the core of observation and if film's material aspect to be a spatial extension. It is only through the weaver's thread of time that paradox is eschewed and transformed into a filmic *chronotopos* (spacetime/timespace), another term which Bachtin borrowed from Einstein's theory of relativity as a metaphor for a narration theory.[3]

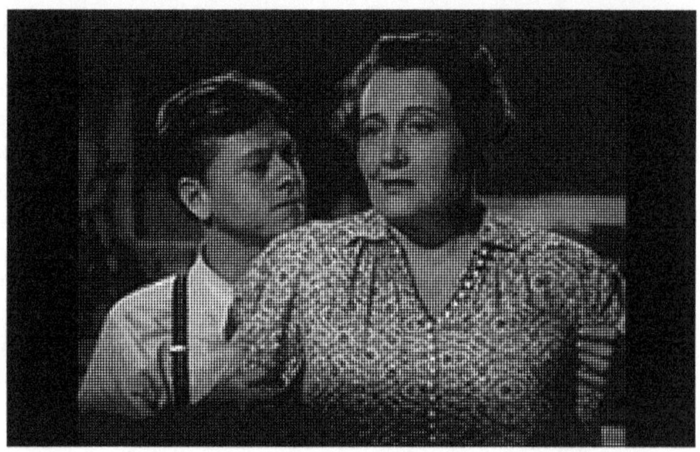

The filmic interaction of technical apparatus and psychological/physiological disposition make matters even more difficult when it comes to name an exact transition from "objective" to "aesthetic" illusion. It is in this interlinking of the technically produced and the psychically/physically perceived in which I see the "aisthetic" quality of film, which is due to it qua its medial characteristics even before "film" gets differentiated into individual objects (e.g. along genre borders etc.). Film's aesthetic dimension is the one constituting illusion.

It cannot be concluded from this, though, that film is a means of constituting illusion aesthetically, in the sense that the very objects we understand as "films" in turn understand the "aesthetic" framework as an "aesthetic" formation. It is exactly this "aesthetic" reflection of the "aesthetic" framework many films are seeking to achieve — e.g. through an experimental blow-up of the flow of motion.

Subsequently, I would like to discuss how aesthetic framings of the filmic dispositive "movement- image" are put at aesthetic disposal with reference to three examples.

Refracting illusion through the production of the "other" image

From the Platonic point of view, images are themselves located on a scale of values which reverts to the idea reproduced in them. A carpenter manufacturing a table comes closer to the idea of a table than the artist painting a table. The table is a reproduction of the idea of "table," the image of the table is a reproduction of a reproduction and thus a more distant relation; and this genealogical chain of negatives can be continued. Therefore, we have to ask if what lies at the core of the idea of making the

3 • Michail M. Bachtin, *Formen der Zeit im Roman: Untersuchungen zur historischen Poetik* (1975), (Frankfurt am Main: Fischer, 1989).

image behind the images visible by producing it practically/ technically is not actually obliged to a Platonic idea of truth which can only comprehend itself as anti-illusionist. Which would mean taking a position that cannot escape the aporias of a genealogical interaction of idealistic claim to truth and its mediatization in the image. Such actions eventually lead to endless regress, as Cavell described with regard to the following problem: If we want to show the camera shooting the images we contemplate in the end as constitutive for the world, we need a second camera showing us how the images are recorded, etc., i.e. the more I want to retrieve the idea which lies behind an object, the deeper I get caught in a web of reproducing reproductions of the primary object, thus losing track of it more and more without ever coming close to breaking up the logic of filmic representation, which would allow me to approach the idea of film as such: "One can feel that there is always a camera left out of the picture: the one working now."[4]

Austrian experimental filmmaker Martin Arnold attempted this kind of filmic cell division in the sense of a psychoanalytic criticism of ideology with reference to selected takes from popular films. For example, he assembled excerpts of three films from the Andy Hardy-series in the film *Alone. Life Wastes Andy Hardy* (1998), thus staging a kind of oedipal drama in which he extended the *Found-footage*-shots by means of a complex technical reproduction, which causes the movement of the figures to condense and the figures to remain stuck in performing movements as though an invisible magnet kept them from altering their position. In this process, the aesthetic pattern of classical narrative cinema, which set such great store by evoking fluent, continuous motion in *continuity editing* is being refracted reflexively at this very point. Instead, the binary code of still and moving images gets dissolved into a hybridization of infinite in-between images, which neither are stills, nor correspondent to the 24 phase images, the projection of which per second produces motion on the screen.

Nevertheless, we are dealing with movement-images here, which are to be comprehended as the aisthetic avatar of the filmic medium. They produce another aesthetics of motion in a retarding bulge, though, which itself leads into a new fiction, namely the one that this very nuances, the hidden subtext between the images, could be heard now, and that we had penetrated into the pre-existent images deeper than the surface of their planned succession would have suggested. Instead of three family films, we now witness the oedipal drama: the boy amorously seeking the mother's touch, the mother incapable of detaching

4 • Stanley Cavell, *The World Viewed: Reflections on the Ontology of Film* (Cambridge, Mass: Harvard Filmstudies, 1979), 126f.

herself from the house's furniture, the father hitting the voluptuous boy. In it, Martin Arnold proves to be a director who may have understood cinematographic motion in the sense of Thierry Kuntzel, but who turns this against the dispositive of illusion for the purpose of ideological criticism, whereas Kuntzel describes it as a characteristics of the motion medium of film and not as the latter's problematic intention. In his essay "Le Défilement," Kuntzel asserted:

> The analysis of movement, this particular instance, could be approached in two ways: the first, a psycho-physiological one, would make it possible, on the basis of a single transformation of an image, to differentiate the elements which are perceived from those which are not (although they are visible when they are not moving) in normal viewing conditions; the second, more semiological, would seek to determine, at the level of the entire film, the logic(s) which control(s) the different transformations. From the view point of the relationship between the film-strip and the film projection, these two approaches would be complementary: the investigation of the visible (and what seems to disappear in movement), and the analysis of the operations of visible elements in the filmic chain.[5]

In his film, Martin Arnold trusts in the digital disruption of cinematographic appearance. He wants to present the medium film in another medium, the digital one, in Apollo's gleam, he wants to pull out the Dionysian as a grotesque from behind oedipal tragedy: "The message which lies deep under the surface of the family idyll, suppressed or lost, is exposed — that message is war."[6] It is not a coincidence that, in achieving this, he preferably uses the iconoclastic techniques of image destruction, "my revenge on film history."[7] Arnold's critical program for an analytic film criticism in digital form becomes problematic exactly at the point where he jealously aims at reducing film's illusionist capacity to the movement image and to a mere fiction.

The example shows two things: on one hand, that aesthetic illusion assumes the form of a *fictitious* filmic body exactly where the two *material* bodies of film are being united: Filmstrip and projector produce the movement-image on the screen. This movement-image, however, doesn't exist beyond what Christiane Voss following Sobchack calls the borrowed body of cinema. A

5 • Thierry Kuntzel, "Le Défilement," in Theresa Hak Kyung Cha (Ed.). *Apparatus* (New York: Tanam Press, 1980), 232–245
6 • Quoted on the cover of the Martin Arnold video edition (ciemnesis, 1999), distributed by Re:voir Video.
7 • Ibid.

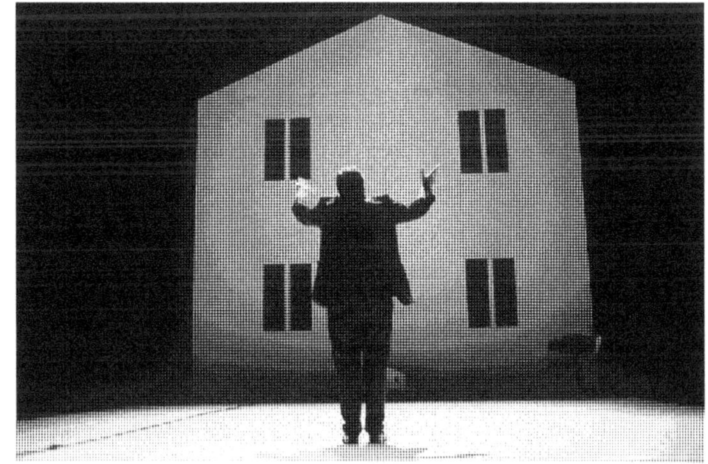

body from which Arnold needs to abstract in order to maintain his program for a technical refraction of visual illusion. For we do again see images of something set in motion, motivated this time not diegetically but psychically, but subject to the same conditions as the vision of movement as a whole. Movement-images are instigated by movement-images (or, be that as it may: Video tapes and liquid crystals produce the movement-image on the screen, and an optical projector produces the movement-image on the wall, etc.).[8]

Arnold has changed the narrative and created another narration about the family without being able to alter the way in which narration through images is possible entirely. From a certain moment onwards, he, too, wants to show something in his images that lay beyond the *Found-footage*-images he used.

Do we see what we think we have to see?
Here, we are talking about those objects which are making the illusionary potential of the filmic dispositive accessible to other arts and media. The confusing and enthralling example of an underlying interlinking of illusion effects and a theatrical aesthetics of presence is a work from Heiner Goebbels' music theatre: *Eraritjaritjaka, The Museum of Sentences* (2004). This play is based on texts by Elias Canetti which are recited by actor André Wilms and accompanied onstage by the Mondriaan quartet. The setting plays on the model of a house, the wall of which finally limits the stage to the rear and which is consequently used as a screen. In the beginning, André

8 • What I think is important here are the aesthetic contexts of movement image and illusion as the core of the cinematographic dispositive and not as an ontology of technical media which are required or enabled by the embodiment of the dispositive. In aesthetic embodiment, the capacity of producing movement images suffices.

Wilms is relatively quickly accompanied by a cinematographer, who follows the actor's walk offstage, through the auditorium and the lobby into a taxi and the door of an apartment, behind which Wilms disappears. Subsequently, we see him within the apartment preparing food etc., watching TV and performing various activities, reciting Canetti accompanied by the music onstage. A clock in the kitchen irritatingly shows the real-time of the performance. Towards the end, the curtains of the stagehouse are opened, and it becomes obvious that the apparently remote apartment, into which Wilms disappeared, is in fact the reverse stage props of the house's wall. In the end, it is clear that the whole performance was based on the production of an illusion effect — which made the audience reflect during the performance's whole length on how the old Aristotelian dramaturgy of spatial and temporal unity was simultaneously questioned and fulfilled here: Was Wilms never gone, but acting behind the wall all the time, while his acting was projected to the front of the wall as a live broadcast (this is what the theatre experts believed) — or was Wilms never gone during the performance, but what we saw was a pre-produced film which was merely accompanied by synchronous live music (this is what the film experts believed)? Do we see, consequently, what we have to see? In any case, it was impossible to precisely reconstruct at what time which theatrical and/or filmic illusion was produced, and how, during the performance, the only thing that was clear was that the aesthetic tension was produced out of this built-in illusion. An illusion which consisted in the creation of a presence which was experienced as an appearance one way or another. By viewing a video recording of one of the performances and by asking Heiner Goebbels directly, the mysterious appearance could be accounted for: It was an impermeable interweaving of theatrical and filmic illusion, which had combined the real-time mode of theatre and live broadcast with the terminated production time of film. In order to achieve illusionist fragilization, exactly one short sequence of the videographed course — the one showing Wilms riding through Berlin in a taxi — had been pre-produced. The time of its projection enabled Wilms to re-enter the stage from the lobby unnoticed by the audience and to reach the setting of the apartment, from where he was projected in a live broadcast onto the front wall in his play.

Eraritjaritjaka approximately means "yearning deeply for what has been lost" in Arana, the language of the Australian Aborigines. What did theatre abandon to film, and what does it have to do with film? The fourth wall, which reclaims the stage and which turns out to be the screen of film, the capacity of illudation in fiction? With this example from contemporary music theatre, we can illustrate that the aesthetics of illusion is not an obsolete technique of delusion for the back rows of mass culture, but points to the centre of poetics, which comes back down to the experience of the dynamization of spatial and temporal horizons, the *chronotopoi*.

Do we see that we have to believe?
The fact that the movement-image is being produced mechanically has lead Henri Bergson, in his chapter on the "Cinematographic mechanism of thinking,"[9] to the premature conclusion that a thinking working cinematographically would remain as much mere mechanics as the cinematograph. Cinema, as far as Bergson is concerned, is an immobile matter, the only movement of which is that of the filmstrip through the projector — and therefore a purely mechanical one, which does not correspond to the environment's motion in any respect. A transposition which Gilles Deleuze subjects to a productive revision in the Bergson commentaries of his cinema-books when he points out that Bergson, in other writings, delivered much more precise implicit descriptions of the filmic. Bergson's critique of film is that it contained movement only in momentary images, which is set into motion illusionistically through the mechanic motion of the projector. Deleuze objects to Bergson with Bergson that the latter had unfolded a more complex construct of movement-*images* already in *Matière et Mémoire* which Deleuze deems applicable to a prefilmic theory of film. Deleuze, too, promotes a kind of aesthetic "correction" of mechanically produced illusion in writing:

> Is the reproduction of illusion, in a certain way, not also its correction? Is it legitimate to conclude from the artificiality of the means to the artificiality of the result? Film works with phase-images, i.e. with immovable cuts [...]. And yet, as stated several times before, it doesn't give us a photogram, but an average image which is by no means supplemented or completed with motion — on the contrary, motion is an immediate given within the average image.[10]

As far as Deleuze is concerned, the vision of motion in film reception is consequently an immediate given, which comes back down to a real, empiric given qua artificial-mechanic mediatization. Space is produced functionally through movement, the camera (like the body in Merleau-Ponty) opens up space in movement, and this movement produces movable, indefinite spaces. It is in this experience of a dynamically and movably

9 • Henri Bergson, *Schöpferische Entwicklung* (Jena: E. Diederichs, 1912), 276.
10 • Gilles Deleuze, *Das Bewegungs-Bild. Kino 1* (Frankfurt am Main: Suhrkamp, 1989), 14.

opened space that film corrects its own mechanical and apparative aprioris into reflexive experiences of the world of the newly opening space in movement. This is the philosophical potential of film, which in this mode produces ever more spaces and is exhaustive of the world again and again in this process. The same way philosophy develops its terms into new ones out of never ending delimitations from themselves, film releases something new in the movement-images. Film updates motion, it doesn't represent it. In this mode of updates, *aisthesis* becomes the aesthetics of film: The motion immediately given becomes the movement-image.

Speaking of the "immediate object," this evokes yet another context: We have to believe in the immediately given in the act of seeing. After André Bazin, Gilles Deleuze was not the first one to position cinema in immediate proximity to Catholicism in that it demands a specific way of believing into the world as it presents itself to us as a creation in which we consider ourselves a part of it. In the second volume of his work on cinema, Deleuze writes:

> Of course, ever since its beginnings, cinema has shared a special relation with religious belief. There is a catholicism of cinema. [...] Is the big show, the staging of things, not part of catholicism? Is cinema not a cult disseminated via cathedrals, as Elie Faure put it? Cinema as a whole seems to be part of the Nietzschean formula of "that in which we are still devout".[11]

And this does not necessarily refer to the catholic origin of individual or a multitude of directors, but to a certain Weltanschauung which was spread by Catholicism and to which many people agree. Apart from revolution, it is Christianity that the mass arts were attracted to, Deleuze states. And this, he goes on to state, "is due to the fact that the cinematographic image [...] illustrates the bond between the human being and the world."[12]

In reverting the Freudian argument about religion as an "illusion," the future of which he denies, Deleuze assumes that cinema contributes to restoring our faith into the world, and this in exactly the moment in which the phenomenological model that once had replaced religion begins to dissolve into skepticism. In view of the fading of metaphysical *truth*, this crucial moment transforms religious belief into the pragmatism of convictions and certainties, which finally cannot be accounted for any longer. Deleuze brings this back to physicality as the last residual of presence:

11 • Gilles Deleuze, *Das Zeit-Bild. Kino 2* (Frankfurt am Main: Suhrkamp, 1991, 223.
12 • Ibid.

Of course belief doesn't mean any longer to believe in another or changed world. Belief solely means this: to believe in the body, to return speech to the body and to reach the body before the speeches, before the words and before the naming of things: to reach the pre-name even before the first name.[13]

It is this creed that forms the basis of the emphasis of the trust in the womb of the pregnant woman and the blink of the newborn child's eyelid in Tom Tykwer's film *Winter Sleepers,* which brings me to my third example.

Deleuze's argumentation is based on the cinema of Rossellini and Bresson, on Dreyer's and Godard's films such as *Je vous salue, Marie* and *Passion*. It might well be interesting, though, to take a look at the works of younger, post-war directors, the cradle of whom where the halls of European author's cinema and whose Sunday school was Hollywood. As opposed to the groups previously mentioned by Deleuze, they have been nurtured by entirely different sources. Their problem is not included into the question whether or not filmic illusion can strengthen a strong belief in the world. They rather start out from the postmodernist problem of metaskepticism, keeping in mind that all knowledge is the temporary illusion of a firm conviction and that any strong conviction such as faith has been lost. Deleuze writes:

> The decisive characteristics of modern times consists in the fact that we do not believe in this world any longer. We don't even believe in the events happening to us: in love and death, as though they only concerned us half. It's not us making the cinema, it is the world that presents itself to us as a bad film.[14]

It's exactly at this landmark that Tom Tykwer sets in: at the conversion of the world of film and the world as film. In *Winter Sleepers,* this formal figure eventually culminates in an infinite surreal spiral movement: The young ski instructor jumps over the edge of the cliff and falls, spins, glides, twists downwards to the valley in slackened and halted velocity, the camera following him from above to disappear in a black fissure in the snow, which evokes both the final impact and the beginning of the next shot. The blackness leads up to a rotating black tunnel. As long as the movement continues, the blackness now appears to be the blackness of a dark room on which the sound of a light switch is dubbed. With the noise it's getting light, a light in which a close-up on an infant appears. Let there be light and there was light, the art of light gives birth to a new beginning,

13 • Ibid, 225.
14 • Ibid, 224.

the conversion of death into life. I propose that this be viewed as the formal conversion of one image into another and thus maybe a narration on cinema itself. Conversion in this context means style — one style of cinema or cinema as a style. This transformatory power relates to: the switchover taking the place of blinding.

The transformatory power of aesthetic illusion
In all three examples at least three modi could be shown under which the production of illusion takes on transformatory qualities by provoking implicit statements from us: either as the reflection of a delusion leading up to a chain of further images which aims at altering our relationship with the processed images, or as manifestations without a cause, which make us ask for the quality of our perception, or as a transformation of skepticism towards believing as the affirmation of a possible relation with the world. ●

Gertrud Koch is Professor of Film Studies at the Freie Universität, Berlin. Recent publications include *Perspektive — Die Spaltung der Standpunkte* (2010) and *Die Mimesis und ihre Künste* (2010, ed with Martin Vöhler and Christiane Voss).

Aisthesis

Art, Aesthetics— Divorce?

Morten Kyndrup

This text is a revised version of a chapter in my book *Den æstetiske relation. Sanse-oplevelsen mellem kunst, videnskab og filosofi* (Copenhagen: Gyldendal 2008). Translated into English by Billy O'Shea.

Art and the artwork

It is an often overlooked truism, even from the perspective of the philosophy of art, that there is a major difference between what can be accepted, experienced and traded under the heading of "art" today, and that which was possible in other eras. The difference is so great that, at its extremes, we can find artefacts from different periods which can be said to have nothing at all in common as objects. Two centuries ago, it would not, for example, have been possible to view the production and estab-lishment of biogas plants in developing countries as an artistic activity, as the Danish art co-operative Superflex regards it. Neither would Jeff Koons' photograph of himself and his then wife, a porn film actress, naked and in a frivolous situation, be regarded as art. On the other hand, a new composi-tion in our day of a typical piece of Viennese classical music, perhaps on the lines of a Mozart symphony, would at best be regarded as kitsch, while a new set of salt cellars in the style of Cellini, although they might provoke admiration for their craftsmanship, would hardly be deemed qualified to be called works of art. Nonetheless — and this is an important point — we undeniably regard both Mozart's symphonies and Celli-ni's salt cellars as belonging to the category of "art."

What, then, has changed? Certain criteria defin-ing what may be considered a work of art seem to have altered

— but not, apparently, with retrospective effect. Aspects of works of art, which, if they were to be created today, would disqualify them from being considered art, are accepted and valued in works from other periods; and this applies not only in a historical or archaeological context, but also in the context of artwork perception today.

To describe the entire historical process of transformation of the status, criteria and tasks of art in modern times would naturally fall outside the scope here; we can however point out certain characteristics. One of these relates to the tasks of art, or in other words, the functions for which art has been responsible in society's organisation of the creation and exchange of meaning.

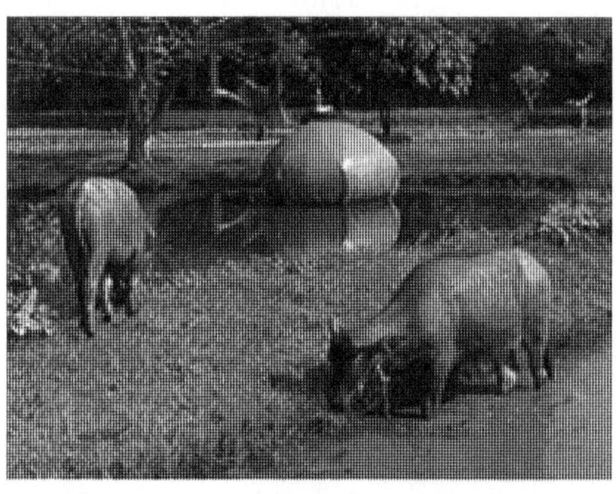

**Superflex,
Supergas, 1996.**

Representational functions, both in a purely mimetic sense and in the context of social stratification, have almost disappeared from the realm of art (which does not mean that these functions have ceased to exist — they are now merely undertaken by other societal integrants). The same applies to the symbolising functions of art, whether in a religious context or in the context of internal societal systems for the organisation of meaning. On the other hand, new functions have clearly been added which are now more or less perceived to be requirements towards the individual work. Art is perceived, and regards itself, as an arena for an especially privileged reflection on the human condition, and in particular the recognition of this condition. It is also seen as entirely natural and predictable that works of art should relate to themselves, i.e. to art as a framework condition or topos in society. The artist still enjoys a particularly privileged — indeed elevated — status, but this is no longer due to his masterly skill in a particular discipline in the physical treatment of the material. *Homo faber* has become *homo significans*; masterful skills in painting, drawing or writing are accepted, but are not viewed as sufficient. Technical mastery is not enough; what is required is soul, spirit, thought, indeed *meaning* — and to such a degree that technical skills are, in principle, superfluous. Artists are to an increasing degree "non-specific" artists; they may paint, write poetry, compose music or conceptualise. A kind of generalisation of media has occurred in artistic skills, while at the same time medialities as such are becoming applied in an ever more specific and effect-conscious manner. Artists who concern themselves only with the actual idea, and leave the material composition to others, can without reservation be acclaimed as brilliant artists. Jeff Koons or Olafur Eliasson, Beuys or Manzoni may serve as examples. At the same time, it is clear that what we might call the *de-objectivisation* of art has occurred. Works of art no longer need to be finite objects such as pictures, verses, or scores for musical or dramatic works. A work of art can also be a situation, an absence, a gesture, a commodity — or, quite simply, anything at all. In addition, something which in one type of situation would certainly not be regarded as art, may in other situations be regarded as art to such a degree that it may be acquired or sold for a fortune — even when there is no discernible objective difference between the item which is accepted as art, and that which is not.

Aisthesis

This entire process is above all symptomatic of a thoroughgoing alteration in the character of art's autonomy, i.e. in its status as a special area in society's overall semantic architecture. This alteration is often misinterpreted, even by professionals, as a sign of a weakening or dismantling of art's autonomy, or a kind of reconciliation between art and society's other semantic communities. This misunderstanding often arises when the declared intentions of the individual works of art are taken at face value, such as in the Superflex example, or so-called "social plastic" in general. Autonomy is thereby viewed in far too narrow a sense, for example as a purely thematic category.

In reality, the opposite is the case: the autonomy of art appears to be even more self-evident and, at bottom, less under threat than ever, and from a semiotic point of view, the discursive framework concept "art" is stronger than it has ever been. However, this autonomy, and thereby the whole question of the borderline between art and non-art, has altered in character. De-objectification has meant that the line between art and non-art, between the artwork and the non-artwork, can no longer solely be ascribed to the character of the object or its stable location, which is to say it can no longer be *territorial* in a physical sense. The autonomy has to an ever-greater extent assumed the character of a framing condition in terms of enunciation or utterance, has become connected to certain types of semantic acts, in which something is declared to be art. This means that

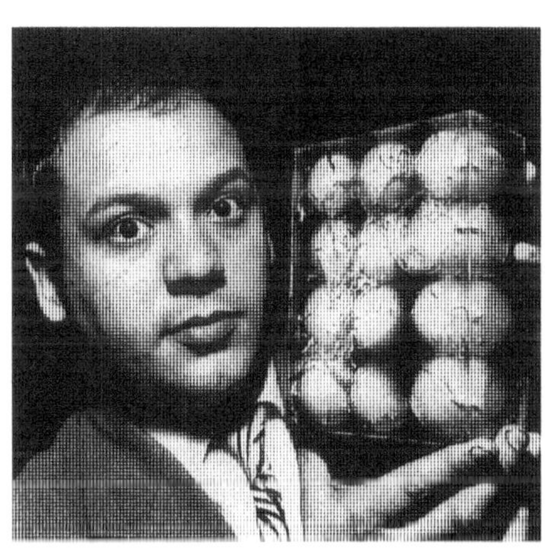

▲
Piero Manzoni and eggs, 1960.

anything at all *is capable* of being art, without this implying
that everything *has become* art. Marchel Duchamp's bottle rack
is a ready-made artwork, while all other bottle racks in the
world, though objectively identical, are not artworks. This
utterance-based condition furthermore implies that all works
of art also refer, either implicitly or explicitly, to their own
conceptual framework, to "art." In this historical process, the
relationship of the individual work of art to "art," or to put it
more precisely, the unending, undecidable *dispute* between
the artwork and "art," has occupied an extremely central position in relation to the agenda of artistic creation. The issues of
ready-made and conceptual art naturally represent flamboyant
examples, but all initiatives and attempts to bring art "back"
to everyday life are in reality also helplessly caught up in this
ongoing dispute between the artwork and art as such.

A very brief summing-up of the historical evolution
of art might therefore be that the work of art today, in all its
relations, functions, and perceptual codes, it is what it is *as art* —
and this in a manner which, from a historical point of view, is
quite new. Its autonomisation has in this sense been completed.
Art today can do anything except cease to be art. The autonomy
of art and its semiotic power are sharper and more potent than
ever; in the wink of an eye, it can quite literally transform shit
into gold. But it cannot escape its own special nature; it cannot
escape itself. And indeed, why should it?

Two different distinctions
The assertion here is that it would be appropriate and adequate
to regard the delineation of art and the delineation of the
aesthetic as two interconnected but fundamentally dissimilar
differentiations; two differentiations, which it has been conve-
nient to regard as essentially identical during a particular
period, for certain reasons and from different positions.
However, more recent developments in the philosophy of art, in
art itself, and in thinking in general, have necessitated a critical
revision in this perspective. Today, a theoretical perspective
which views the special qualities of art and those of the aesthetic
as fundamentally different would appear to be better able to
capture and explain the differences and similarities in the inter-
sections or transitions between these two types of classification,
which are important in order to allow us to understand what is
at stake in our society's overall creation of meaning.

Art, also from a sociological point of view, is delineated as an area, a territory, and a relatively independent
subsystem. Metaphorically, one might describe the delineation
of art as horizontal, since in a number of respects it appears to
fence in its own area, and thereby set up its own special,

self-(re)generating control system. The system of art encompasses a number of precisely defined rules (which are subject to constant change), as well as various classes and participants, and their corresponding utterance positions, which are defined by these rules. The system draws its life from, and through, these defined differences. Here we have the artists; there the various theoretical positions towards art, as expounded by grandstanding commentators, strict academic research and ideologically determined discourse; here we have the critics at various levels and in varying positions; here the administrators; there the collectors — and in particular, here are the audience, the recipients, the users. Art has its own economic circulatory system with particular rules and hierarchies, encompassing a system of institutions. With regard to pictorial art, for example, the museums function like national banks which underwrite the special value of the art and guarantee a "gold standard" for its free circulation. A striking characteristic of this special subsystem is that, in both historical and contemporary terms, the issue of its *boundaries* has been of crucial significance. The relevant players have always been greatly concerned with the question of the boundaries of art — which is hardly surprising, as it is at the borderline of any system that its dynamics and viability are tested, manifested and developed, cf. Niklas Luhmann's work. The constant exploration of the boundaries of art has developed it in particular ways and over time has changed it irreversibly and fundamentally. The challenging of art's boundaries has also maintained and developed art as an autonomous area or system encompassing a number of highly characteristic possibilities for discursive action in the broadest sense. The delineation of art secures it, amongst other things, a special aura — a particular value weight which in turn helps to guarantee (the idea of) art's special epistemological privileges. Above all, art, by comparison with other discursive arenas in our society, possesses a special ability and entitlement to cross between these arenas. (However, as we have seen, it always undertakes these crossover activities *as art*.) This cross-cutting privilege, this "transversality," is one of the most crucial characteristics that art possesses.

The characteristics listed here are of course just cursory notes intended to sketch out the hyper-complex domain and functions of art in modern society. What we can however state with some confidence is that this area, this subsystem, is very much alive. The rumours of the death of art or of the eradication of its boundaries are at best misinterpretations of the processes of change that have taken place, in many cases as a part of the actual border conflicts. The importance of the area of art is in every sense greater today than at any previous historical time. Its economic weight is also considerable and rapidly rising, partly because art, in a derived sense, also supplies raw materials to the so-called experience economy. In semiotic and discursive terms, art is stronger than ever, which is why the question of its boundaries remains the subject of dynamic debate. Furthermore, there is no doubt that the form of the actual boundaries is also undergoing transformation, away from the classical-territorial, and in the direction of more complex, inherent mechanisms of differentiation and thereby transition. We will return to this topic later.

The delineation of *the aesthetic*, as we are attempting to reinterpret it here, is of a quite different type, and could metaphorically be described as "vertical." To view something in an "aesthetic" manner implies choosing one particular form of relationship from among a number of other possible relationships. To enter into an aesthetic relationship with something in this respect means to submit it to the assessment of the senses in a particular evaluating manner, in which the evaluation spans the relationship between that which evaluates and that which is evaluated, in a complicated structure of a "pathway" or "passage," from the "I" through the "it" to an imagined "we." To regard something as "aesthetic" thereby means to undertake a "modelling operation;"[2] which in principle is something that is always available to and accessible by the individual. Sensory-based evaluative relationships of this type (relating to "beauty"), have existed throughout the entire history of civilisation, but in the Modern era they acquire — besides a new, special name — a particular form, not least due to the secularised subject, which is now above all thrown back upon itself. The aesthetic thereby becomes a modus, a dispositive, which, while it certainly delineates a special type of relation which can now be studied and described, does not establish a territorial subsystem in the same respect as art. "The aesthetic" in this sense has a boundary problem of a quite different type. In this case too, the boundary question is certainly vital for the creation and maintenance of the special characteristics of that which is delineated. However, the borders of the aesthetic are, at bottom, borders between different modes of perception which each — and at all times — are available to the individual. Objects, either as a result of shaping, or by convention, may appear more or less suitable for aesthetic perception, i.e. more or less capable of possessing "aesthetic value," but in principle, the aesthetic character of "something" is never either territorially exhaustive nor irreversibly applied. It is a dispositive, a choice, which does not exclude other kinds of relations.

2 • "Modeling operation" comes from W.C. Wimsatt "Generative Entrenchment and the Developmental Systems Approach to Evolutionary Processes," ms. 2000, cited in Wolfgang Iser "Von der Gegenwärtigkeit des Ästhetischen," in Joachim Küpper and Christoph Menke (eds.), *Dimensionen ästhetischer Erfahrung* (Frankfurt am Main: Suhrkamp, 2003).

Viewed in this way, "aesthetic relations" are occupying more and more space in our society. The semiotic or discursive boundary construction is also undergoing change. The increase in quantity occurs not only through the products of the entertainment industry, which very much call forth an aesthetic approach, but also through our surroundings in general; surroundings which to an increasing degree are *designed* — from the packaging, furniture, and devices of which we make use to architecture, urban spaces and the newly calculated "nature" of the landscape. Prescribed aesthetic qualities enter into all this "designedness" as a decisive dimension. More than ever before, the world we encounter invites us to enter into aesthetic relations with it.

The border, the connection

When defined in this way, as two fundamentally different distinctions, what, then, is the relationship between "art" and "the aesthetic," both in general, and with regard to the practical-functional and artefact levels? The relationship is an extremely complex one, and has certainly not been made any easier to analyse and understand by the historical interweaving which has taken place in the past.

If we begin in the world of objects, we may observe that works of art (and thereby art itself) can be much more than merely "aesthetic" in the sense sketched here. Above all, there is reason to point to art's epistemological potential, which it has won and reinforced via its autonomous status in the Modern era. These epistemological privileges — the status, reputation for, and thereby ability to observe and say something particularly true about the world — do not however depend solely upon the fundamental condition of delineation. They are also, at the artwork level, associated with more immediate and phenomenologically observable qualitative features. Here one might first and foremost point to the *representational* qualities of art; its ability to create images in the broadest sense, i.e. to provide replicating references back to the recognizable world. Through the use of fictional constructs in the broadest sense (and in all of the arts), works of art are capable of encapsulating reflexive self-references, such that the recipients see, not merely images of their own world (second-order observation), but also see themselves seeing, which is to say they are confronted with the constructed vision by which their world hereby allows itself to be seen (third-order observation). Among the obvious non-aesthetic qualitative features of art, one could on an entirely different level mention art's express dispute with itself on the relationship of the work of art to art as such, i.e. the

3 • Thierry de Duve, *Kant after Duchamp* (Cambridge, Mass.: MIT, 1996), 301ff.

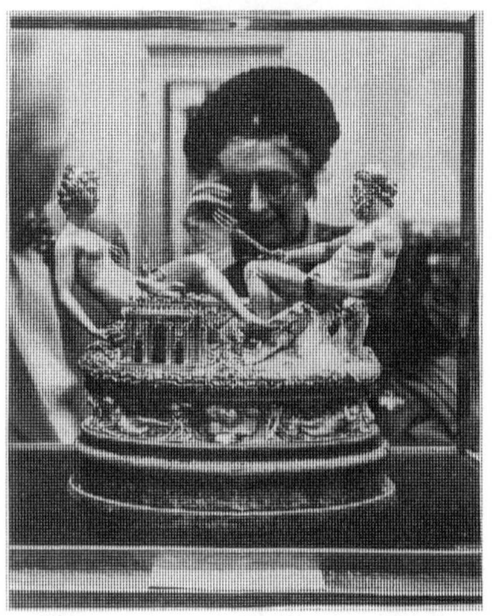

Visitor to the National Gallery Washington, scrutinizing Benvenuto Cellini's *Salt Cellar* on temporary exhibit, ca 1947.

actual work of boundary delineation. Although it has quite rightly been remarked — by Thierry de Duve[3], amongst others — that even the embedded, "this is art" claim of the objectually provocative work has now acquired the character of something resembling a taste judgement via the actual mechanism of its presentation, the issue is, on the part of the work, primarily directed at art as a conceptual area, rather than at the character of the approach of the public as arbiters of taste. This does not of course exclude the possibility of aesthetic relations being established, but that is another matter.

Correspondingly, it is easy to observe that aesthetic relations, in the sense defined here, may be found in many places other than in association with art. At an overall level, our world has entered into a process which could perhaps best be described as a *becoming-aesthetic*. All shaped objects are presented ever more explicitly as being there distinctively for our sake — as *designed* objects in the broadest sense, and thereby things with which we are called upon to establish evaluative relations of an "aesthetic" type. But we also encounter the aesthetic manifested in a number of genres or forms which, while they may to varying degrees draw upon the aura and domain of art, are not in themselves characterised as art, and are not accepted as art in the categorisation of society. The world of fashion is one example (with fashion photography forming a typical hybrid genre [4]); advertising is another. Finally, we must also add so-called natural beauty, i.e. aesthetic relations with (apparently) unworked phenomena such as sunsets, mountain peaks and such things as human beauty.

There is in other words a great deal which falls outside the bounds of art; and yet any work of art, no matter how conceptual, "non-sensual" or epistemologically oriented, remains *also* a potential object of aesthetic relations. The work of art, however, possesses this property, in principle, to a greater extent than any other artefact; it is a potential object of aesthetic relations to a special degree, inasmuch as it is a fundamental rule in art that a work must establish its own individual relationship with the recipient. Right from the start, then, this relationship is already structurally isomorphous with an aesthetic relation.

Conversely, we may also observe

4 • Cf. Charlotte Andersen, *Modefotografi: En genres anatomi* (Copenhagen: Museum Tusculanums Forlag 2006).

that any established aesthetic relationality is capable of claiming its object belonging to the field of "art." It is inherent in the new inclusivity of the 20th century's *n'importe quoi* movement in art that anything can be turned into art by being declared to be so (which is not to imply that so doing necessarily serves the purposes of art or of anything else, but that is another matter, which belongs under the discussion of quality).

AisthesisSeen from this perspective, "art" and "the aesthetic" each span their own separate conceptual arrangements of semantic space — arrangements which are at our disposal as two modelling operations, two possible forms of organisation. They are linked in particular ways, and in terms of type they resemble each other on a number of levels, but they are, however, fundamentally different. They could be metaphorically compared with two vector planes which make it possible to refer a given object to one or the other semantic register, or potentially to both semantic registers at once — just as vector planes intersect each other in every point of space. On the other hand, such intersection neither implies nor permits any conceptual transition between the two planes or registers; they cannot on an overall level be reduced to the same formula, or otherwise be converted into one another. They cannot be made into subsets or complementary sets of each other; *there is no concrete border or localisable transition zone between them.* This applies not least to the individual object, which is otherwise the topos in which the planes meet: you can refer the object to one semantic plane or the other, or you can step back and see the object being (virtually) referred to both semantic planes, but the two planes will actualise different properties or functions of the object. Even though the planes refer to the "same" artefact, it is not possible to localise the double relationship as a *transition* from one to the other, for example from the "aesthetic" aspect of this artefact to its character as a work of art. This may sound like a paradox, but in fact it is not: the perspective quite simply involves taking the existing differentiation seriously, as a difference which does not stem from an original equivalence. This is naturally because, once again, neither of the two qualities refers (any longer) exclusively to the objectual status and characteristics of the objects, even though they are perceived and formulated as though they did precisely that.

The difference derives not least from the fact that the points of origin of the delineations — as we perceive them in this reconstructive re-description — are quite different. The point of origin of art in the Modern era is a socially defined subsystem, which also means that the gesture "this is art" is directed at or assumes a general or exogenous sanction. It is not immediately possible to declare the aims of the gesture to have been met, but

if it succeeds, any utterance-based act of referring something to
this or that area of art is *fundamentally irreversible*. That which
thereby has become art cannot cease to be so — something which
causes the museums enormous conservation problems in relation to some of the (in every sense) transient works of our times,
manufactured from, for example, excreta or margarine.

"Aesthetic relations," on the other hand, are neither
accumulative nor irreversible: although they also institution-
alise conventions, and are institutionalised by them, their point
of origin is their singular availability, and it is the individual
subject, not the social community, which is the first and last
authority. Although both art and the aesthetic can be said to
create pathways or passages, these pathways are fundamentally
different in nature. The pathways can be formed in relation to
one and the same artefact, and will thereby intersect right there.
But they are mutually incongruent in terms of their logics of
extension.

The disciplines

If we accept the distinction between "art" and "the aesthetic" in
accordance with the above reconstructive re-description at the
level of the phenomenon world, this also has consequences at
the level of the disciplines, for the definition of the spheres and
boundaries between scholarly domains such as aesthetics,
philosophy of art and the disciplines of the traditional art forms.

In the Modern era, the philosophy of art — for reason-
ably obvious discursive reasons, cf. Kant — has had chronic difficulty in defining its relationship with philosophy and art,
respectively. Due to the semiotic power of the art system, a
meaningful median position, i.e. a location in the transition
zone, may not even be possible. It would be easy to imagine the
philosophy of art as being clearly a part of philosophy (to the
extent that it is possible at all now to imagine a transdiscursive
discipline of "philosophy," but that is a different question),
which, at the overall and cross-cutting level, would describe and
locate the potentials of art in a "complementary" manner, in
other words in relation to a number of other areas of thought
and meaning production. On the other hand, it would also be
easy to imagine a philosophy of art which viewed itself as
belonging to the overall complex of the art system, in the form
of a discourse which, on the basis of the premises and perspective of art, participated in the maintenance and rebuilding of
art's discursive communications network. The amalgamation
of these two levels, as has occurred in large parts of the Western
continental tradition under the heading of "aesthetics"
(cf. Jean-Marie Schaeffer's "speculative tradition"⁵), makes, on
the other hand, less obvious sense. Viewing the world from

inside the art system does not harmonise well with a minimal philosophical pretension of transdiscursive sovereignty. A philosophical approach which commits itself to being philosophy should not take it upon itself to solve discursive hygiene patrol tasks, whether overtly or covertly, in the service of art. This would controvert the critical distance which is indispensable for a philosophical approach in relation to the "complementary" location of the potentials of art.

Irrespective of whether we speak of one type of "philosophy of art" or the other — and it would probably be appropriate to reserve this label for disciplines which are committed to philosophy rather than art — *aesthetics*, in the form outlined here, must necessarily encompass something quite different, an area which is both greater and smaller. This is because aesthetic relations also exist in other areas besides in connection with works of art.

Aisthesis

If we consider the location of art theory in this disciplinary landscape, a different but structurally equivalent picture begins to emerge. As we know, the sciences of the arts underwent a colossal development during the second half of the 20th century, in the course of which the emphasis moved to (human) "science" as a binding point of departure. This has brought about a shift in the thematic focus from what art and artworks *are*, to what art and artworks *do.* Here, too, a number of discursive bastard constructions have traditionally been forced to choose between utterance positions within the field of art (with all the concomitant obligations this implies in relation to the discipline in question) and to work within the boundaries imposed by a scientific approach with respect to validity, argument, generality, exchangeability and so on.

It is obvious that particular areas of the arts sciences, *die Kunstwissenschaften,* are very closely related to aesthetics in the sense sketched here. This applies to those disciplines which are particularly concerned what one might call the *correlativity* of works of art, i.e. the ways in which they constructionally establish links with their senders and recipients, including their implicit senders and recipients. Art-theoretical disciplines such as narratology and enunciational analysis are therefore extremely relevant to aesthetics. However, the arts disciplines encompass much more than merely correlational aspects. Core areas of arts sciences also for example include the historical development of the constitution and range of epistemological potentials of works of art, not to mention the entire spectrum of analysis of a more "discourse-internal" nature — though still based on scientific premises — which aims to investigate the "collateral"

5 • Jean-Marie Schaeffer, *Art of the Modern Age: Philosophy of Art from Kant to Heidegger* (Princeton: Princeton University Press, 2000), 273ff.

relationship systems of works of art, in relation to other works of art in time and space, and in relation to the medial specificity of the individual art genres.

Aesthetics can naturally provide material for both (art) philosophy and arts sciences, but in our context of argumentation, it seems appropriate here to define aesthetics as an independent discipline *which belongs to the sphere of human sciences.* The field of interest of scientific aesthetics will thus embrace aesthetic relations (both historical and contemporary), and their constitution, phenomenology and potentials, as well as their historical and contemporary weight and significance, both individually and in relation to society. It will also include the conditions of production of aesthetic relations, and their expression as implicit potentials or precepts in objects, artefacts and situations. In particular, it will include the development of methods of analysis for aesthetic relations — both the explicit and the implicitly "prescribed."

"Aesthetics" would thus not be a "part" of arts sciences, but it would share particular areas, disciplines, and, in particular, objects with parts of the arts disciplines, cf. the above. These common areas would furthermore hardly give rise to asymmetrical boundary problems, provided that both disciplines remained within the field of science. The *work of art* would be a primary object of research for aesthetics, too. The work of art has more than anything else been the topos, indeed often the laboratory, for the testing and development of aesthetic strategies, since the work of art, to an exemplary degree, reveals its own implicit relations, and thereby also its potential aestheticity. There are many reasons for this, which are connected with the historical development of the art system — naturally including the role that speculative aesthetics, in the form of the marriage with art, has played in this development. The aforementioned equivalence in the phenomenology of the reception situations between the work of art and all other aesthetically-perceived objects, respectively, is an important factor here. Once again, aesthetics cannot and should not scientifically exhaust the possibilities of the work of art; the work of art encompasses other aspects of pertinence to (art) science besides the construction of its aesthetic relations. Conversely, works of art cannot encompass, and arts sciences therefore cannot exhaust, every conceivable aesthetic relation — neither in principle, nor in its empirical existence in our world. •

Morten Kyndrup is Professor of Aesthetics at the Institute of Advanced Studies at Aarhus Universit. His most recent book is *Den æstetiske relation: Sanseoplevelsen mellem kunst, videnskab og filosofi* (2008).

The Speech of Painting

Pablo Bustinduy Amador

Pure or impure, figurative or not, painting celebrates no other enigma but that of visibility.

Merleau-Ponty, *Eye and Mind*

1. Life of Paintings

Paintings do not stand in front of the viewer like plants or stones. They are so densely traversed by the powers of visibility that they almost seem to bear a life of their own. In painting we assist to an "ongoing birth," says Merleau-Ponty; drawing on the metaphor, he claims later that in the *depth* of painting there is "inspiration and respiration of Being".[1] Strangely enough, Merleau-Ponty is not alone in the use of this analogy. In *What gives*, Jean-Luc Marion says that the painting "breathes in the air of the light of the day," that it "inhales and exhales".[2] And even Gilles Deleuze analyzes the most fundamental processes at work in Francis Bacon's paintings as a twofold movement of "systole" and "diastole," that is, as the fundamental motion of biological pulsation.[3]

In facing this recurrence, we should aim first of all at interrogating this metaphor; indeed, we should ask ourselves if it works as a metaphor at all. For these three rhetorical images do not just aim at some hyperbolic presentation of the expressive power of the artwork. Through them, what we primarily obtain is not a recreation of our subjective aesthetic experience: when we encounter

1 • Maurice Merleau-Ponty, *Eye and Mind,* in *The Merleau-Ponty Aesthetics Reader,* trans. Michael B. Smith (Evanston: Northwestern University Press,1996), 129. Henceforth EM.

2 • Jean Luc Marion, *The Crossing of the Visible,* trans. James K. A. Smith (Stanford: Stanford University Press, 2004), 30, 41. Henceforth CV.

3 • Gilles Deleuze, *Francis Bacon: The Logic of Sensation,* trans. Daniel W. Smith (Minneapolis: University of Minnesota Press, 2004), 29. Henceforth FB.

the painting, they say, when our vision is captured by that enigmatic visibility with which it does not coincide, what we encounter is a presence that is *already* moving, vibrating, breathing "in the light of the day". We could not face the presence of the painting as we would look at a real "still life". Little wonder, then, if one can only stare at such a presence in fascination.

Of course, it is only too obvious to argue that the painting is a produced object, that it is the product of a *techne*, that it is painted by the painter. As a physical artifact or device, its visibility can hence be nothing but the effect or the result of a technical enterprise. But in addition, one may add, the painting is the object not of a single, but of a double intention: first, the intention of the producer, who fabricates it according to an original schema or project; second, the intentional character of its confrontation, of the encounter that constitutes it as

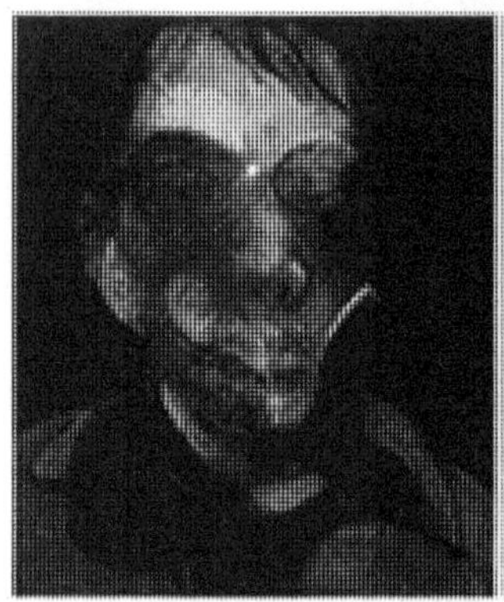
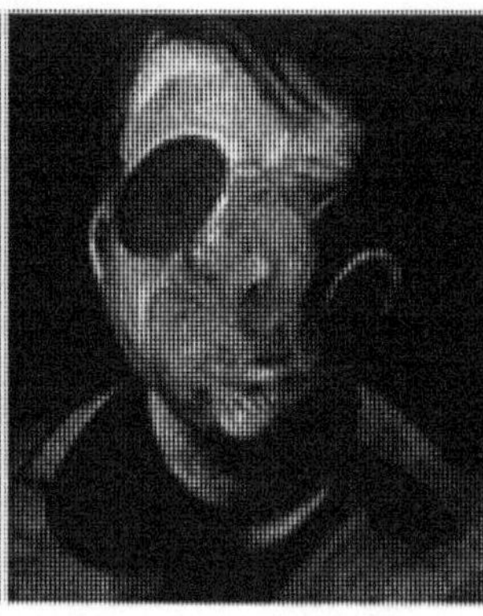
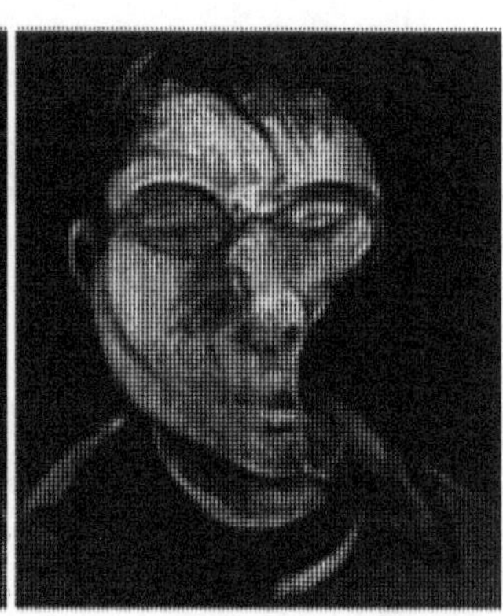

▲

**Francis Bacon,
*Three Studies for
Self-Portrait*, 1976,
Oil on canvas.**

an object of consciousness and experience. Consequently, the painting must be an object doubly subordinated to a will and a look. And no matter what powers it can deploy, it simply cannot escape the framing of this double intentionality.

And yet, in front of the painting we seem to find ourselves in a strange position of passivity: we suffer from an exceptional impact, from an odd and unusual imposition. As Marion puts it, the painting imposes itself "without discussion and by force, but with the sole authority [...] of the unseen that has become visible" (CV, 30). The status of our experience shifts then radically, from the act of an intentional constitution of the object by the viewer towards the very opposite, towards a destitution of the observer by the painting itself. In Marion's thinking of the *icon*, for instance, the experience takes place in which we are "seen" by another gaze, a gaze invisibly emanating through the presence of the painted object as a manifestation of transcendence. And coming from the opposite end, Deleuze characterizes the "logic of sensation" that is at work in painting as a striking, non-mediated action upon our nervous system, as an exceptional collision which destabilizes our own mode of presence. We are passively receiving then the impact of a force — and not an object — that is not mediated by any meaningful, "cerebral" consideration of it.

As we soon learn, however, this passivity of reception is only the effect of a more original submissiveness. For even the painter, the philosophers say, is an agent of passivity. While painting, he is not *intentionally* doing anything. His hand, says Merleau-Ponty, is "nothing but the instrument of a distant will" (EM, 147): distant, that means, not his own, the foreign will of another acting through his own hand. There is something that is "making itself seen within himself," and his actions "seem to emanate from things themselves, like figures emanating from constellations" (129). Merleau-Ponty affirms that this is the core of the experience of the painter: to be assaulted by the very things that will be painted. And it is through the words of an artist that he records this strange symbiosis of the will: he refers to Marchand confessing that "some days I felt that the trees were looking at me, were speaking to me" (129).

The trees look at the painter and speak to the painter. Little wonder, again, if what the painter does is neither the production of a preconceived project nor a re-production of an original existing in the outside, but just a subtle *laissez-faire*. As Marion puts it, the painter simply "allows the forms and features to impose themselves" (CV, 36). It is the things themselves that desire to emerge, to make themselves seen through the work of the painter. Marion qualifies this work as a "passive receptivity," the difficult art of "doing nothing," of letting the unseen appear: "the painting suddenly appears in its own terms, traces its own path" (CV, 37–41). Here a leitmotif of the enigma of painting is touched: like the Kantian genius, the painter does not really know what he is doing. He lends himself, he "gives his body" to an enterprise of which he imposes neither the conditions nor the results that will later appear on the canvas.

This double passivity of painting can be synthesized in Marion's formula: the authentic painting "escapes as much the one who signs it as the one who looks at it" (CV, 32). The painting is, as it were, self-mastered, independent. But this independence is only possible because it springs from a more profound entanglement between the painter and what is to be painted, between the one who sees and that which is seen. It is the original mimesis between the things and ourselves (the world and the painter, the object and the hand that fills the canvas) that allows for this strange communication to erupt.

Merleau-Ponty expresses something like this fundamental contact when he affirms that, in the act of painting, it is impossible to distinguish "who sees and who is seen, who paints and who is painted" (EM, 129). But there is maybe a more profound testimony of this phenomenon, one that appears in *The Logic of Sensation* when Deleuze refers the words of Francis Bacon to a confession of horror recreated by the writer K.P. Moritz. The argument runs as follows: while trying to explain the "pity" that underlies the violent character of his depictions of bodies, Bacon reflects upon a common, everyday activity. "If I go into a butcher shop," he says, "I always think it's surprising that I wasn't there instead of the animal". And Deleuze connects this strange testimony to the words with which Moritz describes the reaction of a person who witnesses the horrible spectacle of a collective execution. Moritz's character feels then strangely involved in the scene, as if he were experiencing himself the horror inflicted on the remains of the executed men, as if he were himself the very meat that was being thrown away. "This discarded meat is we ourselves," paraphrases Deleuze: "the spectator is already in the spectacle". This phenomenon of displaced sensibility, according to him, is neither an arrangement "nor a resemblance; it is a deep identity, a zone of indiscernibility more profound than any sentimental identification" (FB, 22).

Thus it is not merely a question of feelings. The "meat" that constitutes for Deleuze the zone of undecidability between the animal and the human corresponds, like a genus to its species, to another, more general level of indistinctness: that of the things and ourselves, the original mimesis that makes appear, on the surface of a canvas, forms that are not mastered by the one who paints. The mountain and the trees that look and speak to the painter are like the meat in which we suffer, and which probably suffers in us. "Nature is in the inside," say the philosophers quoting Cézanne, and one would be tempted to reply: Meat, our very meat, is also in the outside. It is indeed a matter of indiscernibility, of a radical ambiguity between the life of things in the world and our own. And it is that life what seems to assault us by erupting from the flatness of the painted surface.

Whenever one sees a principle of life animating the presence of a painting, hence, one seems to be seeing something else at the same time. For the life of paintings is not another form of life. It is rather the expression of such profound and fundamental identification, the indetermination of things and beings that turns every intention into a passivity and presents itself on the canvas as the breathing proof of a subtle and radical reversibility, a transitive communication, a common participation in life. Through its mere presence, the painting's excessive visibility would offer nothing other than the evidence of such a living indistinctness, of such a reversibility of life.

The Muteness of Contact

Just as we look at things and speak about things, the trees look and speak to the painter, they look and speak *through* the painter. The "encounter" of the artwork takes place in an indeterminate zone, where the exchange between the life of the painted and our own, between its respiration and ours, is somehow difficult to establish. Thus Merleau-Ponty can think of the image as something different than a copy: it is a visible in the second power, an internal echo of the thing in my body that arises in me "as a diagram of the life of the actual" (EM, 126). But this reversibility can also be thought of as a matter of fundamental violence, like in Deleuze's description of the hysteric reality upon which painting is grounded: a violence in which every organization between an inside and an outside becomes undone or deformed ("the world that seizes me by closing in around me, the self that opens the world itself"; FB, 37). According to Deleuze, the radical affectivity of painting "acts immediately upon the nervous system, which is of the flesh" (FB, 31–37), that is, of meat, of indistinctness.

In both cases, however, what happens in painting is not the formal encounter between a spectator and a lifeless object. The painting is not merely the presentation of something that is seen, but it is something in which we see or sense, through which we see or sense, or which sees and senses in us: the separation becomes difficult to sanction between the seen and the seer, the sensed and the sensing. It is an event of undifferentiation that will become devote communion, at the extreme limit of Marion's thinking of the icon, when we will *see ourselves being seen* by the invisible height of another gaze.

However this contact appears portrayed (echo, sensation, gaze), all its depictions seem to possess at least this one thing in common: what we see in painting is not a retinal or psychological image, not a visible of the eyes. We see an "echo" of life which "clothes vision from within," says Merleau-Ponty (EM, 126); we see beneath the body, we see with eyes that are temporarily located in the stomach or the ear, we see without organs, says Deleuze; we see the explosion of the visible, we contemplate, in the invisible gaze which crosses ours from a transcendence, *that which gives* every other visible to be seen, says Marion. Our seeing is at least synaesthetic, a seeing that spreads throughout the body and the senses; or it is a seeing that goes far beyond what is visually given and discovers that which precedes, neutralizes or makes possible the visible as such. The visibility of painting, the level in which the indistinctness of life comes to manifest itself as an event, seems to produce an extraordinary contact that is precisely not explainable as a mere contact or event.

Thus painting presents us with a tempting paradox. The phenomenological power of its touch is without limit, but somehow its very wealth lies in its capacity to resist description or appropriation. In a certain sense, it is as if the depth of contact defied its very rendition in a philosophical discourse. Deleuze gives us a good example of this tension by exhausting the immense potentiality of painting in the sheer impact of sensation: the *logic* of sensation appears then as a matter of non-mediated violence, as the paradigm of a collision that witnesses for the points of contact or indeterminacy between the body and the outside, producing a collapse of every form of organization, structure or management of the fact:

> Sensation has one face turned toward the subject (the nervous system, vital movement, "instinct"), and one face turned toward the object (the "fact," the place, the event). Or rather, it has no faces at all, it is both things indissolubly [...] at one and the same time I *become* in the sensation and something *happens* through the sensation, one through the other, one into the other. (31)

The fundamental hysteria whose original forces painting captures necessarily neutralizes any dualism between an external "fact" and an internal "synthesis" of the manifold. In the openness of the contact, sensation is not reducible to perception, and it is above all not mediated by any structure of meaning that would receive, order or conceptually organize an intuition. Its dismantling power is so great that it becomes almost meaningless to think of two different things, and perhaps, one may wonder, even to think about it at all.

Merleau-Ponty contributes to this problem with an interesting twist, for he conceives of the painting's contact as a matter of *thought*. That thought, however, is radically distinct from the logical structures of the conceptual: the painting "does not offer the mind an occasion to rethink the constitutive relations of things" (EM, 126); its contact is neither the object of discursive thought nor of any kind of speculation. Painting offers us with a non-conceptual presentation of Being; it is a "mute thought" without words, speechless and non-discursive, drawing in "full innocence" upon a "fabric of brute meaning" (123). Deprived of any intentionality or control, distinct from the powers of the word and the concept, this brute meaning is certainly of a peculiar kind. And in fact, even if Deleuze denies the very possibility of thinking about art in terms of meaning — because true paintings do not even pass through the brain, and if they do, they stick to the "right hemisphere," to the gestural and the expressive, to the "analogical" and never to the "digital" — both philosophers seem to agree at least in one thing: the nearly unspeakable indistinctness that comes to be expressed in painting disrupts every dualism and intentionality of experience without any participation of the *word*.

To Speak without Words

The enigma of the painting's life is closely related to the problem of the word. In a sense, the aliveness of painting appears as the almost exact antipode of the verbal: life speaks without words; the artwork speaks in colors, in depth, in everything but the conceptual. Painting says a lot of things to us, but the fundamental contact that it produces is said to be essentially mute or speechless. In painting, so the story goes, things say things without speaking.

Aisthesis

Opposed to the indistinct mystery of passivity, in fact, the linguistic appears in all its forms as the paradigm of *action*. The one who describes dries up the texture of the world; words operate with colors and lines like science operates with things: they "give up living in them" (EM, 121). Thus the works of true painting must be clearly separated from the works of the concept. Marion provides us with a clear articulation of this distinction: the authentic painting, he says, "exposes an absolutely original phenomenon, newly discovered, without preconfiguration or genealogy, suddenly appearing with such a violence that it explodes the limits of the visible identified to that point" (CV, 25). And against this explosive discovery he identifies the poverty of "academicism," of which conceptual art offers the "exemplary and definitive model [...] not only because the visible itself is defined by the concept — by some exterior understanding in advance — but above all because the work itself cannot and must not appear as such"(CV, 28).

The concept is thus designated as the place of a genealogy, a determination that is the result of a history of anticipations, expectations and intentions. The concept constitutes spectacles, and through them it establishes a desert of appearance, a platitude of vision, a lifeless visible that "sinks in the conception" (34). What painting discovers in the mysteries of its passivity, the concept sterilizes in its grey labor of technical production. What is lost in the transition from the discovery to the spectacle is the "nonmastery" that allows for the irruption of the invisible: when the painting is nothing but a text to be read, no life will emerge to confront us in the manifestation of its presence. An idol, according to Marion, works as a "mere recording [...] of private impressions or spectacles for the desiring gaze, like so many experiences of consciousness being set forth in order to be *read*, indeed, on the support and the surface [...] merely representing the desire to be seen" (34, my emphasis). The idolatrous painting, he will say later, limits itself to inscribe "upon a neutral surface, harmless and available, a complex of foreseen objects, because organized according to the subjective laws of intentional or synthetic imagination" (40). The idolatrous concept, then, must appear as the opposite of the taking place of contact.

Interestingly, Merleau-Ponty agrees to a similar distinction. According to him, painting loses its enigmatic power "if the entire potential of a painting is that of a text to be read, a text totally free of promiscuity between the seeing and the seen" (EM, 132). The text is the paradigm of artificiality, and it is as such intransitive. The text is the blocking of contact, it is the aseptic re-production of the visible, the prohibition of every discovery, a sterilization of life.

A fundamental dilemma seems thus to emerge from this relation between life and words. On the one hand, painting is presented as the exceptional medium in which a radical indistinctness comes to be expressed in the exceptional contact of its visibility. But on the other hand, this possibility is constantly at risk of being colonized, polluted, diverted from its power of witnessing by the mechanics of the text: the conceptual separates and organizes, it sterilizes the painting and enslaves it to the spectacle and the idol, to their labors of anticipation. The "pure" painting of life finds thereby a powerful, "degenerated" enemy that threatens to distort its power by turning the canvas into a mere support, a window or a surface for the inscription of external forms, preconceived objects, and narrative meanings. The "innocence" with which painting works without concepts upon the "brute meaning" of the world seems then to be constantly endangered by the lifeless, textual works of the conceptual.

Deleuze formulates the most radical articulation of this incompatibility between painting and words. The latter are here identified with a whole conceptual family — constituting something like a poetics of narration, figuration and illustration. In synthesis, concepts and words are according to Deleuze tools of *representation*: they inscribe everything into an organization, they unify and structure the manifold, they order and synthesize parts into solid and definite wholes. To represent in painting means above all to establish a series of relations within the visible: it is in the first place a relation of dependence between what is painted and an original object that it is assumed to illustrate, but it is also a set of relations between the images themselves, which are integrated "in a composite whole that assigns a specific object to each of them" (FB, 6). This composite whole introduces a logical connection between the images, figures or forms by constructing a story, an episode or an allegory that refers the presences of the painting to an overarching transcendent meaning.

These poetics of representation inevitably come to pollute the logic of sensation, they render it impossible through their cerebral work of relationality. True painting, Deleuze says categorically, has "neither a model to represent nor a story to narrate" (6). In fact, the purpose of painting is the exact opposite of representation; painting deforms every preconceived organization of things not in order to substitute or replace them with new forms, but to capture non-narrative forces, to make them visible and operative in us through the logic of sensation. Painting, says Deleuze, "directly attempts to release the presences beneath representation, beyond representation" (44). And it releases those presences by acting directly upon the nervous system, by not even passing through the brain. This quarantine of the brain functions thus as an antidote: by sticking to the nervous system, the paint "makes representation [...] impossible" (45).

As a consequence of this assertion, Deleuze identifies on the one side an artificial painting of the bone, a representational art that addresses the brain and aims at illustration, narration, story-telling and relational figuration. On the other, he describes a painting of sensation that overcomes representation and discovers the forces of rhythm and hysteria. By establishing this distinction at the very heart of painting, the Deleuzian argument radically confirms its own diagnosis: in order to preserve the power of contact of the painting, the word must necessarily be kept at a distance. And this gives birth to something like an imperative of painting: painting must above all, in Deleuze's words, "avoid the figurative, break with representation, disrupt narration, escape illustration" (6). Sensation and concepts appear to confront each other as exclusive possibilities.

Here, a fundamental question necessarily emerges. For how can the painter overcome the natural tendency to translate an intention into forms, to inscribe upon the canvas pre-conceived figurative objects, to dominate the act of painting by imposing a prefabricated structure of meaning? According to Deleuze, Bacon's genius consists precisely in his having found an original solution to this problem. Such a solution is nothing other than the "diagram," a technique of composition that, by randomly spreading paint over a limited section of the canvas, works as a plastic distributor of chaos. According to Deleuze, the diagram introduces a specific instance of chance into the process of painting, temporarily subverting the painter's position of rational mastery over the painting. This transitory loss of control, so he says, manages to neutralize the structures of figuration that inevitably tend to slip into the composition, but they leave enough room for the emergence of Bacon's "nonnarrative Figures".

Once again, hence, the works of the word are apparently dismantled by a certain labor of passivity. Painting, according to Deleuze, has to capture and make visible the invisible forces of sensation and rhythm. But in order to do so, it must avoid a double danger: on the one hand, it needs to escape the reign of the word and the cliché, which aspire at taking control over the painting (figuration); on the other, it cannot fall into the absolute abyss in which even sensation is lost in confusion (catastrophe). The challenge is to deal with chaos without disappearing in it: this is, says Deleuze, the fundamental issue that is at stake in modern painting, i.e. that of discovering "what can save man from the abyss, from external tumult and manual chaos," once representation is overcome (85). Abstractionism reduced chaos to a purely optical and symbolic minimum; abstract expressionism extended the diagram to the totality of the painting, generating a violent catastrophe. Bacon embraced chaos while keeping it localized in time and space (84–87); by finding a middle way between the two extremes, his painting provided an original solution to the problem of non-representation.

However, one difficulty arises when we consider Deleuze's presentation at a distance. The difficulty originates from a very simple fact, namely that in order to present Bacon's painting as a *solution*, Deleuze had first to establish the *problem* to be solved. And the issue is not innocent, for the mere articulation of Bacon's diagram as an answer for the "dilemma" of modern painting inevitably inscribes it in the context of a discourse that associates the essence of a medium, the needs of an epoch and the possible ways in which those needs can be satisfied (quoting Wölfflin, Deleuze even says at one point that modern painting could only move "in one of the following two directions: either toward the expression of a purely optical space (...) or, on the contrary, toward the imposition of a violent manual space," 103). By prescribing the abandonment of representation as an imperative for modern painting, in other words, Deleuze is doing nothing but to inscribe Bacon's "solution" within the long odyssey of the figurative and its

victims — a journey that he traces, in its multiple evolutions
and interruptions, from the "pure" origins of ancient Egypt
up to our very days. To put it crudely, Deleuze writes a *history*
of the overcoming of the *stories* that painting used to tell. The
absolute singularity of Bacon's painting, then, is explained by
its relocation in the broader context of another, magnificently
all-embracing narrative.

Hence in the Deleuzian analysis of Bacon's paintings
a very large discursive operation is at work. Even so, the
question could have only a relative importance if Deleuze
were limiting himself to elaborate *post factum* a philosophical
commentary of something (Bacon's paintings) that remained
clearly separate from his account. The problem acquires
another complexity, however, when we notice the role that
Bacon's own voice plays in the development of his analysis. "We
do not listen close enough to what the painters have to say"(FB,
81), affirms Deleuze, and in fact he lets Bacon speak for himself,
he lets his voice explain what he is doing, what he is attempting to achieve, how his own painting faces the "problems" that
it is trying to solve. And it is through Bacon's own words that
Deleuze analyzes the procedures and the functioning of the
diagram; it is Bacon himself, being apparently quite aware of
what he is doing, who explains its origin and its mechanics.
Thus the diagrammatic operation appears now under a different light: Bacon's speech presents it from the offset as an
entirely intentional technique framing the artistic process of
composition. The controlled, limited insertion of chaos into
the painting appears then as the application of something like
Bacon's own poetics of intentional passivity.

So the word is active in Deleuze's presentation of
Bacon's paintings in at least two different ways: first, as the
structuring of a story that explains and redoubles its force,
clothing it with an interpretive apparatus; second, as the exposition of a poetic strategy of creation, an intentional method
or procedure that is previously conceived and applied in the
canvas as a technical operation. The pure singularity of the
painting, its absolute and self-sufficient presence, is thus
inscribed upon the background of this double narrative work:
the first builds a meaningful space of visibility in which the
painting is loaded with a different force; the second informs the
creative process that gives birth to the painting itself. Consequently the question arises: is not Deleuze's logic of sensation
precisely the result of this double labor of the word?

Against the Word?
These problems are not exclusive of Deleuze's account, and
their insistence points in fact towards a more important

question. Marion, for instance, provides us too with something like a "great narrative" of the history of art, one which is in addition dominated by an apocalyptic pessimism. The philosopher wants to trace the scenario of a death of transcendence in the contemporary production of plate idols and homogenized spectacles. And he builds this scenario according to a certain temporality: the history of the image, in which painting seems to be inevitably inscribed, is itself framed by the broader history of metaphysics — from the Platonic condemnation of the image to the Nietzschean affirmation of its absolute self-referentiality (CV, 79–80). The reign of the idol coincides then with the state of complete nihilism in which we live, an era that dissolves art into the narcissist spectacle of idolatry and anticipation. The redeeming power of painting is thus symptomatically integrated within an overarching narrative that combines the determination of its extraordinary properties with a diagnosis of the philosophical problems of our era.

Now, this seems to be quite a framing operation for the absolute spontaneity of the painting's contact. And in fact, one could wonder whether the pure singularity of the artwork, the allegedly unstructured and unintentional character of its presence, could survive its installation in such a titanic historical framework. The enigma of aliveness seems to be threatened indeed by this distribution of contextual meanings and significations, by the discursive search of pictorial solutions for given conceptualized problems. For why would the mute power of painting need the philosophers' words in the first place? Why would the wealth of its naked contact require such a critical addendum or explanation?

These questions are not innocent: by addressing the voice that aims at celebrating the painting's silence, they do nothing but to point at a deep inconsistency. The exceptional visibility of painting is said to depend solely on the powers of its presence, on its enigmatic singularity, on the mystery of its process of emergence. In a sense, this is exactly what the notion of aliveness does: it singularizes the expressive presence of the painting as a small irreducible totality, almost as a close world mysteriously opened to the world, which is nonetheless said to be impermeable to any conceptual operation, to any external ascription or instillation of meaning into the mute event of our encounter with it. This is the affectivity of painting that the philosophers want to defend from the artificial intrusions of the word. And yet, in order to commemorate that muteness they do nothing but to fill it with words.

Marion seems to sublimate the conceptual tonnage of such a discursive operation by redoubling his commitment to the poetics of passivity, as if the submissiveness of the painter could compensate for the extent of his own philosophical intrusion. Thus he affirms the absolute impossibility to shape or control the process of pictorial creation: there is simply no way to organize the irruption of the unseen, which is said to be the involuntary par excellence. Everything the painter (and possibly the spectator as well) can do is to *believe* in the possibility of its taking place, to "beg for the surprise of discovering what he had not dared to foresee" (32). By looking for a referent of transcendence in the Christian tradition of the icon, Marion's "solution" aims hence at neutralizing the problem of the word by subsuming it under the ineffable, by turning the advent and occurrence of contact into a strict matter of hope. The deactivation of the word, in this radical defense of passivity, can only take therefore the exceptional name of *miracle*. But still, the battle is fought at the level of discourse alone. The operation remains unreflective, and Marion never questions the work that his own words are doing while covering the paintings themselves with meanings and significations that they would otherwise lack.

Merleau-Ponty gestures at a more sophisticated solution for the paradox: to radically reinterpret the problem of historicity and the status of art criticism. Unlike Deleuze and Marion, Merleau- Ponty affirms that the history of painting does not admit such thing as a comprehensive account: there are no classifications, no "distinct problems in painting, no really opposed paths, no partial solutions, no cumulative progress" (EM, 148). The historicity of painting is a "hidden" one, it is a labyrinth that cannot be made accessible by a simple exercise of narration (135). Of course, paintings do have meanings, and those meanings change in history; but it is neither the painter nor the spectator (and hence, one should logically conclude, not even the philosopher) who unilaterally attributes or generates them. It is the artworks themselves who produce the evolution of their own meanings, because "the sense we give to them later on has issued from them. It is the work itself that has opened the perspective from which it appears in another light. It transforms *itself* and *becomes* what follows" (139). Painting has an evolutive language of its own — even if that evolution does not follow any apparent direction, scheme or progress. That language is always singular and experimental, it is constantly being made and remade, at each moment beginning anew "in a poetic information of the world which continues after it" (135). The language of painting creates and recreates itself by multiplying its contacts, its equivalencies and mute meanings in an unceasing motion that lacks ends and culminations. This history always comes back to itself, to what has already been painted, to what is still to be painted: the first work of art, says Merleau-Ponty, "went to the farthest reach of the future [...] each creation changes, alters, clarifies, deepens, confirms, exalts, re-creates or creates by anticipation all the others". The enigma of aliveness, then, is one that inhabits the whole history of painting. Being alive with other paintings, every creation truly has its "entire life before itself" (148–9).

Merleau-Ponty's solution is apparently impeccable because it definitively expels the intelligibility of history from the realm of the conceptual. In a certain sense, it truly abandons the idea of a critique of art: the "problems" of painting are wrongly posed because painting deals primarily and above all with a mute opening of Being which lacks a history and a permanent order. However, this denial only happens at the same old price: that of turning once again the painter into an extraordinary being who does not really know what he is doing, the great ignorant who suffers, more than he practices, a "magical theory of vision" (127). One could ask consequently what is the status of the numerous testimonies that Merleau-Ponty uses to illustrate the reality of painting: just like Deleuze, who finds a parallel to Bacon's strategies in the works of Kafka, Proust or Beckett, Merleau-Ponty lets the painters speak, but also the poets and writers (Cézanne of course, and van Gogh or Klee, but also Valéry, Rimbaud or Apollinaire, among others). And just as Deleuze cannot simply dismiss the labors of the word in his presentation of Bacon's painting, in the absence of a miracle Merleau-Ponty cannot avoid the ultimate, inevitable work that these voices, like Deleuze's and his very own, enact towards the presence of the painting: they contribute, at least as much as its colors and lines, to configure the visibilities in which we see it.

The Life of Meanings
The word abandoned long ago its pretense to dominate the painting as the model for a story. What it can never desert, however, is its fundamental presence both at the very heart of the painting and in the eyes that confront it, a presence that is neither dependent nor autonomous from the visible, but rather inevitably indistinct from it. The word does not lie or reside somewhere else, in a different region from which it could come to colonize the fertile lands of artistic spontaneity and aesthetic freedom. The word does not come from abroad: it is rather always already there, inhabiting the same magmatic chaos out of which the meaningful is constantly being re-produced. It roams across the same uncertain landscapes from which great works of art emerge so as to inaugurate new visibilities for themselves and for ourselves.

In a sense, this is precisely the acknowledgement that

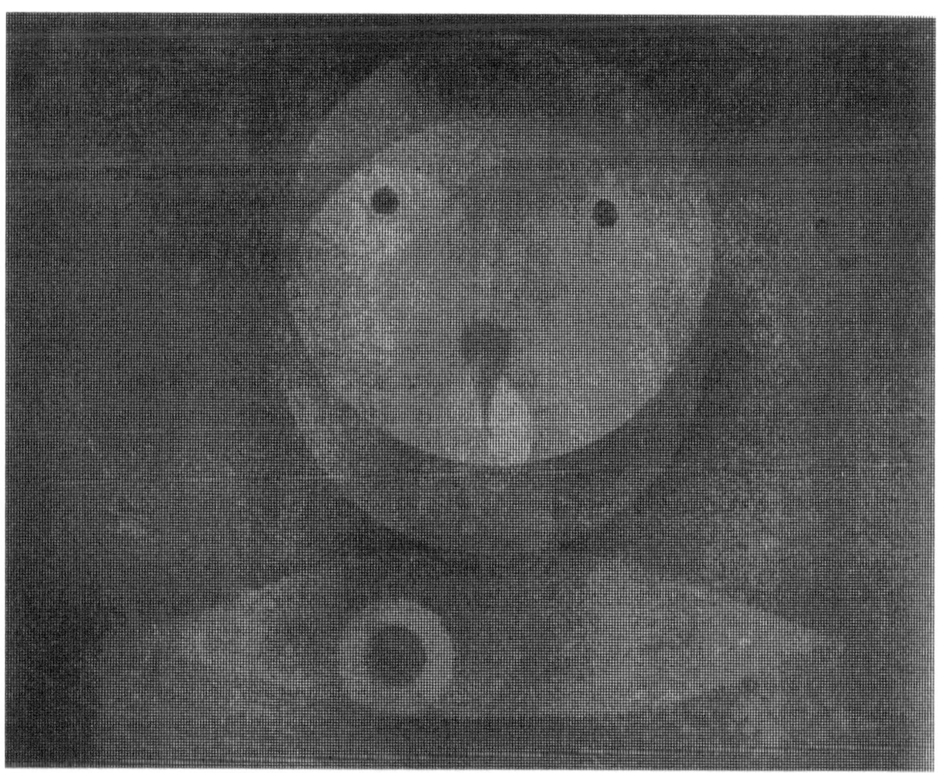

Deleuze emphasizes over and over: there is no such thing as a white surface in painting. Before the painter begins his work, the surface is already filled or invested by images and forms, by the familiar representations and "figurative givens" that have become one with his perception, acting as filters or prisms for his sight and his thought: every painter "paints on images that are already there" (FB, 71). These primeval presences, which Deleuze pejoratively terms "clichés," are already there before one begins to paint because the painter, like all of us, sees and thinks through them, because they order the real around and inside him, because they filter and distribute the *what* and the *as what* of appearance.

Now, this "seeing through" is according to Deleuze the exact opposite of painting: the mission of the painter is to break with these clichés, to deprive them of their illustrative or narrative function, to emancipate oneself from them through a process of figurative destruction and a-signification. But once again, the operation that discerns an imperative for the artistic process has a peculiarly dangerous status. Painting does not have in itself any "must": it does not need any final words (and it is curious that they should be *words*) of order and warning. The surface is always already filled with forms, with figures and relations organized according to complex arrangements and determinations: at any moment, such are the horizons that surround us, such are the conditions of possibility for the meaning of our works. But the life and the force of painting cannot consist in simply ignoring or destroying those inherited fields of meaningfulness. It consists rather in its ability to displace or reinforce, to destabilize or replace, to underline or propose, in a word, to manipulate particular relations which emerge upon that very plane of contingency as the very definition of what is given and what is possible at any given time.

This is why no watchword or mandate will ever be able to establish a priori the essence, the boundaries and the meanings of the operations of painting: if painting had such thing as an essence, it could only consist in subverting time after time the contents that any given definition would try to fix as a determination of its possibilities. This is also why painting has in principle nothing to do with such things as the purity of a medium or the imperative of novelty. Painting has no single mission precisely because its relations to the body, to sensibility and visibility cannot be conceived univocally — as if we still believed that form and content were two separate real entities related according to fixed and pre-established mechanisms. Meaningfulness has no fixed architecture, but depends rather on a cluster of situations in which many elements become entangled according to contingent relations, crystallized into cultural habits and local practices of signification. Those are the situations upon which painting, like any other art, intervenes: it translates (and by now we should know very well that translation is just another name for composition) relations into equivalent dispositions, it displaces affective intensities and directionalities, it re-proposes names and propositions, it erases the boundaries and the articulations of what is meaningful. The artist displaces situations and generates new landscapes of meaning. Likewise, by reflecting upon those landscapes the philosopher does nothing but to keep that motion alive.

This is also why all the "great narratives" on the history or the critique of art are neither wrong nor necessary. They are simply *possible*. They are particular interventions on the surfaces of meaningfulness which have the capacity of making things appear in different ways, to discover new details in what had already been known for a long time, to give new significations to old things and old meanings to new creations. There is no point in opposing painting and words, mediums and concepts, passivity and intention. All of them inhabit one and the same place, they combine and recombine themselves, they meet in articulations that push and displace our meanings into different possible relations. But no word must be expected to ever put each of those elements in its proper place, to establish once and for all what each of them must do: the time for those authoritarian regimes has been gone for ages. All the attempts at doing so are condemned to ignore the effects of their own performance. For they want to organize a field *from above* without realizing that they too are a part of it.

While comparing Bacon's poetics to Beckett's or Proust's, Deleuze himself recognizes that all of them were facing an "analogous situation" (56): they shared the will to emancipate themselves from the mandates of representation. However, Deleuze never analyzes the deep implications of his own comparison: namely, that the emancipation from representation has nothing to do with the nervous system or with a particular technique of composition, but rather with multiple practices and interventions in which words and concepts, far from being ignored, play an equally fundamental role in deforming and displacing the immanent landscapes of meaningfulness — and hence showing once again that its shapes and boundaries are capable of unending growth, i.e. of life. •

Pablo Bustinduy Amador is a PhD candidate in the Department of Philosophy at the New School for Social Research, New York, where he is writing a dissertation on democracy and the critique of space. He is currently working on a book project called *Fiction and Politics: Poetics for a New Antagonism*.

Aisthesis

Notes: In the Beginning Was the Drawing

Marcia Sá Cavalcante Schuback

1 • "Ein Zeichen sind wir, deutungslos. / Schmerzlos sind wir und haben fast / Die Sprache in der Fremde verloren." Friedrich Hölderlin, "Mnemosyne," in *Sämtliche Werke*, vol. 2.1 (Stuttgart: Kohlhammer, 1951), 195 (author's translation).

"**A sign are we,** undeciphered, without pain, our language almost forgotten on foreign shores (...)"[1] With these lines Friedrich Hölderlin introduces his hymn to memory, *Mnemosyne*, the mother of the muses. Here we read of an unread "sign," a description of the human condition as a "we," a being-together constituting each and every one. Each and every one is, as memory, a being-together overlaid upon the self and upon others — the living and the dead, those still to be born and those no longer existing, the like and the unlike, the visible and the invisible, the present and the absent, the near and the far. Undeciphered and without pain are we, writes Hölderlin. We exist almost unnoticed, like signs; with our language almost lost, we find ourselves exiled on foreign shores.

The human has long since been defined as the living creature in possession of language, *logos*; man is understood as the rational animal. Language, in turn, is defined as the articulation between fixed and transparent meanings, on the one hand, and the arbitrariness of signs, on the other, between, that is, content and form. A sign never stands for itself, but for something else — a meaning, a content; a sign means, expresses, or shows something else. Certainly, a sign can mean, express or show something else in many ways, by serving as a mimetic replica, a symptom, signal or symbol.

Regardless of the differences between metaphysical and analytical understandings, between philosophical and logical determinations of the sign, we have nonetheless inherited a way to understand it as a reference to something beyond itself. The sign is thereby something that is by definition noticeable. In the common understanding of what it means to be something noticeable, signs are considered decipherable and, even, painful. Hölderlin writes in his poem that a sign is without interpretation and is painless, once one has made the discovery that a sign is something other than a reference to a something else. A sign describes more than it defines *how* we are ourselves, how existence ex-sists through showing itself when it escapes itself; being "drawing into what withdraws,"[2] to follow Heidegger's interpretation of Hölderlin's poem. That which shows itself through its own disappearance is foremost an appearing. As a way of existing, the sign is the event of appearing in itself and not something that appears to show something else. Here we encounter a phenomenological-hermeneutic definition of the sign: the sign as a "formal indication" of the way of existing. We are signs undeciphered, because there is nothing behind or beyond the very event of existing that could be interpreted in one way or another. The sign is an event of appearing and it is the movement of the gerundive aspect — the "it is happening" — of the event that deciphers the sign. Hölderlin's "undeciphered" neither entails the opacity of the sign nor does it speak of the sign as beyond one's capacity to decipher. The "undeciphered" rather indicates another experience of language: when language reaches its limits, it is accompanied by an experience of its own loss, the loss of meaning. Hölderlin writes that we are "almost," that we are close to, losing language on foreign shores. But this sense of loss is "without pain"; the experience of having been close to, of almost, losing one's language on foreign shores can present itself as a gift when this "almost," this "closeness" carries within itself both the sign's temporality and its spatiality. To have been "close" to, or to have "almost" lost our language, does not entail any limitation or failure; it is rather a way of grasping the event of appearing as such, that which does not let itself be grasped as "something." Like a melody or a comet, the grip of the event of appearing evades, like the vertigo of the "almost" that describes the gripping movement of the event.

Hölderlin's poem about the sign discloses the existential meaning of the abstract, an understanding which gains further specificity with the help of how art understands abstraction. So-called abstract art can be thought as a way of de-realising "reality" in order to sense the "work" of appearing as such. The

2 • Martin Heidegger, *What is Called Thinking?*, trans. J Glenn Gray (London: Harper Perennial, 2004), 18.

abstract is a sign without interpretation, an almost lost language on foreign shores, a distancing from pre-formed forms so as to allow the forming of forms or the de-forming force to appear. The abstract produces both space between spaces and times between times, and is therefore neither univocal nor equivocal. Rather the abstract produces the *inter*-vocal, *das Zwischendeutige*, what is *between* meaning(s). Understood as abstract in this sense, the sign is a kind of drawing, so long as it is understood that the drawing defines the sign and not the sign that defines the drawing.

Aisthesis

The attempt to think the sign from the drawing is at the same time an attempt to think the coincidence of word and image, to get a handle on what the two have in common instead of what separates them. Throughout the philosophical tradition, the opposition between word and image has not only been rendered in terms of the difference between *logos* and *mythos*, between conceptual and visual languages; the difference has also been cast as a difference between sound and silence. Simonides, the Greek lyrical poet (ca 556 BC–468 BC), regarded visual art as mute poetry. In the eighteenth century, Gotthold Ephraim Lessing explained that poetry and visual art should be kept separate, not with respect to sound and silence, but on account of time and space; as an art of the word, Lessing meant that poetry ought to be perceived as an art of time.[3] After innumerable aesthetic and philosophical attempts to divide and unite word and image, the presupposition that both sign and image stand for something other than themselves has remained untouched. Whereas signs are ascribed a metaphysical ground, images are set upon a metaphorical ground, all the same both signs and images exist at the interface between the physical and the spiritual. When, however, signs are understood as arising from the drawing, no longer do they constitute a reference to something other than themselves. Signs are a signing, both a gesticulation and a practice. A high degree of attention is placed on the event of points and lines. In some drafts to an unfinished essay, Walter Benjamin attempts to bring together the sign and the drawing. He observes that the sphere of the sign has many distinctly separated areas and considers that which divides them as "the changing meanings of the line."[4] To these meanings, he counts *the line of geometry, the line of the written sign, the graphic line*, and what he calls *the line of the absolute sign*.[5] In these notes of Benjamin's, which stem from a discussion of Gershom Scholem's essay on painting,[6]

3 • Gotthold Ephraim Lessing, *Laokoon* (Stuttgart: Philipp Reclam, 1964).
4 • Walter Benjamin, "Über die Malerei oder Zeichnen und Mal" and "Malerei und Graphik," in *Gesammelte Schriften*, vol. II. 2 (Frankfurt am Main: Suhrkamp, 1991), 602–607. English translation, "Painting, or Signs and Marks," in *Selected Writings*, vol. 1 (Cambridge, Mass.: Harvard University Press, 2004). I wish to thank Irina Sandomirskaya for inspiring and enlightening conversations about Benjamin's thought, and specifically about these texts.
5 • Ibid, 606.

he describes very sketchily the last of these two lines, the graphic
and the line of the absolute sign, connecting the graphic and the
plastic line with his thoughts on language. These notes can be
read as an example of what Benjamin speaks of in the unfinished essay, namely the way in which a sign comes to be a sign *for*
something. He hints at two fundamental aspects. On the one
hand, the sign is a sign *for somebody*, that is, for the one who sees
it. Here, the way of perceiving the drawing remains paradigmatic, since the question of what the sign is depends on the way
in which it is seen — if, for example, it is seen horizontally or
vertically, whether the gaze is directed upwards or downwards,
if the drawing is hung like a painting in front of the viewer or is
read horizontally like a sheet of paper on a table. A mosaic on
the floor is viewed vertically with the eyes fixed downwards,
while a fresco on the ceiling, requires the gaze to be turned
upwards. The interesting question posed by Benjamin is
whether the image, that is, *the painted image*, is vertical in its
nature, or whether the sign in the meaning of the *drawing* is
horizontal. The verticality of the image, or the painting,
becomes for Benjamin an enchantment or a fabulation, in
contrast to the horizontality of the sign or the drawing, which
takes on the form of an appearance. In this draft he writes apho-
ristically that "Kandinsky's paintings are the simultaneous
occurrence of conjuring and manifestation."[7] We might inter-
pret these words of Benjamin's as meaning that in Kandinsky's
art the distinction between image and sign collapses, as does
that between the painting and the drawing, as well as the verticality (enchantment, metaphysics) together with the horizontality of (that is, the act of making visible or perceptible) the
appearance. Furthermore, the sign is both *a sign of and a sign for
something*. Benjamin argues along similar lines by first distinguishing between drawing and painting and then between the
graphic line and the line of the absolute sign, but doing so in
order to show how they meet. To be a sign *of something* is
discussed by Benjamin as a sign on a surface that cannot be identified with any background. He rather sees this surface as an
Untergrund, an "underground" that does not only have a visual
but also a metaphysical resonance. A sign is drawn or painted,
and the difference between them is defined by Benjamin with
respect to the visual-metaphysical idea of a "ground" that
according to him ought to be kept conceptually distinct from a
white blank surface or an open sky. This underlying ground
cannot be identified with anything, not
even the empty, the colour-less, the open.
Benjamin considers that, for example, the
drawing of the clouds on a sky can be
taken for the purity in the style of the

6 • Ibid.
7 • Walter Benjamin, "Painting,
or Signs and Marks," 82.

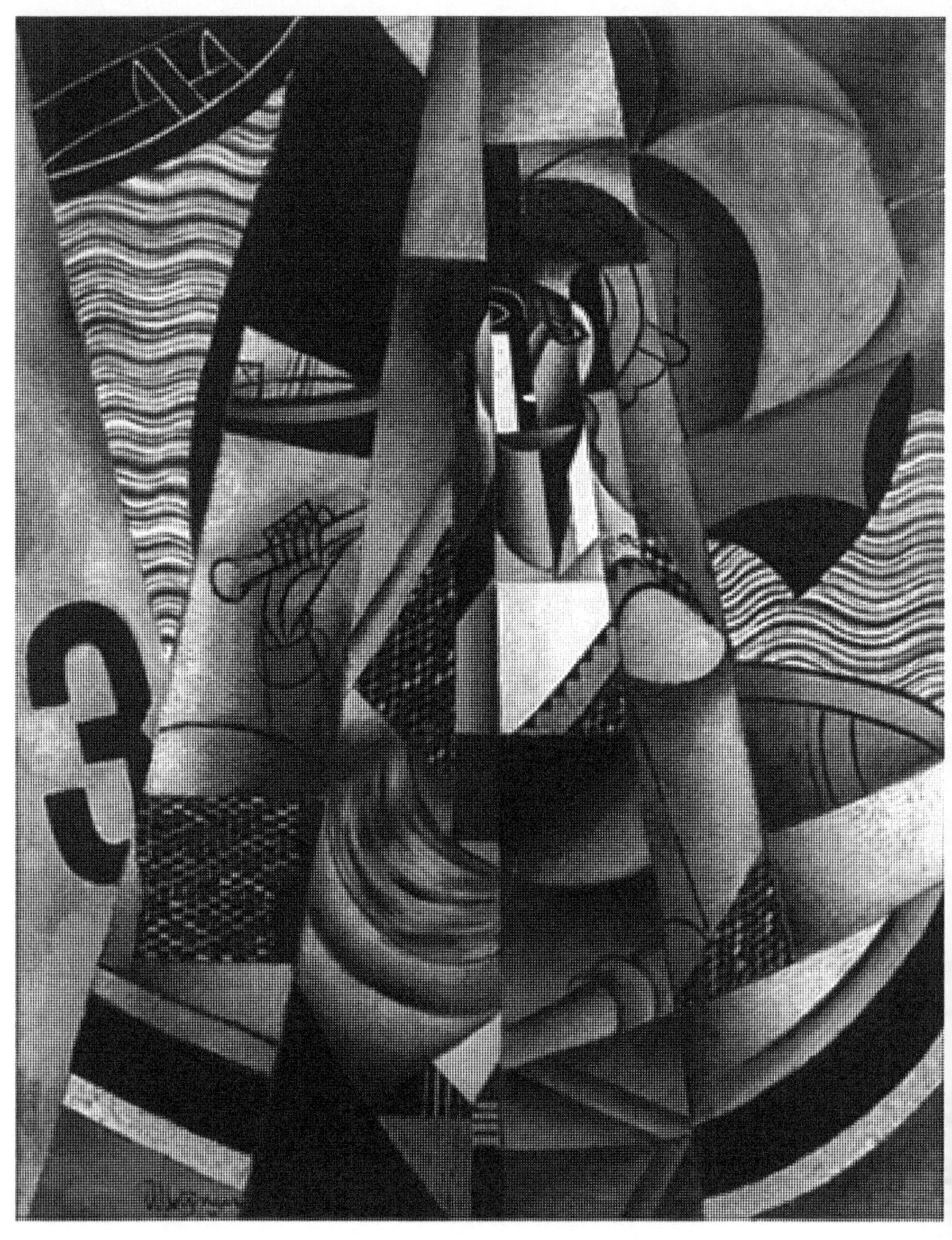

Jean Metzinger, *Le canot*, 1913, oil on canvas, confiscated by the Nazis ca 1936, displayed at the Degenerate Art show in Munich, missing ever since.

drawing,[8] since the utmost, subtle limit between an empty background and this mystical idea of an underground reveals itself. "A graphic line only exists on such an underground,"[9] states Benjamin; it exists as what allows a visual-metaphysical underlying ground appear, giving it its identity.

Benjamin distinguishes the sign from the image, ascribing to the latter *the* pictorial as an attribute. "The picture has no background," he says, "neither does [it] have any graphic line."[10] In the pictoriality of painting we encounter surfaces of colour that are limited by one another but that together create a composition. Benjamin refers in this discussion to Raphael's paintings, and already in the aforementioned letter to Scholem states that he wants to "prove that a painting by Raphael and a cubist painting coincide."[11] He insists that if linear shapes are often so prevalent in a painting it is not a question of the graphic lines that comprise painting as such. A painter does not paint after drawn lines, but after "pictures," surfaces of colour; it would be an aesthetic illusion to assume that a painter first draws lines so as then to paint on them. Here Benjamin refers to Kandinsky, Chagall and perhaps foremost to Klee.[12] Pen and ink drawings constitute, according to Benjamin, the only exception where paint and line co-exist, and where moreover a sense of an "underground" is kept. Distinguishing the sign from the picture Benjamin defines the painted picture as a "mark," in German "Mal." The Swedish word "måleri," "målning" originates from this "Mal," and is related to the Greek word "melas," meaning "black." The Swedish language has not developed any vocabulary from the word "Mal," but in German we can trace its return in words such as *Totenmal*, *Grabmal*, *Denkmal*, *Wundermal*, and *Muttermal*. In Swedish these words are rather described by "mark." Benjamin defines *Mal*, "mark," as the medium of painting,[13] and proposes a conceptual distinction to separate the picture — the pictorial image — and the mark, so as to capture the ambiguity of the picture, according to which the picture is said to refer both to itself and to something other. In a painting the picture cannot just be a "mark," because it always refers to something else. Raphael's pictures are not just marks, that is, tensions between coloured surfaces; they are also "pictures" that depict something, in the same way that a cubist painting or geometrical figures are pictures of figures. According to Benjamin, the mark, *das Mal* — the pictoriality of the picture — is immanent while the image is transcendent in the sense that it constitutes a *beyond of the painting* that nonetheless exists in *the painting's mark*. Benjamin introduces the idea about an

8 • Ibid.
9 • Ibid, 84.
10 • Ibid, 85.
11 • Walter Benjamin, *The Correspondence of Walter Benjamin*, (Chicago: University of Chicago Press, 1994), 100. German original: *Briefe I, 1910–1928* (Frankfurt am Main: Suhrkamp, 1966).
12 • Ibid, 101.
13 • Walter Benjamin, "Painting, or Signs and Marks," 85–6.

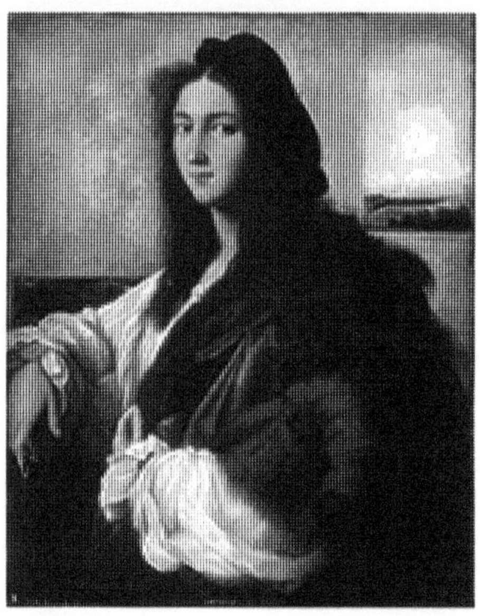

Raphael, *Portrait of a Young Man*, 1513–1514, Oil on panel. Stolen by Nazi Authorities and missing since 1939.

"absolute mark," contrasting this with an "absolute sign."[14] "An absolute mark" is, for Benjamin, related more to "time" than to the personal. It is therefore more proximal to the Swedish word "mål," which in turn refers to the idea of a "specific time," as in "måltid" (meal), and further to a gathering and a communion, as in "modersmål" (mother tongue). The medium of painting, the mark, is more time-bound than "the absolute sign," since the former has little to do with "expression." A mark crops up, whereas a sign gets expressed;[15] while the mark remains tied to the living, "the absolute sign" is closer to what is without life. Since a mark shows up and appears, rather than being expressed — where what is expressed is to a higher degree related to the living — the mark introduces a magical temporality in which the personal dissolves. A mark connects the person to the fullness of life, and to a faith surpassing an individual existence. This way of describing painting as a tension between image and mark interrogates the common idea of representation and depiction. Benjamin's project is to show that Raphael's pictorial images and the work of the cubists have much in common and also to describe how this common ground is shared; he clarifies how Raphael's "figurative images" and Cubism's non-figurative images are "marks." As painting marks these pictures allow for the nature of the mark itself to appear in such a way that they dissolve the undergrounding ground and the personal, both the sign and its expressivity.

In contrast to the mark as a kind of medium of painting, the sign is the element of drawing. Benjamin means that drawing is more closely related to the spatial and the personal.[16] The visual-metaphysical undergrounding ground, understood as the unnamable depth that appears when the spatial and the personal are drawn out, is separated from every idea about a contrastive background or an absolute surface. It cannot exist *beyond* drawing but only be shown *in* drawing. Drawing shows how a sign ascribes a personal identity to somebody, like the signs etched on the Jews' houses during their sufferings in Egypt. These signs of the unmentionable ground personify someone and signify thereby something. Drawn signs are more proximal to the word than a mark. Benjamin's obscure draft presupposes that the drawing of a graphic line in itself explains what a sign is, and that the difference between a sign and a

14 • Ibid, 84–5.
15 • Ibid, 85.
16 • Ibid, 84.

mark, and further, between drawing and painting, can be understood as different ways of relating to word and name. In contradistinction to Lessing's distinction between word and image as an art of time and space respectively, Benjamin tends to connect the drawing or graphics to the spatial and personal expressivity of the word, and the painting to the temporal and impersonal magic of the image.

The relevance of Benjamin's obscure draft lies foremost in the attempt made to define the sign from the graphically drawn line and thus to search for the source of signification in the "nature" of the drawing as such. Benjamin connects up the graphic drawing with the spatial and personal expressivity of the word on the basis of how the personal word is drawn on the unspeakable ground, in the language of the divine.[17] That he chooses to describe signs not temporally but spatially propels us toward a set of different issues, principally because drawing has long been rendered precisely in temporal terms. When, in his "Notes on Painting," Diderot presents his "bizarre thoughts about drawing"[18] he complains of the way in which drawing has been misunderstood by academics as the depiction of models, of slaughtered animals and lifeless models. Diderot argues that the drawing ought to depict "acts" of nature, not "attitudes";[19] drawings should present what is going on in the streets, public scenes, "true movements in the acts of life,"[20] writes Diderot; Diderot shows the modern significance of drawing as a depiction of movements that captures both form and contour rather than their "contents" or determinations. The modern significance differs from the classical view of drawing, which in Vasari's words constitutes a "clear expression for and explanation of a concept that exists in the soul, imagined in spirit or made up in thought." [21] Diderot's realism and the idealist view of drawing expounded by Vasari are united in understanding the drawing as a depiction of the contour and form of things, of the soul of things and the things of the soul. They share a vague idea of drawing as a tendency toward abstraction, like an unfinished and even unclear "image"; such an idea is consonant with the classic aesthetic definition of the drawing as a draft of a later work. At the end of the sixteenth century, Federico Zuccaro (1542–1609) sought to establish a distinction between the internal and the external drawing or plan.[22] The French word *dessin*

17 • Ibid.
18 • Denis Diderot, "Essais sur la peinture," in *Oeuvres esthéthiques*, ed. Paul Vernière (Paris Garnier, 1959), 665–673 (Author's translation).
19 • Ibid, 671.
20 • Ibid, 674.

21 • Giogio Vasari, *Le vite de' più eccellenti architetti, pittori, et scultori italiani da Cimabue, insino a' tempi nostri. Nelle edizione per i tipi di Lorenzo Torrentino, Firenze 1550*, vol. 1 (Turin: Einaudi, 1991), 60.

(drawing) derives from the Italian *disegno,* which does not differ in pronunciation but only graphically from *dessein* (project), meaning purpose. The drawing is understood as a draft toward a goal, a work of projection. This may serve to explain why architecture, sculpting and painting have commonly been considered "arts of drawing,"[23] as was pointed out by Félix Ravaisson.

Today Ravaisson is known to have influenced Henri Bergson, but under the strong influence of German Idealism, generally, and of Schelling specifically, Raviasson penned an inspiring book entitled *Of Habit.*[24] He wrote a book about Leonardo Da Vinci's drawings too,[25] using the same classification he formulated in his article on "drawing" for the dictionary of French pedagogy.[26] Even if in the 1900s the art of drawing was appreciated, it was still defined as a form of "unfulfilled painting," as "draft" or "project" (*dessein*). It was considered principally a depiction of bodies projected against a background or a surface.[27] While, like Diderot, Ravaisson admits that drawing is a "specific talent to exhibit the spirit of the times," on the other hand drawing is recognized as an "unfulfilled painting," per definition a preparation for a later work. Kant's ideas about drawing, which we can glean from disparate passages of both the first and third critiques, is a synthesis of these two ways of regarding the "nature" of the drawing, namely, on the one hand, an almost abstract presentation of the form and contour of things, and on the other a mental image of, and a draft for, a realized future. Kant regards "the drawing" to be a creation of the imagination, which in an unsatisfactory way can be called an ideal drawn from sensibility — in this manner, it remains undifferentiated from the "aesthetic ideas." In the *Critique of Pure Reason* Kant describes such creations of imagination as "monograms." They are, according to Kant, a "floating drawing" (*schwebende Zeichnung*) and "scattered drawn lines." In both cases "monograms" remain distinct from the fixed image.[28] Kant may regard these creations as nonconceptual images existing in the thought of the painter. Nonetheless at the same time he realizes how, in its nature, the drawing floats, how it is comprised of "scattered drawn lines." Kant's employment of the "monogram" can be traced back to

Aisthesis

22 • Federico Zuccaro, *L'idea de' Pittori, Scultori, ed Architetti* (1607) (Florence: Olschki Editore, 1961).

23 • See Félix Ravaisson's article, "Dessin," in *Dictionnaire de pédagogie et d'instruction primaire,* ed. Ferdinand Buisson (Paris: Hachette, 1880), 575–80.

24 • Félix Ravaisson, *Of Habit,* trans. Clare Carlise and Mark Sinclair (London: Continuum, 2008). French original: *De l'habitude* (Paris: Fournier, 1838).

25 • Félix Ravaisson, "Léonard de Vinci et l'enseignement du dessin," in *L'art et les mystères grecs* (Paris: L'Herne, 1985).

26 • See Ravaisson's article, "Dessin," in *Dictionnaire de pédagogie et d'instruction primaire.*

27 • Ibid.

28 • On Kant's understanding of the "monogram," see *Critique of Pure Reason,* A570–571/B598–599. On the subject of Kant's thoughts on signs, see *Critique of Judgement,* trans. W S Pluhar (Indianapolis: Hackett, 1987).

Winckelmann's use of the same word and to his understanding of the drawing as a kind of "drawing of absence." This understanding of drawing as a drawing of absence is consistent with the inherited myth about the origins of the visual arts, according to which the potter Butades is said to have drawn the shadow of his daughter's lover on leaving.[29] Kant considers that "in painting and sculpting, indeed in all visual arts, including architecture and horticulture insofar as they are fine arts, design is what is essential; in design the basis for any involvement of taste is not what gratifies us in sensation, but merely what we like because of its form."[30] The aesthetics of drawing lay, according to Kant, in this privileging of form over colour, in a drawing's ability to perceive the essence of things, and finally in the drawing's kinship with writing; it is this that, for Kant, makes possible the communicability of an aesthetic presentation.[31] In Kant's sober — and, to a greater extent, neo-classic — aesthetics of drawing, a figure emerges — "the floating drawing," "free designs (in which) lines are randomly interlaced"[32] — the appearance of which is neglected in nigh on all aesthetic and art-theoretical reflections on the drawing, namely that what the drawing makes visible is the floating lineations of the hand. Kant's aesthetics of drawing highlights that it first is gesturing, what one could call the mobility of a touching or fingering.

Since the renaissance, attempts have been made within art theory to regard drawing as a representation of movement and as a movement of representation. The drawing is defined as unfulfilled and preparatory, as that which, on the one hand, represents either outer or inner shapes and movements, on the other. Yet what remains unseen in such theorizations is an idea of drawing as the hand's own gesturing, a gesture that can be said to form the unconscious of the sign. In conversation with Valéry, Degas once said that "the drawing does not exist outside of the drawn line, but ... exists within it."[33] As opposed to an understanding of drawing as a representation of both acts of life and movement, Degas' words impress upon us that *the* drawing (the

29 • This myth was told by Plinius the Elder, *Natural History*, vol. 9, Book 35, 43, trans. D E Eicholz (Cambridge, Mass.: Harvard University Press, 1962), 371–373: "It was through the service of that same earth that modeling portraits from clay were first invented by Butades, at Corinth. He did this owing to his daughter, who was in love with a young man; and she, when he was going abroad, drew an outline on the wall of the shadow of his face thrown by a lamp. Her father pressed clay on this and made a relief, which he hardened by exposure to fire with the rest of his pottery; and it is said that the likeness was preserved in the Shrine of the Nymphs until the Corinth by Mummius."

30 • Immanuel Kant, *Critique of Judgment*, §14, 225.

31 • See Jacques Darriulat's discussions of the linkage between Kant's and Condillac's views on the relation between drawing and writing, in "Kant et l'esthétique du dessin," *Revue philosophique de la France et de l'étranger*, No. 2 (2007): 168.

32 • Immanuel Kant, *Critique of Judgement*, 207.

drawn picture) is *drawing* (the act from which the drawn comes to be). It is, as expressed by Dan Karlholm, to acknowledge that the English word "drawing" is really a verb and not a noun, a *drawing of lines*.[34] As *drawing* the drawing is an auto-graphy, a graphics of itself. It indexes its own action and nothing besides. In this regard, the drawing is not a picture — something which Benjamin also insists upon. Here, awareness of how the drawing is indistinguishable from its own act serves to problematize the idea that the drawing is merely a sign of an absent beginning or an imminent completion of a fulfilled picture. Such awareness situates the drawing in its present way of being as a gesturing, and not as a presencing either as what has passed or what is to come. According to Karlholm, the drawing is neither the revelation of an absent beginning nor a portent for an absent end. Perhaps, though, we can still say that the drawing reveals its own act, and that the drawing be so closely tied to the act that it cannot be likened to a *something*. Therefore, the act of drawing is partly conducted blindly, from the place in which the seeing eye cannot see itself. Drawing *qua* the *act* of drawing, is an auto-graphy; just like a blind person, drawing touches the contours of things. It is with this in mind that Degas posited a significant difference between the seeing of things without a pen in the hand and their seeing with drawing hands.[35] To see with drawing hands is to see the closest, even if this means that what is most visible cannot be seen on account of its envelopment with the here and now of drawing. So as to see the closest with drawing hands, the gaze must be transformed into a hand that grips, making the discovery that there exist no object-relations (relations between objects), only relations between drawn lines. Valéry compares the drawing hands with the flight of the bird, discovering such a pattern in da Vinci's drawings of flight. Valéry argues that the drawing hands touch the paper like a blind eye seeking out a form. In the lithe solidity entailed in holding onto the moving contours of forms, drawn lines appear against an underlying surface. Valéry here puts to one side the well-established contradictions between figure and ground and fore- and background, speaking instead of the drawn line and the ground. His descriptions of drawn lines floating towards the ground lead us to Cecco Bravo's captivating drawings. By following this Italian seventeenth century artist, born Franscesco Montelatici (1601–1661), we experience the lines as if they were drawn blind. What becomes vivid is the way in which these drawings, which seem to have been produced in a state of blindness, are comparable to the blindness we experience in our sleep.[36] The naked figures encountered in Bravo's

33 • Paul Valéry, "Degas danse dessin," in *Ouevres II* (Paris: Pléiade, 1960).
34 • Dan Karlholm, "Action Drawing: Notes on the (dis)Revelatory Nature of Drawing," in *Konsthistorisk tidskrift*, vol 78:2 (2009).
35 • Paul Valéry, "Degas danse dessin," 1187.

drawings seem to fall to the ground and to the groundless nothing. This blindness the drawing hand seems to acquire can be interpreted in the same way that the closing of one's eyes is necessary for sleep to reach a dream state. Therefore, drawing can be regarded as disclosing the border of the figurative rather than its negation, analogous to how sleep operates at the border of wakefulness, and not as the negation of wakefulness.

Valéry reports on Degas' description of the drawing as a way of looking upon form. "It may be that the drawing is the most obsessive temptation of the spirit."[37] In a drawing it is rather the hand, and not the eye, that sees, and with this sight acquired through the touch, one is alive to the birth of form in every form.[38] The drawing has, according to Valéry, a higher level of abstraction, inasmuch that abstraction here means the possibility of seeing form from all directions, through all its passages, its gaps and intervals. Rather than generating a form, the drawing tries to rid itself of such a determination: it wishes to unbind rather than to fix new forms. Caesura, *epoche*, openness, sleep, dream, quaking, swindle, fly, fall, threshold — all of these terms can be used in an attempt to describe drawing *qua* the act of drawing, which is to say drawing as the movement of touch or pressing. They contribute to thinking the complex reality of the sign, which resists being reduced to either its counter position to the image or as consisting in spiritual or mental contents. The drawing reveals the sign as a verb in the sense of an act and an event. It lets the word become a verb also, a happening from which a form appears. Drawing gives rise to another linguisticality and mode of signification irreducible to a discursively oriented and communicative language. That which appears is the sign as a thought- and language-form, with both language and thought as movements toward form, revealing the plasticity of form itself.

The notion of the drawing as the birth of the sign is one toward which artistic praxis during the twentieth century has become acutely drawn. We can trace a particular vision of this relationship of sign and drawing, of the word and the drawn line, in the work of Joseph Beuys. In 1974, a collection of drawings by Beuys was exhibited at the Arts Council Gallery in Belfast — and later in Oxford — under the title *The secret block for a secret person in Ireland*. The exhibition showed 266 of the 456 drawings Beuys completed between 1936 and 1972. In an interview with Caroline Tisdall, Beuys recalls that these drawings differ from his other works scattered

36 • See the catalogue *Comme le rêve le dessin*, ed. Philippe-Alain Michaud (Paris: Éditions du Centre Pompidou/ Éditions du Louvre, 2005).
37 • Paul Valéry, "Degas danse dessin," 1211: "Il se peut que le Dessin soit la plus obsédante tentation de l'esprit..."
38 • See Françoise Dastur, À la naissance des choses: Art, poésie et philosophie (Fougères: Encre Marine, 2005) and in particular the chapter "À la naissance des choses: le dessin," 91–110.

Aisthesis

around other different museums; 'the nature of this secret block is different', he remarks, "as a whole it represents my selection of thinking forms in evolution over a period of time."[39] As "thinking forms" these drawings are more proximal to the real in comparison to other ways of approaching reality.[40] In his remarks about this collection Beuys repeats in several places that when he speaks of *thinking*, he means thinking "as form."[41] Thinking does not create reality, it constructs forms. They can be solid like crystals, or they can be light and organic, he adds. Thinking forms are further defined as linguistic forms. "I bring (or deliver) linguistic forms to paper"[42], comments Beuys, by which he means that "drawings are another language form."[43] He implies the connection drawn between thought and language is predicated on the secret of form — which, when the title of Beuys' exhibition is considered, can be called the "secret bloc of form." The drawing presents another language form, through which linguisticality is brought back to the birth of the sign and thus the region of language extended. Beuys describes this expansion of language in terms of "keeping this event of language (*Sprachlichkeit*) in a specific fluidity and mobility, so as to escape the usurpation achieved by culture along with the rationality developed through conceptual language."[44] Beuys' drawings search for an abstraction, an abstraction in the sense of the drawings seeking to detach themselves from any conceptual language. At the same time as conceptual language is detached through abstraction, there is a reactivation of the original sense of the Latin word *conceptio*, meaning origin or birth. Since drawings are "the first thoughts," these thoughts answer to a more fluid and mobile linguisticality, they differ from the idea of "self-expression" as well as from the thought of an "art-product." Drawings signify instead *a living work* (*Werklauf*) as opposed to being part of an author's life-work (*Lebenslauf*), which is to say, as a product of the author; they are *auto-graphical* rather than *auto-biographical*. Like the *secret bloc* of form, these drawings, which Beuys mediates through the title of the exhibition, are dedicated "to a secret person in Ireland." The drawings are *for* somebody in Ireland — a landscape that makes possible another

39 • Joseph Beuys, *The secret block for a secret person in Ireland* (Mosel: Schirmer, 1988), 48.
40 • Ibid.
41 • Ibid.
42 • Beuys to Heiner Bastian and Jeannot Simmen, in the catalogue *Zeichnungen: Museum Boymans van Beuningen, Rotterdam November 1979-January 1980* (Berlin: Staatliche Museen preussischer Kulturbesitz, 1980), 32 note 13.
43 • Joseph Beuys, *The secret block for a secret person in Ireland*, 9.
44 • Beuys to Hans van der Grinten, in *Franz Joseph von der Grinten, Joseph Beuys: Bleistiftzeichnungen aus den Jahren 1946–1964* (Frankfurt am Main: Propyläen, 1973), 17.

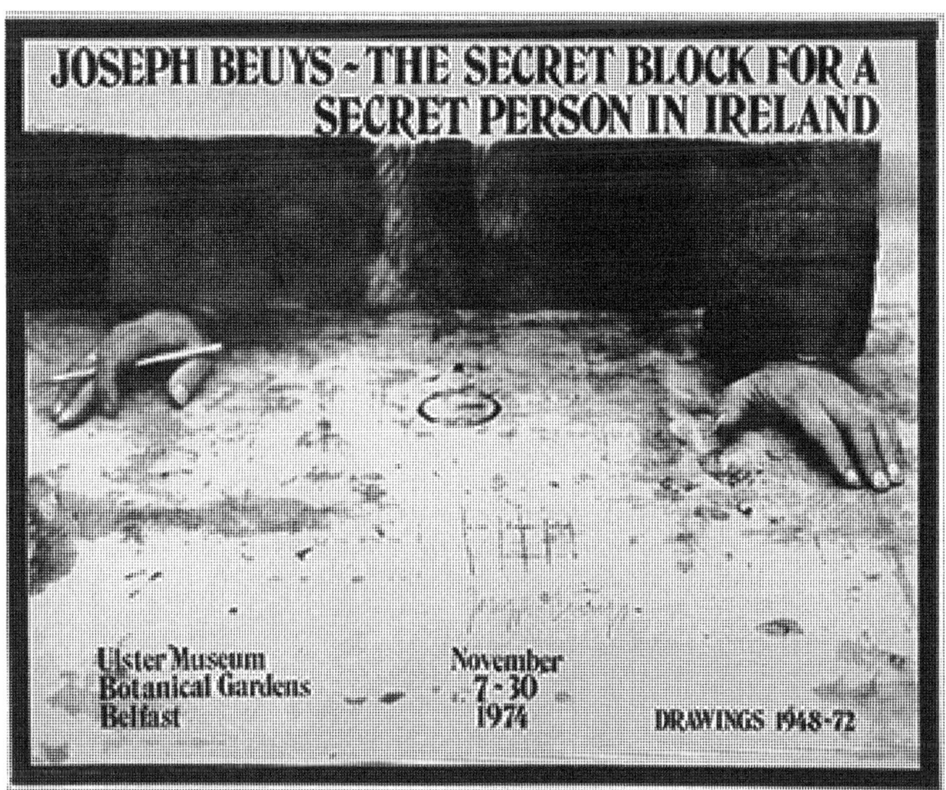

▲

Exhibition Poster,
Joseph Beuys, The
Secret Block for a
Secret Person in
Ireland, Ulster Museum
Botanical Gardens
Belfast, 1974.
© DACS, 2009.

somebody. Maybe this somebody is Joyce's *Ulysses* whose story is about the secret of what it is to be human. The secret is the human, a secret as a question mark; this is what Beuys appears to mean when he writes: "I can see that my researches are most clearly expressed in question marks in. I came to this opinion through drawing."[45] A large part of the drawings of the secret bloc bears two signs as a title: "------?" They show that the drawing is not just a line-drawn but also an interaction between the straight and the curvature of a line, as well as the dot. The presence of the dot in the question mark does not only represent an open and secretive end. More precisely, what it makes visible is *not* the dot as, in the first instance, the absolutely indivisible and the geometrical in-itself that presents an ultimate reference, but a dot as plastic, as a minimal but visible circle. Question marks and stain-marks, line and colour; they coincide in Beuys' secret drawings. Stains of colour from fat or blood show the fat and blood as signs. These secret drawings are inspired by the drawings of Leonado da Vinci and Albrecht Dürer. They follow them in the sense that they show how the drawn line already is a colour, that it is not about depicting symbols but about

45 • Joseph Beuys, *The secret block for a secret person in Ireland*, 48.

making free and visible the "real powers that exist in the world,"[46] standing in "relation to a birth."

Beuys' words about "a relation to a birth" specify the way in which, in his secret drawings, form is a "preparation." But rather than understanding a drawing as a preparation for a later complete form, Beuys' drawings show us that form is itself a preparation. It is hence about the contradictory experience of perfected preparations. We would understand these drawings better were we to regard them as preparations without finality, preparations not striving towards anything other than the continuation to prepare. In this respect, the drawings them-selves are full of new endings. They are "full (of) end." What does all this amount to? Beuys claims "we have not yet reached the art," since that which is called art does not know of any completion but is only the site for innumerable processes of creativity. Beuys speaks not from a standpoint *after art*, but from a *just before art*, from a *before,* or a *not-yet art*. He speaks from a praxis that cannot be defined as having either the completed work or the history of the work as its starting point. It remains an art not derivable from any idea of accumulation. Beuys describes a coming form and not a completed form. A forming form can be said to be a *coming to form*, though in Beuys' case it is not about a becoming that only happens through the constant farewells of previous forms. The forming form is an in-between where a *not yet* meets an *even further*. Hence Beuys understand-ing that "art" is a strange preparation for nothing, rather than for an idealized and determined form. A preparation without teleology, without the rationality of a purpose, is a preparation complete as preparation; preparation itself becomes form. Here, however, another contradiction appears: the formless form. With this contradiction Beuys wishes to shed light on a secret power harboured by the visual arts: a striving for, and the need to come to, a form at the same time as necessarily leaving form behind. The plasticity of the image, which Beuys understands as "preparation" and *not yet* art, is faithful to this secret of life. The forming power of life appears as a strange loss, a loss that supports the search for life forms at the same time as this search-ing force of life can never be satisfied. So as to be able to continue to live vitally, the loss and the longing — the openness of noth-ingness — must endure. Living is indistinguishable from neces-sary interruption and from the ongoing process towards death. A satisfied life is a dead life. In the eyes of vitality, everything that becomes form and action is nothing other than preparation. "Preparation is my life," Beuys insists.[47] This insistence reminds us of Heidegger's famous words: "paths, not works." To shape and to form, but to leave form and image also so as to remain on the routes of becoming, these things constitute the secret of

46 • Ibid, 49.
47 • Ibid, 10.

Beuys' preparations. *The secret bloc* focuses on an attuned insight into the appearing of life. Beuys speaks of metamorphoses, transsubstantializations, incarnations, resurrections, initiations and life actions. "Life course and work course run together but not as autobiography. Initiation through death in shamanism."[48] Beuys constantly speaks about the human being's preparations for humanity, because even human being is as yet to reach humanity — she cannot fulfill that which is not possible to consummate. The human being must always incarnate humanity, embody this not-yet, this *yet-not-now*. But to do this, she must learn to see what is completed as loss and to experience appearance through her own disappearing, as an absence present in a presence. It is about learning to see the event of movement, to cultivate a moving and mobile gaze and body.

The signs for this pedagogy of movement in Beuys' secret drawings are simple. The first image in this series depicts a very simple plant, which in the natural sciences is called *dianthus*, meaning a double plant or double flower. According to Beuys, the plant dianthus traces both an erotics of the flower and the blooming of eroticism. In Beuys way of drawing *dianthus* we can recognize Dürer's drawings. It is as if Beuy's drawings are a citation from the latter; they work, perhaps, as question marks, or maybe rather as the drawings' own citations. In these subtle citations we find a plasticity of being, of being in the middle of the forming of history, a plastic *inter-esse*. The secret drawings show what Beuys learned when, at the age of seventeen, he found a catalogue with reproductions of Wilhelm Lembruck's sculptures: there, every work of art ought to carry within itself traces and residues from the first days of Creation: the smell of soil and the sense of something animalistic.[49] Dianthus' double formation is repeated in endless variations in these drawings. Shown is the coincidence between presumed opposites — the active and the passive, the stone-like and the streaming, the female and the male, light and shade. The opposites coincide in a number of hermaphroditic and androgynous forms, each revealing themselves in each other as elements of life. They appear in each other's life and death, beginning and end, form and formlessness. The dianthus changes into a stream that then transforms into a deer horn, and that, in its turn, transforms into transforming engraved signs. The signs stem from the drawn body and not just from the drawing hands; they are made with drawing feet that show that legs are signs and signs are legs. They depict a nomadic element.[50] In these secret drawings one can discover that earth itself is nomadic. It is Eurasia's ground that is represented as moving transitions rather than depicting movements to walk over. The drawing feet are quick and energetic brisk and jolly, half animal and half vegetal, sketching and

48 • Ibid, 49.
49 • Ibid.
50 • Ibid.

looping, the feet show the nomadism of life out of which a person arises. The body that is drawing reveals the body — that is, the sculpture — as a living drawing, as drawn lines on the foundation of the world. These feet, stains and lines, these underlines and question marks, all of a sudden change into the figure of a hare woman (*Hasenfrau*) in whose empty stomach the formation of this event vibrates like the deer's horns drawn in the air. From the vegetal in the animal to the animal in the vegetal, from the human in the earth and to the earthly in human, Beuys follows "traces and residues of the first days of Creations." The secret drawings have no forms because they *are* the forming movements of form. This movement seeks a completed form, which would make visible their formless forming force. But because such a form would be the death of force, a force that would no longer strive for anything else — it must seek a way beyond form. Beuys once said to his friend, Hagen Lieberknecht, that "the purpose of Western thinking and the science that grew from it was to reach material, but one only does that through death."[51] For Beuys this means that matter is reached in its transformation to stone and in its petrifying transformation. Among the "secret drawings" there are some "self-portraits." Along the drawn-lines that rest on water, lines transformed into stone are visible. We see there the dead person, the human as stone. Life is the forming of matter but this concomitantly means that every material form to which life reaches always remains a preparation, since it is always already beyond itself, it is always already another. "The secret drawings" show that living forms –that which is stone-like or animal, divine or earthly, human or non-human — are preparations for preparations.

The secret bloc collects the gaze in the forming of matter, between absence and presence, time and space, life and death, between what comes and what goes. It is a nomadic gaze. Beuys' drawings show the way in which the human herself is a sign — a sign without interpretation — that has very nearly lost its language on foreign shores. *The secret bloc for a secret person in Ireland* is Beuys' gift dedicated to the secret beginning of things: the sign's drawing movement on the nomadic ground of life. •

Marcia Sá Cavalcante Schuback is Professor of Philosophy at Södertörn University. Recent publications include *Being With the Without* (ed. with Jean-Luc Nancy, 2013), *Phenomenology of Eros* (ed. with Jonna Bornemark, 2012), and *Att tänka i skisser: Essäer om bildens filosofi & filosofins bilder* (2011).

51 • Ibid.

Somatic Materialism or "Is it Possible to do a Phenomenology of Affect?"

Susan Kozel

Writing while standing on my head

I have reached the stage in writing this journal article where I want to throw out all the words. I am also about to give a presentation where I want to avoid all visuals. This is not to say that I dislike words or mistrust visuals. I love words, I relish reading and writing, and I delight in sensuous visual narratives. I swim in words and visuals, but right now they seem to follow patterns that are stifling.

Writing on phenomenology, affect, and somatics is tying me in knots. It is forcing parts of me to stay silent so that other parts may be noticed. It is asking me to do something radically different with words and with the flow of ideas, to invert or turn inside-out the story of what I am doing and why. It is not asking, it is demanding that I do something different. Yelling at me even, and doing what mules or small children do when you ignore them: stubbornly refusing to move. Just not doing what you want them to do. OK. So I stop. What now? "We're going to be late you know." "It seems you don't care." "Let's hum a tune. Look around. Feel our feet. Sit on the ground. Stare at the sky. Get very wet in the rain until you are ready to move. Take a deep breath…"

Perhaps I can write this standing on my head, or while I am shouting very loudly so that I cannot hear my usual narratives, concepts, or arguments. I want to write it from my peripheral vision. (I confess to have written the above paragraphs without my glasses, as a sort of intellectual protest against the usual structures of clarity, the visual blurriness letting my thoughts realign.)

I am aware that this sounds incredibly pretentious.

This writing conundrum is a direct result of an ongoing artistic research process into affect, dance, and mobile technologies in urban. The project is called *AffeXity*; it is a collaboration with screen dance artist Jeannette Ginslov and others.[1] We have set ourselves a challenge of creating short dance improvisations in urban locations that emerge from and reveal affective qualities. These are captured on video, edited, and then will be re-located using an Augmented Reality browser. The AR application running on mobile phones lets us locate the choreography in physical space using either GPS coordinates or small black and white "tags" called QR codes or fiduciary markers. Once the choreography of a fragment of affect is pinned, or tagged, to a spot in a city it can then be visited by anyone who happens to have a phone running the application.[2]

We began by improvising and recording movement sequences in Malmö and Copenhagen, but intend to expand these practices of performing affect to other sites. The choreographies can live in alternate media layers of any city. Not exactly invisible, they exist in Alternate Realities (a better deployment of the letters A and R). Embedded in the city, they are at the same time highly intimate because they live in your city, on your phone, in your pocket. If the project progresses as we intend, the small video choreographies will be augmented not just by the technologies but by people as they add their own choreographies, or annotate and remix existing ones. The AR browsers we are currently exploring are open source and free, and are intended to be used as readily as one might send a text or consult a map application on a phone, but they are not yet as sophisticated in handling video as we would like.[3] As usual, artistic research pushes at the edges of technological functionality.

The *AffeXity* project has the goal of sliding from somatic activity (tapping into affect in our bodies and in the city) to social activity (creating a social practice where people will want to add their expressive physical movement to the cities in the form of short videos in their cities). This journey from the somatic to

1 • Collaborators for the first phase of artistic research include Jeannette Ginslov (screen choreography), Wubkje Kuindersma (dance), Niya Lulcheva (dance), Timo Engelhardt (media application programming), Maria Engberg and Jay David Bolter (technical consultation for Argon AR browser), Karolina Rosenquist (audience development). I provide the artistic direction and some dance improvisation. The project is based at the Medea Collaborative Media Initiative of Malmö Högskola in Malmö, Sweden.
2 • These early artistic research phases are discussed in Kozel,"AffeXity: Performing Affect," *Fibreculture* issue 21 (2012). twentyone.fibreculturejournal.org
3 • Currently we are exploring two augmented reality browsers, Argon (argon.gatech.edu/) and Aurasma (www.aurasma.com/)

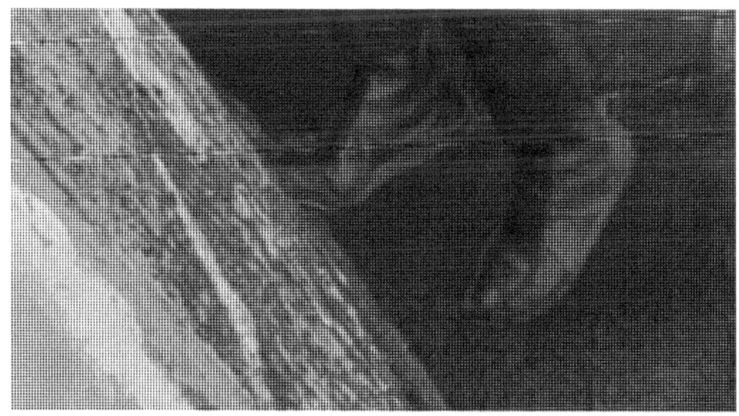

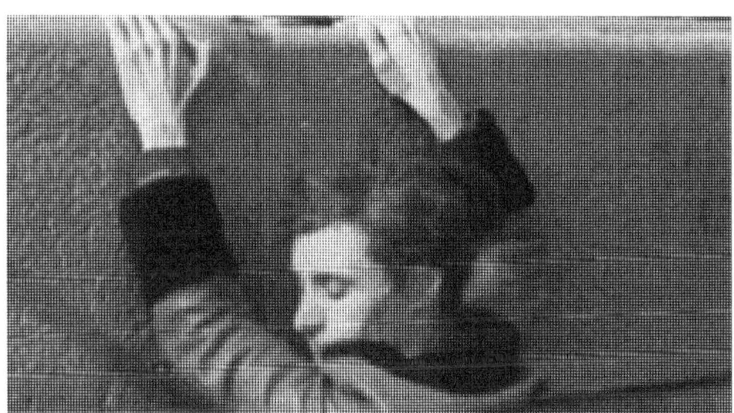

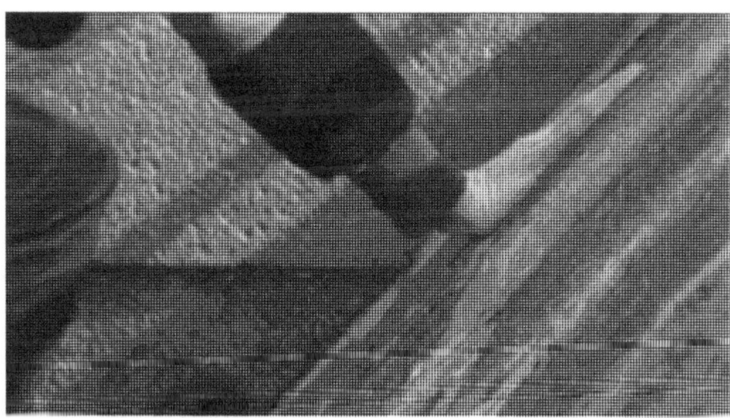

From video of second phase of *AffeXity* development,
images Jeannette Ginslov, Malmö 2012.

the social flows in the opposite direction from most of our media which are filtered through social or public spheres and pound incessantly on our somatic bodies. In the process we will lend a small slice of social media a deeper degree of embodiment and expressivity, at the same time as opening out choreographic impulses into the city using mobile media technologies.

There are multiple ways to situate the somatic, and a resulting lack of clarity around it. This lack of clarity is not surprising since it generally refers to an immanent level of experience, deep within the body, and somewhat resistant to language. Historically, somatics encompasses a set of practices involving touch, internal imagery, or movement that originated in the early twentieth century as a way to overcome physical trauma or to expand expressive range.[4] Somatics attends to the internally perceived body rather than the externally perceived body. There are methodological implications. Observation is accomplished from the first person viewpoint, with importance placed on proprioception, kinaesthesia, and internal visualisation as modes of sensory apprehension. As a result, "a categorically different phenomenon is perceived: the human soma."[5] An analytic stance notes that the somatic body is more than a "hunk of meat" mechanistically conceived and existing in opposition to the activities of the mind. The soma has intelligence, a particular logic, and myriad ways of holding and revealing memory.[6] Further, an ontological layer to somatics is valuable for reminding us that focus is never constrained to the being of an isolated body, but reveals the "embodied-belonging-together-on-the-earth."[7] A scientific perspective was provided by none other than Edmund Husserl in 1912. He established "somatology" as the science of the animate organism: "a material science to the extent that it investigates the material properties of the animate organism."[8] Contemporary approaches to the somatic combine the methodological, analytic, ontological, and scientific to differing degrees.

While devising *AffeXity* I realized I had to move differently as a dancer, to suspend my movement habits. I was dismayed, I will admit, by just how deeply my movement patterns, qualities, or improvisational gestures were engrained. We dancers like to think that when we improvise we are in a golden zone of free creative movement, but it is not so. There exist many techniques and strategies for helping dancers, musicians and theatre practitioners stay in the

4 • Examples include Alexander Technique, Feldenkrais, Rosen Method, Rolfing, Body/Mind Centering, Ideokinesis. See Don Hanlon Johnson, ed. *Bone, Breath, and Gesture: Practices of Embodiment* (Berkeley, CA: North Atlantic Books,1995).
5 • Thomas Hanna, "What is somatics?" in Johnson, *Bone, Breath, and Gesture*, 341.
6 • Johnson, *Bone, Breath, and Gesture*, XV
7 • Jeffrey Maitland, *Spacious Body: Explorations in Somatic Ontology* (Berkeley, CA: North Atlantic Books, 1995), XVIII.
8 • Edmund Husserl, *Phenomenology and the Foundations of the Sciences, Third Book, Ideas Pertaining to a Pure Phenomenology and to a Phenomenological Philosophy*, trans. Ted E. Klein and William E. Pohl (The Hague: Martinus Nijhoff Publishers,1980), 7.

moment, or for short-circuiting predictability or staleness. In deciding to move from affect rather than from form, narrative, impulse or even kinaesthetic sense, I had to stop my self from moving over and over again. Start again, no, start again, no, start again...[9] Patterns of writing and thought are also engrained. With this article, I had to start again, and again, and again, until I was writing (metaphorically) standing on my head.

Aisthesis

You are witnessing in words some of what we experienced as artists in the early stages of this project: the complexity of an artistic research project that avoids formal, aesthetic, and even kinaesthetic starting points in an attempt to work directly from affect. A phenomenology of affect is necessary to better understand the performance of affect, but first it must be argued that it is even possible to do a phenomenology of affect. Then some of the wider political or philosophical motivation for doing so can be unfolded, for affect is not just a pure internal force, it is distributed across bodies of all configurations: physical, social, structural, technological, and institutional.

From phenomenology of the senses to phenomenology of affect

There are many wonderful examples of phenomenological writing that explore, celebrate, or problematise the senses. Witness a memorable description of the taste of stone by architect and theorist Juhani Pallasmaa.

> Many years ago when visiting the DL James Residence in Carmel, California, designed by Charles and Henry Greene, I felt compelled to kneel and touch the delicately shining white marble threshold of the front door with my tongue. The sensuous materials and skilfully crafted details of Carlo Scarpa's architecture as well as the sensuous colours of Luis Barragan's houses frequently evoke oral experiences. Deliciously coloured surfaces of *stucco lustro*, a highly polished colour or wood surfaces also present themselves to the appreciation of the tongue.[10]

Pallasmaa's writing is striking for its sensory descriptions, also its emphasis on the synaesthetic or cross-modal transference across senses, in particular between touch and taste, and between vision and touch. Despite the tongue-on-the-marble-threshold somewhat having the quality of a stunt, or a dramatic gesture to prove a point, it is effective. It is clear that his passion is to expand not just our relation to architecture but to critique certain practices in the creation of physical structures in our environments. With relevance to artistic research, his phenomenologies take in the encounter with architecture as well as its creation. For

9 • Phenomenological descriptions of the processes of dance improvisation, video shooting, video editing and choreographic direction can be found in Kozel, "AffeXity: Performing Affect."
10 • Juhani Pallasmaa, *The Eyes of the Skin: Architecture and the Senses* (Chichester: John Wiley & Sons, 2005), 59.

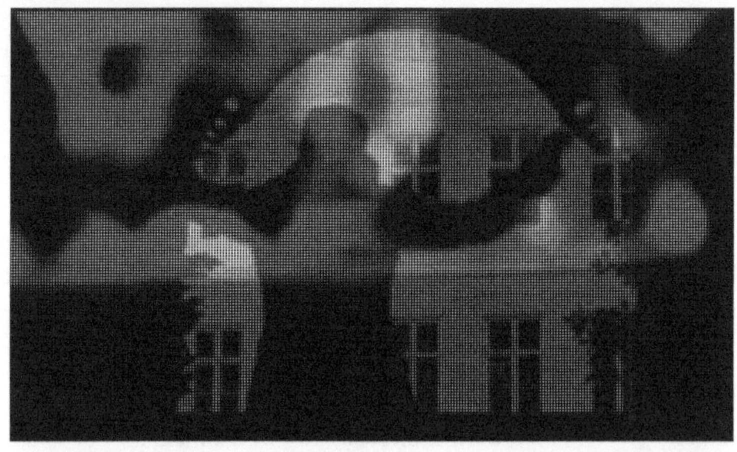

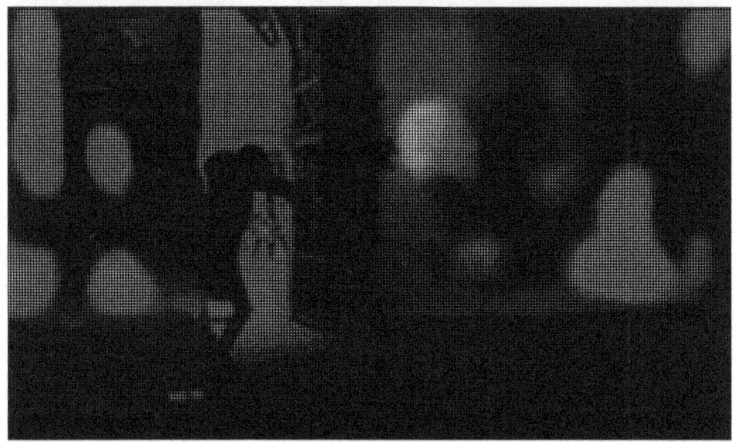

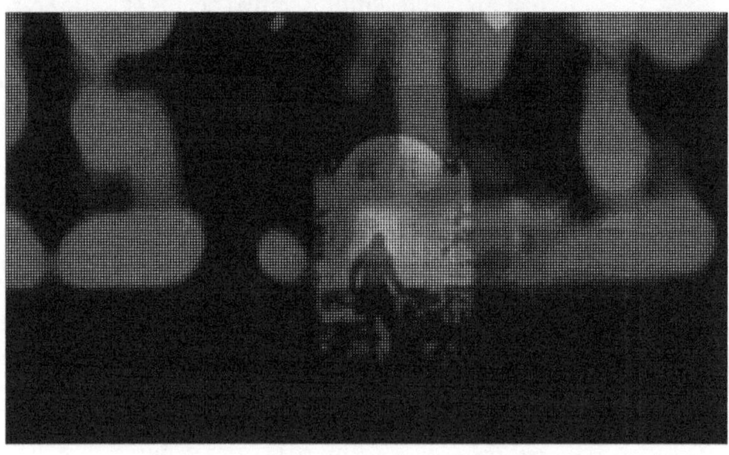

From *AffeXity* first phase, images Jeannette Ginslov,
dance Wupkje Kuindersma, Copenhagen 2011.

him, the problem with many of our dwellings today is that they do not offer potential transactions between body, imagination, senses, and the environment: he traces this absence back to how the design process facilitated by computers and software has become a "retinal journey."[11] The visual process of using software to design buildings has sacrificed the rest of the senses.

Aisthesis

Affect and the sensible are close, even overlapping, but they are not the same. This is also true of affect and the somatic. Affect occupies a different register from sense data, it is reliant on the senses but overspills them. Affect is reduced frequently to emotion but is more than "feelings." Further, it bleeds across the borders of a single body. Affect is more like a cloud: it is as likely to be creepy as euphoric and it does not just come from bodies, but encompasses objects, structures, animals, systems, and all things environmental. Recent research, both practical and theoretical, to refine a definition of affect has left me with this: affect is the passage of forces or intensities, between bodies that may be organic, inorganic, animal, digital, or fictional. It is located in the domain beyond reason, logic, or "conscious knowing."[12] This passage of intensities is like a vibration or a shimmering, in the sense that shimmering is based on change and is not a static state. Viewed this way, affect might travel through familiar states but it may also participate in the creation of something that did not exist previously, in what I am somewhat reductively calling "change."[13] I currently understand affect and the somatic in relation to one another. I hesitate to say whether one is a dimension of the other — perhaps it is too soon to tell, or perhaps that level of conceptual containment is inappropriate for the passage of intensities that characterizes both. I do know that a phenomenology of affect helps to open out, elaborate, and, to a certain extent, explain somatic experience.

In a recent talk at the Medea Collaborative Media Initiative in Malmö, artist and scholar Chris Salter presented his collaborative art installations that challenge the senses by being "just barely noticeable" or by bombarding visitors with overwhelming visual, aural, or tactile stimulation.[14] I asked him about the relation between affect and senses, wondering if they were somehow pinned together like sine curves or if, as with some of his work, they sometimes collided. I saw a collision or a variance between affect and the senses in the moments when very strong affective

11 • Ibid, 12.
12 • Gregory Seigworth and Melissa Gregg, "An Inventory of Shimmers," in Melissa Gregg and Gregory J. Seigworth (eds.), *The Affect Theory Reader* (Durham: Duke University Press, 2010), 1. See also Kozel, "AffeXity: Performing Affect with Augmented Reality."
13 • I notice that the directness of the word change is coming into favour, Peter Sloterdijk's newest book in English is called *You Must Change Your Life* (Cambridge: Polity, 2012).
14 • Medea's activities can be found at medea.mah.se, and an archived video of Chris Salter's talk (18 October 2012) medea.mah.se/2012/10/medea-talks-presents-chris-salter/

qualities were produced by extremely minimal sensations. Thinking on his feet, and basing his response on phenomenological recollections of his and others' experiences, he located senses and affect on a spectrum: indicating that affect is located at either extreme end of stimulation with senses in the middle.

This made me think of infra red and ultra violet, both intensities beyond the visual spectrum. Intensities are experienced somatically. Reflecting on my own experiences, I once saw waves of colour behind my eyelids, mainly indigo and dark electric purple, in the midst of the somatic practice called Rosen Method.[15] Ultraviolet blooms of colour characterised the somatic release, providing a fragment of physical experience to ground the important but otherwise abstract claim that a "processurally oriented materialism" yields "affectual bloom spaces."[16] These colour sensations were not directly pinned to clearly defined physical or emotional qualities. I was vaguely aware that the right side of my body was opening and lengthening but did not have any familiar sensations or memories of similar kinaesthetic or emotional events. Like Salter's suggestion that affect exists in a zone outside of familiar sensations, I was in the domain of affect rather that categorisation. I was experiencing a change in my corporeal schema.

Change is the goal of much somatic practice. Yet, in the worlds of art, design, and cultural discourse change, or transformation, are simultaneously contested and desired outcomes: change for whom? empty or authentic? at what cost? I will locate the possibility for change, for contingency, within the body and say that we can access and understand it by means of a phenomenology of affect; first it is worth seeing just how contentious (and ultimately desirable) this is by taking a philosophical detour through speculative materialism and the event of love.

Speculative Materialism

Pallasmaa relishes the way we encounter and make sense of the world through our bodies: "We behold, touch, listen and measure the world with our entire bodily existence, and the experiential world becomes organised and articulated around the centre of the body,"[17] but philosopher Quentin Meillassoux calls this the correlationist circle and rails against it. In Meillassoux's attempt to craft a new relation between thought and the absolute he is deeply troubled by how the sensible, "whether it be perceptive or affective," can only exist as "a relation between the world and the living creature that I am."[18] The sensible is neither in me nor in the thing-in-itself, it is effectively,

15 • See www.rosenmethod.com/ and the journal www.rosenjournal.org/ The practitioner I am fortunate to work with is Karen Vedel. Vedel is training in Rosen. She is a dance scholar and professor at the University of Copenhagen
16 • Gregg and Seigworth, "An Inventory of Shimmers," 14
17 • Pallasmaa, *The Eyes of the Skin*, 64.

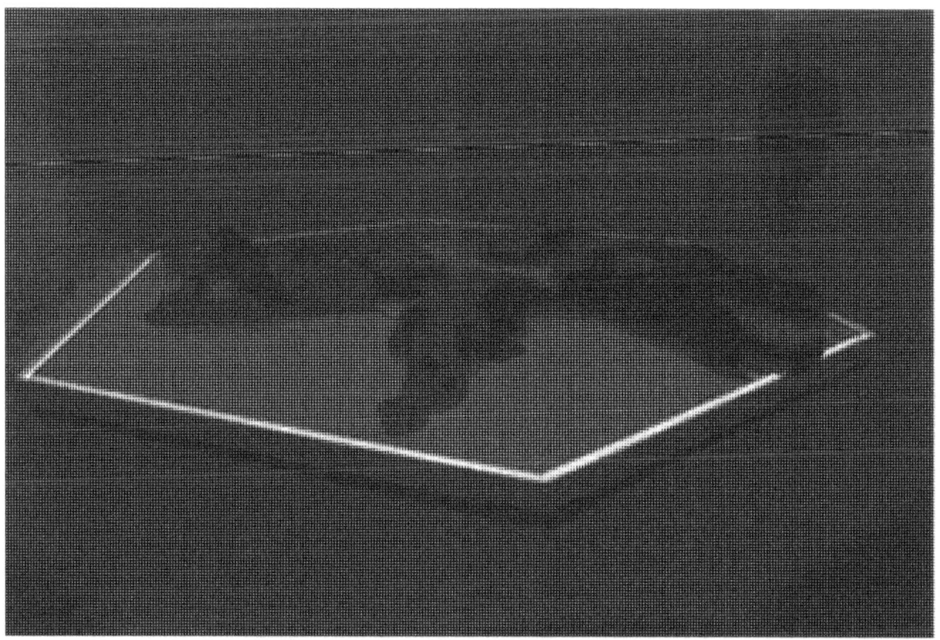

to use his term, a correlation. Meillassoux wants to escape this correlationist circle according to which we can only ever know anything through our own situated embodied perception, thus making it impossible to consider realms of subjectivity and objectivity independently from one another. Phenomenology is the most pernicious and perfidious example of correlationism.

Meillassoux's words reveal a strong sense of claustrophobia; I see it as an affective force behind his rejection of phenomenology. It is troubling for him that a person can only know something through her own perception and cognition, for this means she will always be outside those objects in the world she wants to understand. This yields a strange feeling of imprisonment or enclosure within this very exteriority (the "transparent cage"). For we are all well and truly imprisoned within this outside proper to language and consciousness given that we are *always-already* in it (the "always-already" accompanying the "co-" of correlationism as its other essential locution), and given that we have no access to any vantage point from whence we could observe these "object-worlds," which are the unsurpassable providers of all exteriority, from the outside. But if this outside seems to us to be a cloistered outside, an outside in which one may legitimately feel incarcerated, this is because in actuality such an outside is entirely relative, since it is—and this is precisely the point— relative to us.[19]

18 • Quentin Meillassoux, *After Finitude: An Essay on the Necessity of Contingency*, trans. Ray Brassier (London: Continuum, 2009), 2.
19 • Ibid, 7.

He pins the future of philosophical discourse on the possibility of escaping the correlationist circle, and his book *After Finitude* follows a logical structure of argumentation using the scientific example of ancestrality and an argument around facticity to reveal the instability of the claim that we cannot know the thing-in-itself. Ancestrality refers to science's ability to produce statements about events prior to the advent of life as well as consciousness.[20] In simple terms, if we can comprehend something that so far exceeds our human experience then we have escaped the containment of the correlationist circle.

Those who follow his writing believe that the only way for us to answer the problems facing us as nations and cultures, from global warming to migration, is to escape this containment in order to be able to think the new, or to be able to think a new absolute. This philosophical approach has been called "speculative realism" (a title Meillassoux does not support, preferring the term materialism to realism) and intends to "recuperate the pre-critical sense of 'speculation' as a concern with the Absolute" without denying the progress that was due to the labours of critique.[21] He has become the philosopher of radical change because he asserts "the absolute necessity of the contingency of everything."[22] Even more explicitly revealing the viability of change, he asserts "there is no reason for anything to be or to remain the way it is; everything must, without reason, be able not to be and/or be able to be other than it is."[23]

The celebration of radical contingency at the heart of the philosophical movement speculative materialism/realism can be seen as an attempt to glimpse a crack in what exists so that something else can slip through. Along with so many others, the philosophers who grapple with these ideas exhibit a vision (a desire? a hope?) that things can be otherwise: the philosopher sees his task as levering open a space in which this might happen. (I would normally say "his or her" task, but in the case of the philosophers loosely grouped under speculative realism there are almost no women.) Speculation is a sort of freedom from which other changes or possibilities for unprecedented thought and actions can follow.

In short, necessity constrains us, contingency opens up breathing space. Or does it? Can radical contingency become abstract and overwhelming?

Everything could actually collapse: from trees to stars, from stars to laws, from physical laws to logical laws; and this not by virtue of some superior law whereby everything is destined to perish, but by virtue of the absence of any

20 • Ibid, 9.
21 • Bryant, Levi, Nick Srnicek, and Graham Harman (eds.), *The Speculative Turn: Continental Materialism and Realism* (Melbourne: re.press, 2011), 3.
22 • Meillassoux, *After Finitude*, 62.
23 • Ibid, 69.

superior law capable of preserving anything, no matter what, from perishing [24]

A desire for change, for things to be other than they are, seems to require the abandonment of phenomenology and other sensory approaches to knowledge. Change seems to require an escape from the correlationist circle. However, as Ian Bogost neatly summarises, "speculative realists have not yet concerned themselves with particular implementation," their metaphysics has not yet become a practice, it remains in the domain of grappling with first principles. It is not at all clear how (or if) it is possible to have a "pragmatic speculative realism." [25]

The event of love

On the way to somatics let's be distracted for a moment by love. Alain Badiou discusses love. He praises it. He says that once the One is disrupted by the difference of viewing the world as Two the world is experienced in a new way. This experience gives rise to a risky and contingent form: it becomes an encounter. "Love always starts with an encounter. And I would give this encounter the quasi-metaphysical status of an event, namely of something that doesn't enter into the immediate order of things."[26] There is an implicit sliding scale of disruption from experience (not really offering something new), to encounter (disrupting the order of things), to event (radical contingency). Never far from the surface of discussions of contingency or the event is the deep desire for the possibility of change: perhaps a glimmer; perhaps an explosion.

As a philosophical approach, phenomenology is both vulnerable and frequently under attack, at the same time as it is extremely robust in the ways it is applied by practitioners such as artists, dancers, architects, musicians, pedagogues, and designers. Rarely has a philosophical current been so condemned in some quarters but at the same time so tenacious. Those who are committed to expanding and challenging phenomenology as a practice know the problems with classical or traditional phenomenology. These have been rehearsed (and dealt with) many times: transcendentalist, reduction to *corps propre*, elevation of the male universalist subject, solipsistic, concerned merely with the structures of consciousness, and now correlationist.

However, Badiou's discussion of love, and indeed his entire vast project around logic and the event, opens the most significant critique a pragmatic approach to phenomenology must address: the limitations of experience. He asserts that it is "essential to grasp that

24 • Ibid, 53.
25 • Ian Bogost, *Alien Phenomenology or What It's Like to Be a Thing* (Minneapolis: University of Minnesota Press, 2012), 29.
26 • Badiou, with Nicolas Truong, *In Praise of Love*, trans. Peter Bush (London: Serpent's Tail, 2012), 28.

the construction of the world on the basis of difference is quite distinct from the experience of difference."[27] The mere experience of difference implies that the sensory patterning is only marginally disrupted. In effect, we have our experiences along a continuum. This relates directly to the difficulties of circumventing habit in the improvisations and choreographic patterns around *AffeXity*, or of any use of media in our media-saturated age: media is all around us but how much of it is created or consumed with any critical or disruptive potential? Are our experiences expanded or dampened as they are reproduced? What of that which turns us upside down, which makes us catch our breath, or stop in our tracks in the face of the previously unexperienced? This, for Badiou, is an encounter or an event such as love, "an encounter is not an experience, it is an event that remains quite opaque an only finds reality in its multiple resonances within the real world."[28] It amounts to constructing a world from a "decentred point of view."[29] It does not reaffirm one's own identity.

The event is in need of a recalibration. I agree with Bogust when he expresses concern that for Badiou "events are not commonplace affairs. Rather, they are wholesale changes." Bogust observes that "Badiou's ontology appears incapable of describing the ordinary being of things, limiting itself to the extraordinary being of human change."[30] I can be accused of thinking small. Intimate. Acts of movement or perception that begin with a step, a breath, or a shift of weight. I reject the notion that, with the exception of rare and dramatic moments, change is extraordinary or somehow outside the human's scope. This is where the sensibility of the dancer can help: contingency is motion but not all motion offers contingency. Change is what repetition permits, what many repeated moments of technical execution (lifting a leg) or perceptual awareness (sensing the flow of your body's subtle energies) can yield: contingency within continuity. Somatic experiences offer a glimpse into the event as it is embedded deep within the body. Radical contingency within flesh, or just contingency within flesh?

Somatic Materialism
And here my words begin to falter again. This time because I am only just beginning to explore what somatic materialism might be. In scholarly terms, I am at the beginning of a research programme that has philosophical and artistic currents. When I am at a loss conceptually, or aware that my attempts to force concepts into shape enacts violence upon them prior to the unfolding their actual shape, I turn to experience.

27 • Ibid, 23.
28 • Ibid, 24.
29 • Ibid, 25.
30 • Bogost, *Alien Phenomenology*, 28.

Above I described internally seeing ultraviolet blooms during the practice of Rosen Method. On another occasion while working with Vedel, I had the experience that ignited my fascination with the somatic in terms of phenomenological practice: I felt something that was nothing. I felt and did not feel." She said "look at that," and I felt nothing, but something at the same time.[31] A nothing that was something. To use other words, what I felt was not something I knew *how* to feel, thus grounding the claim that with somatics there is "no knew knowledge, only new knowing."[32] It was beyond my ability to sense, so it felt like an open space. A gap. An openness. It was disconcerting that such a strange void could open up in my body, but also a source of relief and fascination precisely because something so unknown was part of my body. I saw it as the possibility for something new, but it was opaque. In my description of this event it is possible to detect an affective tone of pleasure relating to discovery, but it is also important to state that my initial affective response to this alienness was a desire to shut it down, to run from it, and retrench into the familiar. The affective quality of a somatic event tends to be multiple and contradictory.

A few words on the alien are useful as this article draws to a close. For Bogost, the alien is everywhere around us but a latent assumption in his *Alien Phenomenology* is that we are clear and known to ourselves. We have to look beyond our own bodies for alienness. It is outside of us that is unknown, provoking "benighted wanderings in an exotic world of utterly incomprehensible objects." He sets philosophers the task of amplifying "the black noise of objects."[33] Bernhard Waldenfels in his *Phenomenology of the Alien*, however, sees corporeality and alienness as "intimately connected." Somatic materialism as I sketch it, is consistent with his assertion that a "corporeal being is never entirely present to itself."[34]

Somatic practice reveals that a form of contingency is located in the body. It might not be radical, but if radical contingency is a severance from all we know then it is possible to ask how we can identify it sufficiently to even notice or be aware of it, or as Waldenfels would say, how we might attend to it. There is a dimension to his thought that is consistent with process or practice. "When something comes to a person's attention, at first he does not know with what or whom he is dealing. Attending itself is the first response to the alien."[35] The practice of attending underpins phenomenology.

31 • It is somewhat difficult to describe the directionality of action with Rosen, because the practitioner does not work on the other body, does not manipulate, but works with the body to "meet the tension with her touch, to sink in, show possibilities, and stop if there is resistance." (Vedel email correspondence nov 2012) I see it as a sort of affective duet rather than having someone "do" something to me.

32 • Johnson, 62.

33 • Bogost, *Alien Phenomenology*, 34.

34 • Bernhard Waldenfels, *Phenomenology of the Alien*, trans. Alexander Kozin and Tanja Stähler (Evanston, Illinois: Northwestern University Press, 2011), 43.

35 • Ibid, 58.

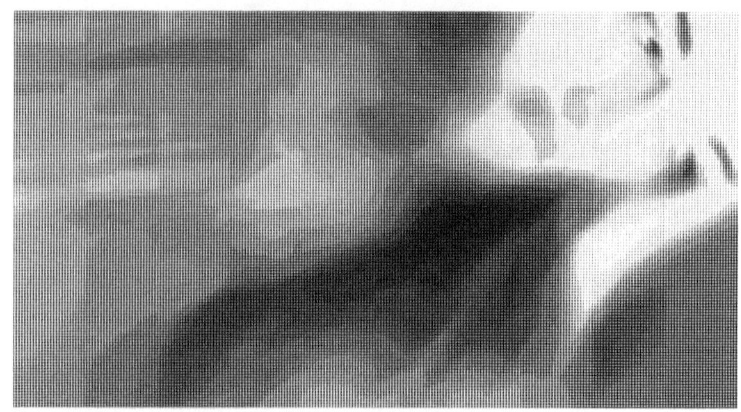

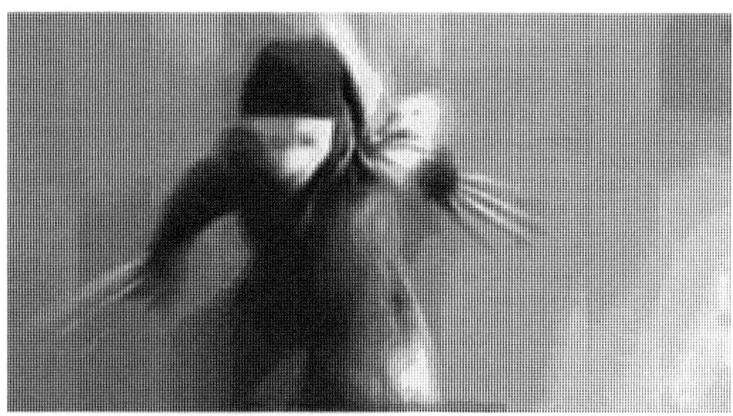

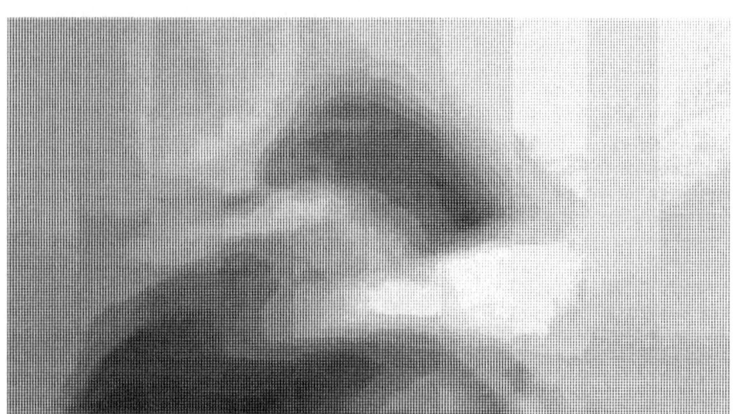

From *AffeXity* first phase, images Jeannette Ginslov,
dance Wupkje Kuindersma, Copenhagen 2011.

As a practical philosophy, phenomenology is not a system, not a dogmatic set of instructions. It is a sensibility and a way of living in the world. In scholarly terms it is concerned with the construction and validation of knowledge, and it is utterly essential for it to be transformed from its original tenets: for it to be challenged, revised, reworked, critiqued, dismantled, and reassembled. This is akin to the artistic process, or what designers do when they set in motion iterative cycles of design. The practicality of phenomenology is that while it is not simply a set of instructions, it is possible to implement it. This responds to a desire for an applied or pragmatic approach to philosophy. My somatic experience of "something that was nothing or nothing that was something" works in counterpoint with the improvisatory practices of *AffeXity* to expand my phenomenological practice from a phenomenology of the senses to a phenomenology of affect. In effect, sense data is replaced with affective intensities. Or they intertwine.

For Badiou, love constitutes a kind of resistance against "the obscenity of the market and the current political disarray on the left."[36] For Meillassoux and those who expand his ideas, the necessary of contingency has a tone of emancipation from the straightjacket of the contemporary intellectual landscape and the insanity of global politics. Somatic materialism, a term I may or may not hold onto, is the corporeal parallel. Contingency, or simply change, can be located in the body and can be, if not exactly understood, touched or explored by a phenomenology of affect — perhaps in the way Pallasmaa touched his tongue to the marble threshold.

Responding to the question: "Is it possible to do a phenomenology of affect?" My answer is yes, with continued refinement of our practices of reflection and capacities for attention, combined with an openness to witness what might arise even if we have no way of immediately understanding, integrating, or even facing it. Somatics has been called fiercely pragmatic.[37] Phenomenology can be that way too. •

Thanks to Jeannette Ginslov, Wupkje Kuindersma and Karen Vedel for permission to reproduce images and words.

Susan Kozel is Professor of New Media at MEDEA Collaborative Media Initiative, Malmö University. Her most recent book is *Closer: Performance, Technologies, Phenomenology* (2007).

36 • Badiou, 95.
37 • Johnson, Bone, Breath, and Gesture, 60.

Media/McLuhan

**Thierry de Duve
Richard Cavell
Wolfgang Ernst
Staffan Ericsson
Dan Karlholm**

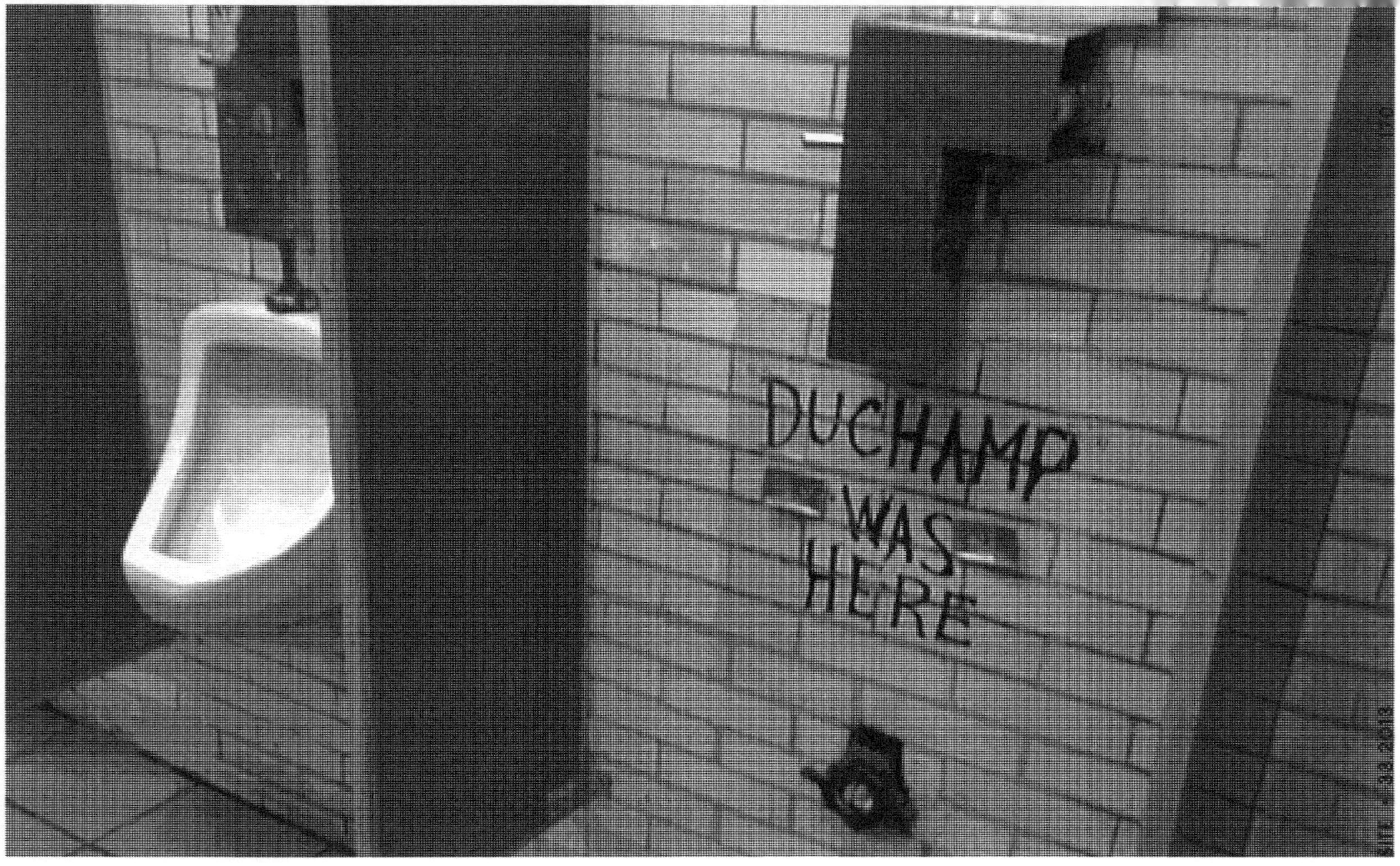

DUCHAMP
WAS
HERE

Media/McLuhan

Duchamp the Messenger of Art Unlimited

Thierry de Duve

As chance would have it, today's invitation came in on the day my colleague, Alexander Nehamas, professor at Princeton, sent me this photo. I also came in the wake of two other invitations, which had imposed themes that prompted my choice of subject. The Akademie der Künste in Berlin has launched a series of lectures under the umbrella title "*Grenzenlos Kunst*". The full English title was "Art Unlimited: Questioning the Issue of Art in the Arts of Today." And for its Graduate Summer Institute, the Film and Visual Arts Department at York University in Toronto also launched a series of lectures, for which it chose the umbrella title "Where is the Medium?" The juxtaposition of "Art Unlimited" and "Where is the Medium?," that is, of a question pertaining to the possible dissolution of the arts (in the plural) into art (in the singular), and a question pertaining to the possible disappearance of medium-specificity in what Rosalind Krauss has dubbed the "post-medium condition" — that juxtaposition, I believe, is not fortuitous. Adorno's *Verfransung* of the arts — their erosion or unraveling at the fringes — seems to be back on the agenda, and with the same whiff of anxiety it had back in 1967, when Adorno wrote "*Die Kunst und die Künste*" (Art and the arts). As you know, Adorno wrote from the perspective of someone who philosophized on art taking music as his paradigm of an art medium.

John Cage was then the most advanced composer Adorno mentioned to illustrate an art practice where increased emphasis placed on spirit or concept paradoxically led to the identification of the medium with the bare phenomenality of its mundane, non-artistic material. For someone like myself who theorizes art taking the visual arts as his paradigm, it was not difficult to see Marcel Duchamp looming behind John Cage. His name condenses the issues that were at stake then and that are apparently at stake again, now. Indeed, in his presentation of the "Art Unlimited" theme at the Berlin Academy, Robert Kudielka referred to "Duchamp's ground-breaking work" as having authorized "a widespread practice of installation and performance art [...] that suspends the aesthetic difference between art and reality." To say that the aesthetic difference between art and reality has been suspended is not unlike identifying the medium with the bare phenomenality of its mundane, non-artistic material. It virtually amounts to saying that anything can be art. Such has indeed been the message Duchamp's "ground-breaking work," or part of his work, namely the readymades, have broadcast. It is to this message that my title, "Duchamp the Messenger of Art Unlimited," refers. It would be exaggerated to the point of absurdity to pretend that Duchamp invented "Art Unlimited" as if it were a new art or a new medium or a new style or a new genre. Given that the gist of the expression "Art Unlimited" is that nowadays anything can be art, it is clear that something like a situation or a condition is thereby designated. Let's admit that "Art Unlimited" names the system we find ourselves in, after Duchamp.

Now, except perhaps in Alexander Nehamas's photo, what we mean by "after Duchamp" is by no means simple. We certainly mean to say that Duchamp's "ground-breaking work," or his readymades, or the concept of the readymade, had an impact on the art world, or on the world *tout court*, if we believe the photo. But this is not as simple as claiming that his work influenced artists who came after him. By the way, when does that start? At his death, in October 1968? When his influence began to be felt? Or when he actually made the work that would later prove to be "ground-breaking"? Whatever the answer, the sense we all have that, after Duchamp, things are no longer the same makes us spontaneously lend him too much. After Duchamp anything can be art, whereas before Duchamp there were rules, conventions, genres, art forms or mediums, in the plural. For something to be art, it had to be a painting, or a sculpture, or a poem, or a piece of music, etc. For somebody to be an artist, he or she had to be a painter, a sculptor, a poet or a musician. But as Allan Kaprow stated, in 1958: "Young artists of today need no longer say, 'I am a painter' or 'a poet' or 'a dancer'. They are

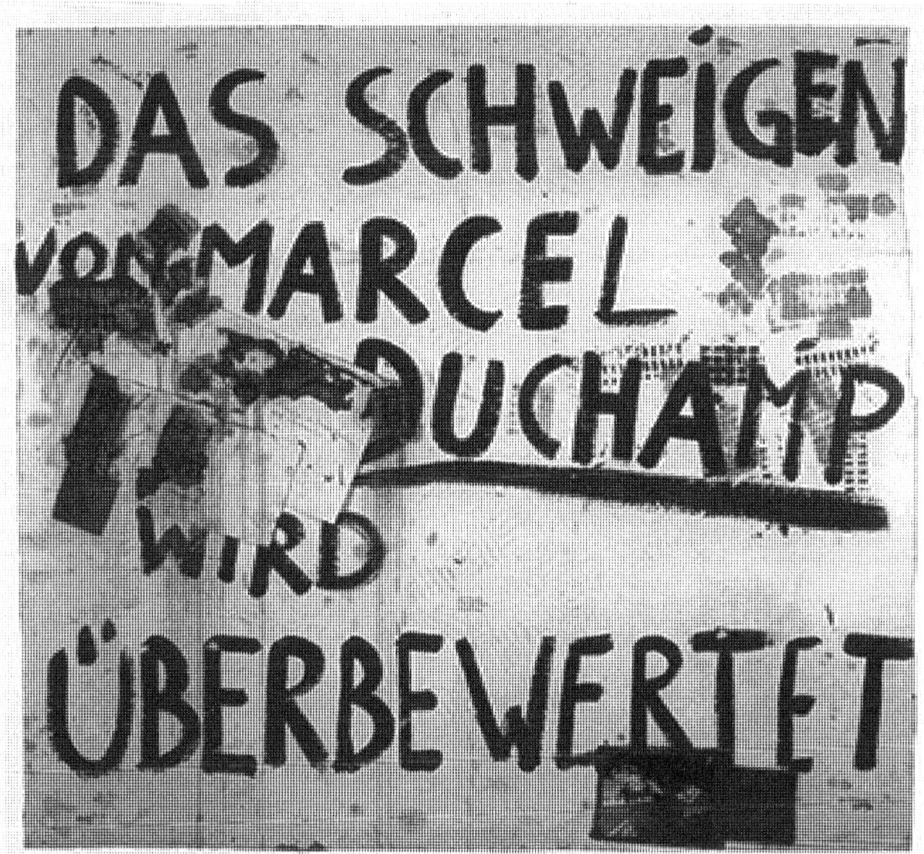

simply 'artists'." Artists, period; artists, unlimited; artists who
are free to make art out of anything and everything. Can a single
individual, even one of Duchamp's stature, be made responsible
for such a sea change in the institution of art? Can he be made to
author, not just a body of work but a whole new definition of art
as well? I don't believe so. Duchamp is not the author of "Art
Unlimited," he is merely its messenger. His achievement is that
he brought us the news that the system of art production, circulation and consumption had changed and that what we call art
became generalized to the point of "unlimitedness".

The subject of my talk is therefore the passage from
one art system to another, the passage, namely, from the Beaux-
Arts system to the "Art Unlimited" system. (Incidentally, I want
"Beaux-Arts" to remain in French, for reasons that will become
clear as I go along.) I will argue in eight points: 1) that the awareness that anything could be art dates from the sixties and has
everything to do with the reception of Duchamp's work and the
sudden fame his readymades acquired for the generations of
Pop, Minimal and Conceptual artists; 2) that on the whole, the

sixties interpreted Duchamp's message in reverse: most artists and critics of the time thought that when anything can be art, then anybody can be an artist, whereas in truth the message spells out: when anybody can be an artist, then anything can be art; 3) that in 1917, when Duchamp's message was mailed in the guise of a urinal titled *Fountain*, the fact that anybody could be an artist was not anodyne: it suggested that the Beaux-Arts system had collapsed; 4) that the collapse of the Beaux-Arts system entailed the passage to a new system, in which we consciously live only since the sixties but unconsciously at least since 1917, and which we may indeed call the "Art Unlimited" system; 5) that the passage in question was symbolically accomplished in 1884, with the creation of the Paris Société des Artistes Indépendants, after which the New York Society of Independent Artists, where Duchamp submitted his famous or infamous urinal, was modeled when it was founded in 1916; 6) that the theoretical condition for the said passage involved a change of paradigm, crystallized at the 1863 Salon des Refusés: the relevant formula for aesthetic judgment ceased to be graded on a continuous scale but instead became an all or nothing binary choice (accepted or refused); 7) that the negative aesthetic judgment by which works were refused at the Salon unwittingly created the category of "non-art," whose invention was subsequently and erroneously credited to Duchamp or the Dadaists in general; 8) that it is only when it became clear, in the sixties, that non-art was a sub-category of art, that the final collapse of the Beaux-Arts system and the advent of the "Art Unlimited" system were acknowledged. So...

1) In 1981, when Ben Vautier did this box-shaped work, what the box stated — *Since Duchamp one can put anything into this box* — was already common knowledge for anyone familiar with contemporary art. Since when was it a fact that anything could enter the box of art, and since when was that fact common knowledge? Those are two different questions: when has Duchamp's message been mailed? And when did it arrive? Excluding two rather obscure shows at the Sidney Janis Gallery in New York in the early fifties, the first public appearance of *Fountain* occurred in Duchamp's very first retrospective, at the Pasadena Museum of Art, in 1963. Success was instantaneous. Signs abound that by the next year the art world as a whole had acknowledged receipt of Duchamp's message. In 1964, a Milan gallerist, Arturo Schwarz, requested from Duchamp the right to issue replicas of a series of some ten readymades, in eight exemplars each. Warhol's exhibition of *Brillo* and other boxes at the Stable Gallery that year was hardly conceivable without the precedent of the readymades. And the same can be said about

Rauschenberg winning the grand prize at the Venice Biennale in the same year: his "Combine Paintings" might not have made such a triumph had the incorporation of readymades into painting not already exploded the boundaries of the medium. But the surest sign that Duchamp's message had been registered is Joseph Beuys's 1964 televised performance in which he painted a sign that said: "*Das Schweigen von Marcel Duchamp wird überbewertet.*"

2) In later interviews, Beuys gave explanations of his 1964 critique of Duchamp:

I criticize him because at the very moment when he could have developed a theory on the basis of the work he had accomplished, he kept silent. And I am the one who, today, develops the theory he could have developed. He entered this object [the urinal] into the museum and noticed that its transportation from one place to another made it into art. But he failed to draw the clear and simple conclusion that every human being is an artist (*Jeder Mensch ist ein Künstler*).

Media/McLuhan

Beuys may have been disingenuous when he claimed to have drawn his theory that "every human being is an artist" from Duchamp's transportation of a urinal into the museum, whereas in fact he derived it from his belief in creativity as *the* fundamental human faculty. But this matters little here. What matters is that Beuys got both the facts about Duchamp and their interpretation wrong. As we shall see in a minute, it is not true that Duchamp transported a urinal into the museum, and it is wrong to claim that the conclusion Duchamp should have drawn was that everyone is an artist. What also matters is that Beuys is far from alone in making this mistake. The sixties are a decade of extraordinarily creative misprisions — creative, yes, but misprisions all the same, inventive misreadings of Duchamp's message. Beuys shares the theory that everyone is or should be an artist with virtually everybody in the sixties, for example with his Fluxus colleague Robert Filliou: "*Oui, oui, voilà, oui! Tout le monde sera un artiste!*," or with art critic Jack Burnham:

Obviously it is no longer important who is or is not a good artist; the only sensible question is — as is already grasped by some young people — why isn't everybody an artist?

Why indeed, since on the art market everybody is free to try his or her luck? Unlike the profession of architect, that of artist — in the sense of painter or sculptor but also in the sense of Kaprow's artist at large — is not licensed. This might have been Duchamp's tongue-in-cheek reply to Burnham, but it certainly wasn't what Burnham had in mind. Burnham meant that when the field of art has become *unlimited* and anything could be art, then it is not just the prospect but also the very status of being an artist that should be open to anybody. Burnham, Filliou, Beuys and many other protagonists of the art world of the sixties and seventies interpreted Duchamp's message in reverse: they noticed that anything could be art, and they concluded that therefore anybody could be an artist. When one takes the historical facts into account, when one studies the actual circumstances in which Duchamp mailed his message, so to speak, then one realizes that the correct reasoning runs the other way: when anybody can be an artist, then it is about time to show that anything can be art.

3) As I said, Duchamp's urinal first appeared publicly in 1963, in the Pasadena retrospective. However, it had made a semi-public appearance in the early forties when it was included, in miniature, in the *Boîte-en-valise*, Duchamp's personally staged mini-museum retrospective consisting of reproductions of his works, reserved for the collectors who were foolish or intelligent enough to buy the *Boîte*. Therein we learn, thanks to a label, that Duchamp was the author of a work entitled *Fountain*, belonging to the category of ready-mades, dated New York, 1917, and signed by the name Richard Mutt. This is enough of an incentive to walk up the historical trail and investigate *The Richard Mutt Case*, as it came to be known. In 1912, the young Duchamp, who was very seriously initiating himself into Cubism, submitted a painting entitled *Nu descendant un escalier* to the Salon des Indépendants in Paris. The hanging committee of the Cubist room, which had Duchamp's brothers sitting on it, rejected the painting, and Marcel felt deeply humiliated. The painting eventually got rehabilitated a year later when Walter Pach selected it for the Armory Show in New York, where it was hailed and lampooned by the local press as the epitome of European avant-garde art. This earned Duchamp a tremendous if scandalous reputation thanks to which, in 1916, he was invited among the twenty founders of the New York Society of Independent Artists and was named chair of the hanging committee of the Society's first show, scheduled for April 1917. Painfully aware that the Paris Indépendants had betrayed their principles — *Ni récompense ni jury* — Duchamp was determined to take his revenge at the expense of their innocent New York counterpart, whose motto likewise stated, *No jury no prizes*. Under the pseudonym of R. Mutt, he submitted a urinal entitled *Fountain*, certain that it

would be censored the way his *Nude Descending a Staircase* had been in Paris five years before. He was right: the urinal was censored and never shown. We know this, not because a scandal occurred there and then — there was no scandal at all during the show — but because Alfred Stieglitz agreed to photograph the rejected *Fountain* and because the photo he took was published in a little magazine called *The Blind Man* (whose main and secret editor was of course Duchamp), accompanied by an editorial that stated:

> They say any artist paying six dollars may exhibit. Mr. Richard Mutt sent in a fountain. Without discussion this article disappeared and never was exhibited.

In reminding the readers that "any artist paying six dollars may exhibit," the editorial was referring to a bylaw written in the statuses of the Society of Independent Artists:

> Any artist, whether a citizen of the United States or of any foreign country, may become a member of the Society upon filing an application therefor, paying the initiation fee and the annual dues of a member, and exhibiting at the exhibition in the year that he joins.

The initiation fee amounted to one dollar and the annual membership dues to five, which explains the editorial of *The Blind Man* but also the sarcasm of the rest of the press. One journalist reviewed the Independents' show with these words:

> Step up, ladies and gentlemen! Pay six dollars and be an artist — an independent artist! Cheap, isn't it? Yet that is all it costs. You and I, even if we've never wielded a brush (...) can buy six dollars worth of wall (...) space at the Grand Central Palace.

And Leila Mechlin, a professional art critic, wrote in the May 1917 editorial of the *American Magazine of Art*:

> Naturally a great many of those who became exposed in this instance had not the smallest claim to the name artists.

4) Leila Mechlin was speaking with the authority of a legitimate representative of the Beaux-Arts system, or of its American avatar, the National Academy of Design. Self-proclaimed independent artists were simply not artists to her eyes. One wonders what she would have said if she had heard of Richard Mutt's

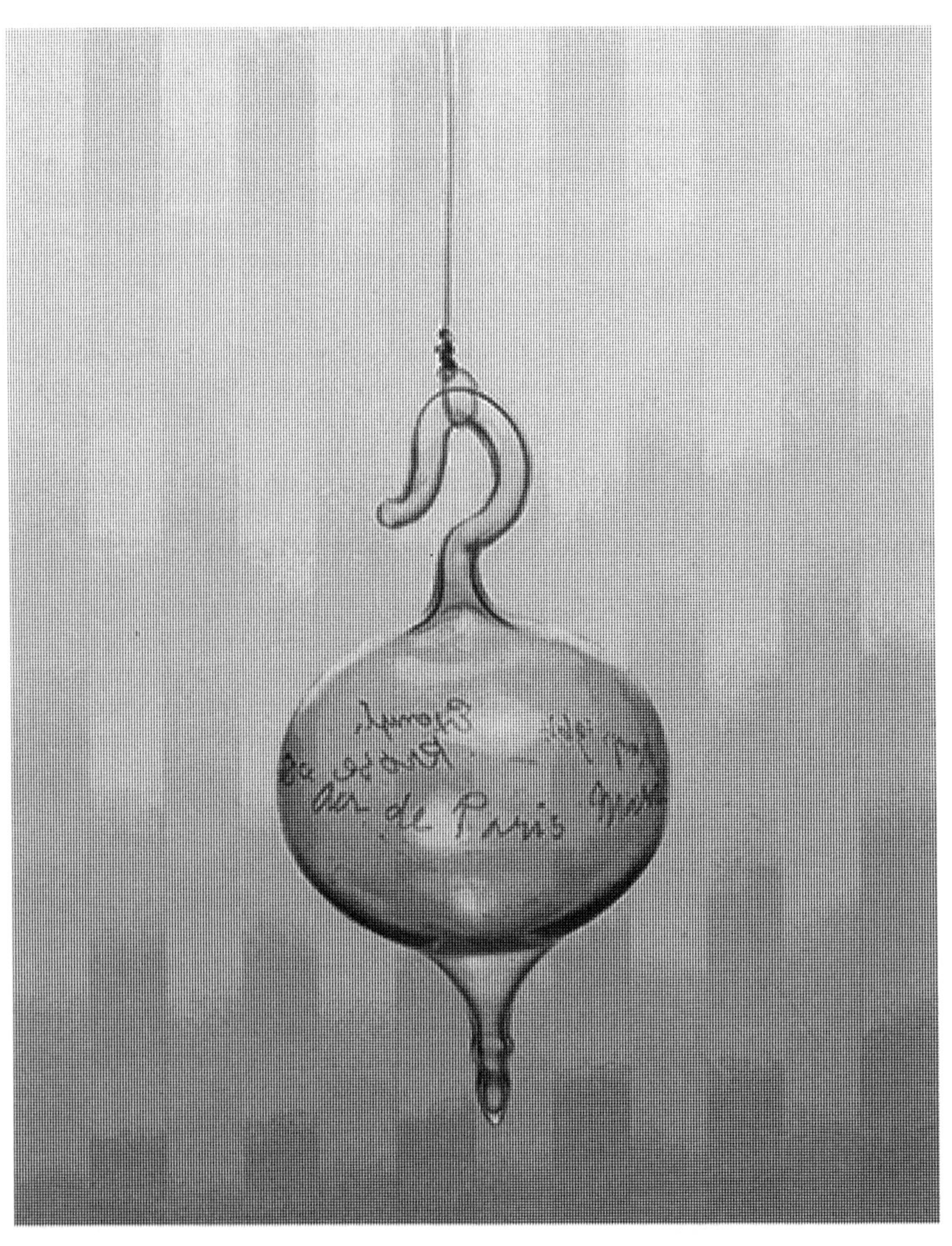

Marcel Duchamp, *Air de Paris*, 1919, Philadelphia Museum of Art.

entry and if, to top it all, she had known that the prankster hiding behind that pseudonym was actually the chairman of the hanging committee and a founding member of the Society of Independent Artists. Clearly, Duchamp had tested the Society on whether or not it would abide by the consequences of its own rules — that when anyone and everyone ready to spend six dollars is allowed membership into the Society, then one should expect its exhibition to contain a bit of anything and everything. *Fountain* was Duchamp's wicked way of welcoming the new "Art Unlimited" system into existence. Of course, he received the rebuttal which he knew from his experience with the *Nude Descending a Staircase* the other founding members would give him. However rebellious they were against the Academy, they did not at all think of themselves as living in the new "Art Unlimited" system. They did not realize, as I think Duchamp did, that the birth of a Society of Independent Artists tolled the knell of the Beaux-Arts system. Duchamp's diabolic intelligence of the situation was level with his desire for revenge and, I believe, exacerbated by it. It was he who advised the founding committee to call their artists' society by the name of "Independents" and to model it after the French *Société des artistes indépendants* — really a double-edged sword, for he knew the *Indépendants* had already betrayed their principles.

5) The *Société des artistes indépendants* was founded in Paris in 1884 by a group of Neo-Impressionist painters with anarchist sympathies gathered around Seurat, Signac and Pissarro. What was their rationale for the creation of an artists' society? More importantly, why claim independence for it? Independence from what? For anyone who knows the 19th century French artistic landscape — Duchamp certainly did — the answer is obvious: independence from the State. From its inception on, in 1648, under the name of *Académie royale de peinture et de sculpture*, and until its demise in the 1880s, the institution which the Directoire had renamed *Institut* and the Restauration *Académie des Beaux-Arts* kept a quasi-absolute monopoly on the education of artists and their access to the profession. Throughout the 19th century, appointed State officials held key positions at the *Académie*, professorships at the *Ecole des Beaux-Arts*, and jury privilege at the *Académie's* annual Salon. Until the Impressionist generation of painters began to refuse to exhibit at the Salon and relied on their private dealers and on influential critics for their careers, anyone aspiring to succeed as a professional painter or sculptor in 19th century France had to undergo the all or nothing verdict of the Salon jury. There were protests against the blunt intransigence of the jury all along the history of the Salon, but when Seurat and his anarchist friends created the

Indépendants, they went way beyond such protest; they essentially declared the tutelage of the State null and void. The situation was ripe: the 1880 Salon had been a complete fiasco, with a jury challenged by most of the artists involved and which, faced with the hue and cry, absolved itself of its responsibilities by accepting almost all the works submitted (7,289 in all!). Add to this a director who hung the worst artists in the best spots in order to disavow the jury, an unbridled criticism, a disgruntled public, and a deficit of about $120,000 in today's currency, and you will understand why, in 1881, Jules Ferry (who was not only Minister of Education but also *ministre des Beaux-Arts*) decided that the Government would no longer be involved with the Salons. That same year the no longer State-sponsored *Société des artistes français* was founded, but it took a mere three years for this body to see its jury challenged in turn by the artists rallying around Seurat, who turned their backs on juries once and for all by founding the *Indépendants*. Meissonier's efforts throughout the 1880s, on behalf of the State, to reconstitute some *"union sacrée"* in view of the *Exposition nationale* of 1890, were to no avail. The official French patronage institution maintained a semblance of vitality and power for yet another forty years, if not more, but for all practical purposes it was dead. Exit the Beaux-Arts system, enter the "Art Unlimited" system. As we shall now see, it is the turning point between those two systems that the critic Paul Mantz unwittingly acknowledged when he gave the motto of the Académie royale, *Libertas artibus restituta* (Freedom restored to the arts) a completely new meaning by attaching it to 1863, the date of the Salon des Refusés.

6) As already noted, what mattered to an artist living in 19th century France and seeking a professional career was acceptance at the Salon. Exhibiting there was virtually the only way of getting one's work across to potential collectors, to stir up public interest via reviews in the press, and to obtain State commissions. This situation had an involuntary collateral effect on the structure of the juries' aesthetic judgments. No matter how subtly the jury members gauged the merits of the works submitted to them, in the showdown they had to phrase their opinion as an abrupt either/or: either the work was accepted, or it was refused. Refusals that were repeated over the years, such as those suffered by Théodore Rousseau or even by Ingres, could have disastrous effects on artists' careers, without informing them in any way as to the nature of the flaws they should correct in order to be co-opted. Needless to say, the public, which flocked to the Salon *en masse*, was no more informed of the jury's criteria than the artists since it could only see what the jury had selected. This changed in 1863, when, for once, Napoleon III authorized a

parallel exhibition of the refused works that made comparison
with the accepted works possible. This was the famous Salon des
Refusés, a structuralist's dream, so to speak, because with it, the
public, which may not have paid much attention to the new
binary phrasing of aesthetic appreciation until then, was
suddenly presented with both sides of the either/or as such.
Mallarmé may have been the first to acknowledge the new structure on behalf of the public when, in an article taking the
defense of Manet after the latter had seen his *Bal masqué à l'Opéra*
rejected from the 1874 Salon, he wrote:

> Entrusted with the nebulous vote of the painters with
> the responsibility of choosing, from among the framed
> pictures offered, those that are truly paintings in order
> to show them to us, the jury has nothing else to say
> but: this is a painting, or that is not a painting. [In
> French: *"Ceci est un tableau," ou encore: "Voilà qui n'est
> pas un tableau."*]

7) Mallarmé wants the public to be the judge and admonishes
the jury to refrain from imposing its own taste but instead to
content itself with setting a minimal standard for acceptance at
the Salon. He does not radically reject the need of a jury, as the
Indépendants would do ten years later, but he challenges its
authority in matters of taste — which is not to say that he denies
the jury *all* right to judge by taste. For the jury to sort "true
paintings" from mere "framed pictures" is not the same operation as for you or me to sort, say, chairs, from objects that are not
chairs. Whereas a framed picture may feature all the characteristics that nominally identify the object as a painting, a true painting must *deserve* to be called a painting, and is only then a work
of art. It is striking how Mallarmé's admonition to the jury
carries echoes of something Théophile Thoré wrote after the
1848 Salon — a most interesting Salon because it took place
between the February days of insurrection and the June days of
repression and was not juried at all. Thoré had been in favor of
the suppression of the jury for some time, but he was appalled
by the quantity of bad work authorized into the Republican
Salon of 1848. And yet he wrote the following:

> In spite of the buffoonery of the present Salon, I am
> not at all convinced of the need for a jury whatsoever,
> except for the hanging. For the next national exhibi-
> tions, I would approve it once again if unlimited free-
> dom were tried out, provided an intelligent committee
> separates the works of art from all this unspeakable
> rubbish.

Comparing Thoré's and Mallarmé's quotes, we note, first, that Thoré proposes to replace the jury with a hanging committee — exactly what the *Indépendants* would do — and second, that besides the hanging he conceives the task of that committee as that of drawing the line between "works of art" and "unspeakable rubbish" — exactly what the hanging committee of the New York Independents thought they were entitled to do when Richard Mutt presented them with a urinal. Compare with Mallarmé, who asks the jury to draw the line between "This is a painting" and "That is not a painting," quasi exactly what the hanging committee of the Cubist room of the Paris *Indépendants* thought they were entitled to do when Duchamp presented them with his *Nude Descending a Staircase*. The *Nude* may have been a painting but it didn't deserve to be called a Cubist painting and, in the eyes of the dogmatic Cubists sitting on the hanging committee, this was tantamount to not being a painting at all. Well, if something is not a painting — "un tableau" — while it is obviously not a sculpture, a poem or a piece of music, then in the Beaux-Arts system it is simply not art. With *Fountain*, Duchamp would prove that such a something either lands into the bin of "unspeakable rubbish" or is redeemed as non-art, and thus as art, but then in the new system of "Art Unlimited" it helped usher in.

8) In today's art world, non-art is the stalest red herring you can buy. No one speaks of non-art anymore or for that matter of its quasi-twin, anti-art. To speak of non-art and anti-art was fashionable in the sixties. By the end of the sixties, Don Judd could claim, "'Non-art,' 'anti-art', 'non-art art', and 'anti-art art' are useless. If someone says his work is art, it's art," without anybody batting an eye. And by the time the YBAs (Young British Artists) were launched in the late eighties, the fact that non-art is art was not even stuff for British tabloids anymore. The sixties were non-art's hour of glory. Yet it was not primarily sixties' artists who earned the title of non-artist. Of all those then competing in the minds of the critics for that title, Duchamp rallied the most votes by far, with the Dadaists (most often not called by name) coming in second and the Neo-Dadaists (as the Pop artists were often called) in third position. The concept of non-art, if it is a concept, appears in the wake of Duchamp's growing reputation after his 1963 retrospective in Pasadena. I would say it is an effect of the reception of the message Duchamp mailed in 1917 in the shape of a men's urinal called *Fountain* and which reached its destination around 1964. As we have seen, the content of the message, its reality, is an altogether different matter. And non-art as part of that content is likewise a different matter. I'd say: non-art is an inadvertent by-product of the binary structure of the one aesthetic judgment that was relevant at the 19th century Salon,

the one that separated the wheat from the chaff by way of "This is a painting" versus "That is not a painting." I am not sure that Mallarmé realized that what he admonished the jury to do, the jury had been doing all along. At the 1874 Salon, it had already separated what it judged to truly deserve the name of painting, Manet's *Gare Saint-Lazare*, for example, from what it must have deemed mere "framed pictures," such as Manet's *Bal masqué à l'Opéra*. And at he 1863 Salon, eleven years before, although the jury had counted Manet's *Déjeuner sur l'herbe* among the mere "framed pictures" that did not deserve to be shown, thanks to Napoleon III it was redeemed at the Salon des Refusés. Whether the jury members of 1863 and 1874 *consciously* refused Manet's pictures the name of painting, and therefore the status of art, is unlikely. I think it more probable that they were suffering from what Leo Steinberg dubbed "the plight of the public," by which he meant "the shock of discomfort, or the bewilderment or the anger or the boredom which some people always feel, and all people sometimes feel, when confronted with an unfamiliar new style." Half the members of the 1863 Salon were state appointees, but the other half were artists, so that when Steinberg further writes that "whenever there appears an art that is truly new and original, the men who denounce it first and loudest are artists," he makes it easy to imagine to what extent the jury members denied the picture the quality of a true painting because they could not stand the betrayal of their taste they saw in it. Recalling his first experience of Jasper Johns's paintings, in 1958, Steinberg has acknowledged that he was on the verge of such denial:

> I disliked the show, and would gladly have thought it a bore. Yet it depressed me and I wasn't sure why. Then I began to recognize in myself all the classical symptoms of a philistine reaction to modern art. I was angry at the artist [...], I was irritated at some of my friends [...], I was really mad at myself for being so dull.

Alone with *Target with four faces*, the painting in the show that depressed him most, Steinberg decided that it was up to him "to evaluate it in the absence of available standards," and wrote:

> It is a kind of self-analysis that a new image can throw you into and for which I am grateful. I am left in a state of anxious uncertainty by the painting, about painting, about myself. And I suspect that this is all right. In fact, I have little confidence in people who habitually, when exposed to new works of art, know what is great and what will last.

I wouldn't rush to accuse the 1863 jury to "know what is great and what will last." We don't have the minutes of the jury's meeting and must therefore rely on indirect sources. But we can infer from the discomfort, the touchiness, the nervousness of many contemporary reviews that the jury's plight when confronted with *Le Déjeuner sur l'herbe* was not unlike Steinberg's before *Target with four faces*. The difference is that the jury members were not willing to perform the kind of self-analysis Steinberg plunged into. In their mouth, "That is not a painting" did not just put Mallarmé's advice in practice, it was a denial — a *Verneinung* — in the Freudian sense. They would pretend to sort paintings from non-paintings the way you or I would sort chairs from non-chairs, all the while knowing well that Manet was "a true painter" (Thoré), "*un tempérament*" (Baudelaire), "one of the greatest personalities of our time" (Astruc), or that he would "triumph some day" (Lockroy). It is by way of such denials that the category of art works we call "non-art" came into being, long before Duchamp and the Dadaists claimed or accepted paternity for it. Non-art is a strange bag containing objects such as chairs and roses, which are quite logically *negated* in their art status because nobody ever claimed they were art, and a few crucial objects, such as Manet's *Déjeuner sur l'herbe*, that are *denied* in their art status because they hurt the jury members' most intimate convictions. Duchamp's genius with *Fountain* and his other readymades is to have pulled out of that bag a few objects nobody ever claimed were art and to have treated them as if they were the equivalent of Manet's paintings.

Coda

To reconnect with the initial occasions having prompted me to write this talk, it seems to me that even though I stuck closely to the title, "Art Unlimited," which framed the series of lectures organized by the Akademie der Künste in Berlin, I gave it an interpretation that doesn't at all address the question, "Where is the Medium?" which framed the series of lectures organized by York University in Toronto. Yet the very content of what I called "Duchamp's message," the fact that today anything can be art, is foreign neither to the question Berlin was asking, the question of the possible dissolution of the arts (in the plural) into art (in the singular), nor to the question Toronto was asking, the question of the possible disappearance of medium-specificity in the "post-medium condition". The question is: are we really in a post-medium condition? Rosalind Krauss's position, which she has defended in an article on James Coleman and in her little book on Marcel Broodthaers, *A Voyage to the North Sea*, before summarizing it in an essay entitled "Reinventing the Medium," interests me a lot. I would feel in sympathy with her desire to

"reclaim the specific from the deadening embrace of the
general" if it were true that we live in a post-medium condition.
But I don't believe that. She speaks of "a fundamental transformation whereby the specificity of the individual medium is
abandoned in favor of a practice focused on what has to be called
art-in-general," crediting me in a footnote for having theorized
"the move from the specific to the generic." Thanks but no
thanks. There is a misunderstanding, here. I too speak of a
fundamental transformation, but one that does not imply at all
that "the specificity of the individual medium is abandoned" or
that the plurality of the arts has been dissolved into art in the
singular. I speak of a change of institution, the passage from the
Beaux-Arts to the Art Unlimited system. In my view, art unlimited, art in the singular, art-in-general or art at large (these are
all equivalent expressions) are not styles or genres or art forms
or practices or media, whether new or old. They are various

Media/McLuhan

appellations for the post-Duchamp condition we live in, a condition where you can make art out of anything and everything.
When such is the case, then you can make art from oil paint on
canvas and analog photography as well as from virtual reality or
institutional critique. And vice versa. There is no medium, new
or old, that holds an a priori monopoly on quality in art. Obsolescence of the medium, which is the kiss of death for some
enthusiasts of the new and a greatly redeeming quality in Rosalind Krauss's conservative account, plays no role at all in mine.
What does play a role is the price we pay for confusing the
unbound liberty of artists with a free for all lacking cultural
pressure, but that is another story. ●

Thierry de Duve is Professor of Aestetics and Art History at the Département d'arts plastiques at
l'Université Lille.

Re-Mediating the Medium

Richard Cavell

Electronic Man approaches the condition in which it is possible to deal with the entire environment as a work of art... This new possibility demands total understanding of the artistic function in society. It will no longer be possible merely to add art to the environment.

McLuhan and Parker, *Through the Vanishing Point* (1968)

For Doug Coupland.

It is entirely appropriate to be considering the "post-medium condition"at the Moderna Museet, since this museum provided the focus for one of Marshall McLuhan's most provocative comments about the nature of art. Writing in *The Medium is the Massage*,[1] published in 1967, McLuhan superimposed his notion that "art is anything you can get away with" over an image of Nikki de Saint Phalle's monumental *She: A Cathedral* (Hon-en Katedral), photographed in its Moderna Museet installation of 1966. This 82 foot / 28 metre long sculpture contained music rooms, a cinema and acquarium, and a milkbar in one of the breasts, and conveys in iconic fashion a number of McLuhan's chief assertions about the function of the work of art in the electronic era: that art was interactive, performative, collective, total, tactile, involving, and, especially, environmental. The risqué nature of the image also encoded McLuhan's notion that the artist was

1 • Marshall McLuhan, with Quentin Fiore and Jerome Agel, *The Medium is the Massage* (N.Y.: Bantam, 1967). For a detailed description of how this book was produced, see Jeffrey T Schnapp and Adam Michaels, *The Electric Information Age Book* (N.Y.: Princeton Architectural Press, 2012).

at once a critic and a renegade — the artist as enemy, as McLuhan's mentor Wyndham Lewis liked to put it.

McLuhan's foundational theory of media was inextricably tied to his ideas about art; in fact, he understood media as a vast work of art which, like de Saint Phalle's sculpture, we had come to inhabit. This notion immediately serves to undermine traditional notions of the separation of art and its cultural contexts and as such raises a number of theoretical questions about art in its post medium condition, a condition where the traditional genres of the "visual" arts — primarily painting and sculpture — no longer seem to hold, and in which we seem to have moved toward a practice-based understanding of the artistic medium. And what can media theory — which, as I have

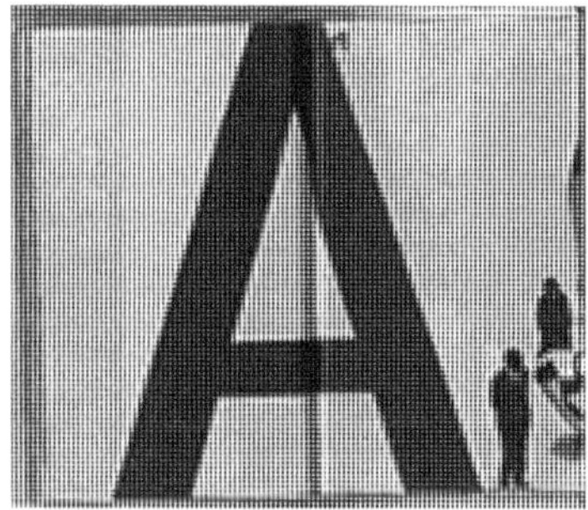
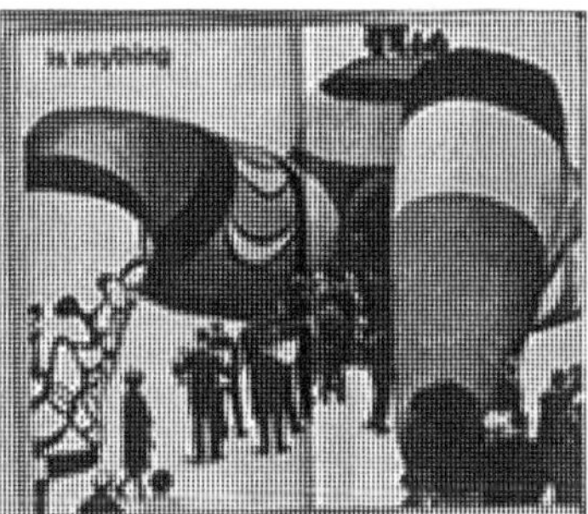
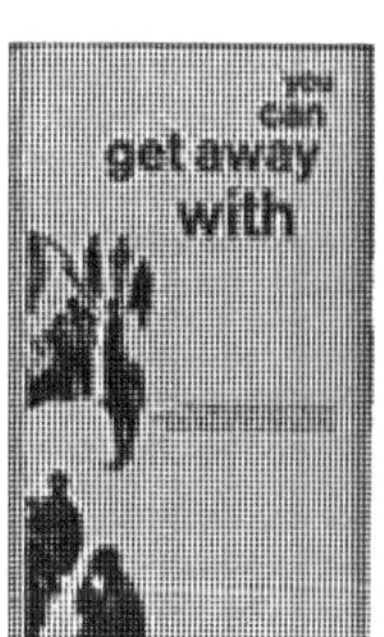

argued elsewhere, can be said to share its pre-history with art theory[2] — tell us about these shifts?

As I have argued in *McLuhan in Space*, McLuhan, by mid-career (that is, post *Understanding Media*, published in 1964), increasingly sought to address himself to artists and, more radically, to be understood as an artist himself — the "intellectual as *vates*"[3] as he put it — the critic as creator. McLuhan argued that "it is the artist's job to *dislocate* older media into postures that permit attention to the new,"[4] and here we approach one of McLuhan's central theoretical pillars, namely that of remediation: the idea that the content of a given medium is a previous medium. This notion is at once historical, critical, and creative, and in McLuhan's theory of mediation, the three elements are co-present, supporting thus an intermediated notion of artistic production.

McLuhan specifically addressed his media theories to artistic discourse in his 1968 book *Through the Vanishing Point: Space in Poetry and Painting*.[5] As the subtitle suggests, McLuhan's central focus is

2 • www.youtube.com/watch?v=N7s31Wr85Nk. See Richard Cavell, *McLuhan in Space: A Cultural Geography* (Toronto: University of Toronto Press, 2002).
3 • www.youtube.com/watch?v=N7s31Wr85Nk. See the section of this title in *McLuhan in Space* 91–97.
4 • www.youtube.com/watch?v=N7s31Wr85Nk. McLuhan, *Understanding Media: The Extensions of Man* (N.Y.: McGraw-Hill, 1964) 254.
5 • McLuhan, with Harley Parker, *Through the Vanishing Point: Space in Poetry and Painting* (N.Y.: Harper and Row, 1968).

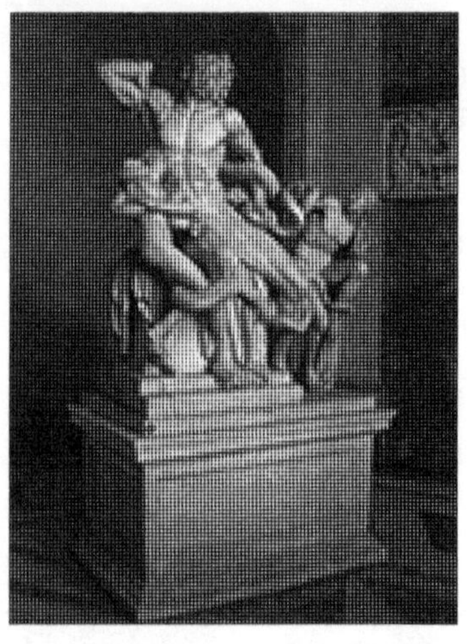

Laocoön and His Sons, Vatican Museum, Rome. Attributed Pliny the Elder to Agesander, Athenodoros and Polydorus. Photo by de:Benutzer:Fb78.

on the classic distinction made by G. E. Lessing in his 1766 book *Laocoön*, where he sought to differentiate poetry as a time-based art and sculpture as a space-based art. Subtending Lessing's argument was the desire to keep discourse about art separate from the art about which it spoke, thus conserving for critical discourse a superior status — criticism of art could say things about art that art itself must remain silent about. As McLuhan's subtitle indicates, he is contesting Lessing's distinction by proposing an interfusion of artistic media, as well as of discourse *about* artistic media (and here the *livre d'artiste* format of *The Medium is the Massage* becomes highly relevant).

By invoking Lessing, McLuhan was entering into a debate on medium specificity within artistic production that had been re-launched by Irving Babbitt's *The New Laokoon*, published in 1910, in which Babbitt lamented what he saw as the confusion of artistic categories within modernist art. Clement Greenberg had taken up the debate by the 1940s, when McLuhan had already established his reputation in the literary and artistic avant garde, being published in *Neurotica* magazine, edited by legendary pornophile Gershon Legman, and in *View* magazine, which also published the work of Joseph Cornell, Brion Gysin, André Breton, Picasso, Klee, and Léger, among others. Greenberg had opted for a "pure" abstraction in art that he proposed as "a salutary reaction against the mistakes of painting and sculpture in the past several centuries which were due to [a] confusion [of forms]."[6] Greenberg's position also implied a *critical* abstraction, placing the critic in a separate and superior category to that of the artist.

By the end of the 1960s, at the height of McLuhan's fame, the "confusion" of the arts was being associated specifically with McLuhan's media theories,[7] as is evident in W. K. Wimsatt's essay, "Laokoon: An Oracle Reconsulted," where he writes that:

> Today's critical "anti-interpreter" rejoices in the trampling of barriers and in a philosophy that understands the non-reality of all art entities and presumably of most natural ones. ... We arrive [thus] at "multimedia," the barrage and "massage," the "super-saturated attack" on the senses, the "overload," the "blitz," contrived with elaborately inventive care in the "total environment"

6 • Clement Greenberg, "Towards a Newer Laocoon," *Partisan Review* 7 (1940) 296–310; this quote 296. See the discussion in Cavell, *McLuhan in Space* 116–7.
7 • I am following, here, my *McLuhan in Space* 116–7.

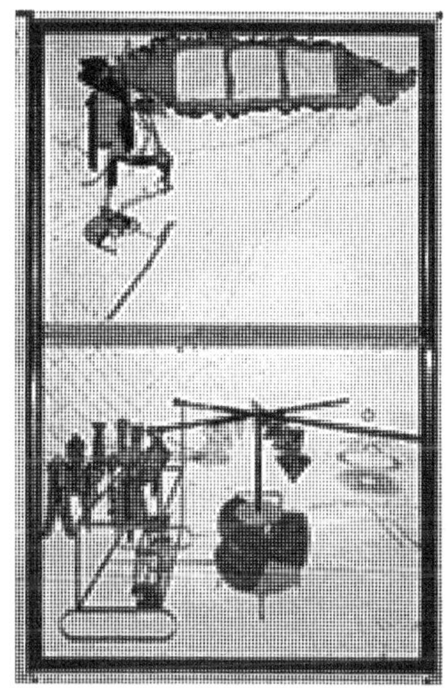

discotheque, at sales meetings, …at electronic theater events, in the halls of Expo and the Royal Ontario Museum: — batteries of pulsing and eye-searing strobe lights, wailing sirens and high-decibel modern rock, flashing and jumping screens, electronically tinted mists, incidental smells and touches, all these for "turning on" the patron–in a total experience which approximates the effect of the psychedelic drug — a deepening and merging of sensory experience, a release of the mind from the rational ordering of perception.

That McLuhan is the intended target of this attack is hard to miss: in addition to the Canadian context invoked by Wimsatt's references to "Expo [67]" (dubbed "McLuhan's Fair") and to the Royal Ontario Museum (where McLuhan's collaborator on *Through the Vanishing Point* was Head of Design and Installations), "massage" is a clear reference to *The Medium is the Massage*, as is "total environment," and phrases such as "sensory experience" invoke well-known McLuhanesque concepts.

Wimsatt's concerns reflect what John C. Welchman has identified as "a kind of subtextual debate on the divisive aesthetic rationale of Lessing's key text. This gave rise to two fields of response to the close zoning of the sign, reproducing that fissure in the formation of the modern between formalist autonomy and self-reference, and non-formalist material and signifying interaction."[8] Dadaist and Surrealist works raised these issues very powerfully, as Welchman goes on to note: "No longer could painting and sculpture be denied access to what Lessing maintained was the exclusive concern of literature: narrative action extending in time. And texts, conversely, were opened up to interactions, [while] visual practice was construed as inseparable from the social, the political, or the personal" (62).

McLuhan's rejoinder to these issues in *Through the Vanishing Point* took as its central argument that the modernist movement in art was a response to 500 years of the spatiality inaugurated by the book, that of three-dimensional space as a concomitant of the foreground/background relationship (deriving from the figure and ground relationship imposed by black type on white paper) and the fixed position of the

8 • John C. Welchman, "After the Wagnerian Bouillabaisse: Critical Theory and the Dada and Surrealist Word-Image" in Judi Freeman, ed., *The Dada and Surrealist Word-Image* (Cambridge, Mass.: MIT Press, 1989) 62 n.8.

viewer. It was this space that was contested by proto-modernist artistic configurations such as the pre-Raphaelite brotherhood, which sought to return to the two-dimensional planar space that had characterized medieval art, which is to say the period in which the manuscript predominated, a form of expression which combined text and image. That combination returned at the beginning of modernism, as cultural production generally began to experience the implications of the end of book culture and the rise of electronic mediation. The book became re-mediated: no longer the dominant cultural form, as McLuhan understood so profoundly, it became the content of the new art.

Media/McLuhan

As McLuhan had argued in *The Mechanical Bride*,[9] his 1951 homage to Duchamp's *Bride Stripped Bare by Her Bachelors, Even*, the newspaper remediated in many ways the medieval manuscript, especially in its juxtapositions of text and image, producing thereby a much more involving space in which one became immersed through the process of reading. As McLuhan puts it in the first essay of *The Mechanical Bride*, "the French symbolists, followed by James Joyce in *Ulysses*, saw that there was a new art form of universal scope present in the technical layout of the modern newspaper. [...] Discontinuity [...] is the visual technique of a Picasso, the literary technique of James Joyce" (3–4; I have reversed the order of the sentences). McLuhan further argued in *Understanding Media* that the newspaper headline invoked the haptic, sculptural quality of typography (which, until the invention of offset, actually impressed the page physically); as he puts it, "ordinary newspaper headline style tends to push letters toward the iconic form, a form that is very near to auditory resonance, as it is also to tactile and sculptural quality,"[10] and, in this context, it is significant to note the uses made of newspaper text not only in early modernist work such as that by Picasso and Georges Braque, but also by postwar artists such as Robert Rauschenberg. The intermediated, involving nature of this art addressed itself to senses other than or in addition to the visual, and the attendant somatic implications became the *cri de coeur* of the art of the 1960s and beyond, from Robert Morris's insistence in his "Anti Form"[11] article that sculpture should represent a "process" to Lucy Lippard's 1966 New York exhibition *Eccentric Abstraction* that polemically asserted the tactile in place of the visual.

Rosalind Krauss has stated that Jackson Pollock, with his large canvases, many of them painted on the ground, is the artist most closely associated with the critique of the "optical mirage"[12] produced by the three-dimensional

9 • McLuhan, *The Mechanical Bride: Folklore of Industrial Man* (N.Y.: Vanguard Press, 1951)
10 • McLuhan, *Understanding Media* 160.
11 • Robert Morris, 'Anti-Form,' *Artforum*, 6.8, April 1968, 33–5.
12 • Rosalind Krauss, *The Optical Unconscious*, Cambridge, Mass. and London, 1993, 123.

spatiality that had been inaugurated by the book. As John Welchman puts it, the "progressive dependence of painters on effects of the surface was seen as a decisive rejection of post-Renaissance verisimilitude and perspective."[13] McLuhan's assessment in *Understanding Media* had been characteristically overarching: "Merely by releasing objects from the uniform continuous space of typography we got modern art and poetry,"[14] where he is thinking not only of early cubism but of poems such as *The Waste Land*, which produce meaning through juxtaposition of discrete texts, rather than through linear continuity–"These fragments I have shored against my ruins,"[15] as Eliot puts it. McLuhan summarized his position in *The Medium is the Massage*:

> Art [...] is shaped by the way space is perceived. Since the Renaissance the Western artist perceived his environment primarily in terms of the visual. Everything was dominated by the eye of the beholder. His conception of space was in terms of a perspective projection upon a plane surface consisting of formal units of symmetry — as an absolute condition of order. This view is deeply embedded in the consciousness of Western art. (56–7)

The effect of electronic mediation, McLuhan suggested, would be a re-integration of the perceptual field of all the senses, not just the visual, which had become dominant in the ear of print. Electronic media thus proposed a return to sensual, affective, involving mediation, including artistic mediation. Hence McLuhan's notion that modern art had gone "through the vanishing point": in eliminating the fixed position of the viewer and the third dimension, modernism sought to involve the viewer as the (co)producer of the work's meaning. This element of involvement was, among other things, part of a much larger sensory revolution that had an apotheosis of sorts in the 1960s via the concept of tactility. And, as McLuhan emphasizes in *Through the Vanishing Point*, the chief aspect of tactility (to which he devotes a concluding essay) is the interval — what he termed "resonance" — as opposed to the continuity posited by print culture. While the visual appearance of two-dimensional space is flat, its sensory dimension is "the opposite of inert. [...] For dynamic simultaneity is the effect of the two-dimensional, and inert homogeneity the effect of three-dimensionality."[16] McLuhan is aware that this

13 • Welchman, "After the Wagnerian Bouillabaisse," 61.
14 • McLuhan, Understanding Media, 289.
15 • T. S. Eliot, "The Waste Land," *Complete Poems and Plays 1909–1950*, New York, 1971, 50, l. 431.
16 • McLuhan, *The Gutenberg Galaxy: The Making of Typographic Man* (Toronto: University of Toronto Press, 1962), 127.

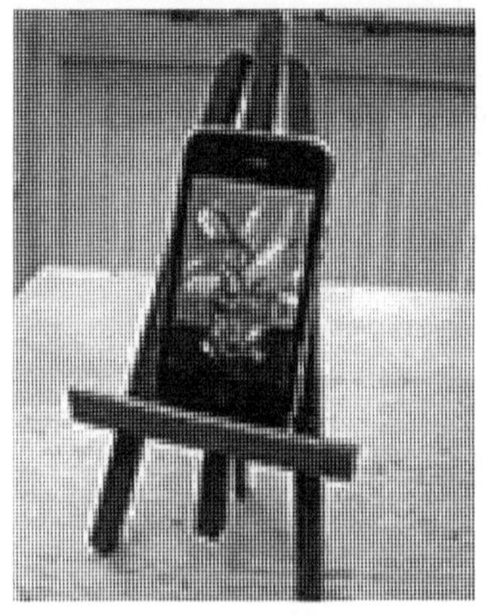

▲

David Hockney,
iPhone art.
Photo: Daily Mail.

argument is counter-intuitive; as he writes, "In a visual culture it sounds quite paradoxical to say that sculpture is primarily tactile and only incidentally visual. In fact, tactility [...] is crucial in the world of the arts."[17] This is so because "[t]actility is the world of the interval, not of the connection, and that is why it is antithetic to the visual world. For the visual is above all the world of the continuous and the connected."[18]

McLuhan's *Through the Vanishing Point* contributed to an aesthetic debate that continues to the present day. One of the major articulations in this debate was Rosalind Krauss's "Sculpture in the Expanded Field," where she writes,

Over the last ten years rather surprising things have come to be called sculpture: narrow corridors with TV monitors at the ends; large photographs documenting country hikes; mirrors placed at strange angles in ordinary rooms; temporary lines cut into the floor of the desert. Nothing, it would seem, could possibly give to such a motley of effort the right to lay claim to whatever one might mean by the category of sculpture. Unless, that is, the category can be made to become almost infinitely malleable.[19]

The danger in this infinite expansion of the field, as Krauss sees it, is that it denies difference by asserting a universal category (in this case, "sculpture,") that is able to encompass all possible manifestations of the form. Like Lessing and his followers, Krauss is thus concerned with category contamination. To this concern she opposes the argument that sculpture is an "historically bounded category and not a universal one"[20] and that sculpture, for much of its history, has been associated with the monument and has thus been site specific. Krauss associates the loss of this site-specificity with modernism itself: "it is the modernist period of sculptural production that operates in relation to this loss of site, producing the monument as abstraction, the monument as pure marker or base, functionally placeless and largely self-referential."[21]

The absorption of the base — thus marking its transportability — and the concomitant self-referentiality, define for Krauss the particular modernity of sculpture, which began to exhaust itself

17 • McLuhan, *Through the Vanishing Point,* 263.
18 • McLuhan, *Through the Vanishing Point,* 264.
19 • Rosalind Krauss, 'Sculpture in the Expanded Field', *October 8,* Spring 1979, 30–44; this quote 31.
20 • Krauss, 'Sculpture', 33.
21 • Krauss, 'Sculpture', 34.
22 • Krauss, 'Sculpture', 34.

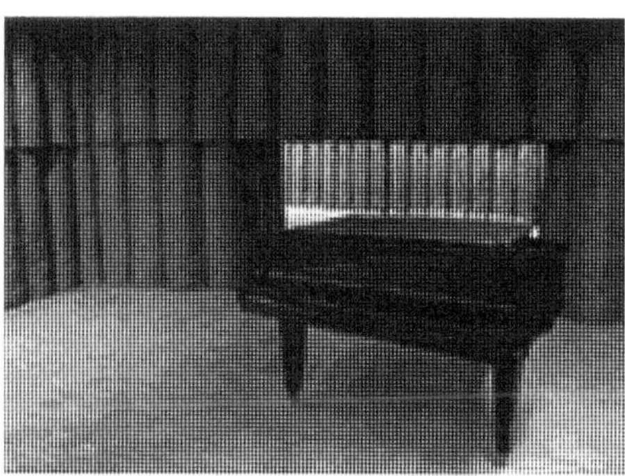

by the 1950s as a sort of "pure negativity."[22] To quote Krauss again: "within the situation of postmodernism, practice is not defined in relation to a given medium — sculpture — but rather in relation to the logical operations on a set of cultural terms, for which any medium — photography, books, lines on walls, mirrors, or sculpture itself — might be used."[23] It is this lack of medium specificity that represents the greatest threat of post-modernism for Krauss; in her latest book, *Under Blue Cup*[24] (2011), Krauss resorts to the notion of "technical support" — the automobile, for example, is the technical support of Ed Ruscha's work — as the contemporary iteration of paint on canvas, a formulation which allows her to extend the notion of medium to post-media practices while denying those media any significance within art historical discourse. Tellingly, however, the automobile is the subject of one chapter in McLuhan's *Understanding Media*, indicating how closely Krauss's critique of post-mediality comes to acknowledging the re-mediation of traditional artistic media. One wonders what Krauss would make of David Hockney's use of the iPhone and iPad to paint pictures of flowers. Hockney wonderfully blurs the art-historical notion of "medium" with the use of the term in media theory when he writes that "I was aware immediately when I started drawing on the iPhone that it was a new medium."[25]

As Joseph Kosuth noted in his 1969 essay, "Art After Philosophy,"[26] Duchamp was pivotal in repositioning the understanding of art as deriving from its physical embodiment (the position that Krauss appears reluctant to give up), to a notion of art as an investigation of the possibilities of art itself, of the medium. Duchamp played throughout his career with this self-referentiality, with its suggestion that the line dividing artist and critic was beginning to blur. This blurring of the critical function has its concomitant in the blurring of artistic media that is the subject of McLuhan's *Through the Vanishing Point*. As we recall, McLuhan argued there that the flat plane of non-perspectival art achieves a multi-dimensionality which he associated with tactility. As Alex Potts comments, such work — work which began to proliferate in the 1960s — "is characteristically sculptural because of

23 • Krauss, 'Sculpture', 42.
24 • Rosalind Krauss, *Under Blue Cup* (Cambridge, Mass.: MIT Press, 2011).
25 • Quoted from *David Hockney's fresh flowers: Drawings on the iPhone and iPad*, a pamphlet accompanying an exhibition of that title at the Royal Ontario Museum, Toronto, in November of 2011, curated by Charlie Scheips and designed by Ali Tayar.
26 • Joseph Kosuth, 'Art After Philosophy', *Studio International*, 178:915-6-7, October, November, December, 1969.
27 • Alex Potts, "Tactility: The Interrogation of Medium in Art of the 1960s," *Art History* 27.2 (2004) 284.

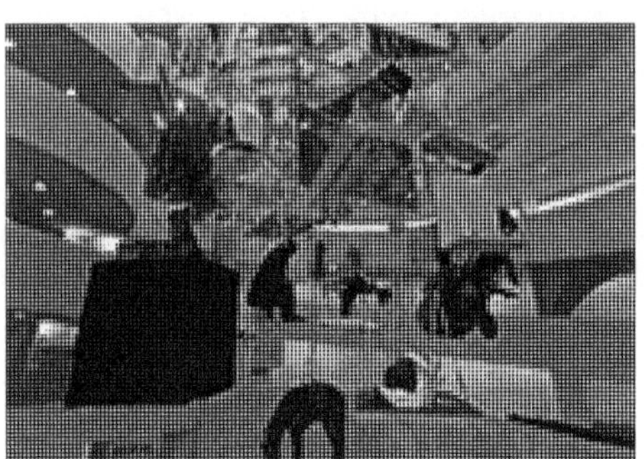

its focus on the tactile substance of objects and materials and the literal properties of its medium. At the same time, through this very focus, it negates traditional conceptions of sculptural form that were seen to constitute sculpture as a distinctive artistic medium."[27] In an era which would increasingly move away from the traditional notion of sculpture, Potts observes, "sculpture, the haptic three-dimensional art, the art of things and objects, is everywhere and nowhere: everywhere in that objects and three-dimensional props are standard features of contemporary art installations; nowhere in that these displays are rarely conceived as falling into the category of sculpture."[28] What is important about these post-medium works is that their "vividly felt sense of tactility displaces any immediate apprehension of structural qualities associated with sculpture as an art form."[29] Joseph Beuys' use of felt, thus, achieves its sculptural qualities through tactility rather than through form. And the everydayness of felt suggests that the notion of artistic materiality has been vastly expanded, as Potts suggests, to embrace "a materiality taken in the broadest sense — to include cultural phenomena, as well as images, voices, sounds and texts, in so much as these constitute the fabric of people's everyday world."[30] It is precisely here that McLuhan's work on "the medium" — a term to which he gave new meaning and new cultural force — gained its purchase: "Rethinking medium seemed to offer a viable way of re-imagining and perhaps even remaking the world for people across the political spectrum — this was, after all, the moment that produced Marshall McLuhan's immensely popular, eccentrically utopian and dystopian speculations on the shaping force of medium in modern culture."[31] Those speculations began with a meditation on typography, on its materiality, and on its material effects on social, cultural and political production in McLuhan's masterwork, *The Gutenberg Galaxy: The Making of Typographic Man* (1962), with its argument that, after 500 years of print culture, electronic mediation would retrieve the qualities of sensuous engagement that had been associated with orality.

We see evidence now of this sensuous engagement in the rise of performance art and also in the expansion of the notion of the aesthetic into our increasingly mediated relationship with the world around us. The supersaturation of contemporary media culture

28 • Potts, "Tactility" 286.
29 • Potts, "Tactility" 286.
30 • Potts, "Tactility" 302.
31 • Potts, "Tactility" 302.

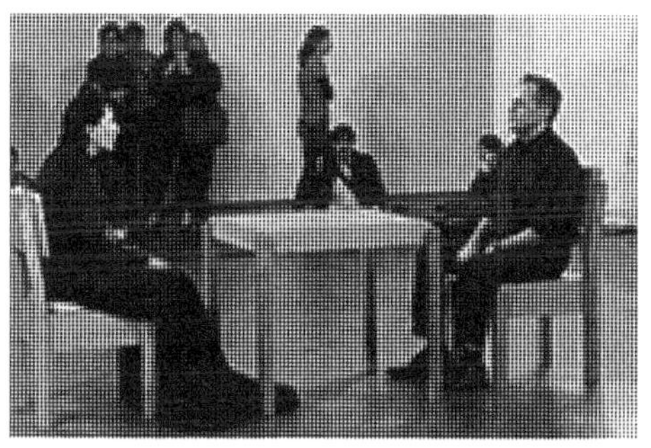

means not only that the traditional artistic media have converged through digitization, but that our being is taking on an aesthetic dimension insofar as computational media are extensions of our consciousness. Domenico Quaranta, in *Media, New Media, Postmedia*,[32] suggests that post-medium art is finding its place not only in the interstices of traditional artistic genres but between the arts and the sciences and between arts and technology: having put our bodies outside ourselves we now inhabit them as artifacts through technologies such as Facebook. The medium, thus, has not disappeared. It has become environmental, as McLuhan suggested in his reading of Nikki de Saint Phalle's installation, and it is important to note here that McLuhan derived the concept of the "environment" from the artistic practice of the installation.

Interestingly, art as environment does not seem to present a threat for artists. Maurizio Cattelan's retrospective installation, shown at the Guggenheim New York in December of 2011, takes all the art off the walls and hangs the works from the ceiling, making the viewer strain and bend and gyrate to see his work. As Nancy Spector remarks in the catalogue for the show, this form of exhibition does not constrain Cattelan's critical position:

> As a child of the 1960s, Cattelan is a product of [the] relentlessly mediated environment, in which the spectacle is no longer "understood as a mere visual excess produced by mass-media technologies" but rather "a world-view ... that has become objective." Cattelan is not at all interested in conquering the totalizing perspective of the spectacle, in opposition to Debord and the other Situationists, critical forebears to his artistic generation. Rather, he infiltrates spectacle culture in order to choreograph its effects from within, with a long-term goal of reclaiming subjectivity and raising consciousness about significant moral issues.[33]

Indeed, the choice of medium says little about the critical potential of a work of art, as Jan Verwoert has noted.[34] If anyone is threatened by such choices it is the

32 • Domenico Quaranta, *Media, New Media, Postmedia: arte e nuovi media nell'era post-mediale* (Milano: Postmediabooks, 2011).
33 • Nancy Spector, *Maurizio Cattelan: All* (N.Y.: Guggenheim, 2011) 108. The internal quotation is from Guy Debord, *Society of the Spectacle* (1967), thesis 1, translated by Ken Knabb, and available on the website of the Bureau of Public Secrets.
34 • Jan Verwoert, "Why are Conceptual Artists Painting Again? Because They Think It's a Good Idea," *Afterall* 12 (2005). Verwoert makes the point that artistic intervention today is made at the level of the environment — the total system of art, which characterizes the work of Cattelan very well.

critics: Cattelan's retrospective has been universally panned. I would argue that a major reason for this negative reaction is that Cattelan denies his critics a fixed standpoint from which to abstractly view his art — the Greenbergian ideal. He demands, rather, that the critic be immersed in the work of art. As Daniel Miller has suggested, "the paradoxical critic appreciates that they hold no transcendent position, but rather remain at ground level, involved in the same system."[35] This is the challenge of so-called post-media art. At the same time that the category of the aesthetic continues to expand, the very notion of the aesthetic becomes paradoxical. As Leonard Koren notes in his recent book, *Which 'Aesthetics' Do You Mean?* "aesthetics is pervasive in our lives and behavior. It's basic, it's primal. The way we dress, style our hair, decorate our homes, prepare our food, give names to things — these are all aesthetic activities. Then there's the novels we read, the music we listen to, the movies we view, the video games we play, the art we make and collect."[36] Through the involving nature of electronic mediation, we ourselves have become artifacts within this environment. As Friedrich Kittler suggested at the end of his career, media are how we configure our being.[37] We are now configuring our being as a work of art. That work of art has become environmental. It is this environment that we call "the media." •

35 • Daniel Miller, review of Boris Groys, Art Power (2008), in Art Margins Online (April 2009), www.artmargins.com, accessed 1 November 2011.
36 • Leonard Koren, *Which Aesthetics Do You Mean? Ten Definitions* (San Francisco: Imperfect Publishing, 2011) 1.
37 • Friedrich Kittler, *Optical Media* (London: Polity Press, 2010).

Richard Cavell is Professor of English at the University of British Columbia and the author of McLuhan in Space: A Cultural Geography.

Printed Letters, Acoustic Space, Real Time Internet: The Message of Current Communication Media, Deciphered with (and Beyond) McLuhan

Wolfgang Ernst

Message, massage: McLuhan's difference to Communication Studies

Although Marshall McLuhan is currently being re-discovered as a thinker of "social media" *avant la lettre*, a kind of prophet of the open source movement within the Internet community, the main lesson to take from McLuhan is still to look behind the computer screens, for a not content-orientated, but hidden message-orientated analysis. This requires — with and beyond McLuhan — a structural analysis of the techno-mathematical conditions of current media practices, to bring out the epistemological layers of such practices.

The message from beyond McLuhan's grave is a critical awareness for media-induced phenomena acting upon humans in implicit ways. McLuhan has inspired neurological studies into mass media perception, that is: the awareness of subliminal processes induced by technical (mechanical and electronic) media, such as later experiments like Herbert E. Krugmann's "Brain Wave Measures of Media Involvement."[1] McLuhan's seminal book *Understanding Media* originally did not develop out of interest in media-epistemological theory, but originated more traditionally in communication studies. *Understanding Media* had been commissioned as an educational report to analyze the impact of watching television on school children. It was "absolutely McLuhan" to turn this study upside down, resulting in a most original analysis of the deep impact of media on human perception on the subliminal level. Understanding media is not about content, but the *message* and *massage* of the medium: the affective, neurological level, analogous to the figure/ground separation as developed in *Gestalt* psychology.

Early 20th century artistic avant gardes have been triggered by media technologies, such as chronophotography and film. As has been pointed out by Clement Greenberg in his writings on art (and later by Michel Foucault in his interpretation of Manet), modernist painting itself has discovered the grounding materiality of the rectangular canvas as the principal message. According to McLuhan, who developed this insight further, it is the media-archaeological task of the artist to uncover such a ground (like according to Martin Heidegger it is the philosopher's task to reveal forgotten ontological substrata), and to communicate these insights in anticipation of what only belatedly becomes apparent to society.

McLuhan's insistence on the ground/figure distinction can be interpreted as the difference between the media-archaeological layering of media against their phenomenological (mass) media appearance on the level of interfaces and other surfaces.[2] This can be extended into the temporal domain, where frequency is the mathematical reversal of physical oscillations. High frequency carrier channels in telecommunication are being modulated by the varying low frequency articulations known to human perception as sound, music or speech, figuring or in-forming the basically *temporal* ground of transmission. Media archaeology is not only about spatial and topological grounds, but also about the floating groundings: "Ground cannot be dealt with conceptually or abstractly: it is ceaselessly changing, dynamic, discontinuous and heterogeneous, a mosaic of intervals and contours."[3]

Having said this, though, McLuhan's focus on the message of the medium *as perceived by human senses* lacks an essential understanding of the inner processes in telecommunication technologies for the second half of the 20th century and since, which are based upon the techno-mathematical theory of information as developed by Claude Shannon in 1948 in his "Mathematical Theory of Communication." McLuhan's critical, almost satirical reading of the Shannon diagram as a simple linear sender/receiver-relation reveals his essential ignorance of the mathematical reasoning involved in digital communication engineering; this makes all the difference between an

1 • Published in *Journal of Advertising Research* vol. 2, no. 1 (1971): 3–9
2 • Interfaces, though, may be treated different from traditional surfaces, since they represent a technical coupling.
3 • Marshall McLuhan and Eric McLuhan, *Laws of Media: The New Science* (Toronto: University of Toronto Press, 1988), 63

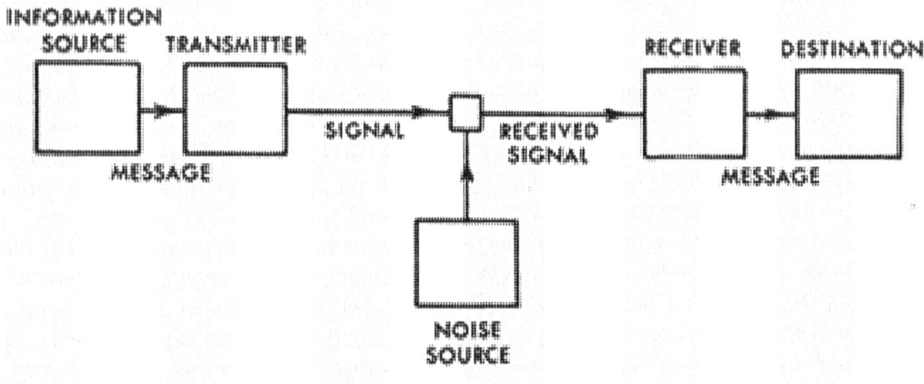

Fig. 1. — Schematic diagram of a general communication system.

▲
Claude Shannon's "Mathematical Theory of Communication," 1948.

analysis of the impact of mass media on audiences on the one side, and media archaeology on the other.

McLuhan's critical comment on Shannon's communication diagram is a disastrous simplification of its mathematical understanding. In his 1978 essay "The Brain and the Media. The 'Western' Hemisphere," McLuhan attributes the Shannon-Weaver model of communication to the predominantly left-hemispheric Gutenberg galaxy.[4] "The Shannon-Weaver model of communication [...] typifies left-brain lineal bias. It is a kind of pipeline model of a hardware container for software content. It [...] assumes that communication is a kind of literal *matching* rather than resonant *making*".[5] This reveals McLuhan's kind of "analogue thinking" from the electronic media age (thus being closer to the analogue computer indeed), as expressed by a follower of McLuhan, the radio scholar Tony Schwartz: "Electronic media have been viewed merely as extensions of print, and therefore subject to the same grammar [...]. The patterned auditory and visual information on television or radio is not 'content.' Content is a print term [...]. As stimuli, electronically mediated communication cannot be analyzed in the same way as print 'content.'"[6]

Can such an interpretation of electronic mass media still be applied to

4 • Quoted Peter Bexte, "Cadillac und Gebetmatte: McLuhans TV-Gemälde," inDerrick de Kerckhove, Martina Leeker, and Kerstin Schmidt (eds.), *McLuhan neu lessen: Kritische Analysen zu Medien und Kultur im 21. Jahrhundert* (Bielefeld: transcript, 2008), 323–337 (citation at 335).
5 • Marshall McLuhan and Eric McLuhan, *Laws of Media*, 86
6 • Tony Schwartz, *The Responsive Chord* (New York: Garden City /Anchor books, 1974), 19

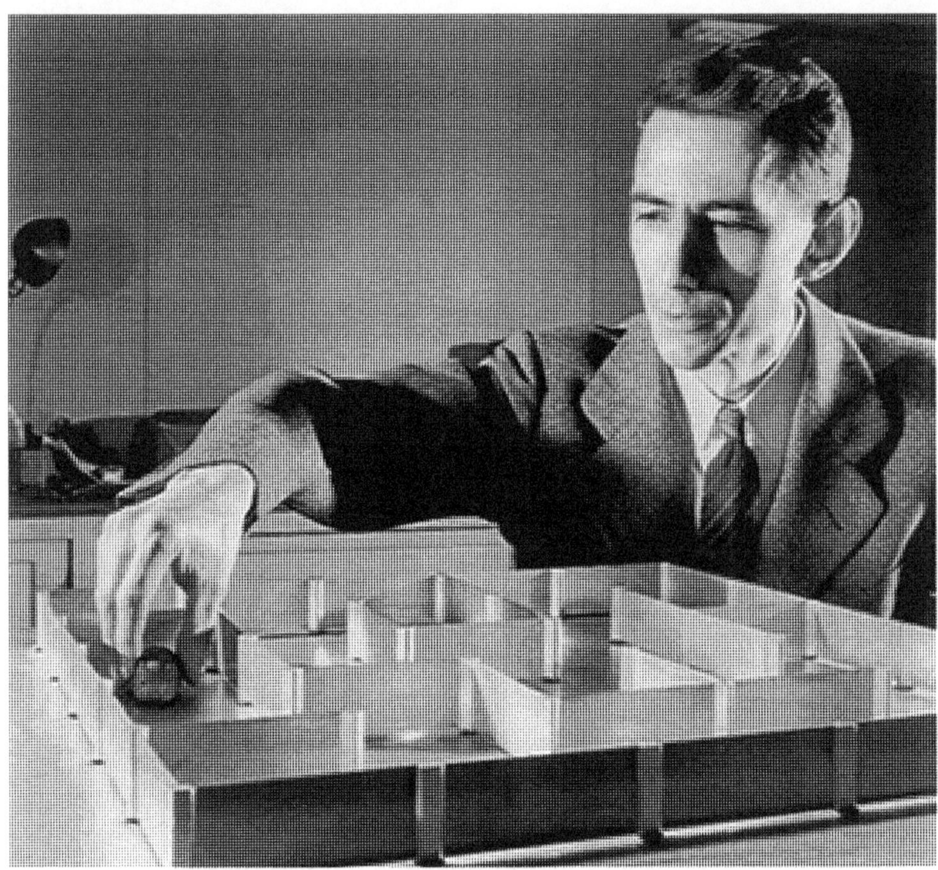

the mathematical theory that rules our digital communication media? McLuhan's brother in mind Schwartz continues:

> The function of a communicator is to achieve a state of resonance with the person receiving visual and auditory stimuli from television, radio, records, etc. Decoding symbolic forms such as [...] written words is no longer our most significant problem. They extract meaning from perception in a manner prescribed by the structure of the language, code this meaning symbolically, and store it in the brain. But the brain does not store everything in this way. Many of our experiences with electronic media are recorded and stored in the same way that they are perceived. [...] since the experience is not stored in a symbolic form, it cannot be retrieved by symbolic cues.[7]

But it is an almost Hegelian irony of technological reason in the history of cultural engineering, that what looks like

7 • Ibid, 24.

non-symbolic (and rather signal-based) audiovisual media in the age of digital communication re-turns in an even more rigid symbolic order. The implicit message of the meta-medium computer is that all former media (especially the signal-based ones) are symbolically transformed from distinct hardware to software, thus: software formats.[8]

A first step in symbolic coding had been spoken language, then writing (especially the phonetic alphabet); these cultural technologies have since been more or less immediate to the human processor. Nowadays though, the alphanumeric programs remain hidden to most users.

Understanding Media in the age of Internet
In order to understand media in the age of the Internet, let us focus on its time-critical aspects, which are the message of Internet-based communication (especially in the form of so-called Web2). McLuhan is not just a historical hero of media theories. As for the Internet and mobile media, it is still useful to follow McLuhan's advice not to ask about the content and its social implications only, but to look equally at the subliminal message or rather massage which is thereby being induced.

McLuhan analyzed the cultural impact of media not on the level of semantic content, as in communication studies, but rather directed attention to their *sublime*, non-figurative message (in the sense of Immanuel Kant and Edward Burke), that is: the ways media act upon and reshape the perceptional schemata within humans. As such, media power operates by "amplifying human sensory preceptors"[9] in their different physiological channels. Among these, the amplification of temporal schemata reigns supreme, but this amplification leads to irritations. Walter Benjamin in his 1936 essay on the work of art in the age of technical reproduction insisted that aesthetic "aura" depends on real presence in space and time. Nevertheless, electronic television, by means of *live* transmission, is able to generate an impression of presence by real signal synchronicity in time across spatial distance. At the same time, human senses have difficulty differentiating *live* from broadcasting of *live from tape* or (nowadays) digital transmission in *real time*:

One can no longer distinguish, visually or aurally, between that which is reproduced and its reproduction [...] not even discern *that* or *when* reproduction or repetition, in the manifest sense of recording or replaying, is taking place. We must be informed whether or not what we are seeing is "live." [...] we cannot distinguish

8 • See Stefan Heidenreich, *FlipFlop: Digitale Datenströme und die Kultur des 21. Jahrhunderts* (Munich and Vienna: Hanser, 2004).
9 • Ibid, 24.

through our senses alone between what we take to be simply "alive" and what as reproduction, separated from its origin, is structurally posthumous.[10]

Samuel Weber discovers for live media what Jacques Derrida once called the "iterability" of the mark.

The liveness of media springs from their temporal effects. In a McLuhanite reading, the essential message of electronic communication transfer is in its temporal field. The previous technical media of storing physical events (photography, phonography, cinematography) have been counter-balanced by media of pure transfer in the 20th century. Prominently ranging among these has been radio based on the electronic vacuum tube and its functional successor (though irreplaceable in the case of the TV monitor tube), the transistor. The thermionic tube has been the defining element of electronics as such. McLuhan neglected this decisive media-archaeological artifact, remaining a philologist rather than an engineer, thus being media scholar only half way. That is how he can write of "electricity" as the paradigmatic energy form of the present, whereas electronics does not simply mean electric energy but the directability, almost governance (both analogue and logical), of free-floating electrons in vacuum space with almost light speed, thus allowing for low-currency-based information engineering.

The characteristic of early radio has been that it transferred music and speech without storing sound at all (electromagnetic waves "store" signals only as a relativistic effect). From that derives a general phenomenological insight: analog mass media like radio and television exist always only momentarily in the "now," being located in time itself. In that sense, radio is a "hot" medium.[11] McLuhan's differentiation between "hot" and "cold" media can be applied to the technical modes of generating temporal affects, ranging between intensive and extensive temporal involvement of the participant. The "live" effect of technical communication takes place since the age of the telephone (whereas telegraphy, intermediated by the inscription paper of dashes and dots, rather represented what we now call differential "live on tape").

Such a time-critically sharpened reading of McLuhan's medium/message theorem leads to new ways of approaching the temporal bias of technical media which is not only a macro-temporal *bias of communication* in a Harold Innis-mode of media theory, "but an intensive microtemporality."[12]

10 • See Stefan Heidenreich, *FlipFlop: Digitale Datenströme und die Kultur des 21. Jahrhunderts* (Munich and Vienna: Hanser, 2004).
11. • Wolfgang Hagen, *Theorien des Radios: Ästhetik und Äther,* www.whagen.de/seminare/AETHER/aether3.htm
12. • See Jussi Parikka, "Operative Media Archaeology: Wolfgang Ernst's Materialist Media Diagrammatics," in *Theory Culture & Society,* September 2011; vol. 28, 5: 52–74.

In a very different way, the temporal message of digital communication media is in temporal deferral: from *live on tape* to media content *on demand*. This is the temporal signature of webcasting.[13] This time-critical sovereignty and immediacy in access means a "tactilization" of what has been non-individual mass media broadcasting before, in fact: an almost *haptic* access to media time (to use one of McLuhan's terms). Something disappears at the same time: the clear distinction between what is present and what is past, what is transmitted "live" and what comes out of the archive. Some online-services of radio or TV channels offer access to commentaries on current news, while at the same time offering access to other commentaries on previous occasions. The delineations of the archive to the present become diffuse, almost fuzzy.

Technical *Eigenzeit* (the temporal logic inherent to media) shapes the collective perception of time; time itself loses its individual character. The study of time challenges media studies.[14] Here is the message of Internet-based communication: the dominant communication platform of today, the World Wide Web, needs to be analyzed on its operative level of temporal processualities and eventualities.

Communication networks are not just topological systems being expressed by hypertextual links, but time-critical processes as well. A symptom of this is a term which does not nominate a new medium but declares the temporal mode its decisive media-theoretical criterion: the *real-time web* which is "a set of technologies and practices which enable users to receive information as soon as it is published [...], rather than requiring that they or their software check a source periodically for updates."[15] The communicative practice of *instant messaging* belongs to this temporal field; in McLuhan's sense the message of the medium here is immediacy serving to create the illusion of a pseudo-co-presence. This recent form of web economy is being defined by communication within the time-critical realm; cyberspace as *docuverse* is being replaced by an extremely accelerated information processing in cybertime.[16] The Internet thus

13 • Andreas Bade, "Radio im Internet: Zwei Wege für die 'Stimme' im Netz," in Bade, *Das Internet als programmbegleitendes Medium des Hörfunks: Historische Entwicklung von Internet, Radio und ihrer Medientheorien* (Hamburg. Diplomica Verlag, 2009), 57–86, available online, www.mediaculture-online.de
14 • "Zeit ist damit auch die Herausforderung einer Medienwissenschaft," Stefan Rieger, *Kybernetische Anthropologie: Eine Geschichte der Virtualität* (Frankfurt am Main, Suhrkampm 2003), 143
15 • en.wikipedia.org/wiki/Real-time_web (accessed January 20, 2010)
16 • "Früher ging es um die Schaffung von Räumen [...] heute geht es um die Zeit selbst, um Chronos, um die Kunst der *longue durée*." Geert Lovink, "Was uns wirklich krank macht," Frankfurter Allgemeine Zeitung No 140, June 21, 2010: 27 (referring to the media theory of Franco Bernardi)

turns out not to be just a topological extension of a generalized archive, but equally as a chrono-technical "compression of time."[17] This requires a close look at time-critical operations on the physical and logistical level of the Internet, for example the "Ping" signal. With the Internet, each data packet into which a document has been sliced is being observed individually; its transfer happens independent from its preceding or successive packages. This procedure is radically time-critical since it takes place within the so-called Time To Live-field which defines the maximal temporal duration in seconds an IP packet is allowed to exist in the Internet. A counter is progressively being reduced during this routing; in case the TTL-counter reaches zero before the packet has reached its destination, it is being annihilated.[18] Media time is not endless.

Communication, in this sense, is about time-sharing (not primarily about exchange of meaning) — just like in physics, engineering and systems theory "communication" is about signal interaction first. This reminds one of a primary scene in media archaeology, the *momentum* of telegraphy, when one of the first messages exchanged on the Morse system in the United States between Baltimore and Washington was a quest for time — with the response indicating local time in almost immediate speed, (almost) without delay.[19] The message of telegraphy in its early, that is: media-archeological phase, is (about) tempor(e)alities — coupling (synchronizing) sender and receiver in the time domain which is, in McLuhan's sense, the tactile temporal affect. What has still been verbal time-communication between human operators on the telegraphic channel later became the technical time signal, with the temporal signal as low frequency modulation of a high frequency signal itself being the message, and not *allegorically* carrying another meaning.

The "acoustic" structure of electronic media

Notwithstanding his confusing electricity and electronics, McLuhan made a crucial discovery. In a letter to P. F. Strawson, author of *Individuals. An Essay in Descriptive Metaphysics* (1959), McLuhan quotes from that work: "Sounds, of course, have temporal relations to each other ... but they have no intrinsic spatial characters."[20]

The immediacy of electricity has been valued essential by McLuhan as the definite difference to the Gutenberg world of scriptural and printed information:

17 • Ibid.
18 • Othmar Kyas, *Internet: Zugang, Utilities, Nutzung* (Bergheim: DATACOM, 1994), 65
19 • The topic of Florian Sprenger's talk "'Intellect hath conquered time': The Presence of Electricity and the Rise of Telegraphy," at the conference *Global Communication Electric. Social, Cultural, and Political Aspects of Telegraphy,* February 18–19, 2001, Museum of Communication, Berlin
20 • Dated April 17, 1969, *Letters of Marshall McLuhan,* selected and edited by Matie Molinaro, Corinne McLuhan, and William Toye (Oxford: Oxford University Press, 1987), 367

Visual man is the most extreme case of abstractionism because he has separated his visual faculty from the other senses.[T]oday it is threatened, not by any single factors such as television or radio, but by the electric speed of information movement in general. Electric speed is approximately the speed of light, and this constitutes an information environment that has basically an acoustic *structure*.[21]

Very media-archaeologically, McLuhan's term "acoustic structure" evidently refers to an epistemological ground, not to the acoustic figure (what ears can hear). This groundbreaking moment took place with the collapse of Euclidean space into Riemann spaces and culminates around 1900 with quantum physical notions (the para-sonic wave/particle dualism, up to the "superstring" theory of today) on the one side, and Henri Bergson's dynamic idea of matter as image in the sense of vibrating waves and frequencies.[22] McLuhan's "acoustic space" is oscillating time and implicitly returns in Gilles Deleuze's "interval" philosophy.

In an epistemological sense, the sonic is not about (or limited to) the audible at all, but a mode of revealing modalities of temporal processuality.

At the speed of light, information is simultaneous from all directions and this is the structure of the act of *hearing*, i.e. the *message* or effect of electric information is acoustic, even when it is perceived as an electronic image, as defined by the video artist Bill Viola in his essay "The Sound of One Line Scanning".[23]

The temporal *punctum* becomes decisive: "The *interval* is where the action *is*"[24]; unwillingly, McLuhan here grasps the essence of binary data processing — the "time of non-reality" (as defined by Norbert Wiener) in switching between Zero and One. In this aspect, McLuhan at first sight misinterprets electronics once more: by understanding the computer as a mere extension of electronics. The point is that the computer conceptually is not dependent on electricity at all but basically a trans-machinic medium, a "paper machine" (in Alan Turing terms). Computer culture as it actually takes place is indeed time-critically bound to electric speed.

"Tetrads": Alternative media historiograms

Marshall McLuhan and his son Eric figure as co-authors of a final work which claims an encompassing theory of media (in)

21 • Letter to Barbara Ward, February 9, 1973, in *Letters of Marshall McLuhan*, 466
22 • Henri Bergson, *Matière et Mémoire* (Paris: Alcan, 1896).
23 • Bill Viola, "The Sound of One Line Scanning," in Dan Lander and Micah Lexier (eds), *Sound by Artists* (Toronto: Art Metropole & Walter Phillips Gallery, 1990), 39–54.
24 • McLuhan ibid.

time: *Laws of Media*.[25] The sub-title of this work ("The New Science") explicitly refers to Giambattista Vico's model of recurrent states in cultural history; for media history, McLuhan calls them "tetrads". Somewhat in the tradition of philosophical phenomenology, McLuhan's tetrads are meant to direct attention to the hidden or unnoticed qualities of technologies in culture — literally media archaeology.

With all his sometimes stupefying imprecisions in media analysis, McLuhan had a stunning sense for alternatives to media historiography as simple history of technologies or cultural history. These alternatives do not result from distant reflection only but from media themselves.

"Just as linear history begins with writing, it ends with TV."[26] In the 1954 version of Marshall McLuhan's pamphlet *Counterblast* the "Media Log" is explicit: "Sigfried Giedion has had to invent the concept of an 'anonymous history' in order to write an account of the new technological culture."[27] In another version of the pamphlet McLuhan declares: "Just as there was no history when there was no linear time sense, so there is post-history now when everything that ever was in the world becomes simultaneously present to our consciousness."[28] Illustrative of this oscillating state (though here paradoxically taking place in a static spatial image form) is the mural painting in McLuhan's seminar room at Toronto university campus: René Cera, *Pied Pipers All* (1969).[29]

Since the dominant mass medium of his age, television, has been McLuhan's research-guiding medium, it is from the time-critical nature of the electronic image that McLuhan derives his insight into the radically temporal message of high-technological media:

You are drawn into that tube, as an inner trip. You're totally involved. You have no objectivity, no distance. And it is acoustic. It resonates. But this is a hidden ground, because superficially people think they're looking at a visual program. And they're not. They're not looking at all — they're absorbed, involved in a resonating experience.[30]

But today, such formerly "acoustic" TV images consist of digital pixels (different from the cathode ray "mosaic" of the iconoscope as referred to in McLuhan's times). In terms of analyzing current computer-based media culture,

25 • Marshall McLuhan and Eric McLuhan, *Laws of Media: The New Science* (Toronto: University of Toronto Press, 1988).
26 • Marshall McLuhan, *Counterblast* (New York: Harcourt, Brace & World, 1969), 122, as quoted in Bexte, "Cadillac und Gebetmatte," 332. This diagnosis has been shared by the media philosopher Vilém Flusser in his writings on the alphabet and on the nature of the technical image.
27 • Recently published on occasion of the media arts festival *transmediale.11* in Berlin (in cooperation with Gingko Press) in 2011.
28 • McLuhan, *Counterblast*, 122.
29 • Photographic color reproduction in: de Kerckhove et al, *McLuhan neu lessen*, 331.
30 • McLuhan in interview with Jerry Brown, in *The CoEvolution Quarterly*, Winter 1977/78; *Letters of Marshall McLuhan*, 177

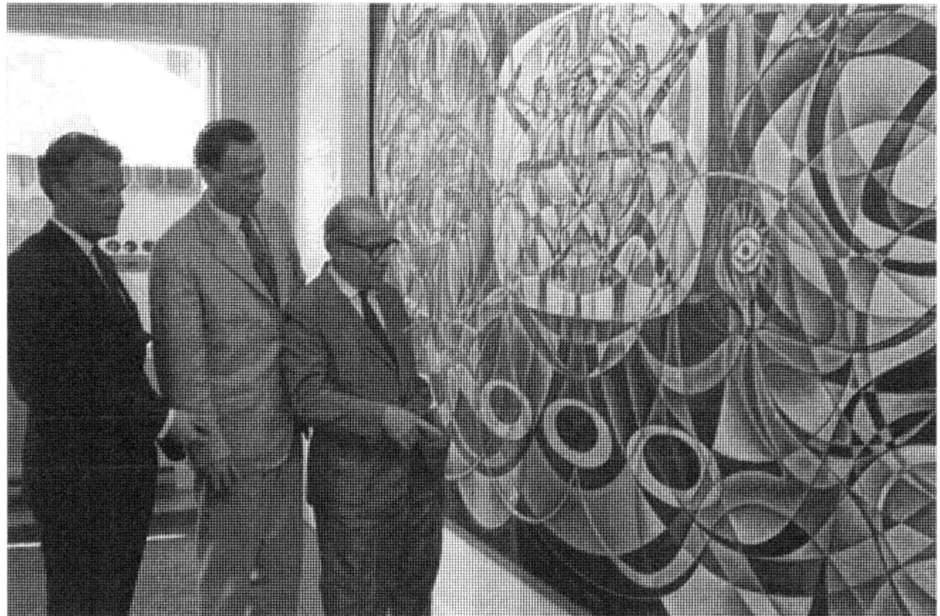

McLuhan's electricity-centered approach seems antiquated. But when it comes to apply his critique of technical communication to the re-thinking of media history, the replacement of scriptural linearity by "sonic" resonance becomes productive. "Resonance" is McLuhan's central figure of dynamic temporality taking place in acoustic space which is "organic and integral, perceived through the simultaneous interplay of all the senses," a kind of "echoland"[31] — sonic time rather than history.

Electromagnetic signals are capable of evoking almost immediate effects in a resonant receiving system. Resonance compares to the dynamic tempor(e)ality of the electro-magnetic field rather than to the mono-dimensional transmission in a linear channel. Such interpretations of electronic communication that intermediates between humans expressively refer to the non-linear epistemology of the sonic temporal field[32] and thus provide a model for non-historic ways of writing media time. In a benevolent re-reading, McLuhan's notion of the "tetrad" suggests a diagrammatic media archaeology dealing with recursive reconfigurations.

The McLuhans (father and son) in *Laws of Media* describe the artists of their time as "the antennae of the race" who "had tuned in to the new ground and begun exploring of discontinuity and simultaneity."[33] This is not meant metaphorically, but uses terms of radio

31 • Marshall McLuhan, "The Playboy Interview: Marshall McLuhan," in:Playboy Magazine, March 1969; reprint in: Eric McLuhan / Frank Zingrone (eds), *The Essential McLuhan* (London; Routledge) 1997), 233–269 (www.columbia.edu/~log2/mediablogs/ McLuhanPBinterview.htm).
32 • "In watching television, our eyes function like our ears," Schwartz, *The Responsive Chord*, 14.
33 • McLuhan and McLuhan, *Laws of Media*, 47.

Bless the fast-talking illiterate American
his face-to-face
ear-to-ear
methods of learning

The crafty cubist J I V E of the daily
press awakening the political appetite of
COSMIC MAN

The starched SHIRT-FRONT symbol of the
printed page
of mass production and commercial
elegance

B L E S S
French Canadian HOCKEY PLAYERS
for keeping art on ice
for our one contribution to
INTERNATIONAL CULTURE

Pages from Marshall McLuhan's
***Counterblast* (1954).**

B L E S S

BLESS the sports page, upholder of
HOMERIC CULTURE

the comic strips, pantheon of
PICKLED GODS and
ARCHETYPES

advertising art, for its pictorial
VITALITY
and verbal CREATIVITY

BLESS the locomotives WHISTLING
on the prairies proclaiming
the SEPARATENESS
Of Man

BLESS FOTOPRINT able to modulate
the printed visual image to the
full range of acoustic space.

technology. They quote from T. E. Eliot's 1917 essay on "Tradition and the Individual Talent" where what Eliot named *historical sense* is — in McLuhan's paraphrase– the awareness of a "resonant interplay". According to Eliot, the whole of the literature of Europe from Homer "has a simultaneous existence and composes a simultaneous order."[34] Instead of historicism, this is short-circuiting epochs that are distant in terms of historical time but immediate to each other media-archaeologically. This modality is genuinely time-bound, thus "acoustic" rather than visual.

Electro-acoustic space

Recent years proclaim — as a counterblast to the so-called "visual turn" or "pictorial turn" as declared by W. J. T. Mitchell long ago — another rebellion against the McLuhanite Gutenberg galaxy, which is the "sonic" or "acoustic turn," accompanied by new methods of making information, and even knowledge, accessible over the long neglected acoustic channel of perception (audio interfaces, methods of sonification of data to the time-sensitive ear). It has been McLuhan who anticipated this turn already, a theorem bound to his analysis of the electronic age which he sharply discontinues from the machinic age.

McLuhan at the borderline of digital computing

But McLuhan's apparent emphasis on electricity hampered him from conceiving the computer in terms other than just anecdotes. Maybe this was the case because he considered the ancient Greek phonetic alphabet responsible for an original sin of the occidental psyche and culture of knowledge, which replaced collective *mimesis* by individualized objectivity and privileged linear, analytic, visually based acquisition of information, resulting in the geometry of control systems.

In chapter 11 of *Understanding Media*, McLuhan defines the nature of the number as "an extension and separation of our most intimate and interrelating activity, our sense of touch"[35] – when fingers are used for discrete counting. But counting in times of mechanized mathematics takes another dimension. McLuhan's *Understanding Media* finishes with a chapter on "automatization"; just up to this limit the author in 1964 perceives the computer.[36]

McLuhan, with his servomechanistic concept of man-machine symbiosis, heavily refers to the cybernetic epistemology of his day, but significantly blinds out the mathematical foundation on which Norbert Wiener always insisted — a mathematization that ultimately

34 • T. S. Eliot, *Selected Essays*, quoted in McLuhan and McLuhan *Laws of Media*, 48.
35 • McLuhan, *Understanding Media: The Extensions of Man* (New York: McGraw-hill, 1964), 107.
36 • See Jens Schröter, "Von Heiß/Kalt zu Analog/Digital; Die Automation als Grenze von McLuhans Medienanthropologie," in: de Kerckhove et al, *McLuhan neu lessen*, 304–320.

replaced McLuhan's vision of a synchronous, instant and resonant "acoustic space" by digital calculation.[37]

The essential von Neumann-architecture of current computing as algorithmic and storage-programmable symbolic machine is acknowledged only in the posthumously edited work *Laws of Media*. But here again, in the best tradition of the central thesis of *Understanding Media*, the McLuhans (both father and son) try to identify the central "message" of the digital computer, less than its social impact, which has been dominated by the "Personal Computer" concept and Graphical User Interface since.

In an uncanny way, McLuhan transforms from a historicized media theorist into an up-to-date model exactly when reading his posthumous work. This after-life is part of the argument already. All of a sudden, McLuhan seems a little bit less dead when reading his identification of computing media as a machine whose essential message is rooted in its delicate time management. Under this aspect, the computer as the dominant medium of today can not only be understood more precisely, but turns out to be a chrono-poet itself, actively reshaping current culture on the basic level (or *a priori*) which George Kubler once described in his *Shape of Time*. Even though this insight has been borrowed from other scholars, as often in McLuhan's fast-processing works, it is directed by a remarkable skill to identify the crucial and original arguments: "Jeremy Rifkin shows that, thanks to the computer, visual centralized time is a s obsolete as visual space. The Central Processing Unit orchestrates a ballet of operations in simultaneous times, chronology in counterpoint."[38] This is an understanding of *mousike* in its ancient Greek sense. Here, McLuhan comes close to what has recently been termed the "algorhythmic" (Shintaro Miyazaki)[39] — carrying his notion of "acoustic space" into the digital kernel.

Thus the computer is not just time-based as performing arts and technical media before, but itself becomes chrono-poetical. A distinguishing feature of the computer is "its temporal creativity".[40] Referring to David Bolter's *Turing's Man*[41], McLuhan points out "that while clocks are all set to the same exacting sequence, duration, and rhythm, the computer is free to manipulate all three of these temporal dimensions by merely changing the program"[42] — which is true especially for the von Neumann architecture of computing, a concrete embodiment of the algorithms as being-in-the-world, and thus in time.

37 • See Martina Leeker, "Camouflagen des Computers: McLuhan und die Neo-Avantgarden der 1960er Jahre," in de Kerckhove et al, *McLuhan neu lessen*: 345–374, citation at 357.
38 • Marshall and McLuhan *Laws of Media*, 53.
39 • Shintaro Miyazaki, "Das Algorhythmische. Microsounds an der Schwelle zwischen Klang und Rhythmus," in Axel Volmar (ed), *Zeitkritische Medien* (Berlin: Kulturverlag Kadmos, 2009), 383–396
40 • McLuhan and McLuhan *Laws of Media*, 53.
41 • David Bolter, *Turing´s Man: Western Culture in the Computer Age* (Chapel Hill: The University of North Carolina Press, 1984), 38f.
42 • McLuhan and McLuhan, *Laws of Media*, 53.

"With this new timepiece, time is no longer a single fixed reference point that exists external to events. Time is now 'information' and is choreographed directly into the programs by the central processor"[43]; this choreography is media theatre in its dramatic, time-operative sense.

With computers we enter the age of "multiple times"; every program here has its own unique sequences, durations, rhythms, its own unique time. [...] The clock dial is an analogue of the solar day, an acknowledgement that we perceive time revolving in a circle, corresponding to the rotation of the earth. In contrast, computer time is independent of nature: it creates its own context[44]

— up to so-called Internet Time. Genuine media time is *Eigenzeit*, just like in acoustic space "every thing or event creates its own space, and time."[45] "The computer imprints a unique temporality into every program,"[46] which makes all the difference between an algorithm written with pencil on paper (like a musical score) and its implementation as an actually running program (like a musical performance differs from its symbolic score). The message of the computer as medium is not just its temporality, but more: its different hard- and software-biased tempo realities. The totalizing cultural and semantic reference "time" implodes. It is the timing mechanism within the computer which brings it close to what Aristoxenus once coined *chronoi* for measuring the temporal duration in music, dance and prosodic speech.[47] Media theory, today, thus needs to be algorhythmic itself, just as the conventional concept of media history is being replaced by chrono-archival reconfigurations and media-archaeological recursions. Thus, re-reading McLuhan still sets media theory in motion. •

Lecture on occasion of the conference *McLuhan revisited* at the Fritt Ord Foundation, Oslo, April 12, 2011

Wolfgang Ernst is Professor and Chair at the Institute for Musicology and Media Studies, Humboldt-Universität, Berlin.

43 • Ibid. Refering to David Bolter.
44 • Ibid.
45 • Ibid.
46 • Ibid.

47 • Aristoxenus, *Elementa Rhythmica: The Fragment of Book II and the Additional Evidence for Aristoxenian Rhythmic Theory*, ed. Lionel Pearson (Oxford: Clarendon Press, 1990).

Media and Maelstroms

Staffan Ericson

1 • Marshall McLuhan, *Understanding Me: Lectures and Interviews* (Cambridge, Mass: MIT, 2003), 172.

I have always been very careful never to predict anything that had not already happened. The future is not what it used to be. It is here. And when you look into the rearview mirror what you ordinarily see is not the car you passed but the truck that is coming up on you fast.

Marshall McLuhan, 1970

The most common explanation of the current interest in Marshall McLuhan is his apparent gift for making predictions. Already in 1970, in the television interview quoted above, Tom Wolfe offers a checklist of McLuhan predictions from the early 1960s, which all seemed to have come true by the end of that decade. McLuhan shrugs this suggestion off, resisting, as he did often, the role of a prophet, insisting, as always, that the rearview mirror will provide poor navigational aid: "Never look back [...] The present includes the past and the future."[1]

This is peculiar advice, coming from someone whose legacy rests on a series of historical distinctions (tribal culture, print culture, electronic culture), and whose reputation as a prophet has been growing ever since. While most items on Wolfe's lists may by now be forgotten, the 21st century has been offered a new set of premonitions to be confirmed, by those very same McLuhan texts: online-surfing, post-humans, pro-sumers, glocalisation.

And just how did he do that? If we are to believe the

man himself, McLuhan learnt just about everything he knew about media from modern artists. From James Joyce, Wyndham Lewis, Charles Baudelaire, people who knew to adjust their sensory awareness to the present, and to avoid the sort of hindsight that would obstruct insight. Already in his 1940s dissertation on Renaissance poet Thomas Nashe, McLuhan introduced the theme of the "impercipience of the ubiquitous"[2]: the way in which our environment under normal circumstances will remain invisible to us, like water to fish. This theme will remain in place throughout most of his media theory. For instance, *The Gutenberg Galaxy* (1962),[3] McLuhan's book on print culture, is declared to have been written at a point when that galaxy was no longer ubiquitous as environment, when the glow of its stars was actually fading. Thus, the full scope of its constellation was distinctly intelligible (as rational logic, visuality, nationalism, individualism, cities, assembly lines). While the galaxy or environment that gradually had engulfed the 20th century, the electronic, remained invisible. This is the condition that invites the unfortunate habit of "looking back": "We march backwards into the future. Suburbia lives imaginatively in Bonanza-land."[4] "Every age creates as an Utopian image a nostalgic rear-view mirror image of itself, which puts it thoroughly out of touch with the present."[5]

If McLuhan was right about this (too), our current fascination with him may follow less from how the world has moved in directions he once predicted, and more from how we prefer to view the "content" of our own present in the "form" of an older environment (i.e. by living imaginatively in "McLuhanland," a "global village" where "the medium is the message," much like McLuhan's contemporaries lived in "Bonanza-land," i.e. the wild west of the 19th century).

The claim that "the present includes the past and the future" is by no means unique for modern times (one need only think of Augustine), but McLuhan's version is historically specific, and well in tune with how others have framed the modernization of time itself: with the acceleration of social and technological change, historical experience shrinks into presentism, "the

2 • Marshall McLuhan, *The Classical Trivium: The Place of Thomas Nashe in the Learning of his Time*, ed. W. T. Gordon (Corte Madera, Gingko Press, 2006), 68.
3 • Marshall McLuhan, *The Gutenberg Galaxy: The Making of Typographic Man* (Toronto: The University of Toronto Press. 1962).
4 • Marshall McLuhan & Quentin Fiore, *The Medium is the Massage: An Inventory of Effects* (New York: Random House, 1967), 74–75.
5 • Quote from a televised conversation between Norman Mailer and McLuhan, broadcasted by CBC in 1968.
6 • Marshall McLuhan, *Understanding Media: The Extensions of Man* (Berkeley: Gingko Press, 1964/2011), 25.

sequence yields to the simultaneous."[6] A jet plane, McLuhan notes, needs no rearview mirrors. At jet speed, the foreseeable future is already there, at the moment you decide to take a look. To "look back" under such conditions is to take a position that McLuhan often will mock, as well as use at times: the position of a "prophet turned backwards" (Schlegel). A predicament famously acknowledged and illustrated in Walter Benjamin's reading of Klee's *Angelus Novus*, in which the wings of an "angel of history" are caught in the storm of "progress," a storm that "irresistibly propels him into the future to which his back is turned," history appearing before his eyes, not as a chain of events, but as "one single catastrophe which keeps piling wreckage upon wreckage and hurls it in front of his feet."[7]

Like McLuhan, Walter Benjamin is a twentieth-century media theorist who, for many, appears as particularly sustainable for orientation in the twentyfirst. Just how did *they* do that? And just how did these two, as often noted,[8] "think alike" (one a Jewish Marxist, schooled in the aesthetic philosophy of German romanticism, the other a conservative Catholic, schooled in classical Trivium and Cambridge practical criticism)? As for mutual influences, both had sent early drafts or publications to the same man: the Swiss historian of architecture, Sigfried Giedion. In Benjamin's case, the work in preparation was the *Arcades Project*, and the source of inspiration was Giedion's *Bauen in Frankreich* (1928). In McLuhan's case, the inspiration was Giedion's *Mechanization Takes Command* (1948), and the work in preparation was McLuhan's first major publication: *The Mechanical Bride* (1951). Its preface touches on many aspirations of Benjamin's *Arcades Project*. In both, the premise is that the modern world is saturated with myths: "a sort of a collective dream" (McLuhan), a "*Zeit-Traum*" for the sleeping collective (Benjamin). In both, the task is to devise a trick to interrupt its context and continuity: in Benjamin, a "dialectics at a standstill," leading to "historical awakening"; In McLuhan, a "reversing of the process" leading "out of the labyrinth": "A whirling phantasmagoria can be grasped only when arrested for contemplation. And this very arrest is also a release from the usual participation."[9]

7 • Walter Benjamin, "Theses on the Philosophy of History," in *Illuminations* (New York: Schocken, 1950/1969), 257–258
8 • See Richard Cavell, *McLuhan in Space: A Cultural Geography* (Toronto: University of Toronto Press, 2002); John Durham Peters, "McLuhan's Grammatical Theology," *Canadian Journal of Communication*, Vol. 36 (2011); Judith Stamps, *Unthinking Modernity: Innis, McLuhan, and the Frankfurt School* (Montréal: McGill-Queen's Press, 1995).
9 • Marshall McLuhan, *The Mechanical Bride: Folklore of Industrial Man* (Corte Madera: Gingko Press, 1951/2002), v.

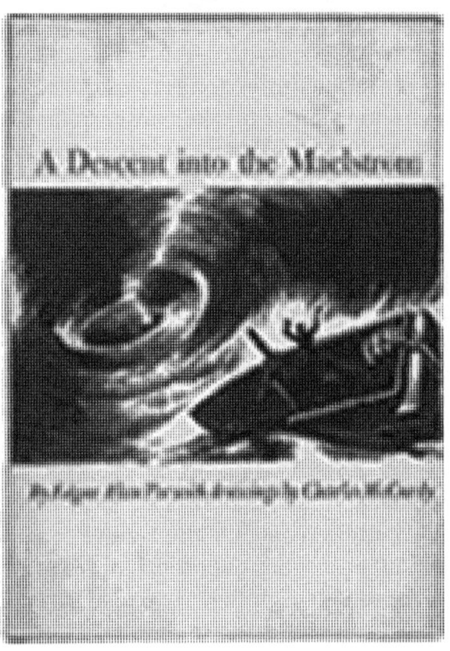

Cover of *A Descent into the Maelstrom*, with drawings by Charles McCurdy.

In the first passages of this preface, McLuhan illustrates his method by referring to a short story (one he keeps referring to, until his very last lecture, in 1979). The writer is Edgar Allan Poe; the story is "A Descent in the Maelstrom".[10] It is the story told by a Norwegian fisherman, to a visitor of Lofoten. While out fishing with his two brothers, the fishermen's boat gets caught in the "Moskoe maelstrom," a mighty "vortex" formed by the flux of ebb and flood under stormy conditions. This whirlpool sucks large vessels and whales into the depths of the ocean, drags them towards destruction at its bottom, and returns debris and fragments to the surface. While the teller of the tale loses both of his brothers in this whirlpool, he manages to save himself by leaving the boat during its descent, and attaching his body to a smaller cask, shaped in a form that will return unscathed to the surface. McLuhan provides only brief commentary on this story, as if the allegory was obvious: to survive in the whirlpool of information, we must not only resist it, but learn to master it, ride its currents, literally "surf" its waves. As discovered by the fisherman at the most critical of moments, this skill will involve a sort of "pattern recognition" that goes beyond ordinary sensory perception (which is what artists are good at, and why they may provide the rest of us with navigational aid/warning systems).

In the Poe story, the fishermen's encounter with the maelström is caused by a malfunction of chronometrics:

> I dragged my watch from its fob. It was not going. I glanced at its face by the moonlight, and then burst into tears as I flung it into the ocean. *It had run down at seven o'clock! We were behind the time of the slack, and the whirl of the Ström was in full fury!*

With Benjamin and McLuhan, any "awakening" from the dream or "release" from the whirlpool, will involve the suspension of a time that is linear, sequenced, and progressive. Inside Poe's maelstrom, time seem out of joint: the fisherman looks up, and notices how the moon above and the foam of the water form "a magnificent rainbow, like that narrow and tottering bridge which

10 • Edgar Allan Poe, "A Descent in The Maelström," in *Great Short Works. Poems, Tales, Criticism* (New York: Harper & Row, 1841/1970).

Musselmen say is the only pathway between Time and Eternity."
He looks down, and senses how "progress" must lead to "dreadful doom": the coming of the last hour. At this point, he becomes "possessed with the keenest curiosity of the whirl itself."

> I positively felt a *wish* to explore its depth, even at the sacrifice I was going to make. [...] I now began to watch, with a strange interest, the numerous things that floated in our company. I *must* have been delirious — for I even sought *amusement* in speculating upon the relative velocities of their several descents towards the foam below.

Benjamin and McLuhan have both routinely been characterized as being "positive" or "optimistic" in regard to modern media technology and culture — to Guy Debord McLuhan appeared as "the spectacle's first apologist [...] the most convinced imbecile of the century."[11] In both cases, the claim will run into difficulties upon closer scrutiny. But there is certainly some positive "wish" and some "amusement" in their respective attempt to "follow the collective" into the *Zeit-Traum* of fashion and advertising (Benjamin), to "set the reader at the center of the revolving picture" of press, radio, movies (McLuhan). Without such immersion, the trick might fail. For the trick is precisely, in Benjamin's terms, to turn the immediate *Erlebnis* of modern man into true, historical *Erfahrung*. While McLuhan in 1951 still may use the term "contemplation" for the right grasp, he will soon replace it, even oppose it, with the exploration of other sensory registers: more tactile-audile than visual, more subliminal than rational, more collective than individualistic. Here, too, Benjamin was a fore-runner: according to the artwork essay,[12] "contemplation" was for auratic paintings, while film was a "field of practice" for "distracted" and "tactile" perception, the sort that increasingly engaged collective experience and artistic production.

But as the point of the trick was getting out of the dream/mastering the whirlpool, involvement must somehow lead to detachment. The fisherman is getting close, while speculating about those floating objects: "It was not a new terror that thus affected me, but the dawn of a more exciting *hope*. This hope arose partly from memory, partly from present observation." The fisherman's memory has produced images of the shores of Lofoten, covered by objects coming out of the *Ström*, most of them shattered to splinters and fragments, but some not disfigured at all. His "present observations" concern the movement of objects inside the

11 • Guy Debord, *Comments on the Society of the Spectacle* (London: Verso, 1990), 33.
12 • Walter Benjamin, "The Work of Art in the Age of Mechanical Reproduction," in *Illuminations* (Schocken: New York, 1936/1969).

Media/McLuhan

whirlpool, "the natural consequence of the forms of the floating fragments": the descent of objects that are large and have spherical shape being more rapid, while any cylindrical shape would descend slower. When memory and observation conjure, hope turns into action: the fisherman strips himself to a cask and throws himself into the water.

To "seize hold of a memory as it flashes up at a moment of danger,"[13] was one of Benjamin's strategies for "historical awakening". To practice pattern recognition was McLuhan's strategy for surviving the maelstrom. For Poe's fisherman, memory interplays with observations on "forms of floating fragments." When it comes to form, both Benjamin and McLuhan have been branded as "technological determinists" and/or "aesthetic formalists." What actually seems to unite them, is a category of "form" that may engulf all sorts of "content," may expand into perceptions, technologies, worldviews, and "environments." In this capacity, not in isolation, form will register historical change: how Greek tragedy differs from baroque allegory (Benjamin), how tribal culture differs from print culture (McLuhan). If anything, their take on form seems to gravitate towards what now is called "reception," or "performance": for Benjamin, baroque allegory is a form for those who mourn, not a form that causes mourning. Modern allegory (Brecht) is a form to be integrated by its audience, not a form that integrates it. For McLuhan, the ultimate "content" of any medium is the user, the co-maker, the public. Media are, first and last, "extensions of man."

Their observations on "form" also proceed in a similar fashion: they avoid pre-existing genres (Benjamin), "contents" (McLuhan), and conceptual classifications (both). They collect scattered "fragments," which often will translate as "quotes" (few other writers use quotes as extensively, as capriciously, as McLuhan and Benjamin). When interrelated, the discontinuity of such fragments must be preserved: in figures of thought that are sudden, explosive (with McLuhan, "probes," "puns," "counter-environments," with Benjamin, "dialectical images," "awakenings," "profane illuminations"), in patterns that display "mosaics" (McLuhan), "montages" (Benjamin), or "constellations" (both); which present "configurations rather than sequences of events"[14] (McLuhan), in which "chronological movement is grasped and analyzed in a spatial image"[15] (Benjamin).

When it comes to space and time, however, this catalogue of similarities might end. As Richard Cavell has demonstrated, McLuhan's thinking is consistently engaged with space.[16] (As for

13 • Benjamin, "Theses on the Philosophy of History": 255.
14 • McLuhan, *The Gutenberg Galaxy*, 216.
15 • Walter Benjamin, *The Origin Of German Tragic Drama* (London: Verso, 1928/1977), 92.
16 • Cavell, *McLuhan in Space*

time, McLuhan's compression of past, present, and future seem to leave us with the "pathway between Time and Eternity" glimpsed by the Norwegian fisherman.) In contrast, all of Benjamin's categories, while rejecting conventional historiography, are to be fulfilled within an elaborate philosophy of history. To John Durham Peters, "McLuhan sought timelessness; Benjamin sought timefulness."[17]

It is therefore of interest, that when Benjamin first introduces his main historical category, the *Ursprung,* he places it, not inside a dream, but inside a *Strudel*; a whirlpool, an eddy, or a maelstrom (translations differ). This is the passage, from the preface to *The Origin of the German Tragic Drama* (1928):

Origin (*Ursprung),* although an historical category through and through, has, nevertheless, nothing in common with emergence (*Entstehen).* In Origin, what is meant is not the becoming of something that has sprung forth (*Entsprungenen),* but rather that which springs forth out of coming-to-be and passing-away (*dem Werden und Vergehen Entspringendes).* Origin stands in the flow of becoming as a maelstrom (*Strudel),* that irresistibly draws the stuff of emergence into its rhythm. In the bare manifestation of the factual the original is never discernible, and its rhythm is accessible only to a double insight. It is recognizable on the one hand as restoration, as reinstatement, and precisely in this as on the other hand incomplete, unfinished. In every original phenomena the form (*Gestalt)* is determined, in which again and again an idea confronts and struggles with the historical world, until it lies there in the totality of its history. Consequently, origin will not arise from the findings of fact, but will rather concern their fore- and after-history (*Vor- und Nachgeschichte).*[18]

To Benjamin, there was no such thing as "art history" (in terms of intentionality, causality, continuity). Within its own time, the profound understanding of a work of art would be severely limited, maybe unavailable[19] (c.f. the impercipience of the ubiquitous). The task that remained, for interpretation, critique, and commentary, was to reveal the "historical indexes" of works, in terms of their "fore- and after- history." To look for origins, then, was not to confirm

17 • John Durham Peters, "McLuhan's Grammatical Theology": 235.
18 • Benjamin, *The Origin Of German Tragic Drama*, 45; translation altered via Samuel Weber, *Benjamin's Abilities* (Cambridge: Harvard University Press, 2008).
19 • Cf. Sandor Radnoti,: "The Early Aesthetics of Walter Benjamin," *International Journal of Sociology* Vol. 7, No. 1, Spring, 1977.

Media/McLuhan

emergence through historical facts, but to recognize the rhythm of what is standing "in the flow of becoming." With this conception, "change" may be directed towards both past and future, the present is "split"[20] into what is being restored and what will remain unfinished, into that "which springs forth out of coming-to be and passing-away." To say that, for example, Charles Baudelaire "stands in the flow of becoming" of modernism, is to say that his works exposes this split, the rhythm of that double insight, in which we may recognize the fore- and after-history of modernism. This rhythm need not be perceived by its original writer or audience, it may only become legible at a later time, and not by the work in isolation, but by the accumulating history of its reception: "it is their post-history which illuminates their pre-history as a continuous process of change."[21] Thus, it is a split to be reinterpreted, again and again — as for Benjamin, the true picture of the past "flits by"[22], as it is "the present that polarizes the event into fore- and after-history,"[23] as the founding concept of historical materialism was "not progress, but actualization."[24] In the 1930s, to Benjamin, Baudelaire's modernism had a fore-history in baroque allegory, and an after-history in *Jugend*.

Let us assume that McLuhan approached historical observation in a similar fashion. To say that, for instance, the "global village" stands as an "origin" of an era of instant information, would be to say that it recognizes a split in the "flow of becoming," something which is being "restored," and something which remains unfinished. Not only as manifested in historical facts, but in a "rhythm," which exposes a double insight. The expression "global village" certainly seems to pick up its rhythm from within a split: that between the fore-history of orality and tribal culture, and the after-history of communication beyond time and space. This rhythm runs all the way through *The Gutenberg Galaxy*, which may be why that book is doing something more, something different, than "looking back" at the fading configuration of one bygone era, "the making of typographic man." What it may do, in Benjamin's term, is to present historical circumstance as "a force field in which the confrontation between its fore-history and after-history is played out."[25] McLuhan imagines that force field as a "*Ström*," a "whirling phantasmagoria," one that is set spinning by changes of technology and media, one in which "all physical, psychic and social processes merge in

20 • Term introduced in Samuel Weber's reading of the passage.
21 • Walter Benjamin & Knut Tarnowski: "Eduard Fuchs: Collector and Historian," *New German Critique*, No. 5 (Spring, 1975): 28.
22 • Benjamin, "Theses on the Philosophy of History": 255.
23 • Walter Benjamin, *The Arcades Project* (Cambridge: Harvard University Press, 1982/1999), N7a 8.
24 • Benjamin *The Arcades Project*, N2, 2.
25 • Ibid, N7a 1.
26 • Eric McLuhan and Marshall McLuhan, *Media and Formal Cause* (Houston: Neopoiesis Press, 2011), 43.

constant play and replay."[26] His recurrent trick is to look inside it, for form, patterns and use (not for content), for "gaps" and "missing links" (not for linear development), in which this process "flips," retrieves, makes obsolete, enhances. In that sort of current, like in the coming-to-be-and-passing away of Benjamin's origin, history is always on the verge of repeating itself, and always on the verge of starting anew. In that sort of current, all sorts of pasts may be drawn in, all sorts of futures might emerge (tribal drums, Chinese calligraphy, jazz, front page news, the planet as art form, auditory space — the scope should be familiar to McLuhan's readers).

Still, there is a method. To Benjamin, the "fore-history" may be illuminated by the "after-history." McLuhan used to propagate a method of "working backwards," and illustrate this with how Poe's detective stories would register the present effects of the crime, rather than the past cause, to get at the solution. Actually, the same technique of registering effects that Poe's fisherman uses in *ascending* from the maelstrom: a reading of present observations in the shadow of coming events. Still "working backwards," in a sense, since to McLuhan, "causes" do not necessarily precede "effects." For example: if intensified road traffic is to be regarded as an "effect" of railroad and cars, McLuhan assumes that the environment preceding these "causes" already anticipated this effect, in ways that were hidden, but possible to register. This is why McLuhan claimed to never predict "something that had not already happened." This is why the radar of artists may pick up the future from the present.

Late in his life, McLuhan attempted to clarify this (admittedly paradoxical) notion of causality by referring to Aristotle's account, in which there are four different ways of answering a "why?" question. The frequent characterizations of McLuhan as a "technological determinist" suggest that he was taken to discuss media as either "material" or "efficient" cause; in the classic example, that out of which a statue is produced (bronze), or its primary source of change (the art of bronze-casting). In 1979, McLuhan tries to set the record straight: in a letter to a journal that had reviewed Elizabeth Eisenstein's *The Printing Press as an Agent of Change,* he claims this book to be concerned with "efficient causality," while his own *Gutenberg Galaxy* had been concerned with "formal causality and the study of effects, with reception aesthetics."[27]

With Aristotle, the "formal" cause is an account of what a-statue-is-to-be, in terms of its form or shape. To McLuhan, a formal cause is not concerned with "contents," nor with value judgments. A formal cause is non-sequential and non-linear. If anything, its way of relating cause-effect is simultaneous, "out of time". But while formal causality is best revealed in the "effects," method (and art) must "work backwards": be aware of "effects" that precede "causes," and acknowledge that "the child is the father of the man."

In Aristotle's doctrine of change, "formal cause" also tends to converge with "final cause" (the end, *telos*, that for the sake of which the statue is made). When the child "fathers" the man, the formation of early years must merge with some (preexisting) totality of a fully developed life. To describe the combination of being-at-work and being-at-an-end, Aristotle invented the term *entelecheia* (alluding to *endelecheia*, persistence, but inserting *telos*, completion; McLuhan might have called it a "pun"). Interestingly, Leibniz adapts this Aristotelian term for his *Monadologie*, in which any single monad is all-inclusive in terms of its potential "history," is "laden" with past and "pregnant" with future. And Benjamin turns to Leibniz to elaborate his own notion of "idea" in the *Ursprung* book, in which any idea/monad, according to the quote above, "confronts and struggles with the historical world, until it lies there in the totality of its history." As for McLuhan, "entelechy" and "formal cause" might have been what media was all about: "Marshall McLuhan's idea of a medium as an invisible, ever-present *vortex* (my emphasis) [...] is exactly that of formal cause."[28] This according to his son Eric McLuhan, who also claims that an alternative term for "vortex" in the sentence above would be "entelechy".

If one should instead insert "origin" for that vortex, the kind that "stands in the flow of a becoming as a maelstrom," McLuhan's "timeless" idea of a medium might meet up with Benjamin's exposition of "historical indexes" (while also acknowledging the role of memory, in Poe's tale of the fisherman). Not necessarily, though, the sort of history sought by McLuhan himself. In 1975, McLuhan published a short article on "The Laws of Media,"[29] in the journal *Technology and Culture*. His purpose was to invite, ironically, a criticism more concerned with the "content" of his thoughts than with his "rhetoric". Further, he wanted to "test the validity of my laws in terms of history." Not being a historian, his postulates had been formulated in a "synchronic" approach, in which all aspects of form were simultaneously present. He now invited historians of technology to provide the "diachronic" approach, to prove or disprove his postulates through historical data, and to send their material to the journal, or to him personally. These "laws" are phrased as four questions, aimed at four types of effects assumed to accompany every "technology" (from clocks to zippers to computers):

28 • Ibid, 129.
29 • Marshall McLuhan, "McLuhan's Laws of the Media," *Technology and Culture*, Vol. 16, No. 1 (1975): 74–78.

What does the new thing enlarge or enhance or
amplify?
What does it retrieve or bring back in a new way?
What, when it is pressed to an extreme, is the area of
reversal?
What does it sideline or make superfluous or obsolete?

As an analytic of the media (rather than as its "laws"), or, as Eric
McLuhan suggests, an analytic of "formal causes," these questions present a fairly systematic approach. What has been
suggested here is that its object and method may already be
"historical" in registering the fore- and after-history of technology within a "flow of becoming". If so, one suspects that McLuhan waited in vain for those historical validations. With Benjamin, a historical index would not only concern the time to
which an original phenomena belonged (to be confirmed by
historians of art or technology). It would concern its *legibility*, at
any later time. In other words, the "validation" of McLuhan and
Benjamin's historical observations, would now involve us. And
what the prolonged life of their texts in our time may suggest, is
not necessarily that they provided predictions with particular
accuracy, nor that we are in need of their particular pasts, for
walking backwards into the future. It may suggest that they
provided a "field of practice" for the *actualization* of history, in
exposing a rhythm of coming-to-be-and-passing-away, which
may still be picked up today (along with a glimmer of hope). •

Rosalind E. Krauss, Under the Blue Cup

Dan Karlholm

1 • Rosalind E. Krauss, *"A Voyage on the North Sea": Art in the Post-Medium Condition* (London: Thames & Hudson, 1999); Krauss, "Reinventing the Medium," *Critical Inquiry* 25 (Winter 1999): 289–305; Krauss, *Bachelors* (Cambridge, Mass.: MIT Press, 1999).
2 • *Under Blue Cup* (Cambridge, Mass.: MIT Press, 2011). Henceforth cited in the text with pagination.

The year 1999 was an eventful one for Rosalind Krauss. Not only did she publish her now famous book *"A Voyage on the North Sea": Art in the Age of the Post-Medium Condition*, the essay "Reinventing the Medium" and a collection of earlier essays on women artists entitled *Bachelors,*[1] she was also struck by an aneurysm, "an exploded artery launching a cataract of blood into the brain, disconnecting synapses and washing neurons away". In her latest book, *Under Blue Cup*, [2] from which this medical description derives, she uses her brain's hard drive crash and the memory loss that ensued to follow up on her analysis about the "post-medium condition" of the art scene from around the turn of the millennium. What she invokes is a form of looking, not just in terms of an obsolete preoccupation with some putative essence of a traditional medium such as painting or sculpture, but as a mode of remembering. Her efforts to recover and regain her own memory intersect here with an argument against the effects of the post-medium condition — devastating, according to the author — which in turn leads her to propose a group of artists as "knights" of the aesthetic medium in its self-differing specificity, or, in other words, in highly divergent understandings of "mediums". It is no longer a question of pointing to specific uses of a received, generally acknowledged artistic medium, but of ways to invent a plurality of media or mediums, each singular and specific with respect to their particular artistic use. To get an immediate sense of the author's focus, it is worth quoting the opening lines of her Acknowledgments: "Incited by over a decade of disgust at the spectacle of meretricious art called installation, this book was made possible by fortuitous encounters with what I saw as its strong alternatives."

The title of this book requires some explaining. It refers to the legend on a flash card from one of the first cognitive therapy lessons the author was exposed to. It has no deeper meaning outside of its use-value as a mediation between memory and temporary amnesia. The title is thus a medium in the conventional sense of an intermediary, as well as a linguistic sign for the recovery of a lost memory, which ultimately reminds us not to forget about art's defining involvement with differing mediums. Compared to the structure of the book, however, the title is straight-forward. The book is divided into three parts, but sliced into shorter sections throughout these divisions as well. The reader is faced with a structure that looks familiar even to small children: A(neurysm), B(rain), C(hessboard), D(iscursive unity), E(xpansion), etc. Okay, we get it: the alphabet's arbitrary-yet-predictable automatism will structure this text, in a sense congenial to its non-historical essay form as well as the author's attempts to recompose herself. And this beat goes on, up to a point, but then the following continuation of the series unfolds: F, G, H, I, J, K, L, M, Z, N, V, V, A, L, L, M, N, O, O, P, Q, R, S, T, T, U, V, W, X, Y, W, W, F, V, W, X, U. Given that I have no idea how to decipher this code, unless of course this structure performs the very thesis of the book (as an invented scriptural medium in the form of a well-known sequence that is interrupted and re-composed according to a set of new rules for the production of this particular work), I will focus on discussing Krauss' most explicit argument on mediums and memory and her critique of contemporary art.

What connects the author's loss of memory, including other difficulties of this eruption and the state of contemporary art, is the word *memory*. "Why Are There Several Arts and Not Just One?," Jean-Luc Nancy asked in a well-known essay.[3] Krauss connects this question to an "emphasis on the medium as a form of remembering, since the various artistic supports, each represented by its individual muse, serve as the scaffolding for a 'who you are' in the collective memory of the practitioners of that particular genre — painting, sculpture, photography, film"(2).

Now, do several mean nine or a potentially unlimited number? A lot about this discussion hinges upon what we mean by general and specific, respectively, as well

3 • Jean-Luc Nancy, *The Muses*, trans. Peggy Kamuf (Stanford: Stanford University Press, 1996).

as about the one and the other or the many. Artistic mediums in general and medium specificity in particular are then discussed. For example, that the rules of cubist practice gave birth to the grid, itself a kind of echo of the chessboard structure that Hubert Damisch has connected with Renaissance perspective. A distinction is made with regards to Clement Greenberg's idea of an empirical, physical substance to be successively reduced, whereas Krauss is more interested in connecting to the rules of the old craft guilds, on the one hand, and to certain structures of modern mass-culture, on the other. She links her definition of medium to "discursive unity" (Michel Foucault) and "automatism" (Stanley Cavell), and her key term "technical support," which rings open and rather mechanical, is seen as a substitute for the traditional idea of a physical medium and a means with which to overcome many jaded connotations of the word medium today. Having said that, however, the m-word should perhaps be understood as the almost physical if invisible support of the scaffold "technical support": "It is only the word *medium* that conjures the recursive nature of the successful work of art. The artists who discover the conventions of a new technical support can be said to be 'inventing' a new medium, the way [Michael] Fried saw [Frank] Stella 'inventing' *shape* as a new medium" (19, italics in original).

With such an interestingly wide conception of medium, however, why not also consider Boris Groys' proposition that the medium of installation is space, something very material, according to him?[4] Krauss would never go there, of course, since "installation art" is anathema to her. She apparently decided long ago (at least as early as 1999) that the historical sequence of aesthetic disaster reads like the following: conceptual art (Joseph Kosuth in particular), institutional critique, installation art, relational art and (new) media art or computer-based art. The order of appearance here may perhaps be adjusted, and some of these phenomena are clearly worse than others, but as an outline of Krauss' trajectory of artistic decline, it should suffice. Compare, for instance, the following allegations: "The post-medium condition of our age resembles the radical dispersal of '70s sculpture, as installation art, now updated as relational aesthetics — both of them variants of institutional critique — opens contemporary practice to a profusion of forms joined by conceptual art's contempt for specificity."(18) And: "*Under Blue Cup* is a polemic, adamantly shouting 'fake' and 'fraud' at the kitsch of installation. The effect of the genuine is not lost to memory, not swept away. A polemic is a call to remember, against the siren song of installation to 'forget'." (69) While the author was once

Media/McLuhan

4 • Boris Groys, "Politics of Installation" (www.e-flux.com/journal/view/31) (2009).

famous for scrutinizing "Modernist Myths," her current position as "an unreconstructed modernist" points to the post-medium condition as a "monstrous myth."[5]

There are eight artists in particular with which Krauss deals in the present book, most of whom she has written about for years now: Ed Ruscha, Marcel Broodthaers, James Coleman, Bruce Nauman, William Kentridge, Christian Marclay, Harun Farocki and Sophie Calle. Since many of them work explicitly with installation, the wholesale rejection of this category is odd, to say the least, and as they are all clearly "contemporary" artists, the following is also puzzling: "If such artists are inventing their medium, they are resisting contemporary art's forgetting of how the medium undergirds the very possibilities of art. If *Under Blue Cup* is about one idea, this is what it is about." (19) Is this to imply that contemporary artists in general (with the exception of this group) "forget" the ways of the medium? Are they not, rather — many of them — using various forms of installation as a multifaceted medium in its own right, each instance of which differs from all other instances as well as from the ones of other artists employing similar means? Perhaps the whole formulation of a post-medium condition, as a pretty descriptive diagnosis at first but increasingly transformed into *the* disaster of the "contemporary art" scene, is misleading (also for Krauss)? Many seem happy to embrace the idea of an aftermath of the whole bag of media from within which to work, and this condition comes to resemble Arthur Danto's post-historical situation of anything goes,[6] but what makes the phrase apt, as I read it, is the way it captures that from a certain point in time in the postwar period, no singular medium could command and direct the practice of an "art" or a genre, such as painting or landscape painting, for example. In the post-medium condition, surely, any artist can paint landscapes, but they can just as well present ready-mades with sound effects in a shopping mall (as a medium) to earn their (high) art credits. It is not a question of the author describing, much less celebrating, a state of "post-media" in the plural, although the introduction of the readymade supposedly amounted to a "ditching" of the medium (32), which may be a historically accurate thing to say about the infamous events of 1917 or thereabouts. For a redefinition of medium today, however, it is less convincing. The remark calls to mind the traditional, physical notion of artistic medium, as if a readymade post-1960 or so, because of its un-crafted nature perhaps, could not constitute its own,

5 • Cf. Krauss, *The Originality of the Avant-Garde and Other Modernist Myths* (Cambridge, Mass.: MIT Press, 1985); Krauss, "Some Rotten Shoots from the Seeds of Time," in Terry Smith et al (eds.), *Antinomies of Art and Culture: Modernity, Postmodernity, Contemporaneity* (Durham: Duke University Press, 2008), 69; Krauss, *Perpetual Inventory* (Cambridge, Mass.: MIT Press, 2010), xiv.

6 • Arthur C. Danto, *After the End of Art: Contemporary Art and the Pale of History* (Chicago: University of Chicago Press, 1998).

singular medium. I can't see why not, unless there is a hidden agenda about what may qualify as a proper medium in this account. Krauss is silent about how far the concocted mediums of the eight artists can be seen as representative of ways in general to expand and proliferate the concept of medium, or whether they are now the received and approved new ways within which to work. If the latter sounds preposterous, and I hope it does, I fail to see why certain media somehow fall short of this medium-definition. What predetermined rules might there be by which to sort what rules are OK or interesting to use artistically? Installation art, according to Krauss, means introducing "ordinary components," such as readymades or perhaps "mere real things" (Danto), in the art context to ask what makes them art. (32) But this ceased to be a hot issue on the art scene some fifty years ago. Today, it remains an interesting question for the philosophical subculture of analytic aestheticians involved in fine-combing definitions of art in relative obliviousness to current art practices.

By referring to her favorite artists as "knights" of the medium, a word that occurred already in "'*A Voyage on the North Sea*'," they are here associated with chessboard characters, on the one hand, and plain medieval heroes on the other. Such "knights" appear to be the king's keepers of memories, rather than inventors of their own kingdoms. But who would be king? And what are the memories? Perhaps the king is dead, and the memories are akin to phantom pain in a limb no longer there? Or is the term "knight," in 2011, meant to imply a kind of Don Quixote character, involved in a combat unacknowledged as worthwhile by the rest of the world? As this text unfolds, Krauss does come to resemble a quixotian knight herself, battling her windmills of installation.

Perhaps we could say that *the* medium is no longer operative, while *a* medium remains essential. I would neither have a problem with that, nor with the idea that artists invent their medium, but when they are also accredited with "discovering" the rules of this practice, I have a hard time following. Are not rules also made up or literally invented, just like when small kids play games of their own making (not football, tennis, etc.)? And, was this not part of the discourse of the genius in eighteenth-century aesthetics? The verb *discover* seems to suppose that rules are somehow already in place, just waiting to be found, even for such idiosyncratic inventions as James Coleman's constructed slide tape with a synchronized sound track. Other examples of these invented mediums or self-proscribed rules cover Ed Ruscha's use of the automobile as a medium and William Kentridge's set up of drawing and erasure as captured by a film camera, for example. The medium is seen by Krauss as a kind of frame, a structure, like the sides of a swimming pool against which the swimmer kicks off in new directions (25), and of course she is reluctant to accept the alleged demise of the "white cube," which does resemble a kind of swimming pool for both artists and the public, who splash around for a while in the pond of art before returning to the street or the real world. This part of her, in many ways untimely, critique leads Krauss to blame one swimmer in particular on the contemporary ocean of art for declaring the white cube obsolete: Catherine David. Krauss's relies on a 15-year-old film about documenta X (1997), in which David utters the following provocation: "Unless you are naïve, or a hypocrite, or stupid, you have to know that the white cube is over." (58) This could be interpreted as a kind of bone to the media vultures to draw attention or perhaps to mark a clear distance to the modernist traditionalists, the philistines or all of those who mistrusted her as a foreign woman in charge of this important mega-exhibition. In any event, the remark triggers Krauss to hunt down and cut this "Frenchwoman" to pieces in the following pages. "Catherine David has become the antagonist to this book's crusade — its resistance to the collapse of the white cube." (84) This is not only a rather weak rhetorical strategy, it is a bit like crucifying not *the* but *a* messenger, rather than reaching the heart of the matter: the art made by artists that are hailed by the art world for their practices against, in conflict with or negligence of, the quintessential modernist white cube. Not even the latter stand, however, necessarily indicates that "the white cube is over" (as if it were a temporal moment and not a kind of space, charged with the energies of the neutral). On the contrary, this metaphoric cubicle continues to exert its paradigmatic spell also on the varied negations and innumerable resistances to this model for presenting art in a non-artistic, and thus ideally art-defining space.

Time and again, the author returns to what she sees as the horrible kitsch of "installation art". To me, this is actually a point of agreement. The phrase "installation art" is kitsch, since this is not a specific kind of art, although it is sometimes mentioned as a distinct flavor in the list comprising minimal art, land art, body art, performance, video art, etc., as if most of these practices were not involved one way or another with installation. I would go as far as to propose that installation art does not exist, but art does not exist either unless it is — one way or another — installed (as art). This, of course, is the outcome of a relatively new regime of art, which Thierry de Duve has termed art in general, generic art and the like, and which merely stipulates that there are no longer internal or specific limits to what could become art in certain art world circumstances, within the system or institution of art.[7] Within this immense spectrum, however,

7 • Thierry de Duve, *Kant after Duchamp* (Cambridge, Mass.: MIT Press, 1996).

individual media and specificities do count. In his highly interesting paper "Duchamp the Messenger of Art Unlimited," included in the present issue of *SITE*, de Duve claims — rightly — to be misunderstood, when Krauss thinks that he has theorized the movement of artistic practice from the specific to the general, or away from medium-specificity to its demise in a post-medium state of generalities. But de Duve seems to misunderstand Krauss, in turn, when he maintains that Krauss sees redemptive qualities in a state characterized by "obsolescence of the medium," i.e. the post-medium condition. The redemption she finds is in artists, a handful of fairly canonical figures, who — *despite* and not due to the dire conditions of the post-medium situation — manage to construct new ways to base their art on a specific medium, without any kind of general, conventional and historically accumulated investments characteristic of the medium in Greenberg's account. Krauss' perspective may indeed be called conservative, but perhaps reactionary is more appropriate. Hers is literally a reaction to the development of advanced art practices in the West since she first started out as a critic in the 1960s, not an attempt to return to something or simply wipe out recent history. She is just as concerned to reconstruct the phenomenon of medium with respect to Greenberg, as well as to his cadre of postmodern opponents flippantly waving goodbye to media as such. Her definition salvages the basic character of a medium (with a memory, i.e. self-differing or reflective), while discarding the superstructure of presumed essences and conventional connotations. While so doing, however, I think she overstates her case by restricting her scope to a small group of master artists, as if claiming the position of an old-fashioned art critic, rather than the analyst of larger structures she once was. It is easy, however, to sympathize with her proclaimed urgency to remember, necessary not only to reassemble herself, but as a critique of art practices seemingly oblivious of the structure of memory and history on the field of art that, at the end of the day, is the only thing that will be able to support them as art when the artworks themselves have become indistinguishable from culture or kitsch at large. ●

Dan Karlholm is Professor of Art History at Södertörn University.

Architecture and Urbanism

Tim Anstey
Sten Gromark
Sarah Stanley
Staffan Lundgren

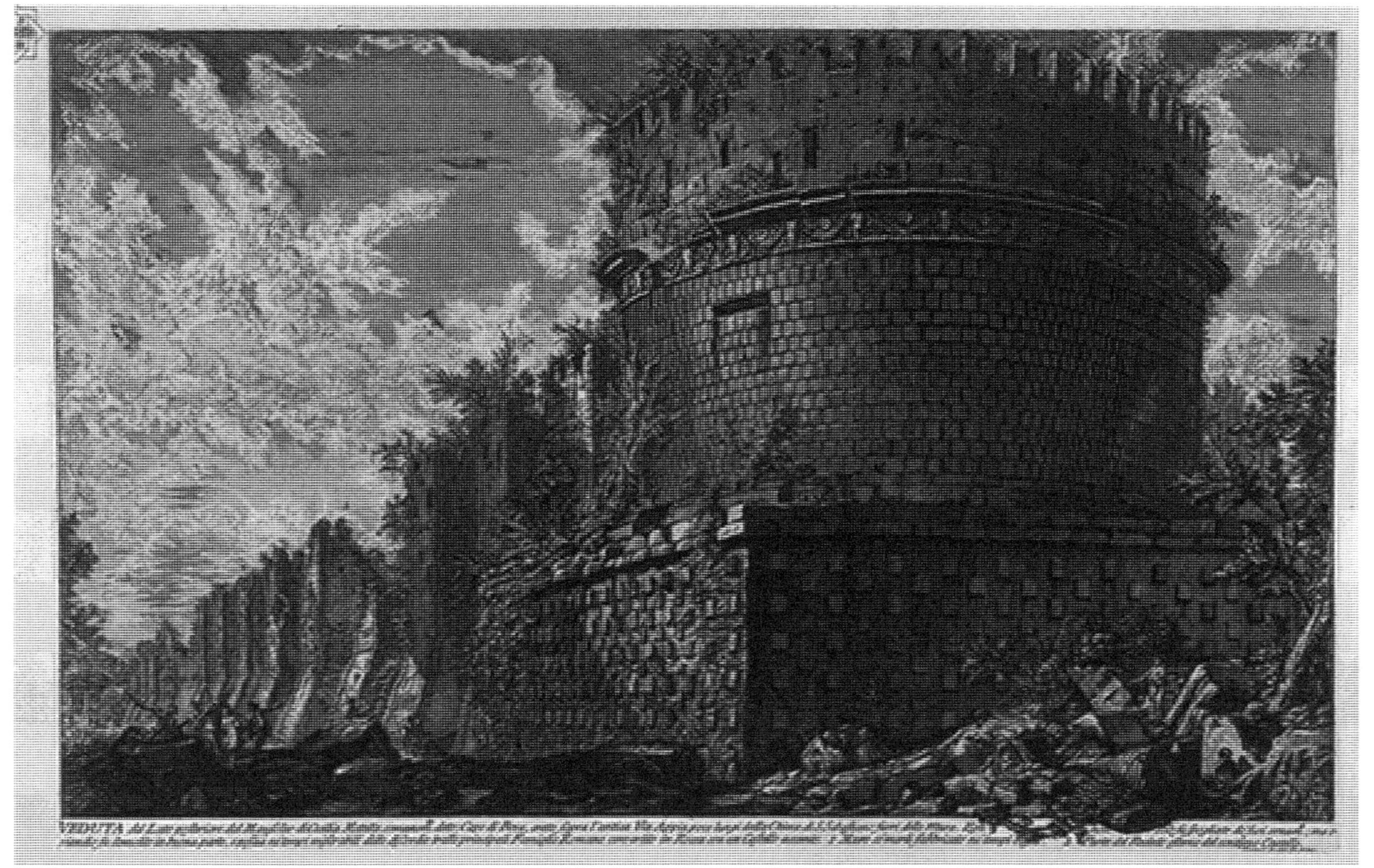

Against the Empire: Pier Vittorio Aureli On the Possibility of an Absolute Architecture

Tim Anstey

◄

In a world of flows, of facebook and free-markets, one dreams of the full stop. For a period, starting with Pliny, including Virginia Woolf's childhood trips to St Ives and ending somewhere in the 20th century, one could be pretty certain that this possibility of arrest could emerge through transporting yourself out of the metropolis. Physical distance from the conurbation allowed the perception that one was outside the sea of flows that drove it. Hence Pliny's villa; hence Talland House, which would be fictionalised in Woolf's novel *To the lighthouse* as the summer residence of Mr and Mrs Ramsay. In this model certain characteristics remained constant; the identification of the urban space with unmitigated flow; the need for some kind of barrier against emersion in this sea; the location of an architecture — a house, a villa — as that locus of retreat; and the situation of this fastness beyond the confines of the urban.

The possibility of creating even a proxy experience of life outside the flow of capital and exchange has changed in the last few years. Sitting in a field 480 kilometers from Stockholm, without "mains services"(the physical tentacles of light, water, communication and power that the conurbation spreads), I am still as connected to the flows of the urban condition as if I were sitting downtown. The treacherous sun, via a solar panel and an iphone, connects me back. I can check synonyms, definitions, references online, but also the share prices; my pension fund; the weather; a sea of pornography. Relying on distance to create barriers against this "urbainformation" is no longer a possibility. What remains is the dream of the full stop — of a place outside the system — and the half articulated sense that a spatial organisation still has the potential to create this sanctuary.

Can architecture serve as an exemplar for how this longed for stoppage is to be claimed? *The Possibility of an Absolute Architecture*,[1] which is published as part of the excellent MIT *Writing Architecture* series edited by Cynthia Davidson, addresses this problem. The method of exploration is to make a wide historical traverse: Greek *polis* versus Roman *urbs*; Palladio's work in Vicenza and Venice; Nolli and Piranesi in Rome; the French revolutionary architect Boullé and the Spanish theorist of urbanism, Cerdà. The aim is to advance a thesis that architecture has the potential to be something more than an index of the systems of power, capital and incorporation that characterise the urban condition. And the *loci* Aureli chooses are all situated in what might be called the "hinterland": spaces within conurbations where neither a single controlling idea nor an evolutionary chaos hold sway, but in which systems of all kinds merge and mingle — the fringe of the Veneto; the border between the "abitato" and the "disabitato" in Rome during the 17th and 18th century; Revolutionary Paris; Berlin after the wall.

To ground the analysis Aureli asks "What sort of significant and critical relationship can architecture aspire to in a world that is no longer constituted by the idea and the motivation of the city, but is instead dominated by urbanization?" The adversarial divide between these two, and particularly a critique of the latter, are the subject of the opening chapter. The distinction between the city and the urban Aureli relates *in gestato* to that between the Greek *polis* — the "democratic" space of the political collective, which permits the articulation and resolution of conflicts among a populace defined as equal to each other and different to everyone else — and *oikos* — the "economic" space of the household, subject to the despotic rule of an individual, whose agency is based on survival and self-interest. Critically for this argument, the space of the *polis* cannot be conceived without walls, and these at two levels: an external wall, that makes possible the definition of the group that seeks to resolve its conflicts, and an inner line that separates the "democratic" interests of the *polis* from the "economic" interests of the *oikos*. Both these introduce into the city-as-*polis* a notion of the absolute stop; the space that permits reflection and allows rational decision needs boundaries.

1 • Pier Vittorio Aureli, *The Possibility of an Absolute Architecture*, Cambridge, Mass. and London: MIT Press, 2011.

This notion of stoppage, *qua* Aureli, is foreign to the functional system of the *oikos*. Despotic power based on self-interest can, in theory, be exercised infinitely; in and of itself, a household can grow to any size. To suggest the implications of this conclusion Aureli pairs the greek notion *oikos* with the Roman notion of *urbs*. *Urbs*, which the Romans used to describe the physical manifestation of communal habitation — blocks of houses and the shared space between them — like *oikos* does not *per se* imply any boundary. Provided with a sufficiently good infrastructure of "mains services" — spies, roads, letter bearers, aquaducts — *urbs* can continue indefinitely. Rome, which makes itself felt powerfully as a presence through the whole book (Aureli grew up on the outskirts of the city close to EUR and attended the architecture school there during its last period as a site of political agitation during the early 1990s), can be seen as the first place on earth where the notion of self-interest, the ruling principle of the *oikos*, came to dominate a very large physical and power structure that resembled a city but which constituted the world. Two thousand years before Ildefons Cerdà formulated the theory of urbanization, in Aureli's eyes urbanization as a phenomenon began.

For Aureli, Cerdà was percipient and correct in his conclusion as to why just the Roman *urbs* provided the best root and model for this radical idea of the modern condition, the "vast swirling ocean of persons, of things, of interests of every sort, of a thousand diverse elements". The reconstitution of the city-state in the West after the dissolution of the Roman empire is seen by Aureli as a reification of how *oikos*, a system of despotic economic self interest, coupled with *urbs*, a collective and unlimited space of habitation, came to provide the model for urbanization. For Aureli this prompts fundamental questions:

> One can argue that the notion of urbanization presupposes the fundamental substitution of politics with economics as a mode of city governance to the point that today it is reasonable — almost banal — to ask not what kind of political power is governing us, but whether we are governed by politics at all — that is, whether we are living under a totalitarian managerial process based on economy, which in turn uses different political modes of public governance ranging from dictatorship to democracy to war [...] At the centre of this principle, from Cerdà on, the fundamental space of human association shifts from the political space of the city to the economic space of the house.

From the paragraphs above you get a good sense of the vertiginous quality in Aureli's writing — and of its aspiration. Its likely that historians of all kinds — ideas, religion, politics, philosophy — will have difficulty getting past several of the full stops in the text. To dispense with two thousand four hundred years of development in Western civilisation in ten densely packed pages might seem cavalier to some. But arrogant though it may be, this construction of a world history emerges out of a very real concern with what it means to live within the system that urbanization has created today: "the actual modern city has become a shopping mall, where value-free pluralism and diversity — the totalizing features of its space — have made urbanization the perfect space of mass voluntary servitude to the apolitical democracy imposed by the market."

Aureli's claim is that architecture can be used both to understand and provide a platform for refuting that condition, to find "highpoints" within the mess of the now from which sense can be made. It's worth stopping and noting what "architecture" is in this claim. Aureli contributes to a long tradition that identifies "architecture" with the architectural project — the description, made usually via projective drawings, about how the world, or at least significant sections of it, might be arranged. Thus rather than talking simply of houses or buildings or segments of actual construction, Aureli's argument is situated around proposals, manifestos and plans. These architectural projects create a space of reflection above the capitalist sea of urbanization through their potential to provide a critical perspective on that sea. Aureli's term for suggesting how this notion of "vantage" might play out spatially is to refer to the condition of architecture as creating "islands within an archipelago" — a metaphor which becomes more central as the book proceeds.

To demonstrate the potential of this thesis, Aureli concludes the introductory chapter by grouping Cerdà's *General Theory of Urbanisation* with architectural projects that illustrate defining characteristics he associates with the modern urban condition. Ludwig Hilberseimer's *Hochhausstadt* (from 1927, the same year that Virginia Woolf published *To the Lighthouse*) identifies how "any distinction between public space and private space, between political space and economic space, collapses in favor of a totalizing, organic understanding of the city as devoid of any limit"; Archizoom's *No Stop City* (1968–72) adumbrates the "disappearance of architecture " as a significant structuring device, because of its intractability to consumerist principles; Rem Koolhaas' *City of the Captive Globe* (1972) identifies two "collateral effects" which emerge from urbanization: "the landmark and the enclave". Although all these architectural projects are about urbanization, they lay claim to a ground that is, specifically, higher than the level of the urban through their creation of a critical space. It is this potential within the architectural project that lies at the centre of the book.

There is much to enjoy in the ensuing chapters that examine architectural projects from the sixteenth to the twentieth centuries, both built and imaginary, searching for a "general construction of the idea of a city [...] by starting from the limits of the architectural form itself." If Aureli is likely to offend the rest of historical studies through the kaleidoscopic nature of his first chapter, there's no doubt that architectural historical toes will be trampled in the ensuing march. The light skip from *oikos* to *urbs* to urbanization to radical late 60s Italian Marxism (performed in the first chapter) is matched by the equally ambitious scope of the rest of the book. Andrea Palladio *and* Rem Koolhaas; the Giovanni Battista's Piranesi *and* Nolli; Étienne Louis Boullé *and* Oswald Mattias Ungers. Yet although Aureli often reads only the canonical sources that relate to these cases — sources among which Tafuri looms — out of this in many senses narrow source material he anyway fabricates a radical proposition. Like an architectural Alan Turing, he looks at the problem, makes his own pattern out of the evidence at hand, and only when he has formulated his findings, does he worry much about what others have made of it.

If one does want to gain historical insight from reading this book the final chapter, which charts the collaboration between Rem Koolhaas and Oswald Mattias Ungers, is the most valuable. This for several reasons. Ungers, whose voice was influential in the architectural debates of the 1960s and 70s that laid the foundation for the intellectual culture around architecture towards the end of the 20th century, was also the most radically and quickly forgotten by much of that culture. Aureli does a strong service in recovering his voice. But at the same time, Aureli's careful historical scholarship, which outlines the connections and nuances of difference between the work of Ungers, the Cornell based theorist Colin Rowe, Koolhaas and the Italian architect, theorist and father of architectural postmodernism Aldo Rossi, recovers a sense of continuity between two periods in architectural criticism (the 1960s and the 1980s) that are sometimes seen as too distinct.

I had always been curious that Koolhaas' *Delirious New York* and the English translation of Rossi's *The Architecture of the City*, shared the same year of publication: 1979. I understood the commons in the channels of publication and dissemination — Rossi was published through the *Oppositions* series under the editorship of Peter Eisenmann, Anthony Vidler and others who were involved in the context of American architectural research

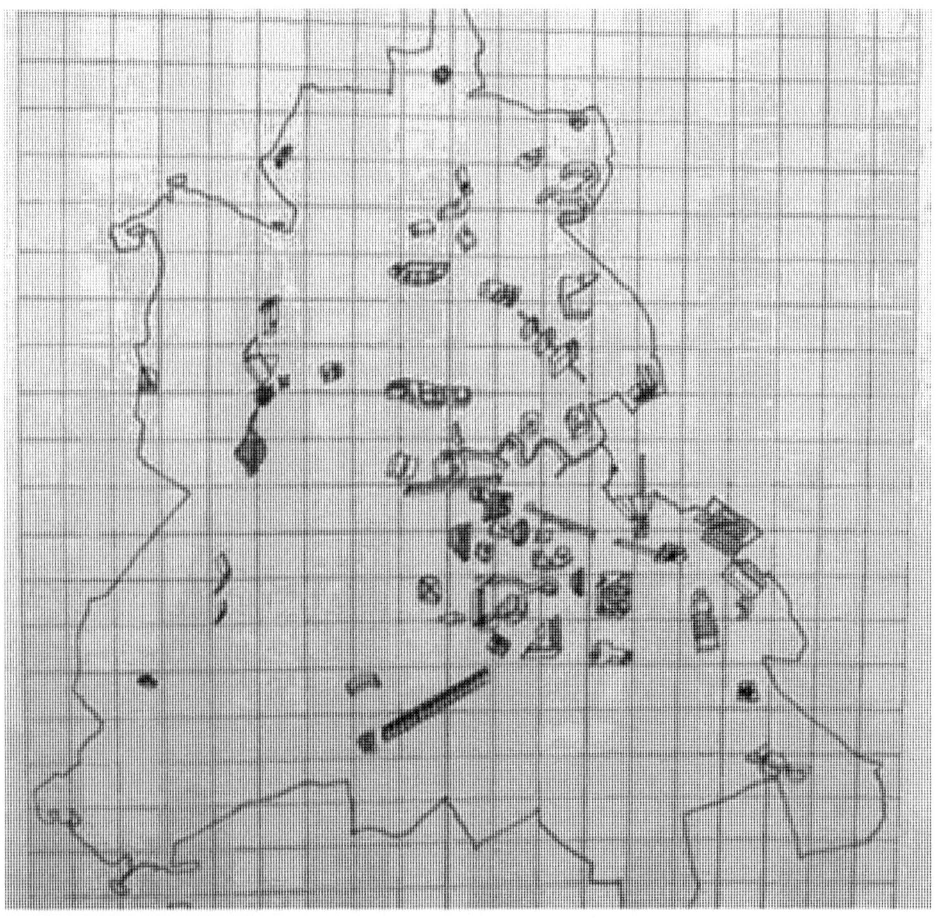

that lead to *Delirious New York*. Yet the two pieces of work seemed to articulate some kind of fundamental break, Rossi pointing to concerns anchored in the 1960s; Koolhaas forwards to the discourse of the 80s and 90s, and the hiatus caused by the assimilation of ideas from French philosophy — particularly deconstructivism — into the mainstream architectural debate. Aureli's analysis provides a platform for understanding the continuity that actually existed in the major influences that worked on architecture during the later part of the century, and in so doing escapes a major problem for historical analysis of that period — the problem of how much of a 'break' the introduction of a system of analysis based on the idea of breakage — deconstruction — actually created.

Most importantly, Aureli recovers a direct political strand in architectural thinking that analyses of that period of architectural post-modernism often lack. Particularly the text is valuable in outlining the contrast between the politically situated ideas that drove Ungers and the *laissez faire* attitude to the political evident in the work of the British born Rowe. Although Rowe and Ungers taught together at Cornell (where they were joined by the young Koolhaas), and although their ideas about the city led to some shared concerns — particularly about how the forms and architectural morphology of the past could be used in projecting the future — their motivations were quite different. Rowe assumed the benevolence of western liberalism and denied architecture any critical potential in relation to it. "The only context Rowe acknowledges is morphological collage: the possibility of combining radically different architectural figures [from the past] in a pleasant composition." Ungers on the other hand rejected "this image of the city of accumulation, the concrete result of free-market politics."

The distinction between Rowe and Ungers can be exemplified by juxtaposing two images created during the period they were most associated. In *Collage City*, published in 1976, Rowe illustrates the city of "pleasantly juxtaposed fragments" with a plan from London. In terms of Aureli's thesis, the "collage" condition of that city can be read as an index of *oikos*-based self-interest and political *laissez faire*. The great "fragments" of urban planning that jostle together in London faithfully trace the boundaries in private land-ownership among the great estate holders — the Bedfords, the Portmans, the Cadogans and the Grosvenors — who developed the city. These boundaries in turn reflect an even earlier *oikos* — like division, for each of these aristocratic "households" (and that was the literal name of these extended family organisations in medieval and renaissance England) were holding land previously owned by monastic orders. Thus each site in the patchwork of London had been controlled from the start by a self-sufficient economic unit, and the architectural form of each site reflected its despotic control by a private source of power.

In contrast to this Ungers' project for *Berlin as a Green Archipelago*, made in collaboration with Rem Koolhaas among others in 1977, produces very different readings of the possibility of the city. Aureli reproduces the "essential" map of Berlin created by Ungers, showing the form of the city in an abstracted diagram. Here "set pieces" of architectural composition float as separated islands in an undifferentiated sea. These fragments are not the product of any private or *oikos*-like pattern of ownership or control; neither do they relate directly to the picturesque sense of the city as experienced. Rather they are selected because they are "characteristically the products of precise ideological intentions about living and working in the city." They include areas that were diverse and separated, from Friedrichstadt Süd and the abandoned Görlitzer Park Station in the north, to Onkel

Toms Hütte in the south, all products of city-wide agency in government and intellectualised ideas about planning. Each provides an "embodiment of an idea of the city different to the others" — they are, in short *polis*-like constructions, dependent on containing boundaries, defining differences.

These images are not directly comparable. Rowe is making an analysis of an existing condition and Ungers is illustrating a projected arrangement (*Berlin as a Green Archipelago* envisioned the future condition of the city with a dramatically reduced population and subject to radical demolition). Yet in order to understand the different political wills of these two theorists, the juxtaposition works well. Rowe chooses to extract from London precisely the map that most clearly suggests it as a city where human association is based on the "economic space of the house"; Ungers envisages the preservation, isolation and reinforcement of those existing fragments of Berlin that articulate human association within "the political space of the city."

It was Ungers, Aureli shows, not Rowe who developed a symbiotic relationship with the young Rem Koolhaas, the architect whose impact on the architectural discourse of the late twentieth and early twenty-first century was to become legendary. Ungers' thinking was inherited into the early paper projects of OMA, the Office of Metropolitan Architecture (whose name, Aureli points out, played on Ungers own initials OMU) that Koolhaas founded together with Madelon Vriesendorp and Elia and Zoe Zenghelis. Particularly his ideas are evident in projects such as *Welfare Island*, made in 1976 and strongly connected to the idea of the "city within a city" developed through collaboration on *Berlin as a Green Archipelago*. Aureli finds his desired model for the recovery of a sense of *polis,* and the connection of that model to the idea of the archipelago, precisely in these projects. "Koolhaas called his model an archipelago: the grid is a sea and the plots are islands. The more different the values celebrated by each island, the more united the total grid or sea that surrounds them. Hence the plots are not simply buildings but are cities in minature or, as Koolhaas calls them, quoting Oswald Mattias Ungers, "cities within cities."

In tracing the evolution of this position, and relating this specifically back to his own desired rediscovery of a way to articulate political space through the architectural project Aureli shows Ungers' debt to ideas of communitarianism. Partly, Aureli observes, Ungers position emerged out of studies of secessionist groups like the Shakers, who established self sufficient communities that were still able to create a space "outside" urbanized modern America even in the late twentieth century (remember Harrison Ford in *Witness* [1985]). Such spaces of course relied on an apparent physical separation — like Pliny's Villa or Woolf's

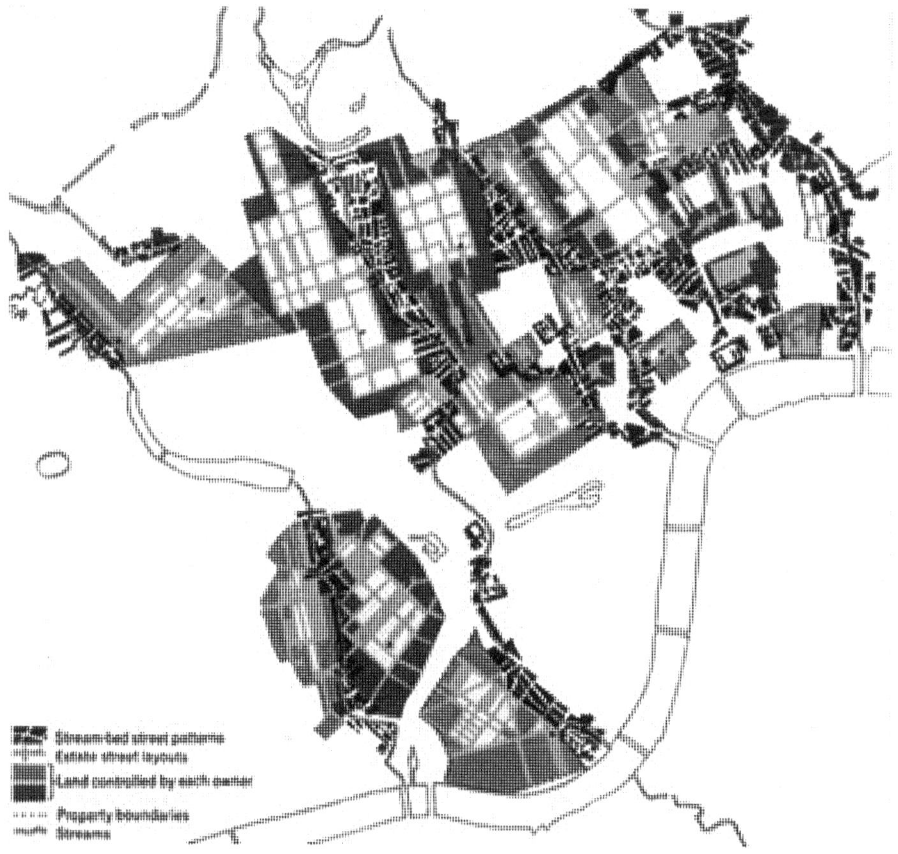

▲

Oswald Mattias Ungers, Rem Koolaas, Hans Kollhoff, Arthur Ovaska and Peter Riemann, The City within the City — Berlin as a Green Archipelago, 1977.

Talland House they were surrounded by "green"; their quality as fastnesses against urbanization was articulated partly through physical separation from the conurbation. But importantly for Aureli's thesis, these ideas in Ungers are to be traced also through his concern with set pieces of development found within existing conurbations. Particularly Aureli returns to Unger's examination of the "superblocks" developed for worker's housing within the existing urban grain of Vienna during the 1930s. These, for Aureli, epitomise Ungers idea of a "city within the city"; the notion that an architectural organisation could somehow contain, provided with legislative help, a political space even in the midst of inescapable urbanization based in the power of capital and self interest.

Here, *The Possibility of an Absolute Architecture* leaves the reader with a very real question. For who, and how is this political space, the archipelago of "islands" that Aureli claims architecture can provide, created? There is a difference between using architecture to create physical and social boundaries that inform and condition the everyday lives of citizens, and the notion of an architecture of projects that creates a critical space of reflection through discourse. Seen through other eyes than Aureli's, the built examples of the Vienna superblocks, that provided physical patterns and organisations for the everyday life of many, have a different kind of potential agency than the unbuilt projects of Ungers, Hilberseimer, Koolhaas, or of Aureli himself. These paper projects operate primarily through the space of rhetoric and discourse. They question urbanization and can operate globally, but only indirectly and on an informed and specialised audience. Real buildings are limited in their effect, and as Aureli points out, are dependent on a distinct political will conditioning the surrounding city. As with the superblocks of "red" Vienna, or the architectural set pieces Ungers examined in Berlin, they are the manifestation of decisions made through governing the city as a whole, and point back to the necessity of a *polis*-like space existing in the city at large.

Aureli argues that the formal organisation of architecture — of projected spaces and buildings — can neutrally span between these two different registers of agency. This would suggest that the experimental morphologies of the paper projects, conditioned by their positioning within a rhetorical critique of urbanization, contain a guarantee in terms of how to create built political space on the ground. The arguments of *The Possibility of an Absolute Architecture* are predicated on this claim, but not they do not categorically support it. Among Aureli's examples, the two that are most suggestive in this regard are his disquisition on the American period in Mies van der Rohe's work (as if Palladio, Nolli, Piranesi, Boullé, Koolhaas, Rowe, Rossi, Hilberseimer and Ungers were not enough) and his identification of the class of the "architectural commons" — of the anonymous spaces of commercial Modernism — as significant models for architectural production.

I will not follow Aureli through that analysis here. Rather, I return to the thought that this sense of a space outside the flow of markets and self-interest can now only be achieved through mediating the experience of a built architecture. One needs to put a label on one's experience in order for it to be acknowledged. We know of the potency of Pliny's Villa or of Virginia Woolf's experience of Talland House only through the curative practice of description in relation to how they created a space outside the flow of the city. Pliny must write his Diaries; Talland House must be transformed in *To the Lighthouse*. The resulting kinds of construction are most ambiguous as they are formed out of the paradoxical articulation of both conditions — urbanization and the space outside it — at once.

There is a beautiful passage in *To the Lighthouse* that suggests how architecture — building — might still be implicated, fundamentally, in such an articulation. Mrs Ramsay's friend Mr. Bankes talks to her on the telephone, she at her Hebrides fastness outside the city; he in his flat in London (almost certainly, in Woolf's mind, in Bloomsbury, one of the *oikos*-like set pieces of urban development that make up the collage of that city). As he talks and hears her over the wire, Mr Bankes sees Mrs Ramsay in his mind's eye in far off Scotland — he is almost achingly present in the space outside the urban — at the same time as he watches workmen building an hotel — a flow of materials and labour constructing the most fluid and urbanized of programmes:

> He saw her at the end of the line, Greek, blue-eyed, straight-nosed. How absurd it seemed to be telephoning to a woman like that. The graces assembling seemed to have joined hands in meadows of asphodel to compose her face.
>
> Yes, he would take the 10.30 from Euston. "But she's no more aware of her beauty than a child," said Mr. Bankes, replacing the receiver and crossing the room to see what progress the workmen were making with an hotel which they were building at the back of his house. And he thought of Mrs. Ramsay as he looked at that stir among the unfinished walls. For always, he thought there was something incongruous to be worked into the harmony of her face. She clapped a deer-stalker hat on her head; she ran across the lawn in galoshes to snatch a child from mischief. So that if it was her beauty merely that one thought of, one must remember this quivering thing, the living thing (they were carrying bricks up a little plank as he watched them), and work it into the picture.

In this scene the technologies of urban communication — telephones and trains — allow the space of repose outside, beyond urbanization to be created directly as part of the "stir among unfinished walls" within the conurbation. The sense of a protected space, as in Aureli's examples, is communicated by the experience of being within and outside the surrounding sea of urbanization simultaneously. Architecture here is defined, in one way, as merely another element in the net of infrastructure — telephones and trains, bricks and wheelbarrows, hotels — that forms the urbanized background for the space in Mr Bankes mind. But in another sense Mr. Bankes is constructing that space — setting one thing against another to create the effect — precisely through his experience of the urban. The "shivering" articulates Mrs Ramsay's remote, disinterested beauty that so moves Mr. Bankes, and the still place that contains that beauty; but it is produced by his experience of the little plank, flexing under a moving load. Architecture *qua* building provides the frame and boundary.

Perhaps, finally this notion of islands of experience, of architecture as a series of actions experienced "in construction," might add to Aureli's analysis. The final image one takes away from his book is that of the landscape around Rome, one which clearly haunts Aureli himself, in which the abandoned, "unfinished walls" of enormous architectural set pieces, linked by a decaying infrastructure of roads and aquaducts, are juxtaposed in the *campagna*. At a seminar in Stockholm discussing *The Possibility of an Absolute Architecture* Aureli's closing comment was this: we must build among those ruins. •

Tim Anstey is Professor and Head of the PhD Programme at the Oslo School of Architecture and Design. His research, which bridges between architectural history, theory and technology, focuses on the role of the architect and how ideas about that role have been inscribed into architectural discourse.

A Third Wave of Receptions: Space as Concrete Abstraction Łukasz Stanek on Henri Lefebvre

Sten Gromark

Many of the concepts once forged by Henri Lefebvre (1901–1991) will forever be written into our unconscious when we relate to urban and architectural issues, professionals and laymen alike, whether we are familiar with them or not; when we ask ourselves what the true social nature is of the space-time realities we constantly experience in our lives; when we are confronted with the concrete abstractions of the material world we dwell in. Henri Lefebvre initiated a distinct turn in our ways of understanding the social implications of an overwhelming urban society and of *social space*, as well as the rethinking of social time.

Łukasz Stanek, researcher and teacher at ETH in Zürich, architect and philosopher, with an academic history in Poland, Holland, France and Switzerland, has recently delivered a refreshing and impressive close-up account of this legend of post-war reconsiderations of architecture and the city in a social world. His book, *Henri Lefebvre on Space*, is a thorough re-reading, to be particularly commended, because as I understand it, this endeavor has been executed primarily based on original text documents,

1 • Among the flood of similar attempts still the most fundamental book with an inside look on the subject is without any doubt Remy Hess, *Henri Lefebvre et l'aventure du siècle* (Paris, Éditions A.M. Métailié, 1988). It was elaborated in collaboration with Henri Lefebvre. Equally Stuart Elden's *Understanding Henri Lefebvre: Theory and the* *Possible* (London: Continuum, 2004), is to be recommended. There is also a quite recent dissertation on the same subject in France by Silvain Sangla with a similar approach and orientation, *Politique et Espace chez Henri Lefebvre* (Paris, l'Université de Paris 8 Saint-Denis, 2010).

extensive archive material and conversations with key personalities formerly related to the philosopher. This attempt reveals so far undetected aspects of the philosopher and presents a broader and far more detailed picture of an astounding actor and voice in twentieth century intellectual discourses, events and actions.[1] The chapters focus on, first of all, *The Production of Theory* and then *Research, Critique,* and finally — symptomatically in the case of Lefebvre — *Project*. The published book is a re-edition of a PhD thesis defended in Delft Faculty of Architecture in 2008 under the auspices and supervision of Arie Graafland.[2]

This significant achievement is particularly striking for me since my academic career started with the reading — and the constant rereading, over and over again — of *The Production of Space*, originally published in France in 1974, and in English as late as 1991. This book has left a long-lasting impression and has been an inspiration, ever since, towards my understanding of architecture and urban development. And in hindsight I can remember the time when Lefebvre was considered with outright scorn as a "romantic revolutionary" or a ridiculous "social philosopher" by authorities of urban sociology like Manuel Castells, Jean Lojkine or Edmond Preteceille and in particular by the most renowned urban scientist of the older generation: Paul-Henry Chambart de Lauwe. In the contemporary debate he was caught with an unclear position in crossfire between Sartre and Althusser. Commissioned on the one hand by the French Communist Party (PCF) to reveal the disturbing mystique of existentialism,[3] and on the other without interruptions fighting the Stalinist structuralist interpretations of Marx, his ideas were therefore simply not valid and would soon be forgotten, even if it was acknowledged they provided some "inspiration" for research orientations.

Stanek rejects these hackneyed arguments and objections, which include the notion that Lefebvre's qualitative concepts were not based on any objective empirical evidence and thus not passable as reliable and serious research, nor science in a restricted sense. He provides substantial evidence that this is not altogether the case, while acknowledging that Lefebvre's most convincing scientific approach remains his focus on extremely creative and valid conceptualisations and qualitative research methodologies, as well as promoting the excessive need for trans-disciplinary research collaboration in order to fully grasp the huge complexities of interpretations related to urban architecture within a social science perspective. As Stanek formulates

2 • *Henri Lefebvre on Space: Architecture, Urban Research, and the Production of Theory* (Minneapolis: University of Minnesota Press, 2011); *Henri Lefebvre and the Concrete Research of Space: Urban Theory, Empirical Studies, Architecture Practice* [diss.] (Delft, Delft University of Technology, 2008).

3 • Henri Lefebvre, *L'Existentialisme* (Paris: Editions du Sagittaire, 1946).

Lefebvre's firm conviction, methodologies must be adapted to the fact that "space is not only produced by economic and material practices but also on the level of conceptual, aesthetic, symbolic and phantasmatic appropriation,"[4] not only of basic objective *needs*, but as much of hidden, unfulfilled, highly subjective *desires,* in Lefebvre's own phrasing. On account of his qualitative approach, he never abandoned his belief in "the irreducible and singular experience," but paid particular attention to it as a vital part in any scientific investigation.[5]

However, I was once among those convinced early on that Henri Lefebvre's writings, along with his actions, would ultimately prevail, and that they had such a level of relevance that in the end they would be resurrected for a renaissance and posthumous celebration in academia, which Stanek's book actually proves.[6] Another argument for the relevance of Lefebvre in a historical context is, as it is argued in a recent similar philosophical dissertation, that his concepts were confirmed to a large degree while the hardcore Marxist orthodox urban sociology was never empirically confirmed.[7] That is why it is so stimulating to take part in this serious and successful attempt by Łukasz Stanek, by a new generation, to project a more solid re-reception and a refreshed take on this whole vast and irreducible contribution to urban architectural research. The special value of Stanek's approach is that he provides a reading with a particularly insightful focus on Lefebvre's unique relation with the architectural profession as a philosopher and sociological researcher.

A most interesting, and I believe to many minds also surprising, aspect of Stanek's presentation is the importance he puts on the key notion and analysis of *dwelling* as the very starting point for the creation of Lefebvre's conceptual universe, besides his early dedication to rural and somewhat later urban studies. The urban and rural realities must be understood from the level of residential experiences, needs and desires in Lefebvre's terms, as the constituent elements of either an urban or a rural culture. As the author argues, one of the most crucial texts indirectly initiating the turmoil following May '68, is a unique research project published by the team led by Henri Raymond, the close collaborator and successor, in 1966 as *L'habitat pavillonaire,*[8] which had far-reaching importance for renewed social orientations of residential architecture designs. This extensive

4 • Stanek, *Henri Lefebvre on Space,* 149.
5 • Ibid, IX
6 • Cf. Gromark, "A Crucial Moment of Transgression: Henri Lefebvre and the Radical Metamorphosis of Every Day Life in the City," in *Nordisk Arkitekturforskning* No. 4 (1999), and Gromark, "Henri Lefebvre; Vardagligheten och Staden," postface in Lefebvre, *Staden som rättighet,* trans. Peter Einarsson (Stockholm: Bokomotiv, 1982).
7 • See Sangla, *Politique et Espace chez Henri Lefebvre.*
8 • See Henri Raymond, Nicole Haumont, et al, *L'Habitat pavillonaire. Préface de Henri Lefebvre* (Paris: Centre de recherche d'urbanisme 1966 [1971]); Henri Raymond, Marie-Geneviève Dezès, et al, *L'habitat pavillonaire. Préface d'Henri Lefebvre* (Paris: L'Harmattan, 2001 [1966, 1979]).

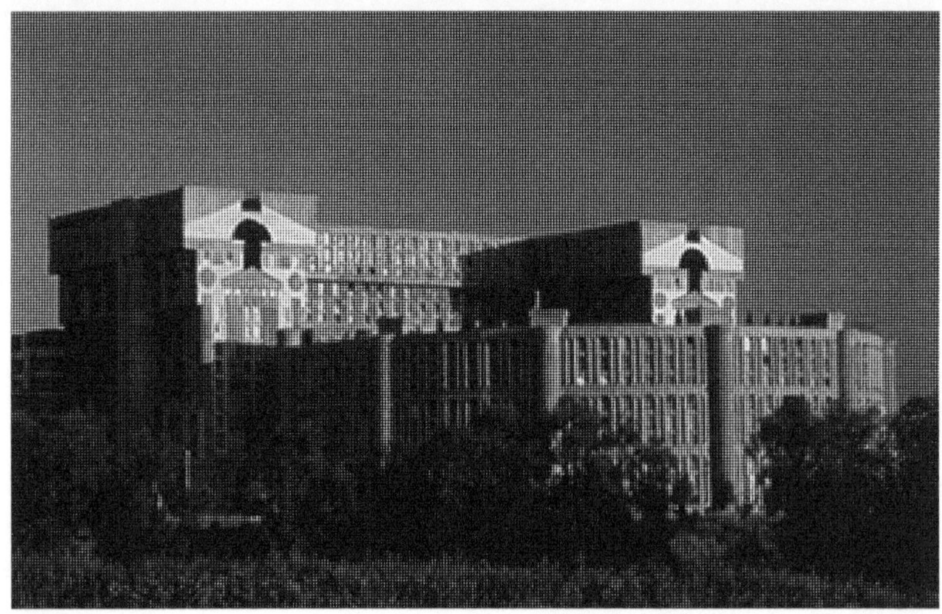

research focuses surprisingly on and reveals the life world and perceptions of families in traditional detached single family housing areas, the *pavillon*, conceived as preferred ways of residing *"chez soi"* put into relation to the abstract ways of residing introduced and imposed in large collective housing estates. This work should be put to the forefront and beside the more well-known and often mentioned titles in this period, like *The Society of the Spectacle*, *The Right to the City*, or *The Consumer Society* by respectively Debord (1967), Lefebvre (1968) and Baudrillard (1970).

Stanek also stresses the seldom-acknowledged fact that Lefebvre was a paramount initiator for the redefinition of the architectural profession, perhaps even the main source for a distinct and crucial moment of transgression for a whole generation of architects and urban planners. He was active in project designs, in competitions and competition juries, as well as in the educational reform of architecture schools post '68, alongside his extensive publishing and editing efforts. He also initiated early attempts to develop research as mentioned above devoted to combined architectural and sociological studies focused on residential issues.

Stanek's book is in many regards dedicated to providing evidence for the vital role played by Lefebvre in the architectural design profession's reorientation towards the profound questioning of the profession itself, in the broadest understanding of the word. The vast repercussions from this distinctive leap are far from difficult to identify in contemporary projective practices. Providing background for the numerous architectural experiments conducted in France in the late-1970s and early-1980s, Stanek writes that "the disciplinary identity of architecture, its formal techniques, conceptual frameworks, and social obligations were revised, providing orientation points for discourses and designs until today."[9] This contributed to a radicalization of professional convictions in the architectural community that would by the late 1960s amount to the explicit credo that the ability "to proceed from the real toward the possible" is the sole and specific competence of architectural practice, thus primarily contributing to radical social and cultural *change* through the architectural act and project design.[10] For Lefebvre, "to think the impossible is to embrace the whole field of potential possibilities."[11] On top of that, when Lefebvre on one occasion compares himself with architects, he conceives of them as *intellectuals* of architecture and urban transformations, and Stanek concludes, "this statement pointed to a shift in architectural culture, with the architects claiming the position of intellectuals,"[12] something so far in history rarely advocated with the same emphasis. These events in the transforming self-image of the profession represent a major change of profile from a technical and aesthetic expertise towards the new image of a dedicated actor in cultural and social transformations.

Stanek's analysis of Lefebvre is based on the presentation of extensive new graphic material, in particular related to projects that Lefebvre was an active supporting partner in, like the early experimental and seminal utopian works of Constant Nieuwenhuys' *New Babylon*, Ricardo Bofill and the early explorations of the *City in Space* (*La ciudad en el espacio*)[13] in the late-1960s in Madrid and later abandoned, before the illustrious and highly questionable *Palaçio d'Abraxas* residential complex in Marne-la-Vallée in 1980, and Jean Renaudie with the much admired radical and seminal Ivry-sur-Seine urban residential project, *Danielle Casanova* 1962–82.[14] During this writing endeavor he also apparently had the occasion to come close to witnessing the events around Lefebvre and his collaborators in their everyday life, drawing on precious accounts gathered in lengthy discussions with key personalities, sociologists and architects, such as Serge Renaudie, Ricardo Bofill, Henri Raymond, Jean-Louis Cohen and Anne Querrien.

The most important point in this refreshed approach

9 • Stanek, *Henri Lefebvre on Space*, XI.
10 • Ibid, XIII.
11 • Lefebvre quoted in Gromark, "Guy Debord och Situationens politiska estetik," in Gromark and Fredrik Nilsson (eds.), *Utforskande arkitektur: situationer i nutida arkitektur* (Stockholm, Axl Books, 2006), 69.
12 • Stanek, *Henri Lefebvre on Space*, XI.
13 • Ibid, 204–219
14 • Irénée Scalbert, *A Right to Difference: The Architecture of Jean Renaudie* (London Architectural Association, 2004).

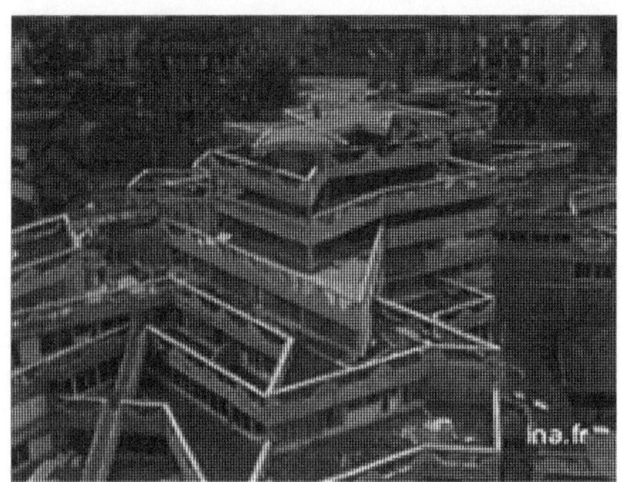

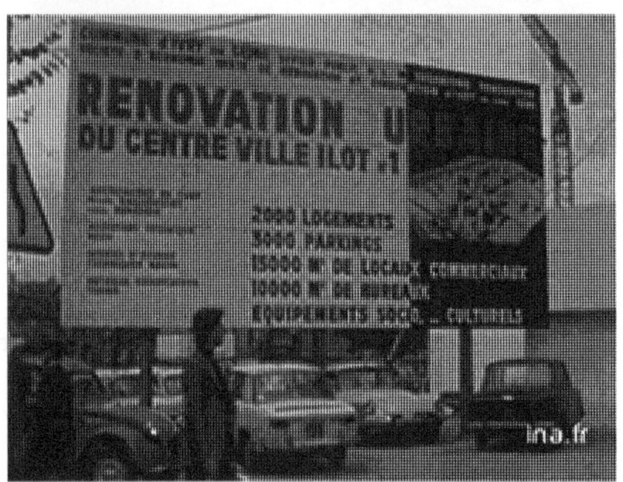
RENOVATION
DU CENTRE VILLE ILOT
2000 LOGEMENTS
3000 PARKINGS
15000 M2 DE LOCAUX COMMERCIAUX
10000 M2 DE BUREAUX
EQUIPEMENTS SOCIO CULTURELS

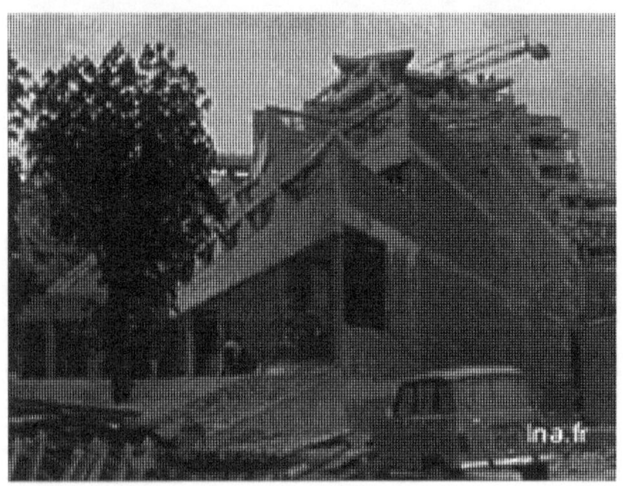

is the author's ambition to go beyond the first wave of receptions — David Harvey in the 1970s — and the second wave — Edward Soja in the 1980s — predominantly confined to the Anglo-American context of Academia and to situate Lefebvre's venture firmly on European soil and intimately related to French, German and Italian, as well as Central European, intellectual language and academic contexts. This apparently opens up for a more profound and just future implementation of Lefebvre's legacy, making it possible to ground his still most valid conceptual reorientations further and better on empirical investigations.

The most interesting and original aspect focused in the book is the discussion around Lefebvre's concept of space as *concrete abstraction* under the chapter heading of *Critique*, even if it is quite demanding to follow this somewhat obscure reasoning. Departing from Karl Marx and *Das Kapital*, where labor is considered the key object of analysis, in abstract and concrete terms, Lefebvre identifies the notion of space in its concrete and abstract sense as the key object of analysis in researching the intermediating and conditioning character and nature of social practices and societal interrelations. In a society where the material world around us is more and more conceived in abstract terms by social agents with specific agendas, perceived and lived through by the consumer in concrete spaces, in this *urban* society, space as concrete abstraction becomes a predominant aspect of everyday life in structural as well as in symbolic terms. For Lefebvre, the everyday life world's confrontation with abstract space, *l'espace abstrait*, was the result, effect and consequence in spatial terms of a capitalist society, a mode of production, reproduction and consumption, initially attempting to organize social life in an extremely rational manner, as exposed in urban residential projects, the "archipelagos of programmed and imposed space-time consumption modes" and detailed structural analysis optimizing at best the use-value of every single square centimeter in minimal apartments. This capitalist space was considered double-sided: "homogenized but also fragmented," concrete but also abstract. This meant that Lefebvre positioned himself in many regards as an extreme *anti-modernist*, if not a mere postmodernist, next to the devastating critique of modernity delivered by the Situationists and Guy Debord, both refusing to see the emancipatory and liberatory powers, elements and convictions present in the modern movement that he was himself constantly searching for elsewhere.

Another possible interpretation you might make, and that I think Lefebvre also had in mind, could be that *architecture as concrete abstraction* means that architecture obviously is concrete in sensual, material terms, seemingly neutral and innocent, but that under the surface it carries within itself intrinsically hidden, whether intended, accidental or unintended, abstract messages and mediations of an abstract and profound social and cultural nature, that speak to us non-verbally, without words, but yet sometimes with tremendous and overwhelming seducing or coercive power, whether critically transgressed, perceived intellectually or just lived through on a basic existential level.

Finally we might ask ourselves as Stanek concludes, could Lefebvre be regarded as a theorist delimited, confined to and isolated within his own particular glorious time frame, the dynamic 1960s and 1970s, as an historic and intellectual relic? How relevant is his perspective today? Stanek helps us to see that there is indeed a lot to question in his situation-based assumptions and preferences, when we confront them with contemporary culture and the radically different political and urban situation of the present day. For example, Stanek states, we need to revise "his belief in dwelling as the paradigmatic practice of production of space in view of the increasing privatization and gentrification of urban spaces modeled according to domestic interiors; challenging his theorization of difference in the face of the cultural logics of consumption as differentiation." The list is long.[15]

A voice somewhat akin to Henri Lefebvre's in its tone, that of Zygmunt Bauman, puts these recent situational changes in the prevalent mode of consumption into a relevant perspective in an attempt to characterize contemporary societies where, citing in his turn premonitions expressed by Pierre Bourdieu another twenty years ago, and indeed echoing Lefebvre himself: "coercion has by and large been replaced by stimulation, the once obligatory patterns of conduct by seduction, the policing of behaviour by PR and advertising, and normative regulation by the arousal of new needs and desires."[16]

We must be very grateful for this very solid account and thorough discussion, as well as elaborated critical interpretation of the key concepts of Henri Lefebvre grounded in the empirical world he encountered, the people he met and collaborated with. It opens for a far more complete image of the philosopher, and for renewed implementations of his research approaches toward the growing, and today even more accentuated, relevance of spatial aspects of our modern reality. These approaches are on the verge of including the intriguing and pressing aspects of time consumption in a united scientific and political framework — towards the potential critique of the political economy of time consumption. •

15 • Stanek, *Henri Lefebvre on Space*, XIV.
16 • Zygmunt Bauman, *Consuming Life* (London: Polity Press, 2007).

Sten Gromark is Professor of Architecture at Chalmers School of Architecture.

Architecture
and Urbanism

The Japanese Were Never Modern: Metabolism's Supra-Modernity

Sarah Stanley

Tokyo Data Flows, Infrastructure

Despite efforts by the Japanese government to decentralize the economy and population outside of Tokyo since the 1950s, it contains a viral urbanism set to 'automatic replicate'. This urban predicament involving the scale, density and future growth of Tokyo became the focus of a group of architects in the 1960s that called their movement Metabolism. The name placed emphasis upon living systems and processes that then became the basis for generating design models. When taken in combination with the nonmonumental sensibility of the cultural products of Japan that favor ephemerality over permanence, the Japanese do not fit squarely into Western architectural modernity. Nevertheless, this infiltration of life sciences into architectural thinking was one of the first cases of an ecological design model. The organicism to be found in Japanese architecture that had mesmerized Frank Lloyd Wright and Bruno Taut is perhaps what had first pointed the Metabolists towards ecological design. This, in conjunction with rebuilding after the Atomic bomb, propelled an enduring ecological orientation that deserves further attention.

Metabolist ideas were first published in the manifesto "Metabolism 1960," which was sold at the entrance of the 1960 World Design Conference in Tokyo (WoDeCo). The

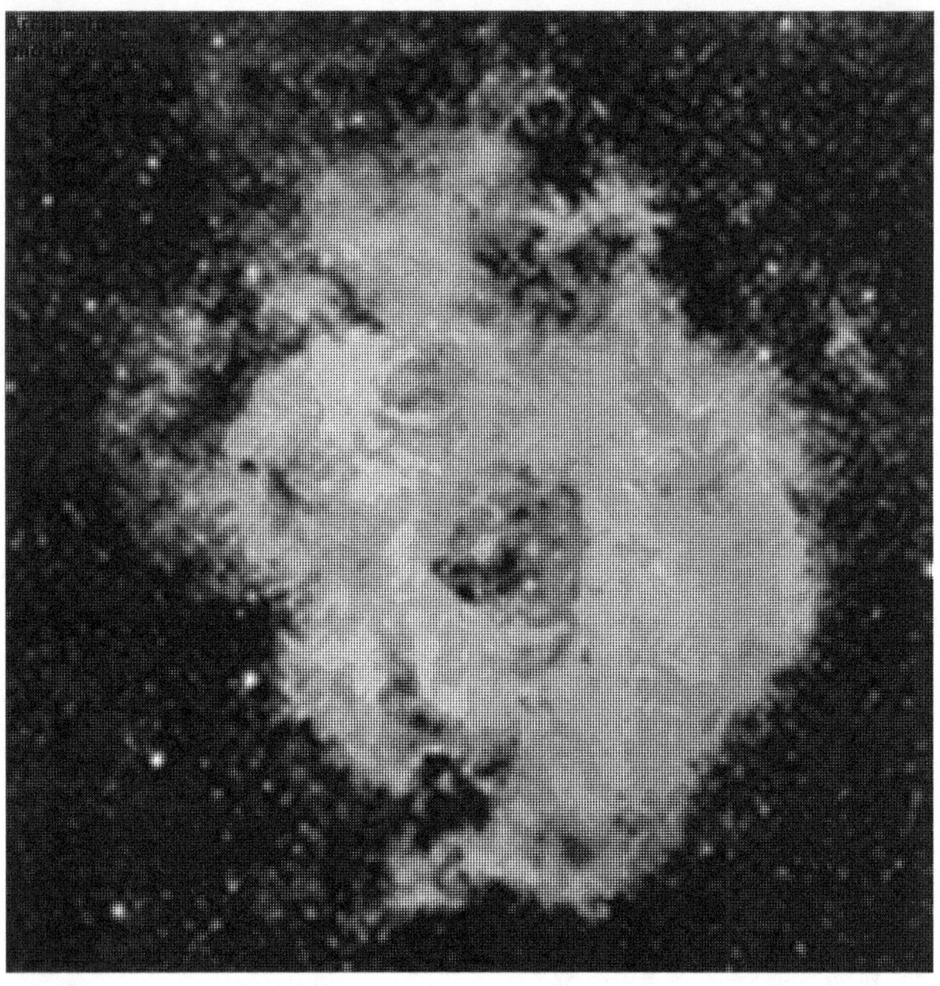

▲
Page from Metabolism 1960. Image from +ACNE.

emergence of Metabolism happened amidst a flood of mechanical inventions in Japan (pocket transistor radios [1951], Suzuki lightweight cars [1955], Fujitsu Computers [1956], Tokaido Shinkansen bullet trains [1964] and fiber-optic communications [1963]). In this small press publication architecture follows the logic of high-speed rail, radio broadcast transmissions ("brainwave receivers") and industrial floating cities. The basic problem of living environments and the home were folded into overarching concerns with urban mobilities. What was categorized as "move-nets," from movable appliance systems within houses to movable city blocks, were actually a type of hardware that could double as urban infrastructure. The capsule towers that contained interchangeable, industrially produced living units epitomize these ideas. Kisho Kurokawa succeeded in manufacturing the capsule units and built two towers, one in Tokyo and the other in Osaka. The compact, efficient organization of the living unit was informed by the research done by NASA regarding bodily efficiency when operating control panels. In 1972, after Japan had emerged as a major manufacturer and exporter of automobiles, each capsule unit was designed to be manufactured at the same price as a Toyota, and each was fitted with a radio, telephone and reel-to-reel tape deck. The capsules, preceding the personal computer, were defined by the idea that a person could be 'plugged in' to their communication apparatus at all times.

  The key to Metabolist thinking was the mapping of biological design models onto urban growth to produce a networked informational system. For these architects, architecture was no longer a singular building but a much vaster region that could stretch out along the length of Japan, or could form a network of spine-like bridges over the Bay of Tokyo. Many of the models generated by Metabolism function as a type of scaffolding that could hold the various components, resembling an animal or plant's cellular partitions. If organic life depends upon the need to consume, process and store energy, these processes also describe the inputting, storage and retrieval of an informational archive. Following from this emphasis, the city of Tokyo was studied through socio-economic data collected, examined and relayed into design methodologies. This meant that urban architectural sites had to be designed at the scale of infrastructure. The technical system capable of organizing urban living conditions, including informational ones, was the megastructure. The idea of superstructures had been pervasive in modernist visions for a newly electrified city, such as Soviet constructivist El Lissitsky's horizontal skyscrapers. Arata Isosaki's contribution of office buildings for Tange's Plan for Tokyo 1960 use massive slabs suspended between joint core structures across the Bay of Tokyo, which Isosaki continued to use for other master planning projects in Shinjuku and Shibuya. Fumihiko Maki's Golgi Structures also spread fan-like in linked clusters above the existing urban infrastructure [1968]. Megastructures, and the practice of large-scale master planning, are derived from the aerial perspective associated with the imagery of aerial bombardment. In fact, Metabolist megastructures first appear in a photomontage that shows a tangle of architectural mutations resembling metallic tumbleweed that drift over a nuclear landscape. In other ways, the idea of megastructures were practical in one of the world's most seismically active areas, prone to earthquakes, fires and flooding. It is within these ephemeral conditions that the Japanese first began to build in far shorter cycles than other countries (26 years against the 44 in the USA and 75 in the UK).

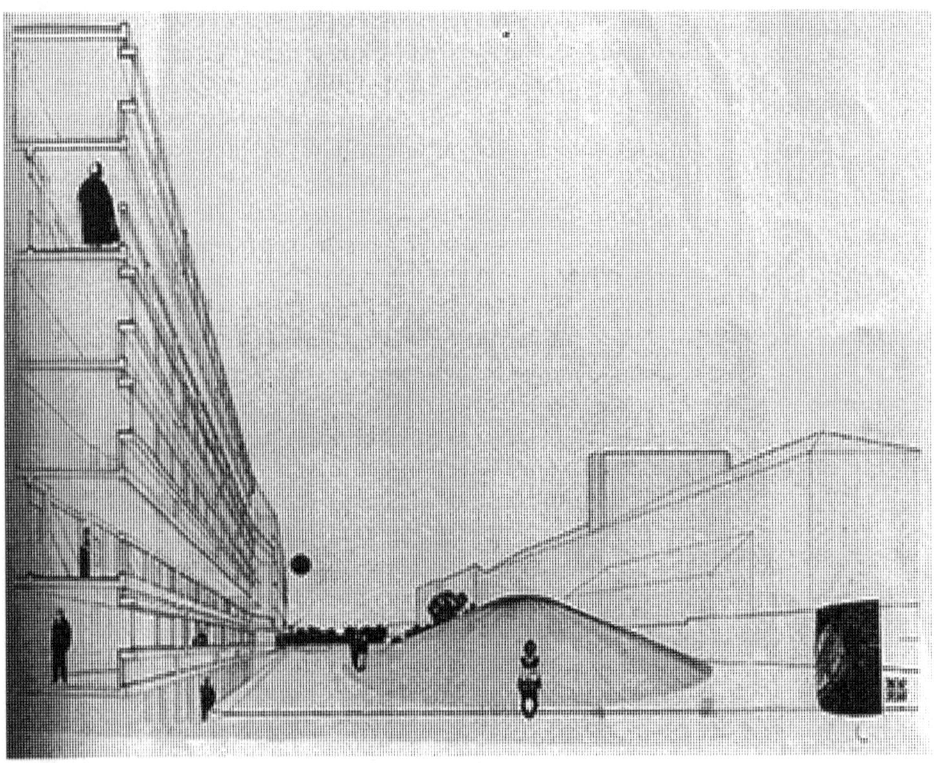

As the largest metropolitan area in the world (35 million), Tokyo expands by eating itself: sliver-thin subdivisions cut from larger plots in low-rise areas. Despite its rapid, intensive growth, Tokyo is still today a low- to mid-rise city compared with other capitalist global cities in Asia, such as Taiwan, Hong Kong or Singapore. The problem with suburban sprawl in Tokyo is the long commuting times for those who live in areas farthest from central business districts, most often those with lower incomes. This has led to a condition of intensive concentration of the working population located in an urban belt on the Eastern coast that joins Tokyo, Nagoya and Osaka. Kenzo Tange announced his Tokaido Megalopolis plan in 1964 that made the Tokyo-Osaka continuum into a single massive city, which was then refined in 1971 as "21st Century Japan — A Vision of the Future on National Land and Living". Tange's graphic atlas processed statistical data gathered from throughout Japan so that informatics was coupled with emphasis placed by the government on the development of urban and regional infrastructure. This is a transitional period for Japanese architects as they begin to integrate their designs with regional planning, a research emphasis later adapted in the 1990s by European architecture offices like Rem Koolhaas/OMA and later by MVRDV,

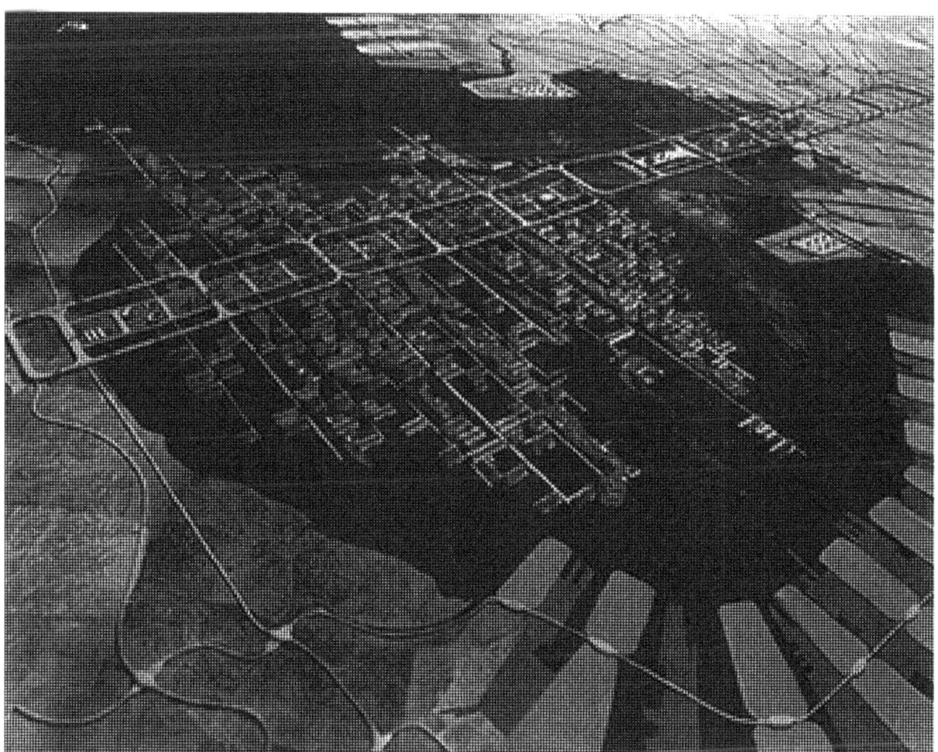

Dutch architects also beset with concerns about density and intensive urbanization. This approach provided a strong impetus for an architecture that can integrate urbanism rather than focus only upon institutional, private or corporate programs.

Japanese Metabolism's Alternative Modernities

The main tenets of Metabolism were first presented as a graphic exercise, ones that drew upon technical science imaging of mass media, a design trend in the 1950s also found in exhibitions organized by Gyorgy Kepes at MIT. (Tange taught at MIT in 1959). Crick and Watson's double-helix diagrams of the DNA in 1953, as one example, were then incorporated into Kurokawa's Helix City Tokyo (1961). However, this engagement with images does not automatically turn design into aesthetics as architectural historians often diagnose it.[1] It may be that the emergence of design science stole back the creation of images from aesthetics through a focus upon patterning that emphasized flows of energy and information. Metabolist design methodologies were searching for more complex model through diagrammatic rather than static images. The Metabolist discussion of

1 • Reinhold Martin considers the Geodesic dome to be a collapsing of art and science in "Crystal Balls," Any 17 [Forget Fuller?], 1997: 35. Mark Wigley calls the use of pattern "an aesthetic criterion" in "Planetary Homeboy," Any 17: 19.

processing systems also became their strategy for promotion. International in outlook from the beginning, Japanese architects' unique contributions were made known through the staging of interactions with international groups, both by traveling to CIAM meetings and by inviting these international groups and design figures to design events in Tokyo (Expo 70, WoDeCo 60). Japanese Metabolists made use of media, similar to Archigram's emphasis on graphic communication, such as small print publications, allowing the machinic morphologies that inhabit the designs to be maximized through the dissemination of information. This engagement with media networks points to yet another layer of storage and retrieval systems built into the Metabolist informational archive.

Commentators often imply that modern architecture was invented in Europe and America and transferred to places like Japan. Yet, the Japanese may have outpaced Western modernity through advanced technologies, especially through cinema and animation, without any need to topple historical memory and the monument.[2] While the Italian architects of Superstudio took an ironical approach to city planning by proposing monuments that covered over the entire city, as a criticism of architecture as a monumental edifice, it becomes clear that classical monumentality never shaped architectural modernity in Japan. A few of the Metabolist architects, and the generation prior, did study, work or teach with icons of the Modern movement, such as Fumihiko Maki with Josep Sert and Walter Gropius at Harvard. Despite this, according to Maki's own accounts, his contributions to Metabolism stem from a two-year research tour through Asia, Europe and the Middle-East, the period he had first developed the use of Golgi structures for high-rise towers. Likewise, Maki's concept of the 'genetic' emerged from an intensive scrutiny of vernacular architectures, which were analyzed as urban topographies in relation to climate.

The standardized structures produced by industrial prefabrication were already present in much of Japanese architecture, such as prefabricated wood components used to build Japanese houses along with the "Six-Mat Room," which denotes a standardized measuring system for houses, both from the sixteenth century. The tatami itself is the size of an average height of a person while lying down, exhibiting a very early effort to standardize architectural components tailored to the human body. Furthermore, a schematic drawing that presents the long, intersecting wooden enclosures that define the Japanese temple or shrine complex describes Mies van der Rohe's concept of the generic, long before the architect used the term to describe a modern architecture without features.

2 • Trond Lundemo, "Tokyo and the Monument," *SITE* 7–8, 2004.

Metabolism projects often played with additions that could be built according to expanding operations over time, similar to the 1620 Katsura Detached Palace in Kyoto, raised up on pilotis, which is rebuilt every twenty years. Similarly, the structures that emerged from Metabolism's design production were all highly changeable, multiplying only as required for expanding operations. Despite this continued reliance upon traditional building practices, Tokyo had already been built as a modern city with the first concrete and steel frame construction used in mass-produced housing after the widespread devastation caused by the 1923 Kanto Earthquake. The implementation of land redistribution policies and industrialization in the aftermath of World War 2 set loose a second wave of modernization during the American occupation.

Guattari considers it to be a "machinic eros" that drives the Japanese to great heights of commercialism that is broadcast loudly across the luminous cubes that sit atop buildings in Shinjuku or Shibuya. "Might Japanese capitalism be a mutation resulting from the monstrous crossing of animist powers inherited from feudalism during the 'Baku-han' and the machinic powers of modernity to which it appears everything here must revert?"[3] If modernity signifies a rupture with the past or traditional cultures, often associated with the emergence of scientific rationalism, then the Japanese were never modern. For Bruno Latour, what defines modernity is the purifying practices of science that make absolute distinctions between nature and society, human and thing.[4] The mixing of these categories is what defines animism. Architect Toyo Ito addresses these disjunctions by saying, "I can't help feeling that the deeper we go into this information age, the further we go into the virtual realm, the further we will be returning to a primitive experience."[5]

Animistic practices rests less in faith in a singular soul or God, then on repetitive actions performed as an automatic system concerned with immediate causes and effects, just as Metabolist investigations of urban networks through megastructures were organized through the repeating programs of bacterial contamination, DNA coding or Gogli protein storage. Following the same trajectory as Metabolism, the Japanese artist Yayoi Kusama begins to make repeating patterns in her paintings, referencing design and architecture in the 1950s. She begins making architectural environments using soft sculpture in

3 • Felix Guattari, "Tokyo the Proud," trans. Gary Genosko and Tim Adams, *Deleuze Studies* 1 (2) 2007: 93–99. Félix Guattari visited Japan throughout the 1980s to give lectures and to engage in a series of conversations and collaborations with Japanese intellectuals, artists and architects.
4 • Bruno Latour, *We Have Never Been Modern*, trans. Catherine Porter (Cambridge: Harvard University Press, 1993).
5 • "Glimpses of the Invisible City," A Conversation between Toyo Ito and Hans Ulrich-Obrist, *SITE* 5, 2003: 5.

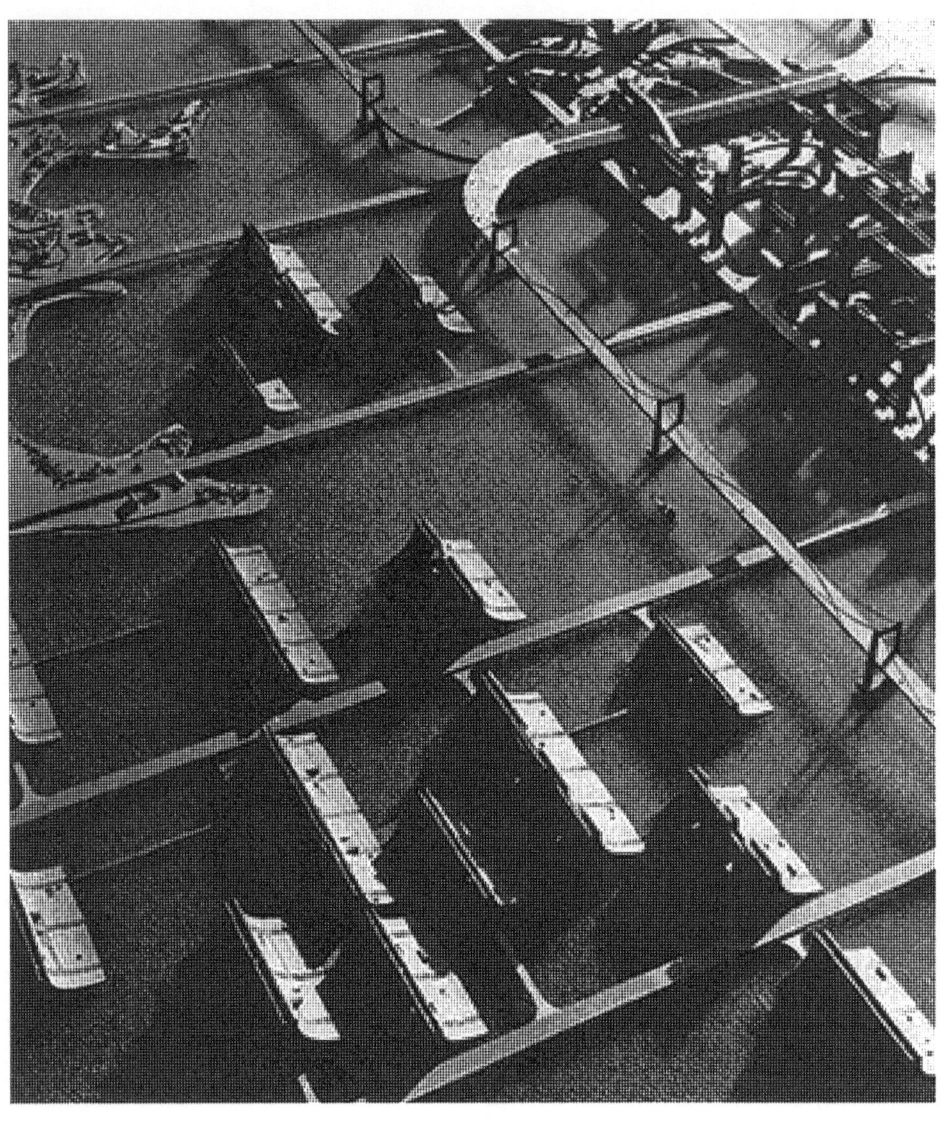

Plan for Tokyo, 1960. Details of the model. Kenzo Tange.

1961, characterized by the repetition of rounded tentacles painted with circular dots, which are inserted into chairs or mirrored rooms (Endless Love Room, 1964). The omnidirectional mirroring achieves a vertiginous melting of the boundaries between body and environment, so that the entire cosmos is vibrating through this turning inside out of embodiment. In order to engage the invisible, the life or spirit of things must be reanimated on a continual basis. What is found in every small corner of contemporary Tokyo is the prescribed habits or gestures upon entering a Shinto and Buddhist shrine, such as washing at the fountain, ringing the gong at the entrance, clapping the hands, bowing; all this is executed as quickly as consuming a bowl of Udon.

Nuclear Modernity
In post-Atomic Hiroshima the founder of Japanese Metabolism Kenzo Tange was brought in soon after the blast to begin to plan a new city. Tange eventually won the competition to build the Hiroshima Peace Memorial, his first design commission, an iconic modernist building located at ground zero completed in 1955. Tange's Peace Memorial makes a cameo appearance while under construction by an all-women crew in the film *Children of the Atom Bomb* (Kaneto Shindo, 1952), the first film allowed to depict Hiroshima and its destruction by the Atom bomb. Images of ecological devastation, including burning trees, plants and wildlife are reoccurring. One sequence follows two young boys who work as shoe shiners running through the war-torn city. The mother is working with primitive tools as her young son runs up the stairs of the memorial because the father is now finally dying of radiation sickness. The dust and steady hammering noise rising from the raw concrete building lends to the scene's misery. In the next shot, the family mourns the loss of the patriarch in a diminutive wooden house, an austere contrast to the overbearing monumentality of the Peace Memorial. The cinematic climax of this scene exposes something of the relations between modern architecture and the destruction wrought by atomic warfare. The memorial succeeded in creating an artillery for remembering, a site that instantly became global in orientation, appearing in several movies, including Alain Resnais' *Hiroshima Mon Amour* (1959), and eventually becoming one of the centers for the anti-nuclear movement.

In relief exposure, Japan's nuclear power industry was launched during the same period as the emergence of Metabolism. It was rationalized at the time as necessary due to destroyed thermal generators, grids and transformers in urban areas during the war. It seems unlikely that a country that had been devastated by the Atom bomb would so readily accept

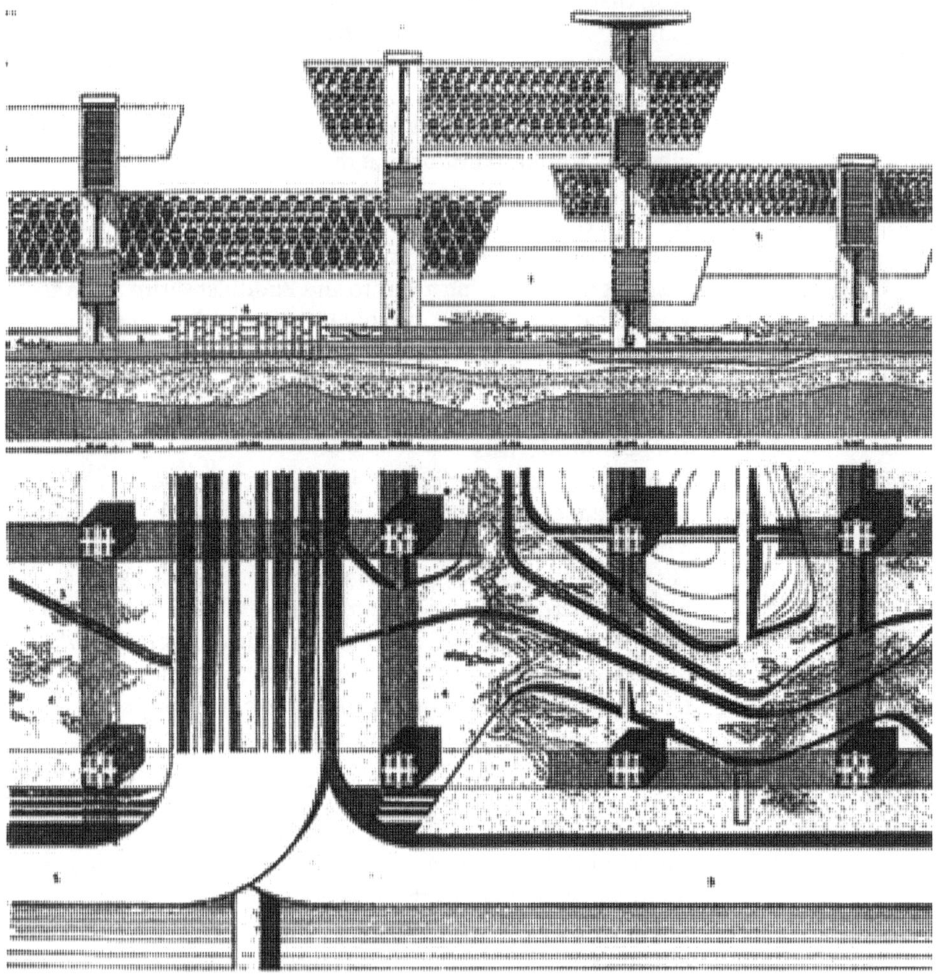

Plan for Tokyo, 1960. System piles and nuclei. Kenzo Tange.

6 • Tetsuo Arima, *Nuclear Power, Shoriki and the CIA* (Tokyo: Shinchosha 2008).

nuclear power, alongside the obvious risks due to earthquakes and tsunami. Tetsuo Arima, a professor of media studies at Tokyo's Waseda University, studied declassified documents on postwar relations to establish links between the CIA and media outlets in Japan.[6] Among the CIA's Japanese allies in the propaganda effort was Matsutaro Shoriki, owner of the Yomiuri newspaper, the world's largest, and Nippon Television, Japan's first commercial TV station, who published a series of pro-nuclear articles starting in January 1954 and aired Disney's *Our Friend the Atom* (1953). Alongside the emergence of Japanese Metabolism, in many ways an ecological response to the devastation and death caused by the Atom bomb, was a nuclear power industry that was planning facilities in risk-prone earthquake and tsunami zones. Tange's Peace Memorial has become yet again the focus of the anti-nuclear movement, with protests planned regularly in Hiroshima, Tokyo and elsewhere in Japan.

Metabolism in Contemporary Tokyo

The members of Metabolism do not so readily distinguish aesthetic matters from other philosophical, technological or scientific categories or even more practical dimensions of living. Consequently, the Metabolists chose to design in relation to large-scale infrastructure in ways that merged the practical with the fantastic. The kernel of the idea for an unbroken landscape between streetscape and building is found when city blocks and walkways climb up the sloping side of a building's roof (Kurokawa, Wall City, 1959). Today this has become a common design strategy, found in the undulating surfaces of the Yokohama International Port Terminal. Both Kurokawa and Tange at various times proposed huge A-frame roofs that provided ecological advantages of ventilation slots and shade that were eventually realized in Singapore by students of Metabolist architects.[7] Even if realized projects never can measure up to the ambitions that take shape in conceptual renderings and models, it is one of the most important methods that architects have to generate new models for design. When examining the entire spectrum of the Metabolist projects, many of the design projects worked out through various media, yet never formally realized, may have found openings in the planning and construction of Tokyo. By the early 1970s building and construction was largely taken over by multinational corporate entities responsible for building Tokyo's infrastructure.[8] Preceding this period, Japanese Metabolists had been commissioned by the government throughout the 1960s to produce multi-billion yen urban planning studies that were then ostensively handed off to an advanced building industry, one that contributes 17.9% of Japan's GDP (higher than the United States and Europe combined).[9] A concrete example of this is Tange and Kurokawa's separate proposals for an urban core to extend between Tokyo, Nagoya and Osaka taken up by the end of the 1980s using "Maglev" 500 kilometer per hour train lines and the eventual adhoc land reclamation of Tokyo Bay.

One way Tokyo's architecture might be described is "real modernism". If in the areas of Roppongi, Ginza and Shibuya exclusive brands produce designer architectures that appear in every other luxury shopping district worldwide, the majority of Tokyo resembles more the computer game Tetris,

7 • OMA/AMO, *Project Japan* (Koln: TASCHEN 2011), 608.
8 • Ibid, 603.
9 • Livio Sacchi, *Tokyo: City and Architecture* (Milan: Skira Editore S.p.A, 2004), 69.

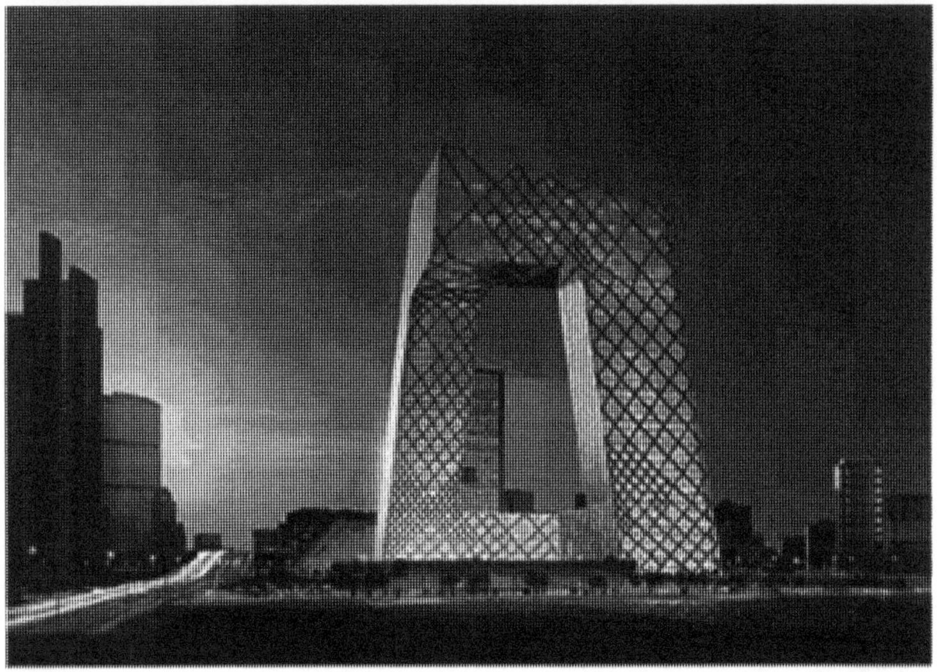

where any piece can be plucked out and replaced by any other. What may be the actual legacy of Metabolist thinking is the detachable and interchangeable building parts that can be snapped into place, newly fitted and changed as warranted by wear. For instance, perhaps due to the temperate climate, stairwells and movement corridors are often built as separate modules outside many mid-rise buildings; some of these emerged from Metabolist prototypes. Consequently any assessment of the impact of Metabolism should not be based upon the percentage of any individual architect's built projects based on interviews with Metabolists today. Many of the group's proposals took shape in the infrastructure of Tokyo, a city that has produced the greatest number of bridges, viaducts and tunnels per unit of distance in the world.

It is as if the building of megastructures above the city, as the Metabolists had envisioned, became the spiraling multilevel networks found today in Tokyo. It becomes clear almost immediately that it is food and drinking establishments that organize these urban transport passageways below ground. "To cross the city (or to penetrate its depth, for underground there are whole networks of bars, shops to which you sometimes gain access by a simple entryway...)"[10] Every sweet, sour, hard or crunchy snack or condiment, dried or fresh fish, what seems like miles

10 • Roland Barthes, *Empire of Signs* (New York: Hill and Wang, 1982), 39.

of it, line these underground networks. Tokyo's urban metabolism is therefore connected with the deep Japanese sensibility regarding alimentary processes, ones that often evoke design. Naming this the Twilight of the Raw, Roland Barthes writes an hermeneutical exegesis of Japanese cooking and eating: "the cucumber's future is not its accumulation or its thickening, but its division." and "the foodstuff has for its envelope nothing but time."[11] These underground corridors with multiple levels connect up with train stations, retail shopping of all varieties, service centers and above ground office complexes. All these are combined through multi-level platforms that weave into buildings several stories above street level. This multidirectionality is displayed as a series of overhead signs that list 50 to 100 names at informational checkpoints to direct circulation provided by escalators, elevators and people movers. All of these flows congregate around the station as the 'empty center' that Barthes claimed shares a kinship with the imperial ring: "Thus each district is collected in the void of its station."[12] This hyperinformatic way finding continues even into the multi-storied department stores. For instance, Labi's numerous locations exhibit floor plans with the same superimposition of maps and information that is liable to induce vertigo in a visitor — the station level maze of signage is continued through color-coded lines on the floor that point to a product's location.

Coda: OMA's *Project Japan* and Mori Art Museum's *Metabolism, City of the Future* (2011)

The importance of design in this potent mix of architecture, urbanism, information systems and ecology happens on several levels. Metabolism has reemerged now for some of the same reasons that Buckminster Fuller's models were pulled from the archive and placed back onto museum tables beginning in the 1990s. The Mori Art Museum's 2011 exhibition about Metabolism opened around the same time the OMA research project was released as *Project Japan*, a book compilation about Metabolism including interviews with its members. Although both the Mori show and *Project Japan* were planned well in advance of the Fukushima disaster of March 2011, it nevertheless forms the backdrop for both the venue and the book about Metabolism. The Fukushima disaster lent additional weight to the Mori Art Museum's entrance galleries containing the first Metabolist projects in response to Hiroshima-Nagasaki. Likewise, the ecological devastation increases the urgency for an ecological design approach explored by the Metabolists.

OMA's *Project Japan* follows the discourse networks that enabled Japanese architects, loosely gathered as members of Metabolism, to gain international prominence. The Mori Art

11 • Ibid, 11—15.
12 • Ibid, 39.

Museum showed many of the same films, books and models discussed at length in *Project Japan*, so both the exhibition and the book feed on and process many of the same information bundles in ways that complement each other. Museum exhibitions and publications dedicated to architectural research make use of the same informational systems invoked by design, creating efficient feedback systems with the viewing public. Both the exhibition and the book are as much an information-jammed junk space of modernity as Tokyo itself. The "Blade Runner" views of Tokyo from the top floor of the Mori Tower, with its hefty machinic profile, provided an appropriate setting for wall-sized screens showcasing newly created animations of Metabolist megastructure models. In the case of OMA's CCTV tower in Beijing, the Metabolist philosophy of the megastructure has become a reality in other parts of the globe. Megastructures, considered by many architectural historians as a bothersome pastime of visionary architects, or relegated to "artistic speculation," have entered the realm of possibility in other parts of the globe. It can be recognized in the outlines of Japanese Metabolism that design must maintain a connection to life. Similar to genetic mutations, divisions between technology and nature were successfully merged in the urban tissue of contemporary Tokyo.

Sarah Stanley is a writer based in New York and Berlin.

The Digital Dissolution of Disegno

Staffan Lundgren

1 • Michael Graves, "Architecture and the Lost Art of Drawing," *New York Times*, September 1, 2012, accessed February 12, 2013, www.nytimes.com/2012/09/02/opinion/sunday/architecture-and-the-lost-art-of-drawing.html?_r=5&pagewanted=all&.

Michael Graves — the architect behind the Portland Public Service Building, which could be considered the emblem of Fredric Jameson's notion of pastiche — recently published an opinion piece in the New York Times entitled "Architecture and the Lost Art of Drawing." "What has happened," Graves asks, "to our profession, and our art, to cause the supposed end of our most powerful means of conceptualizing and representing architecture?" That which is threatened, in Graves' view, is the drawing and that which is threatening it is "computer-aided design software with names like AutoCAD and Revit, a tool for 'building information modeling.'" [1] As a discipline architecture has always, as other disciplines within the realm of representation, rested heavily on the deployment of technologicies and to an equal degree, with a few historical exceptions, on the notion of authorship. The discipline's mathematical and geometrical essence is inscribed in it by means of its tools — the drafting machine, the scale ruler, orthographic projection, the velo, or the computer. At first, therefore, it is hard not to dismiss this claim of loss as merely the conservative, perhaps even reactionary, outburst of an architect who sees his prime tool of representation being outdated and outgunned — a generational shift that also entails a transition of power. Marshall

McLuhan's analysis of the mechanism of tribalization in regard to the advent of new technologies and/or media seems to fit Graves' critique exactly: "Specialist technologies detribalize. The nonspecialist electric technology retribalizes. The process of upset resulting from a new distribution of skills is accompanied by much culture lag in which people feel compelled to look at new situations as if they were old ones".[2]

However if Graves' stance is seen as just another avant-garde vs. avant-garde battle, as a kind of naive prolongation of Heidegger's "authentically acting hand," as an "obstinate Luddism"[3], of the consequences of what is now often called the digital turn in architecture are lost. That turn entails, it could be argued, a shift from technique to technology within architecture in a more fundamental way than earlier technological deployments hitherto had. A paradigmatic shift evident in Graves' comment that "[b]uildings are no longer just designed visually and spatially; they are 'computed' via interconnected databases" — that is, in a new way of design that implies an opaqueness of authorship (and agency) that will, whether one affirms it or not, transform the authoritarian art of architecture. Understood in this way, Graves' somewhat alarmist and bitter critique of computer-aided design tools might also help to bring to fore a set of underlying and constitutive concepts advocated by both the propellants of the drawing and the digital.

The Divinity of Design

In *The Alphabet and the Algorithm,* Mario Carpo demonstrates convincingly the extent to which architecture since Alberti has considered the design of a building as the original and the building as its copy.[4] A copy, it might be added, that, at least up until now, has been bound to be imperfect. Counter-intuitively given that we often think of architecture as buildings with mass that occupy space, architecture as a discipline, at least since the renaissance, is one of the most Platonic of the arts and is so by means of its claim of *drawing* over *building*. However, this Platonism must also be understood in relation to its mediation.[5]

2 • Marshall McLuhan, *Understanding Media* (New York: Routledge Classics, 2001), 26–7.
3 • Pablo Miranda Carranza, "Out of Control: The Media of Architecture, Cybernetics and Design," in *Material Matters Architecture and Material Practice*, ed. Katie Lloyd Thomas (Oxon: Routledge, 2007), 152. "Besides unconditional acceptance and consumption of these new 'tools', or otherwise an obstinate Luddism — praiseworthy, perhaps, in its critical resistance but not all that practical in the face of contemporary CAD dominance — there is a need to look at the longer-term effects of the use of computation in architecture and at the relation between architects and their technologies."
4 • Mario Carpo, *The Alphabet and the Algoritm* (Cambridge: The MIT Press, 2011), 26.
5 • As Pablo Miranda Carranza has noted in "Out of Control: The Media of Architecture, Cybernetics and Design," 153: "Through an almost literal implementation of the archetypical Platonic allegory of the cave, the mechanisms of projection inscribe Platonic discourse into the technologies and media of architecture."

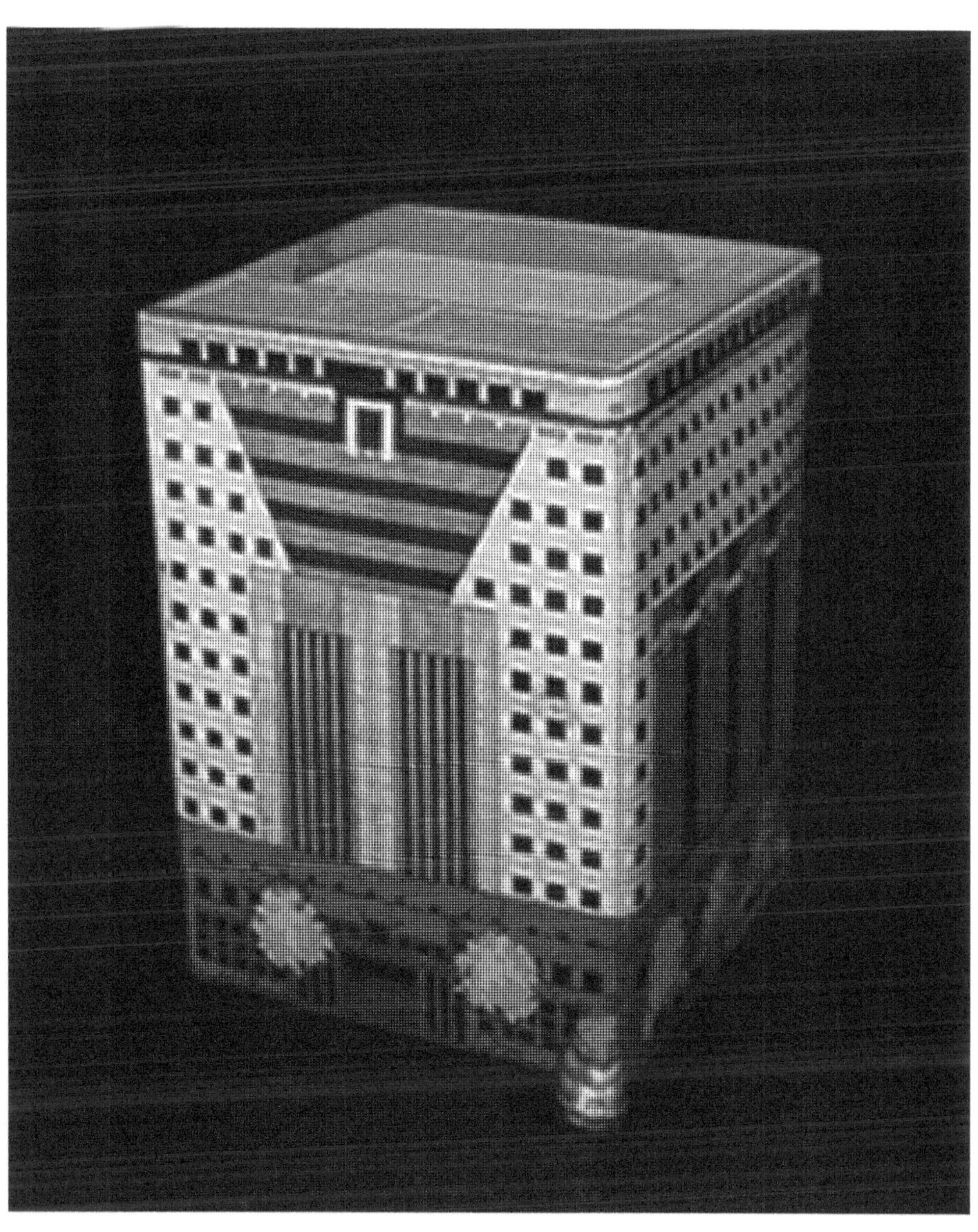

Michael Graves, Portland (Municipal Services) Building
opened and dedicated on October 2, 1982.

It is worth noting how both the "drawing over building" hierarchy and the "projective inscription" could, and perhaps should, be understood in relation, and translated, to the distinction and rivalry, between *disegno* and *colore*. The sixteenth century debate stood primarily over the value of painting being that of the idea (*invenzione*) with its origin in the mind of the artist materializing through *disegno*, defined by Lodovico Dolce as "the form with which the painter presents his material"[6], *colore,* on the other hand, represented the more lively diversity of nature through variation and color materializing through the act of painting (rather than drawing). In the words of Federico Zuccari (1542–1609) *disegno* "is not matter, not body, nor affection, nor substance, it is a form, idea, rule boundary, or the object of the mind."[7] However ideal these qualities might seem, *disegno* is not confined to the mind, but may just as well be a drawing on a paper — *disegno* extends from the internal to the external as Zuccari makes a distinction between *disegno interno* and *disegno esterno*.[8] "One should remember," Zuccari writes, "that there exist two kinds of operations: external ones like drawing, outlining, shaping, carving, building [*disgno esterno*], and internal ones like reasoning and desiring [*disegno interno*]."[9] *Disegno interno*, he argues further, is an "example and shadow of the divine," a "spark of divinity" common to all men. The manifestations of *disegno esterno* — though exemplified by drawing, outlining and shaping — is not to be regarded a completed work of art as the "external design is nothing but that which is circumscribed by form without corporeal substance."[10] The ambiguities and peculiarities of *disegno*, relating to the distinction between original and the copy in the Albertian sense and between *disegno interno* and *disegno esterno,* not only haunt Quattrocento accounts but are implicit in contemporary discussion on drawing versus digital.

There is however not just one digital turn in architecture but two. Already towards the end of the first coming — with its origin dating back as early as 1963 with the development of the first CAD (Computer Aided Design) program[11] — Nicholas Negroponte in 1969, in his discussion of the architectural machine, highlights some implications of the digital turn that holds true also for its second coming:

6 • See Jane Turner, *The Dictionary of Art*, Vol. 9 (New York: Grove, 2006), 6.

7 • Federico Zuccari, cited in Moshe Barasch, *Theories of Art: From Plato to Winckelmann* (New York: Routledge, 200), 299.

8 • See Barasch, *Theories of Art*, 295ff.

9 • Barasch, *Theories of Art*, 299.

10 • Barasch, *Theories of Art*, 301.

11 • For a thorough account of this, see Pablo Miranda Carranza, "Out of Control: The Media of Architecture, Cybernetics and Design."

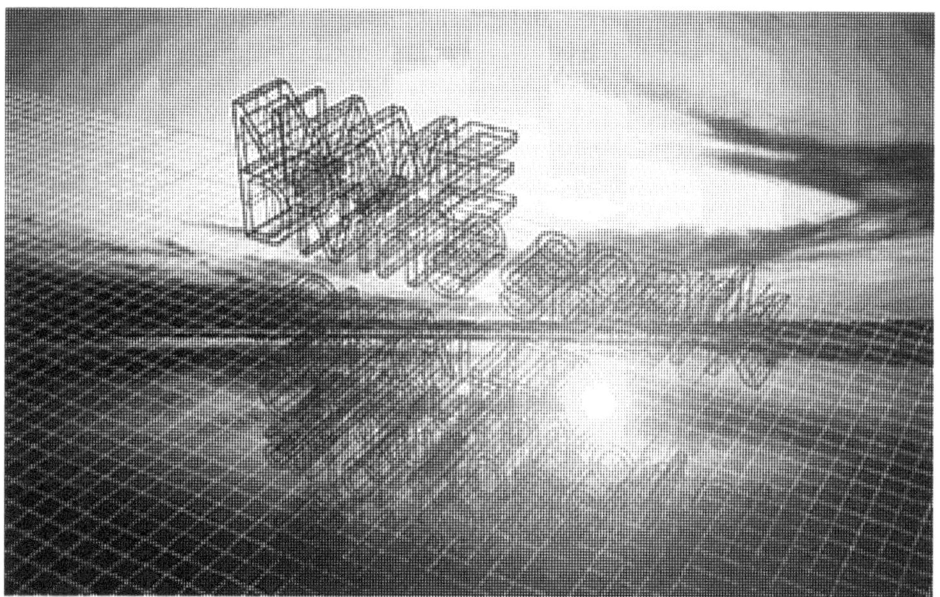

When a designer supplies a machine with step by-step instructions for solving a specific problem, the resulting solution is unquestionably attributed to the designer's ingenuity and labors. As soon as the designer furnishes the machine with instructions for finding a method of solution, the authorship of the results becomes ambiguous. Whenever a mechanism is equipped with a processor capable of finding a method of finding a method of solution, the authorship of the answer probably belongs to the machine.[12]

From Design to Drawing to Diagram to Digital

In their highly influential text, "Notes Around the Doppler Effect" (2002), Robert Somol and Sarah Whiting address the topos of engagement and autonomy. Their discussion critiques K. Michael Hays' view of critical architecture as a position "between culture and form," asserting the (im)possibility of such a position. Now a decade old, Somol and Whiting's text has gained both critique and endorsement in a way only a few texts of its kind have. Together with Michael Speaks' "Design Intelligence," "Notes Around the Doppler Effect" has become seminal to what is known as the post-critical stance in architectural discourse that opposed the possibility of criticality in both architectural design and discourse. A stance that in the words of George Baird considers the critical "as obsolete,

12 • Nicholas Negroponte, "Toward a Theory of Architecture Machines," *Journal of Architectural Education* Vol. 23, No. 2 (Mar., 1969): 9..

as irrelevant, and/or as inhibiting design creativity."[13]

The inhibiting force of critique for Somol and Whiting lies in Hays' view that critical architecture is something between culture and form: "The proposition of a critical realm between culture and form is not so much an extension of received views of interpretation as it is a challenge to those views that claim to exhaust architectural meaning in considerations of only one side or the other."[14] Thus Hays' position is oppositional: first to positions that "emphasize culture as the cause and content of built form; [where] the task of the interpreter, then, becomes the study of objects and instruments of cultural values"; second, to the idea of "Architecture as autonomous form," which begins "with the assumption that the only alternative to a strict, factual recovery of the originating situation is the renunciation of a single 'truth,' and advocates a proliferation of interpretations based solely on form."[15] Hays closes his description of the position-in-between by concluding that: "If critical architectural design is resistant and oppositional, then architectural criticism — as activity and knowledge– should be openly contentious and oppositional, as well."[16]

While the Haysian betweenness could be regarded as a position of both/and, Whiting and Somol articulate yet another position in terms of a neither/nor. This position, they argue, would allow for an escape from the impossibilities of the critical past by evoking the diagram.[17] The diagram "'imposes a particular form of conduct on a particular multiplicity.'"[18] and should also be understood as a means of "investigation of the frame structure" (a reference to Rem Koolhaas' project the Downtown Athletic Club). To Somol and Whiting, this opens for a distinction between the critical and the projective, where the latter "'proceeds through the diagram'"[19].

As Hélène Frichot has noted in "Drawing, Thinking, Doing: From diagram work to the superfold," "Although there is no explicit mention by Somol of emerging digital architectures, I would argue" — and I agree — "that these new

13 • George Baird George Baird, "Criticality and Its Discontents," *Harvard Design Magazine*, No. 21, Fall 2004/Winter 2005: 1.
14 • K. Michael Hays, "Between Culture and Form," *Perspecta* Vol. 21 (1984): 15
15 • Hays, "Between Culture and Form," 16.
16 • Hays, "Between Culture and Form," 27.
17 • As Hélène Frichot has pointed out the diagram — with direct reference to the diagrammatic workings of Deleuze and Guattari's abstract machine — by architectural thinkers and designers of the 1990s was considered "as a generative tool to bring

forth the possibility of new and ever-transforming built worlds." See Hélène Frichot, "Drawing, Thinking, Doing: From diagram work to the superfold," *ACCESS Critical Perspectives on Communication, Cultural & Policy Studies* Volume 30(1) 2011: 2.
18 • Robert Somol and Sara Whiting, "Notes Around the Doppler Effect," in *Constructing a New Agenda. Architectural Theory 1993–2009*, ed A. Krista Sykes (New York: Princeton Architectural Press, 2011), 196.
19 • Somol and Whiting, "Notes Around the Doppler Effect," 196.

technologies are part of what have contributed to the shift that Somol identifies between drawing and diagramming."[20] The implications of this were first laid out in the "Folding in Architecture" issue of *Architectural Design* from 1993. In the opening text, symptomatically titled "Unfolding Folding," Kenneth Powell cites Mark Wigley referring to deconstructive architecture as "'devious' and 'slippery' — and disturbing [...] It had to disturb, to be subversive, in order to break the hold of the old order."[21] "In practice," Powell continues, "architecture cannot be engaged in a process of permanent revolution, it has practical and formal as well as speculative and philosophical [*sic.*] ends to pursue." [22]

In elaborating on the proposed generative side of the diagram Somol and Whiting also make use of Marshall McLuhan's distinction between "Media Hot and Cold":

Architecture and Urbanism

There is a basic principle that distinguishes a hot medium like radio from a cool one like the telephone, or a hot medium like the movie from a cool one like TV. A hot medium is one that extends one single sense in "high definition". High definition is the state of being well filled with data. A photograph is, visually, "high definition." [...] Telephone is a cool medium, or one of low definition, because the ear is given a meager amount of information.[23]

Considering the diagram a cool media, in combination with their understanding of the productive side of the diagrammatic, Somol and Whiting argue for its ability to open up the architectural discipline. In their critique of the hitherto dominant and critical stance in architectural discourse Somol and Whiting conclude that:

One could say that their definition of disciplinarity is directed against reification rather than toward the possibility of emergence. While reification concerns itself with the negative reduction of qualitative experience to quantification, emergence promises that serial accumulation may itself result in the production of new qualities. As an alternative to the critical project — here linked to the indexical, the dialectical and hot representation — this text develops an alternative genealogy of the projective — linked to the diagrammatic, the atmospheric and cool performance. [24]

20 • Frichot, "Drawing, Thinking, Doing," 5.
21 • Kenneth Powell, "Unfolding Folding," *Architectural Design*, Profile 102 "Folding in Architecture" (London: Academy Editions, 1993) 7.
22 • Powell, "Unfolding Folding," 7.
23 • Marshall McLuhan, "Media Hot and Cold," in *Understanding Media* (New York: Routledge Classics, 2001), 24.
24 • Somol and Whiting, "Notes Around the Doppler Effect," 193.

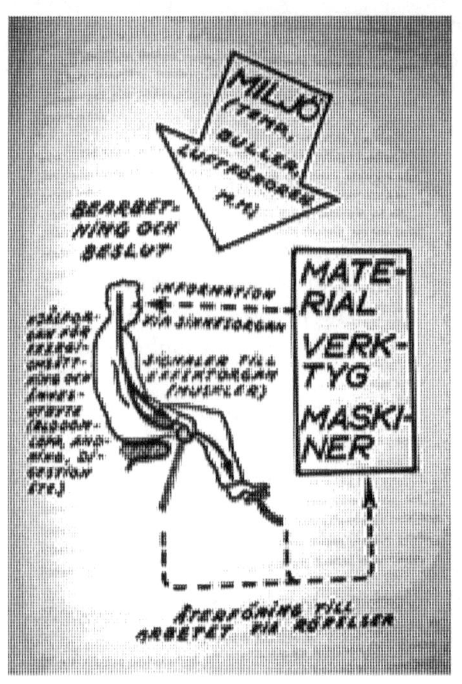

The implications of Somol and Whitings text can be unfolded and act as a lens through which to see how the changes that occured during the second digital turn were indeed fundmental and discipline changing. In Macluhan's terms Somol and Whitings claim that their's is a "cool" rather than a "hot" methodology can and should be disputed as their argument rests heavily on this distinction.

Following McLuhan the question is if it really is the "indexical and the dialectical" that we are to understand as a reifying force? Following how Fredric Jameson in the afterword to *Aesthetics and Politics* describes reification as "a process that affects our cognitive relationship with the social totality," a process that, "renders society opaque" [25] is it not rather the "diagrammatic and atmospheric" that should be understood in terms of reification?

In the diagrammatic and atmospheric lays an all-encompassing idea of architecture that extends beyond the avant-garde's will to gain ground to the furthering of the discipline. A will that is present already in Robert Somol's "Dummy Text, or The Diagrammatic Basis of Contemporary Architecture":

> Working diagrammatically — not to be confused with simply working with diagrams — implies a particular orientation, one which displays at once both a social and a disciplinary project. And it enacts this possibility not by representing a particular condition, but by subverting dominant oppositions and hierarchies currently constitutive of the discourse. [26]

With McLuhan I would argue that the claim of a ubiquitous atmospheric quality expressed in the orientation towards both a social and disciplinary projecthood should be understood in terms of a hot medium rather than a cool. Hence, in contrast to Somol and Whiting's "alternative genealogy of the projective," I

25 • Fredric Jameson, "Reflections in Conclusion," in *Aesthetics and Politics*, (London: NLB, 1977), 212.
26 • Robert Somol, "Dummy Text, or The Diagrammatic Basis of Contemporary Architecture," in *Diagram Diaries* ed. Peter Eisenman (New York: Universe, 1999), 23.

would like to suggest that rather than to understand the projective, the atmospheric and the diagrammatic as emergence, it should be understood in terms of reification. That the notion of atmosphere can be attached to an idea of reification — of providing the controlling means for the realisation of things — is evident in Mark Fishers understanding of capitalist realism: "It is more like a pervasive atmosphere, conditioning not only the production of culture but also the regulation of work and education, and acting as a kind of invisible barrier constraining thought and action."[27] For what are the atmospheric workings of the diagrammatic — that which "'imposes a particular form of conduct on a particular multiplicity'" — if not reification in the Jamesonian sense described above? Perhaps then the projective stand should simply be regarded as yet another ideological mystification of the workings of late capitalism.

In "Dummy Text" Somol also argues that "In general, the fundamental technique and procedure of architectural knowledge has seemingly shifted, over the second half of the twentieth century, from the drawing to the diagram."[28] But how are we to understand this shift from drawing to diagram? Is Somol here thinking of the drawing as something like the diagram also in its diagrammatic sense or is he reducing the diagram to a form of representation? In the latter case with McLuhan one could argue that yes, if the diagram is to be understood in the sense of a two-dimensional representation of a process or an account of data etcetera it surely is to be understood as a cold medium, just as the low definition drawing is. However this is not the kind of diagram Somol (and Whiting) are thinking about, rather it is, as noted above, a diagram which "imposes a particular form of conduct on a particular multiplicity". This "imposition of a particular form of conduct on a particular multiplicity requires" — even as it rests on the historical working of *disegno interno* and *disegno esterno* — a new interface that is not to be reduced only to a simple "graphical user interface" but also must be understood as a more fundamental disposition of society as a whole.

To unfold this, it is necessary to look into the techno-scientific ideological framework mentioned above, that is the relation between society, science, and technology in connection to Max Weber's understanding of rationalization as a "purposive-rational action" that "aims at the establishment, improvement, or expansion of systems of purposive-rational action themselves."[29] In discussing Herbert Marcuse's view of the concept of rationalization, Jürgen Habermas concludes that to Marcuse "what Weber

27 • Mark Fisher, *Capitalist Realism. Is There No Alternative?* (Winchester: Zero Books, 2009), 16.
28 • Somol, "Dummy Text," 7.
29 • Jürgen Habermas, *Toward A Rational Society*, trans Jeremy J. Shapiro (Boston: Beacon Press: 1970), 81.

called 'rationalization' realizes not rationality as such but rather, in the name of rationality, a specific form of unacknowledged political domination."[30] Aiming at establishing, improving, and expanding a system of purposive-rational action — constructing an "evolutionary system" — we can see how Nicholas Negroponte's architecture machine fit well into such a framework:

> This discussion is not about machines that necessarily can do architecture; it is a preface to machines that can learn about architecture and perhaps even learn about learning about architecture. Let us call such machines architecture machines; the partnership of an architect with such a device is a dialogue between two intelligent systems — the man and the machine — which are capable of producing an evolutionary system. [31]

If technology and science are to be understood as ideology in the sense proposed above we can also see how this ideology acts as a vanishing mediator, just as Protestantism to Weber once served as the mediator between the medieval and modern (capitalist) world that later withdrew its defining properties and remained unacknowledged. This phenomenon could also explain the temporal discrepancy that constitutes the first and second digital turn in architecture. As Slavoj Žižek has shown, in a dialectical process, form stays behind content as "the crucial shift occurs within the limits of the old form" until the work is done and the old form can fall off.[32] The process of rationalization — that both instills a new cognitive order and destroys old forms of legitimizing processes — will also give rise to the *science* of architecture expressed for instance in the will to supersede the old legitimation found in the humanistic and/or anthropomorphic, toward the post-human, projective, performative, and biomimetic.

It is hard not to understand this development in relation to Heidegger's concept of enframing (Ge-Stell) that, in the words of Sven-Olov Wallenstein, should be understood "as a systemic, auto-regulating, and totalizing quality."[33] Neither is it hard to find in Negroponte's ideological architecture machine an affinity and close relationship to another form of machine, the abstract machine described by Delueze and Guattari as follows:

30 • Habermas, *Toward A Rational Society*, 82.
31 • Negroponte, "Toward a Theory of Architecture Machines," 12.
32 • Slavoj Žižek, *For they Know Not What They Do: Enjoyment as a Political Factor* (London: Verso, 2008), 185.
33 • Sven-Olov Wallenstein, *Nihilism, Art, Technology* (Stockholm: Axl Books, 2011), 68.

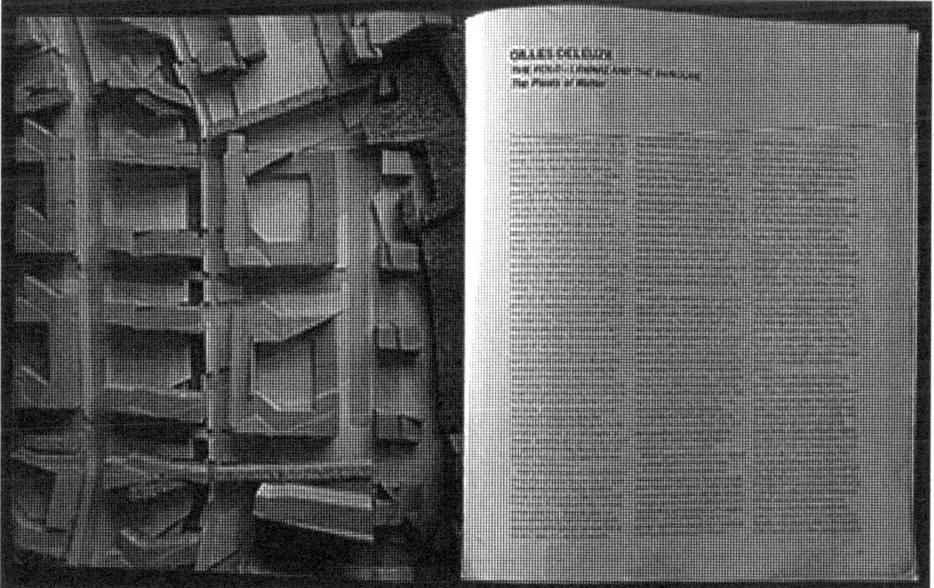

▲
Spread from "Folding in Architecture" (*Architectural Design*, 1993).

it is the reinvention of a machine of which human beings are constituent parts, instead of subjected workers or users. If motorized machines constituted the second age of the technical machine, cybernetic and informational machines form a third age that reconstructs a generalized regime of subjection: recurrent and reversible "humans-machines systems" replace the old nonrecurrent and nonreversible relations of subjection between the two elements; the relation between human and machine is based on internal, mutual communication, and no longer on usage or action. [34]

It is important to stress here that recurrent and reversible cybernetic and informational machines, freed from usage or action, continue to produce an evolutionary system, just as in Negroponte's architecture machine. The "dialogue between two intelligent systems" fully adheres to the "purposive-rational action" although this action is no longer — as in the second age of the technical machine — to be understood as mans domination over nature and man.

The mutual constitution of, and the reciprocal relation between, the abstract and architecture machine is then a prerequisite of a certain paradigm described by Douglas Spencer as follows: "For many thinkers of the spatiality of

34 • Gilles Deleuze and Felix Guattari, *A Thousand Plateaus. Capitalism and Schizophrenia*, trans. Brian Massumi (Minneapolis: University of Minnesota Press, 2005), 458.

contemporary capitalism, the production of all social space tends now to converge upon a single organizational paradigm designed to generate and service mobility, connectivity and flexibility."[35]

Presumably in the background of Somol's argument is the realisation that drafting in the architectural profession is gradually being superseded by computer aided design and a whole promising raft of new modelling and animation softwares."[36] It seems as if the diagrammatic and digital turns have in common both a notion of a "total situation," and the concern with effect (and affect) over meaning. A phenomenon that McLuhan identifies with hot media: "Concern with *effect* rather than *meaning* is a basic change of our electric time, for effect involves the total situation, and not a single level of information."[37] The "hot representations" of the previous avant-garde that the "projectives" seek to overcome is present also in the diagrammatic, however not in the same representational way. Instead it is manifest by way of the immersive "hotness" of the mathematical/geometrical ontology in Deleuze's reading of the Baroque. As Mario Carpo has put it:

> Owing to a bizarre series of events that is still to be reconstructed, Deleuze's *pli*, when exported to America, morphed into the Deleuzian Fold and merged with the visualization of Leibniz's differential calculus that computers now made available to most architects, regardless of their mathematical talents. As a result, algorithmically generated continuous functions soon became an almost ubiquitous component of architectural design.[38]

One of the most prolific examples of the relation between the diagrammatical and the digital turn is the *objectile,* the name Gilles Deleuze gave to the research done by Bernard Cache into how to industrially produce nonstandard objects. In *The Fold* Deleuze writes:

As Bernard Cache has demonstrated, this is a very modern conception of the technological object: it refers neither to the beginnings of the industrial era nor to the idea of the standard that still upheld a semblance of essence and imposed a law of constancy ("the object produced by and for the masses"), but to our current state of things, where fluctuation of the norm

35 • Douglas Spencer, "Architectural Deleuzism. Neoliberal space, control and the 'univer-city'," *Radical Philosophy* 168, July/August 2011: 9.
36 • Hélène Frichot, "Drawing, Thinking, Doing: From diagram work to the superfold," in *ACCESS Critical Perspectives on Communication, Cultural & Policy Studies* Volume 30(1) 2011, 5.
37 • Marshall McLuhan, "Media Hot and Cold," 28.
38 • Mario Carpo, "Post-Hype Digital Architecture: From Irrational Exuberance to Irrational Despondency," *Grey Room* 14, Winter (2004): 103.

replaces the permanence of a law; where the object assumes a place in a continuum by variation; where industrial automation or serial machineries replace stamped forms. The new status of the object no longer refers its condition to a spatial mold — in other words, to a relation of form-matter — but to a temporal modulation that implies as much the beginnings of a continuous variation of matter as a continous development of form.[39]

The affirmation of the "current state of things" that lays in the neither/nor can of course be considered as an emergence of something radically new. However it can also be seen as a defense of status quo by the internal or immanent forces of the abstract machine expressed through the workings of the architecture machine and its production of an "evolutionary system".

Rendering the Real

There is a global convergence in recent avant-garde architecture that justifies the enunciation of a new style: *Parametricism*. The style is rooted in digital animation techniques. Its latest refinements are based on advanced parametric design systems and scripting techniques. This style has been developed over the last 15 years and is now claiming hegemony within avant-garde architecture. It succeeds modernism as a new long wave of systematic innovation. The style finally closes the transitional period of uncertainty that was engendered by the crisis of modernism and that was marked by a series of short lived episodes including Postmodernism, Deconstructivism, and Minimalism.[40]

Owing its existence to the digital turn of the 1990s *parametricism* has over the last half decade or so been raised to stardom, mostly through the advocacy of Patrik Schumacher. As the quote above suggests, the claims of the parametric avant-garde are far-reaching. Describing his 2011 book *The Autopoiesis of Architecture* as "an attempt to create a comprehensive and unified theory of architecture" Schumacher — in the same lecture, held at SCI Arc in September 2010 — also argues: "Parametricism continues the autopoesis of architecture, which is the self-referential, closed system of communications that constitutes architecture as a discourse in contemporary society."[41] To Schumacher it seems then as if the unified theory of parametricism is not only to become the savior of the discipline of

39 • Gilles Deleuze, *The Fold. Leibniz and the Baroque*, trans Tom Conley (London: The Athlone Press, 1993), 19.
40 • Patrik Schumacher, "Parametricism — New Global Style for Architecture and Urban Design". Published in *AD Architectural Design Digital Cities*, Vol 79, No 4, July/August 2009. Here retrieved and read from www.patrikschumacher. com/Texts/Parametricism%20-%20A%20 New%20Global%20Style%20for%20Architecture%20and%20Urban%20Design.html
41 • Schumacher, "Parametricism And the Autopoiesis Of Architecture." *Log* 21 2011: 63.

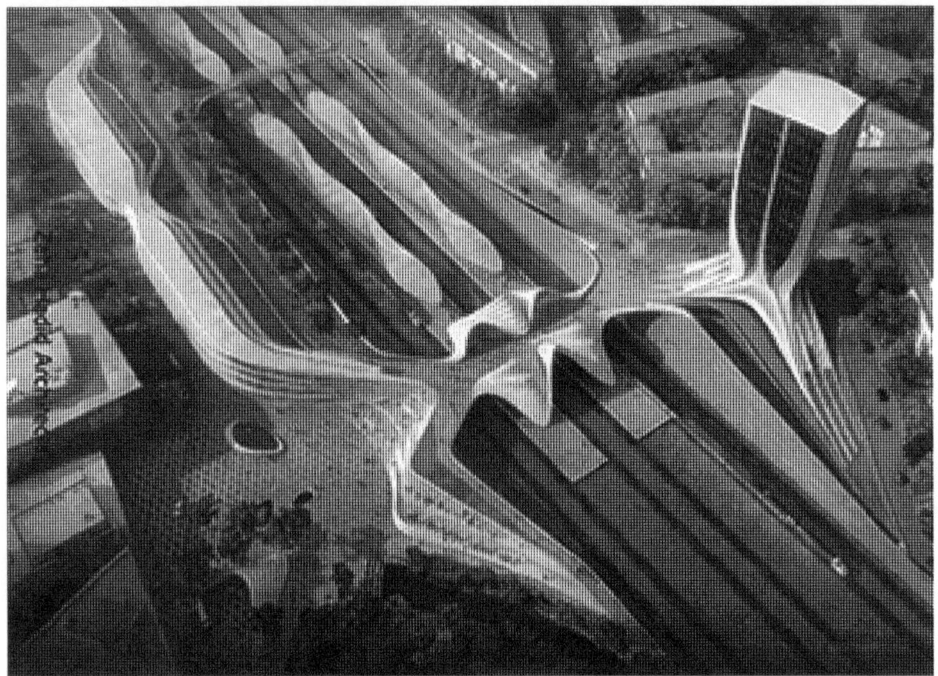

▲
**Zaha Hadid
Architects, proposal
of a remaking of
the station area in
Upplands Väsby
(Stockholm region).
Copyright Zaha
Hadid Architects.**

architecture but also to reinstate its autonomy. An autonomy, that is, that does not recognize the authority of politics, clients, science or morality but is "the autonomy to adapt to an environment and to stay relevant in it,"[42] an autonomy that is of social resilience.

So how are we to understand the seemingly contingent but still defining and authorative environment Schumacher refers to in his creed for autonomy? This question becomes even more accute since the construction of such an aesthetic ideology is in line with what Martin Jay, with a sense of despair, refers to as a "*l'art pour l'art* tradition of differentiating a realm called art from those of other human pursuits, cognitive, religious, ethical, economic, or whatever."[43] How to address and confront an aesthetic ideology strengthen by its techno-scientific claims in a post-political society permeated by a cybernetic telos of progress as a means to counter organic and inorganic entropy?

As yet another result of the effects and affects[44] of the diagrammatic-digital turn of the 1990s it seems as architecture, at least as it is understood by the propellants of the projective and later the parametric, has turned into a form of "image-building". As Hal Foster has noted with regards to the global style of

42 • Schumacher, "Parametricism And the Autopoiesis Of Architecture," 65.
43 • Martin Jay, "The Aesthetic Ideology" as Ideology; Or, What Does It Mean to Aestheticize Politics?," *Cultural Critique* No. 21 (Spring, 1992): 43.
44 • For a thorough overview of the affective and affirmative in relation to vitalism, the late Foucault, and critical theory see Sven-Olov Wallenstein's "Noopolitics, Life, Architecture" in his forthcoming *Architecture, Critique, Ideology: Essays on Architecture and Theory* (Stockholm: Axl Books, 2013).

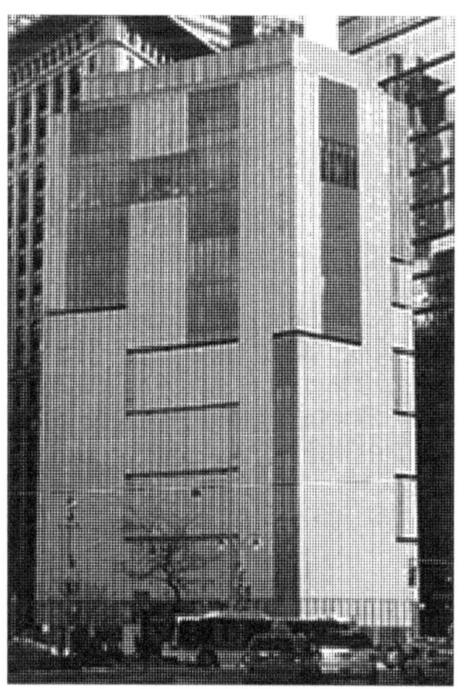

▲
The Museum
of Arts and
Design at 2
Columbus Circle
in Manhattan,
New York City.
Photo: Beyond
My Ken. Source:
Wikimedia.

contemporary architecture it is characterized by its "'banal cosmopolitanism'," that implies that, "even as its signal buildings respond to local conditions and global demands at once, they often do so in a manner that produces an image of the local for circulation to the global."[45] With this turn to the image some rather remarkable transformations have occurred in terms of the relation between concept and representation. Not only, as Peter Eisenman recently stated in an interview, is the digital "inhabited by what I call the phenomenological, or the thought of materials in a nostalgic and romantic way" but it also seems to take advantage of the implosion of *disegno* and *colore* into *inventione* by means of the digital, allowed as a result of the collapse of the representational in the wake of the diagrammatic and digital upheaval of interior and exterior.

A stark contemporary example of this has been brought to fore by John Hill in the August 2012 issue of the journal *Clog* ("Rendering") where he shows how the office Allied Works Architecture (AWA) chooses to present their work on The Museum of Arts and Design in New York, not in concordance with how it was built but how it was designed. This is neither something new nor extraordinary in terms of how architects traditionally have understood the final work. However, as we shall see, AWA's presentation fundamentally differs in the way in which it carries out the task of showing the work. In one of the photos presenting the project a part of the façade has been fundamentally altered in Photoshop in order for the representation to manifest the *disegno* rather then building as built. But why at all claim the mimetic force of the photographic image in order to represent the project, if the realized project does not represent the *disegno*? It seems as if the two visual regimes of *disegno* and *colore* have collapsed into each other through the mediation of the possibilities rendered by advanced digital technologies and architecture machines of the early twentyfirst century. This also implies a reversal or even upheaval of Zucchari's diagram as this rested on the idea of difference and "mechanisms of projection". When "the relation between human and machine is based on internal, mutual communication, and no longer

45 • Hal Foster, The Art-Architecture Complex (London: Verso, 2011), X.
46 • Deleuze and Guattari, A *Thousand Plateaus*, 458.

on usage or action"[46] the distance necessary to critique has dissolved. As a paradox it also seems as the disciplinary credo of both the projectives and paramatrecists renders authorship obsolete or at least contingent. With the totalizing claims expressed in the idea of Schumacher's "unified theory of architecture" in synthesis with the "social and a disciplinary project" of Somol and Whiting made possible by the technologies of late capitalism — and as a technology of late capitalism — the withdrawal of authorship and agency and with it the possibility of responsibility is, to say the least, worrying in its implications to both the disciplinary and the social.

Somol and Whiting end "Notes Around the Doppler Effect" by concluding that the projective program "does not necessarily entail a capitulation to market forces, but actually respects or reorganizes multiple economies, ecologies, information systems, and social groups."[47] To a certain extent, this is obviously true: the projective and parametricist programs do not entail a capitulation to market forces but rather are a prerequisite for them. ●

47 • Somol and Whiting, "Notes Around
the Doppler Effect," 202.